Programming Spiders, Bots, *and* Aggregators *in* Java

Programming Spiders, Bots, *and* Aggregators *in* Java™

Jeff Heaton

SYBEX

San Francisco · London

Associate Publisher: Richard Mills
Acquisitions and Developmental Editor: Diane Lowery
Editor: Rebecca C. Rider
Production Editor: Dennis Fitzgerald
Technical Editor: Marc Goldford
Graphic Illustrator: Tony Jonick
Electronic Publishing Specialists: Jill Niles, Judy Fung
Proofreaders: Emily Hsuan, Laurie O'Connell, Nancy Riddiough
Indexer: Ted Laux
CD Coordinator: Dan Mummert
CD Technician: Kevin Ly
Cover Designer: Carol Gorska, Gorska Design
Cover Illustrator/Photographer: Akira Kaede, PhotoDisc

Library of Congress Card Number: 2001096980

ISBN: 0-7821-4040-8

Software License Agreement: Terms and Conditions

This book is dedicated to my grandparents: Agnes Heaton and the memory of Roscoe Heaton, as well as Emil A. Stricker and the memory of Esther Stricker.

Acknowledgments

There are many people that helped to make this book a reality, both directly and indirectly. It would not be possible to thank them all, but I would like to acknowledge the primary contributors.

Working with Sybex on this project was a pleasure. Everyone involved in the production of this book was both professional and pleasant. First, I would like to acknowledge Marc Goldford, my technical editor, for his many helpful suggestions, and for testing the final versions of all examples. Rebecca Rider was my editor, and she did an excellent job of making sure that everything was clear and understandable. Diane Lowery, my acquisitions editor, was very helpful during the early stages of this project. I would also like to thank the production team: Dennis Fitzgerald, production editor; Jill Niles and Judy Fung, electronic publishing specialists; and Laurie O'Connell, Nancy Riddiough, and Emily Hsuan, proofreaders.

It has also been a pleasure to work with everyone in the Global Software division of the Reinsurance Group of America, Inc. (RGA). I work with a group of very talented IT professionals, and I continue to learn a great deal from them. In particular, I would like to thank my supervisor Kam Chan, executive director, for the very valuable help he provides me with as I learn to design large complex systems in addition to just programming them. Additionally, I would like to thank Rick Nolle, vice president of systems, for taking the time to find the right place for me at RGA. Finally, I would like to thank Jym Barnes, managing director, for our many discussions about the latest technologies.

In addition, I would like to thank my agent, Neil J. Salkind, Ph.D., for helping me develop and present the proposal for this book. I would also like to thank my friend Lisa Oliver for reviewing many chapters and discussing many of the ideas that went into this book. Likewise, I would like to thank my friend Jeffrey Noedel for the many discussions of real-world applications of bot technology. I would also like to thank Bill Darte, of Washington University in St. Louis, for acting as my advisor for some of the research that went into this book.

Contents at a Glance

Contents

Introduction

A tremendous amount of information is available through the Internet: today's news, the location of an expected package, the score of last night's game, or the current stock price of your company. Open your favorite browser, and all of this information is only a mouse click away. Nearly any piece of current information can be found online; you have only to discover it.

Most of the information content of the Internet is both produced and consumed by human users. As a result, web pages are generally structured to be inviting to human visitors. But is this the only use for the Web? Are human users the only visitors a website is likely to accommodate?

Actually, a whole new class of web user is developing. These users are computer programs that have the ability to access the Web in much the same way as a human user with a browser does. There are many names for these kinds of programs, and these names reflect many of the specialized tasks assigned to them. *Spiders, bots, aggregators, agents,* and *intelligent agents* are all common terms for web-savvy computer programs. As you read through this book, we will examine how to create each of these Internet programs. We will examine the differences between them as well as see what the benefits for each are. Figure I.1 shows the hierarchy of these programs.

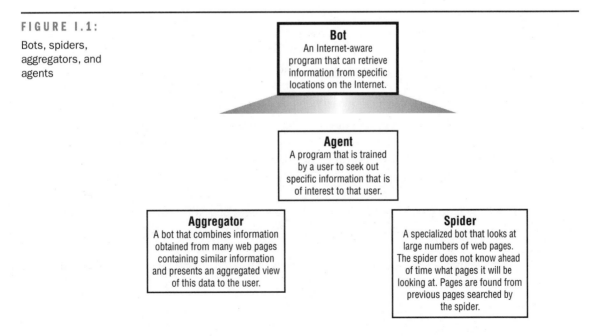

FIGURE I.1:

Bots, spiders, aggregators, and agents

Bot
An Internet-aware program that can retrieve information from specific locations on the Internet.

Agent
A program that is trained by a user to seek out specific information that is of interest to that user.

Aggregator
A bot that combines information obtained from many web pages containing similar information and presents an aggregated view of this data to the user.

Spider
A specialized bot that looks at large numbers of web pages. The spider does not know ahead of time what pages it will be looking at. Pages are found from previous pages searched by the spider.

What Is a Bot?

Bots are the simplest form of Internet-aware programs, and they derive their name from the term *robot*. A robot is a device that can carry out repetitive tasks. A software-based robot, or bot, works in the same way. Much like a robot on an assembly line that will weld the same fitting over and over, a bot is often programmed to perform the same task repetitively.

Any program that can reach out to the Internet and pull back data can be called a bot; spiders, agents, aggregators, and intelligent agents are all specialized bots. In some ways, bots are similar to the macros computer programs, such as Microsoft Word, give users the ability to record. These macros allow the user to replay a sequence of commands to accomplish common repetitive tasks. A bot is essentially nothing more than a macro that was designed to retrieve one or more web pages and extract relevant information from them.

Many examples of bots are used on the Internet. For instance, *search engines* will often use bots to check their lists of sites and remove sites that no longer exist. Financial software will go out and retrieve balances and stock quotes. Desktop utilities will check Hotmail or Yahoo! Mail accounts and display an icon when the user has mail.

In the February 2001 issue of *Windows Developer's Journal*, I published a very simple library that could be used to build bots. I received numerous letters from readers telling me of the interesting uses they had found for my bot foundation. One such use caught my eye: A father wanted to buy a very popular and recently released video game console for his son's birthday. As part of a promotion, the manufacturer would place several of these game consoles into public Internet auction sites as single bid items. The first person that saw the posting got the game console. The father wrote a bot, based on my published code, that would troll the auction site waiting for new consoles. The instant the bot saw a new game console for sale, it would spring into action and secure his bid. The plan worked and his son got a game console. The father was so delighted he wrote to tell me of his unique use for my bot. I was even invited to stop by for a game if I was ever in Maryland.

This story brings up an important topic that arises when you are working with bots. Is it legal to use them? You will find that some sites may take specific steps to curtail bot usage, for example, some stock quote sites will not display the data if they detect a bot. Other sites may specifically forbid the use of bots in their terms of service or licensing agreement. Some sites may even use both of these methods, in case a bot programmer ignores the terms of service. But, for the most part, sites that do not allow bot access are in the minority. The ethical and legal usage of bots is discussed in more detail in Chapter 12, "Using Bots Conscientiously."

WARNING As the author of a spider, bot, or aggregator, you must ensure that it is legal to obtain the data that your bot seeks, and if you are still in doubt after conducting such a study, you should ask the site owner or an attorney.

What Is a Spider?

Spiders derive their name from their insect counterparts: spiders spin and then travel large complex webs, moving from one strand to another. Much like the insect spider, a computerized spider moves from one part of the World Wide Web to another.

A spider is a specialized bot that is designed to seek out other sites based on the content found in a known site. A spider works by starting at a single web page (or sometimes several). This web page is then scanned for references to other pages. The spider then visits those web pages and repeats the process, continuing it indefinitely. The spider will not stop until it has exhausted its supply of new references to additional web pages. The reason this process is not infinite is because a spider is typically given a specific site to which it should constrain its search. Without such a constraint, it is unlikely that the spider would ever complete its task. A spider not constrained to one site would not stop until it had visited every site on the World Wide Web.

The Internet search engine represents the earliest use of a spider. Search engines enable the user to enter several keywords to specify a website search. To facilitate this search, the search engine must travel from site to site trying to match the keywords. Some of the earliest search engines would actually traverse the Web while the user waited, but this quickly became impractical because there are simply too many websites to visit. Because of this, large databases are kept to cross-reference websites to keywords. Search engine companies, such as Google, use spiders to traverse the Web in order to build and maintain these large databases.

Another common use for spiders is *website mapping*. A spider can scan the homepage of a website, and from that page, it can scan the site and get a list of all files that the site uses. Having a spider traverse your own website may also be helpful because such an exploration can reveal information about its structure. For instance, the spider can scan for broken links or even track spelling errors.

What Are Agents and Intelligent Agents?

Merriam-Webster's Collegiate Dictionary defines an agent as "a person acting or doing business for another." For example, a literary agent is someone who handles many of the business transactions with publishers on behalf of an author. Similarly, a computerized agent can access websites and handle business for a particular user, such as an agent selling an investment position in response to some other event. Other more common uses for agents include "computerized research assistants." Such an agent knows the types of news stories that its master is interested in. As stories that meet these interests cross the wire, the agent can clip them for its master.

Agents have a tremendous amount of potential, yet they have not achieved widespread use. This is because in order to create truly powerful and generalized agents, you must have a level of artificial intelligence (AI) programming that is not currently available.

There is a distinction between an intelligent agent and a regular agent. A *nonintelligent agent* is nothing more than a bot that is preprogrammed with information unique to its master user. Most news-clipping agents are nonintelligent agents, and they work in this way: their master user programs them with a series of keywords and the news source they are to scan.

An *intelligent agent* is a bot that is programmed to use AI to more easily adapt to the needs of its master user. If such an agent is used to clip articles, the master user can train the agent by letting it know which articles were useful and which were not. Using AI *pattern recognition* algorithms, the agent can then attempt to recognize future articles that are closer to what the master user desires.

NOTE   This book specifically deals with spiders, bots, and aggregators—the bots that deal directly with web pages. Intelligent agents are programs that can make decisions based on a user's training, and therefore they are more of an AI topic than a web programming topic. Because this book deals mainly with the types of bots directly tied to web browsing, intelligent agents will not be covered.

What Are Aggregators?

Aggregation is the process of creating a compound object from several smaller ones. Computerized aggregation does the same thing. Internet users often have several similar accounts. For instance, the average user may have several bank accounts, frequent flyer plans, and 401k plans. All of these accounts are likely held with different institutions, and each is also secured with different user ID/password information.

Aggregators allow the user to view all of this information in one concise statement. An *aggregator* is a bot that is designed to log into several user accounts and retrieve similar information. In general, the distinction between a bot and an aggregator can be understood by the following example: if a program were designed to go out and retrieve one specific bank account, it would be considered a bot; if the same program were extended to retrieve account information from several bank accounts, this program would be considered an aggregator.

Many examples of aggregators exist today. Financial software, such as Intuit's Quicken and Microsoft Money, can be used to present aggregated views of a user's financial and credit accounts. Certain e-mail scanning software can tell you if messages are waiting in any of several online mailboxes.

NOTE   Yodlee (http://www.yodlee.com) is a website that specializes in aggregation. Using Yodlee, users can view one concise view of all of their accounts. The thing about Yodlee that makes it unique is that it can aggregate a diverse range of account types.

The Java Programming Language

The Java programming language was chosen as the computer language on which to focus this book because it is ideally suited to Internet programming. Many programming techniques, which other languages must use as third party extensions, are inherently part of the Java programming language. Java provides a rich set of classes to be used by the Internet programmer.

Java is not the only language for which this book could have been written because the bot techniques presented in this book are universal and transcend the Java programming language; the techniques revealed here could also be applied to C++, Visual Basic, Delphi, or other object-orientated programming languages. In addition, some programming languages have the ability to use Java classes. The Bot package provided in this book could easily be used with such a language.

This book assumes that you are generally familiar with the Java programming language, but it doesn't require you to have expert knowledge in the Java language. This book does not assume anything beyond basic Java programming. For instance, you aren't required to have any knowledge of sockets or HTTP. You should, however, already be familiar with how to compile and execute Java programs on your computer platform. Given this, a good Java reference, such as *Java 2 Complete* (Sybex, 1999), would make an ideal counterpart to this book.

This book was written using Sun's JDK 1.3 (JS2SE edition). Every example, as well as the core package, contains build script files for both Windows and UNIX. The JDK is not the only way to compile the files, however. Many companies produce products, called *integrated development environments (IDEs)*, that provide a graphical environment in which to create and execute Java code.

You do not need an IDE in order to use this book. However, this book does provide all the necessary project files that you could use with WebGain's VisualCafé. The source code is compatible with any IDE that supports JDK1.3. Once a project file is set up, other IDEs such as Forte, JBuilder, and CodeWarrior could also be supported. Microsoft Visual J++ only supports up to version 1.1 of Java and, as a result, it will have some problems running code from this book. It is unclear, as of the writing of this book, if Microsoft intends to continue to support and extend J++.

Wrap Up

As a reader, I have always found that the books that are the most useful are those that teach a new technology and then provide a complete library of routines that demonstrate this new technology. This way I have a working toolbox to rapidly launch me into the technology in question. Then, as my use of the new technology deepens, I gradually learn the underlying techniques that the book seeks to teach. That is the structure of this book. You, the reader, are provided with two key things:

- A reusable bot, spider, and aggregator package that can be used in any Java or JSP project (hereafter referred to as the *Bot package*). This package is found on the companion CD.

- Each chapter contains examples of how to use the Bot package. These examples are also contained on the companion CD.

Complete source code to the Bot package is included on the companion CD. Additionally, the chapters provide an in-depth explanation of how the Bot package works.

CHAPTER 1

Java Socket Programming

- Exploring the world of sockets

- Learning how to program your network

- Java Stream and filter Programming

- Understanding client sockets

- Discovering server sockets

The Internet is built of many related protocols, and more complex protocols are layered on top of system level protocols. A *protocol* is an agreed-upon means of communicating used by two or more systems. Most users think of the Web when they think of the Internet, but the Web is just a protocol built on top of the Hypertext Transfer Protocol (HTTP). HTTP, in turn, is built on top of the Transmission Control Protocol/Internet Protocol (TCP/IP), also known as the sockets protocol.

Most of this book will deal with the Web and its facilitating protocol, HTTP. But before we can discuss HTTP, we must first examine TCP/IP socket programming.

Frequently, the terms *socket* and *TCP/IP programming* are used interchangeably both in the real world and in this chapter. Technically, socket-based programming allows for more protocols than just TCP/IP. With the proliferation of TCP/IP systems in recent years, however, TCP/IP is the only protocol that is commonly used with socket programming.

The World of Sockets

Spiders, bots, and aggregators are programs that browse the Internet. If you are to learn how to create these programs, which is one of the primary purposes of this book, you must first learn how to browse the Internet. By this, I don't mean browsing in the typical sense as a user does; instead, I mean browsing in the way that a computer application, such as Internet Explorer, browses.

Browsers work by requesting documents using the Hypertext Transfer Protocol (HTTP), which is a documented protocol that facilitates nearly all of the communications done by a browser. (Though HTTP is mentioned in connection with sockets in this chapter, it is discussed in more detail in Chapter 2, "Examining the Hypertext Transfer Protocol.") This chapter deals with *sockets*, the protocol that underlies HTTP.

Sockets in Hiding

When sockets are used to connect to TCP/IP networks, they become the foundation of the Internet. But because sockets function beneath the surface, not unlike the foundation of a house, they are often the lowest level of the network that most Internet programmers ever deal with. In fact, many programmers who write Internet applications remain blissfully ignorant of sockets. This is because programmers often deal with higher-level components that act as intermediaries between the programmer and the actual socket commands. Because of this, the programmer remains unaware of the protocol being used and how sockets are used to implement that protocol. In addition, these programmers remain unaware of the layer of the network that exists below sockets—the more hardware-oriented world of routers, switches, and hubs.

Sockets are not concerned with the format of the data; they and the underlying TCP/IP protocol just want to ensure that this data reaches the proper destination. Sockets work much like the postal service in that they are used to dispatch messages to computer systems all over the world. Higher-level protocols, such as HTTP, are used to give some meaning to the data being transferred. If a system is accepting a HTTP-type message, it knows that that message adheres to HTTP, and not some other protocol, such as the Simple Mail Transfer Protocol (SMTP), which is used to send e-mail messages.

The Bot package that comes with this book (see the companion CD) hides this world from you in a manner similar to the way in which networks hide their socket commands behind intermediaries—this package allows the programmer to create advanced bot applications without knowing what a socket is. But this chapter does cover the lower-level aspects of how to actually communicate at the lowest "socket level." These details show you exactly how an HTTP request can be transmitted using sockets, and how the server responds. If, at this time, you are only interested in creating bots and not how Internet protocols are constructed, you can safely skip this chapter.

TCP/IP Networks

When you are using sockets, you are almost always dealing with a TCP/IP network. Sockets are built so that they could abstract the differences between TCP/IP and other low-level network protocols. An example of this is the Internetwork Packet Exchange (IPX) protocol. IPX is the protocol that Novell developed to create the first local area network (LAN). Using sockets, programs could be constructed that could communicate using either TCP/IP or IPX. The socket protocol isolated the program from the differences between IPX and TCP/IP, thus making it so a single program could operate with either protocol.

NOTE   Although other protocols can be used with sockets, they have very limited Internet browsing capabilities, and therefore, they will not be discussed in this book.

When it was first introduced, TCP/IP was a radical departure from existing network structures because it did not follow the typical hierarchical pattern that was used before. Unlike other network structures, such as Systems Network Architecture (SNA), TCP/IP makes no distinction between client and server at the machine level, instead, it has a single computer that functions as client, server, or both. Each computer on the network is given a single address, and no address is greater than another. Because of this, a supercomputer running at a government research institute has an IP address, and a personal computer sitting in a teenager's bedroom also has an IP address; there is no difference between these two.

The name for this type of network is a *peer-to-peer network*. All computers on a TCP/IP network are considered peers, and it is very common for machines on this network to function both as client and server. In a peer-to-peer network, a *client* is the program that sent the first network packet, and a *server* is the program that received the first packet. A *packet* is one network transmission; many packets pass between a client and server in the form of requests and responses.

Network Programming

You will now see how to actually program sockets and deal with socket protocols. Collectively, this is known as *network programming*. Before you learn the socket commands to affect such communications, however, you will first need to examine the protocols. It makes sense to know what you want to transmit before you learn how to transmit it.

You will begin this process by first seeing how a server can determine what protocol is being used. This is done by using common network ports and services.

Common Network Ports and Services

Each computer on a network has many sockets that it makes available to computer programs. These sockets, which are called *ports*, are numbered, and these numbers are very important. (A particularly important one is port 80, the HTTP socket that will be used extensively throughout this book.) Nearly every example in this book will deal with web access, and therefore makes use of port 80. On any one computer, the server programs must specify the numbers of the ports they would like to "listen to" for connections, and the client programs must specify the numbers of the ports they would like to seek connections from.

You may be wondering if these ports can be shared. For instance, if a web user has established a connection to port 80 of a web server, can another user establish a connection to port 80 as well? The answer is yes. Multiple clients can attach to the same server's port. However, only one program at a time can listen on the same server port. Think of these ports as television stations. Many television sets (clients) can be tuned to a broadcast on a particular channel (server), but it is impossible for several stations (servers) to broadcast on the same channel.

Table 1.1 lists common port assignments and their corresponding Request for Comments (RFC) numbers. RFC numbers specify a document that describes the rules of this protocol. We will examine RFCs in much greater detail later in this chapter.

TABLE 1.1: Common Port Assignments and Corresponding RFC Numbers

Port	Common Name	RFC#	Purpose
7	Echo	862	Echoes data back. Used mostly for testing.
9	Discard	863	Discards all data sent to it. Used mostly for testing.

Continued on next page

TABLE 1.1 CONTINUED: Common Port Assignments and Corresponding RFC Numbers

Port	Common Name	RFC#	Purpose
13	Daytime	867	Gets the date and time.
17	Quotd	865	Gets the quote of the day.
19	Chargen	864	Generates characters. Used mostly for testing.
20	ftp-data	959	Transfers files. FTP stands for File Transfer Protocol.
21	ftp	959	Transfers files as well as commands.
23	telnet	854	Logs on to remote systems.
25	SMTP	821	Transfers Internet mail. Stands for Simple Mail Transfer Protocol.
37	Time	868	Determines the system time on computers.
43	whois	954	Determines a user's name on a remote system.
70	gopher	1436	Looks up documents, but has been mostly replaced by HTTP.
79	finger	1288	Determines information about users on other systems.
80	http	1945	Transfer documents. Forms the foundation of the Web.
110	pop3	1939	Accesses message stored on servers. Stands for Post Office Protocol, version 3.
443	https	n/a	Allows HTTP communications to be secure. Stands for Hypertext Transfer Protocol over Secure Sockets Layer (SSL).

What Is an IP Address?

The TCP/IP protocol is actually a combination of two protocols: the Transmission Control Protocol (TCP) and the Internet Protocol (IP). The IP component of TCP/IP is responsible for moving packets of data from node to node, and TCP is responsible for verifying the correct delivery of data from client to server.

An IP address looks like a series of four numbers separated by dots. These addresses are called IP addresses because the actual address is transferred with the IP portion of the protocol. For example, the IP address of my own site is 216.122.248.53. Each of these four numbers is a byte and can, therefore, hold numbers between zero and 255. The entire IP address is a 4-byte, or 32-bit, number. This is the same size as the Java primitive data type of int.

Why represent an IP address as four numbers separated by periods? If it's really just an unsigned 32-bit integer, why not just represent IP addresses as their true numeric identities? Actually, you can: the IP address 216.122.248.53 can also be represented by 3631937589. If you point a browser at http://216.122.248.53 it should take you to the same location as if you pointed it to http://3631937589.

If you are not familiar with the byte-order representation of numbers, the transformation from 216.122.248.53 to 3631937589 may seem somewhat confusing. The conversion can easily be accomplished with any scientific calculator or even the calculator that comes with

Windows (in scientific mode). To make the conversion, you must convert each of the byte components of the address 216.122.248.53 into its *hexadecimal* equivalent. You can easily do the conversion by switching the Windows calculator to decimal mode, entering the number, and then switching to hexadecimal mode. When you do this, the results will mirror these:

Decimal	Hexadecimal
216	D8
122	7A
248	F8
53	35

Now that each byte is hexadecimal, you must create one single hexadecimal number that is the composite of all four bytes concatenated together. Just list each byte one right after the other, as shown here:

D8 7A F8 35 or D87AF835

You now have the numeric equivalent of the IP address. The only problem is that this number is in hexadecimal. No problem, your scientific calculator can easily convert hexadecimal back into decimal. When you do so, you will get the number 3,631,937,589. This same number can now be used in the URL: `http://3631937589`.

Why do we need two forms of IP addresses? What does 216.122.248.53 add that 3631937589 does not? Mainly, the former is easier to memorize. Though neither number is terribly appealing to memorize, the designers of the Internet thought that period-separated byte notation (216.122.248.53) was easier to remember than the lengthy numeric notation (3631937589). In reality, though, the end user generally sees neither form. This is because IP addresses are almost always tied to hostnames.

What Is a Hostname?

Hostnames are used because addresses such as 216.122.248.53, or 3631937589, are too hard for the average computer user to remember. For example, my hostname, `www.heat-on.com`, is set to point to `216.122.248.53`. It is much easier for a human to remember `www.heat-on.com` than it is to remember `216.122.248.53`.

A hostname should not be confused with a Uniform Resource Locator (URL). A hostname is just one component of a URL. For example, one page on my site may have the URL of `http://www.jeffheaton.com/java/advanced/`. The hostname is only the `www.jeffheaton.com` portion of that URL. It specifies the server that will transmit the requested files. A hostname only identifies an IP address belonging to a server; a URL specifies some specific file on a server. There are other components to the URL that will be examined in Chapter 2.

The relationship between hostnames and IP addresses is not a one-to-one but a many-to-many relationship. First, let's examine the relationship of many hostnames to one IP address. Very often, people want to host several sites from one server. This server can only have one IP address, but it can allow several hostnames to point to it. This is the case with my own site. In addition to www.heat-on.com, I also have www.jeffheaton.com. Both of these hostnames are set to provide the exact same IP address. I said that the relationship between hostnames and IP addresses was many-to-many. Is there a case where one single hostname can have multiple IP addresses? Usually this is not the case, but very large volume sites will often have large arrays of servers called *webfarms* or *server farms*. Each of these servers will often have its own individual IP address. Yet the entire server farm is accessible through *one* hostname.

It is very easy to determine the IP address from a hostname. There is a command that most operating systems have called Ping. The Ping command has many uses. It can tell you if the specified site is up or down; it can also tell you the IP address of a host. The format of the Ping command is PING <hostname | IP>. You can give Ping either a hostname or an IP address. Below is a Ping that was given the hostname of heat-on.com. As heat-on.com is pinged, its IP address is returned.

```
C:\>ping heat-on.com

Pinging heat-on.com [216.122.248.53] with 32 bytes of data:

Reply from 216.122.248.53: bytes=32 time=150ms TTL=241
Reply from 216.122.248.53: bytes=32 time=70ms TTL=241
Reply from 216.122.248.53: bytes=32 time=131ms TTL=241
Reply from 216.122.248.53: bytes=32 time=120ms TTL=241
```

This command can also be used to prove that my site with the hostname jeffheaton.com really has the same address as my site with the hostname heat-on.com. The following Ping command demonstrates this:

```
C:\>ping jeffheaton.com

Pinging jeffheaton.com [216.122.248.53] with 32 bytes of data:

Reply from 216.122.248.53: bytes=32 time=80ms TTL=241
Reply from 216.122.248.53: bytes=32 time=80ms TTL=241
Reply from 216.122.248.53: bytes=32 time=90ms TTL=241
Reply from 216.122.248.53: bytes=32 time=70ms TTL=241
```

The distinction between hostnames and URLs is very important when dealing with Ping. Ping only accepts IP addresses or hostnames. A URL is not an acceptable input to the Ping command. Attempting to ping http://www.heat-on.com will not work, as demonstrated here:

```
C:\>ping http://www.heat-on.com/
Bad IP address http://www.heat-on.com/.
```

Ping does have some programming to make it more intelligent. If you were to just ping `http://www.heat-on.com` without the trailing "/" and other path specifiers, the Windows version of Ping will take the hostname from the URL.

WARNING   Like nearly every example in this book, the Ping command requires that you be connected to the Internet for this example to work.

How DNS Resolves a Hostname to an IP Address

Socket connections can only be established using an IP address. Because of this, it is necessary to convert a hostname to an IP address. How exactly is a hostname resolved to an IP address? Depending on how your computer is configured, it could be done in several ways, but most systems use domain name service (DNS) to provide this translation. In this section, we will examine this process. First, we will explore how DNS transforms a hostname into an IP address.

DNS and IP Addresses

DNS servers are server machines that return the IP addresses associated with particular hostnames. There is not just one central DNS server, however; resolving hostnames is handled by a huge, diverse array of DNS servers that are set up throughout the world.

When your computer is configured to access the Internet, it must be given the IP addresses of two DNS servers. Usually these are configured by your network administrator or provided by your Internet service provider (ISP). The DNS servers may have hostnames too, but you cannot use these when you are configuring the servers. Your computer must have a DNS server in order to resolve an IP address. If the DNS server you have was presented using a hostname, however, you're in trouble. This is because the computer doesn't have a DNS server to use to look up the IP address of the one DNS server you do have. As you can see, it's really a chicken and egg–type of problem.

But requiring computer users to enter two DNS servers as IP addresses can be cumbersome. If the user enters any piece of this information incorrectly, they will be unable to connect to any sites using a hostname. Because of this, the *Dynamic Host Configuration Protocol (DHCP)* was created.

Using the Dynamic Host Configuration Protocol

Very often, computer systems use DHCP instead of forcing the user to specify most network configuration information (such as IP addresses and DNS servers). The purpose of DHCP is to enable individual computers on an IP network to obtain their initial configurations from a DHCP server or servers, rather than making users perform this configuration themselves. The network administrator can set up all the DNS information on one central machine, the DNS server. The DHCP server then disseminates this configuration information to all user computers. This provides conformity and alleviates the users from having to enter network configuration information. The DHCP server has no exact information about the individual computers until they request this configuration information. The user computers will request this information when they first connect to the network. The overall purpose of this is to reduce the work necessary to administer a large IP network. The most significant piece of information distributed in this manner is the DNS servers that the user computer should use.

DHCP was created by the Internet Architecture Board (IAB) of the Internet Engineering Task Force (IETF; a volunteer organization that defines protocols for use on the Internet). Because of this, the definition of DHCP is recorded in an Internet RFC, and the IAB is asserting its status as to Internet Standardization.

Many broadband ISPs, such as cable modems and DSL, use DHCP directly from their broadband modem. When the broadband modem is connected to the computer using Ethernet, the DHCP server can be built into the broadband modem so that it can correctly configure the user's computer.

Resolving Addresses Using Java Methods

Earlier, you saw that Ping could be used to determine the IP address of a hostname. In order for this to work, you will need a way for a Java program to programmatically determine the IP address of a site, without having to call the external Ping command. If you know the IP address of the site, you can validate it, or differentiate it from other sites that may be hosted at the same computer. This validation can be completed by using methods from the Java `InetAddress` class.

The most commonly used method in the `InetAddress` class is the `getByName` method. This static method accepts a String parameter that can be an IP address (`216.122.248.53`) or a hostname (`www.heat-on.com`). This is shown in Listing 1.1, which also shows how an IP address can be converted to a hostname or vice versa.

Listing 1.1   **Lookup Addresses (Lookup.java)**

```java
import java.net.*;

/**
 * Example program from Chapter 1
 * Programming Spiders, Bots and Aggregators in Java
 *
 * A simple class used to lookup a hostname using either
 * an IP address or a hostname and to display the IP
 * address and hostname for this address. This class can
 * be used both to display the IP address for a hostname,
 * as well as do a reverse IP lookup and  * give the host
```

```
 * name for an IP address.

 *
 * @author Jeff Heaton
 * @version 1.0
 */
public class Lookup {

  /**
   * The main function.
   *
   * @param args The first argument should be the
   * address to lookup.
   */
  public static void main(String[] args)
  {
    try {
      if ( args.length==0 ) {
        System.out.println(
                        "Call with one parameter that specifies the host " +
                        "to lookup.");
      } else {
        InetAddress address = InetAddress.getByName(args[0]);
        System.out.println(address);
      }
    } catch ( Exception e ) {
      System.out.println("Could not find " + args[0] );
    }
  }
}
```

The actual address resolution in Listing 1.1 occurs during the execution of the following two lines:

```
InetAddress address = InetAddress.getByName(args[0]);
System.out.println(address);
```

First, the input address (held by arg[0]) is passed to getByName to construct a new Inet-Address object. This will create a new InetAddress object, based on the host specified by args[0]. The program should be called by specifying the address to resolve. For example, looking up the IP address for www.heat-on.com will result in the following:

```
C:\Lookup>java Lookup www.heat-on.com
www.heat-on.com/216.122.248.53
```

Reverse DNS Lookup

Another very powerful ability that is contained in the InetAddress class is *reverse DNS lookup*. If you know only the IP address, as you do in certain network operations, you can pass this IP address to the getByName method, and from there, you can retrieve the associated hostname.

For example, if you know the address 216.122.248.53 accessed your web server but you don't know to whom this IP address belongs, you could pass this address to the InetAddress object for reverse lookup:

```
C:\Lookup>java Lookup 216.122.248.53
heat-on.com/216.122.248.53
```

With the basics of Internet addressing out of the way, you are now almost ready to learn how to program sockets, but first you must learn a bit of background information about sockets' place in Java's complex I/O handling system. You will first be shown how to use the Java I/O system and how it relates to sockets.

Java I/O Programming

Java has some of the most complex input/output (I/O) capabilities of any programming language. This has two consequences: first, because it is complex, it is quite capable of many amazing things (such as reading ZIP and other complex file formats); second, and somewhat unfortunately, because it is complex, it is somewhat difficult for a programmer to learn, at least initially.

But don't be put off by this initial difficulty because Java has an extensive array of I/O support classes, which are all contained in the java.io package. Java's I/O classes are made up of *input streams*, *output streams*, *readers*, *writers*, and *filters*. These are merely categories of object, and there are several examples of each type. These categories will now be examined in detail.

NOTE   Because the primary focus of this book is to teach you the Java network communication you will need in order to program spiders, bots, and aggregators, we will examine Java's I/O classes as they relate to network communications. However, much of the information could also easily apply to file-based I/O under Java. If you are already familiar with file programming in Java, much of this material will be review. Conversely, if you are unfamiliar with Java file programming, the techniques learned in this chapter will also directly apply to file programming.

Output Streams

There are many types of output streams provided by Java. All output streams share a common base class, java.io.OutputStream. This base class is declared as abstract and, therefore, it cannot be directly instantiated. This class provides several fundamental methods that are needed to write data. This section will show you how to create, use, and close output streams.

Creating Output Streams

The OutputStream class provided by Java is abstract, and it is meant only to be overridden to provide OutputStreams for such things as socket- and disk-based output. The OutputStream provided by Java provides the following methods:

```
public abstract void write(int b)
  throws IOException

public void write(byte[] b)
  throws IOException

public void write(byte[] b, int off, int len)
  throws IOException

public void flush()
  throws IOException

public void close()
  throws IOException
```

NOTE   Other Java output streams extend this class to provide functionality. If you would like to create an output stream or filter, you will need to extend this class as well.

We will first see how the abstract write method can be used to create an output stream of your own. After that, the next section describes how to use the other methods.

Creating an output stream is relatively easy. You should create an output stream any time you would like to implement a *data consumer*. A data consumer is any class that accepts data and does something with that data. What is done with the data is left up to the implementation of the output stream.

Creating an output stream is easy if you keep in mind what an output stream does—it outputs bytes. This is the only functionality that you must provide to create an output stream. To create the new output stream, you must override the single byte version of the write method (void write(int b)). This method is used to consume a single byte of data. Once you have overridden this method, you must do with that byte whatever makes sense for the class you are creating (examples include writing the byte to a file or encrypting the byte).

An example of using an output stream to encrypt will be shown in Chapter 3, "Securing Communications with HTTPS." In Chapter 3, we will need to create a class that implements a base64 encoder. *Base64* is a method of encoding text so that it is not easily recognized. We will create a filter that will accept incoming text and output it as encoded base64 data. This encoder works by creating an output stream (actually a filter) capable of outputting base64-encoded text. This class works by providing just the single byte version of write.

There are many other examples of output streams provided by Java. When you open a connection to a socket, you can request an output stream to which you can transmit information. Other streams support more traditional I/O. For instance, Java supports a `FileOutputStream` to deal with disk files. Other `OutputStream` descendants are provided for other output streams. Now, you will be shown how to use output streams using some of the other methods of the `OutputStream` class.

Using Output Streams

Output streams exist to allow data to be written to some data consumer; what sort of consumer is unimportant because the output stream objects define methods that allow data to be sent to *any* sort of data consumer.

The `write` method only works with the `byte` data type. Bytes are usually an inconvenient data type to deal with because most data types are larger numbers or strings. Most programmers deal with the higher-level data types that are composed of bytes. Later in this chapter, we will examine filters, which will allow you to write higher-level data types, such as strings, to output streams without the need to manually convert these data types to bytes.

NOTE   Even though the `write` methods specify that they accept `int`s, they are actually accepting bytes. Only the lower 8 bytes of the `int` are actually used.

The following example shows you how to write an array of bytes to an output stream. Assume that the variable output is an output stream. You will be shown how to actually obtain an output stream later in this chapter.

```
byte b = new byte[100]; // creates a byte array
output.write( b ); // writes the byte array
```

Now that you have seen how to use output streams, you will be shown how to read them more efficiently. By adding buffering to an output stream, data can be read in much larger, more efficient blocks.

Handling Buffering in Output Streams

It is very inefficient for a programming language to write data out in very small blocks. A considerable overhead occurs every time a `write` method is invoked. If your program uses many `write` method calls, each of which writes only a single byte, much time will be lost just dealing with the overhead of writing each byte independently. To alleviate this problem, Java uses a technique called *buffering*, which is the process of storing bytes for later transmission.

Buffering takes many small `write` method calls and combines them into one large block of data to be written. The size of this eventual block of data is system defined and controlled by Java. Buffering occurs in the background, without the programmer being directly aware of it.

But sometimes the programmer *must* be directly aware of buffering. Sometimes it is necessary to make sure that the data has actually been written and is not just sitting in a buffer. Writing data without regard to buffering is not practical when you are dealing with network streams such as sockets. This is because the server computer is waiting for a complete message from the client before it responds. But how can it ever respond if the client is waiting to send more data? In fact, if you just write the data, you can quickly enter a deadlock situation with each of the components acting as follows:

Client   Has just sent some data to the server and is now waiting for a response.

Output Stream (*buffered*)   Received the data, but it is now waiting for a bit more information before it transmits the data it has already received over the network.

Server   Waiting for client to send the request; will time out soon.

To alleviate this problem, the output stream provides a flush method, which allows the programmer to force the output stream to write any data that is stored in the buffer. The flush method ensures that data is definitely written. If only a few bytes are written, they may be held in a temporary buffer before being transmitted. These bytes will later be transmitted when there is a certain, system-defined amount. This allows Java to make more efficient use of transfer bandwidth. Programmers should explicitly call the flush method when they are working with OutputStream objects. This will ensure that any data that has not been transmitted yet will be transmitted.

If you're dumping a certain amount of data to a file object, buffering is less important. For disk-based output, you simply dump the data to the file and then close it. It really does not matter when the data is actually written—you just know that it is all written once you issue the close command on the file output stream.

Closing an Output Stream

A close method is also provided to every output stream. It is important to call this method when you are done with the OutputStream class to ensure that the stream is properly closed and to make sure any file data is flushed out of the stream. If you fail to call the close method, Java will discard the memory taken by the actual OutputStream object when it goes out of scope, but Java will not actually close the object.

WARNING   Not calling the close method can often cause your program to leak resources. Resource leaks are operating system objects, such as sockets, that are left open if the close method is not called.

If an output stream is an abstract class, where does it come from? How do you instantiate an OutputStream class? OutputStream objects are never obtained directly by using the *new* operator. Rather, `OutputStream` objects are usually obtained from other objects. For example, the `Socket` class contains a method called `getOutputStream`. Calling the `getOutputStream` method will return an `OutputStream` object that will be used to write to the socket. Other output streams are obtained by different means.

Input Streams

Like output streams, there are many types of input streams provided by Java, which share a common base class, `java.io.InputStream`. This base class is declared as abstract and, therefore, cannot be directly instantiated. This class provides several fundamental methods that are needed to read data. This section will show how to create, use, and close input streams.

Creating Input Streams

The `InputStream` class provided by Java is abstract, and it is only meant to be overridden to provide `InputStream` classes for such things as socket- and disk-based input. The `InputStream` provided by Java provides the following methods:

```
public abstract int read()
   throws IOException

public int read(byte[] b)
   throws IOException

public int read(byte[] b, int off, int len)
   throws IOException

public long skip(long n)
   throws IOException

public int available()
   throws IOException

public void close()
   throws IOException

public void mark(int readlimit)

public void reset()
   throws IOException

public boolean markSupported()
```

We will first see how the abstract `read` method can be used to create an input stream of your own. After that, the next section describes how to use the other methods.

Creating an input stream is relatively easy. You should create an input stream any time you would like to implement a *data producer*. A data producer is any class that provides data that it got from somewhere. Where this data comes from is left up to the implementation of the output stream.

Creating an input stream is easy if you keep in mind what an input stream does—it reads bytes. This is the only functionality that you must provide to create an input stream. To create the new input stream, you must override the single byte version of the read method (int read()). This method is used to produce a single byte of data. Once you have overridden this method, you must do with that byte whatever makes sense for the class you are creating (examples include writing the byte to a file or encrypting the byte).

Usually you will be using input streams rather than creating them. The next section describes how to use input streams.

Using Input Streams

There are many examples of overridden input streams provided by Java. For example, when you open a connection to a socket, you can request an input stream from which you can receive information. Java also supports a FileInputStream to deal with disk files. Still other InputStream descendants are provided for other input streams.

The InputStream class uses several methods to transmit data. By using these methods, you can transmit data to a data consumer. The exact nature of this data consumer is unimportant to the input stream; the input stream is only concerned with the function of moving the data. What is done with the data is left up to which type of input stream you're using, such as a socket- or disk-based file. These methods will now be described.

The read methods allow you to read data in bytes. Even though the abstract read method shown in the previous section returns an int, the method is only reading a byte at a time. For performance reasons, whenever reasonably possible, you should try to use the read methods that accept an array. This will allow more data to be read from the underlying device at a time.

NOTE   Note even though the read methods specify that they return ints, they are actually returning bytes. Only the lower 8 bytes of the int are actually used.

The skip method allows a specified number of bytes to be skipped. This is often more efficient than just reading bytes and discarding their values. The available method is also provided to show how many bytes are available to be read.

Java also supports two methods called mark and reset. I do not generally recommend their use because they have two weaknesses that are hard to overcome. Specifically, not all streams support mark and reset, and those streams that do support them generally impose range limitations that restrict how far you can "rewind." The idea is that you can call a mark at some point as you are reading data from the InputStream and then you continue reading. If you ever need to return to the point in the stream when the mark method was called, you can call reset and return to that position. This would allow your program to reread data it has already seen. In many ways, this is a rewind feature for an input stream.

Closing Input Streams

Just like output streams, input streams must be closed when you are done with them. Input streams do not have the buffering issues that output streams do, however. This is because input streams are just reading data, not saving it. Since the data is already saved, the input stream cannot cause any of it to be lost. For example, reading only half of a file won't in anyway change or damage that file.

Input streams do share the resource-leaking issues of output streams, though. If you do not explicitly close an input stream, you run the risk of the underlying operating system resource not being closed. If this is done enough, your program will run out of streams to allocate.

Filter streams are built on the concept of input and output streams. Filter streams can be layered on top of input and output streams to provide additional functionality. Filters will be discussed in the next section.

Filter Streams, Readers, and Writers

Any I/O operation can be accomplished with the InputStream and OutputStream classes. These classes are like atoms: you can build anything with them, but they are very basic building blocks. The InputStream and OutputStream classes only give you access to the raw bytes of the connection. It's up to you to determine whether the underlying meaning of these bytes is a string, an IEEE754 floating point number, Unicode text, or some other binary construct.

Filters are generally used as a sort of attachment to the InputStream and OutputStream classes to hide the low-level complexity of working solely with bytes. There are two primary types of filters. The first is the *basic filter*, which is used to transform the underlying binary numbers into meaningful data types. Many different basic filters have been created; there are filters to compress, encrypt, and perform various translations on data. Table 1.2 shows a listing of some of the more useful filters available.

TABLE 1.2: Some Java Filters

Read Filter	Write Filter	Purpose
BufferedInputStream	BufferedOutputStream	These filters implement a buffered input and output stream. By setting up such a stream, an application can read/write bytes from a stream without necessarily causing a call to the underlying system for each byte that is read/written. The data is read/written by blocks into a buffer. This often produces more efficient reading and writing. This is a normal filter and can be used in a chain.
DataInputStream	DataOutputStream	A data input/output stream filter allows an application to read/write primitive Java data types from an underlying input/output stream in a machine-independent way.
GZIPInputStream	GZIPOutputStream	This filter implements a stream filter for reading or writing data compressed in the GZIP format.
ZipInputStream	ZipOutputStream	This filter implements input/output filter streams for reading and writing files in the ZIP file format. This class includes support for both compressed and uncompressed entries.
n/a	PrintWriter	This filter prints formatted representations of objects to a text-output stream. This class implements all of the print methods found in `PrintStream`. It does not contain methods for writing raw bytes, for which a program should use unencoded byte streams.

The second type of filter is really a set of filters that work together; the filters that compose this set are called *readers* and *writers*. The remainder of this section will focus on readers and writers. These filters are designed to handle the differences between various methods of text encoding. Readers and writers, for example, can handle text encoded in such formats as ASCII Encoding (UTF-8) and Unicode (UTF-16).

Filters themselves are extended from the `FilterInputStream` and `FilterOutputStream` classes. These two classes inherit from `InputStream` and `OutputStream` classes respectively. Because of this, filters function exactly like the low-level `InputStream` and `OutputStream` classes. Every `FilterInputStream` must implement at least a `read` method. Likewise, every `FilterOutputStream` must implement at least a `write` method. By overriding these methods, the filters may modify data, as it is being read or written. Many filter streams will provide many more methods. But some, for example the `BufferedInputStream` and `BufferedOutput-Stream`, provide no new methods and merely keep the same interface as `InputStream` and `OutputStream`.

Chaining Filters Together

One very important feature of filters is their ability to chain themselves together. A basic filter can be layered on top of either an input/output stream or another filter. A reader/writer can be layered on top of an input/output stream or another filter but never on another reader/writer. Readers and writers must always be the last filter in a chain.

Filters are layered by passing the underlying filter or stream into the constructor of the new stream. For example, to open a file with a `BufferedInputStream`, the following code should be used:

```
FileInputStream fin = new FileInputStream("myfile.txt");
BufferedInputStream bis = new BufferedInputStream(fin);
```

It is very important that the underlying `InputStream` not be discarded. If the `fin` variable in the preceding code were reassigned or set to null, an error would result when the `Buffered-InputStream` was used.

Proxy Issues

One very important aspect of TCP/IP networking is that no two computers can have the same IP address. Proxies and firewalls allow many computers to access the Internet through one single IP address, though. This is often the situation in large corporate environments. The users will access one single computer, called a *proxy server*, rather than directly connecting to the Internet. This access is generally sufficient for most users.

The primary difference between a direct connection and this type of connection is that when a computer is directly connected to the Internet, that computer has one or more IP addresses all to itself. In a proxy situation, any number of computers could be sharing the same outbound proxy IP address. When the computer hooked to the proxy is using client-side sockets, this does not present a problem. The server that is acting as the proxy server can conceivably support any number of outbound connections.

Problems occur when a computer connected through the proxy wants to become a server. If the computer hooked to the proxy network sets itself to become a server on a specific port, then it can *only* accept connections on the internal proxy network. If a computer from the outside attempts to connect back to the computer behind the proxy, it will end up trying to connect to the proxy computer, which will likely refuse the connection.

Most of the programs presented in this book are clients. Because of this, they can be run from behind a proxy server with little trouble. The only catch is that they have to know that they are connected through a proxy. For example, before you can use Microsoft Internet Explorer (IE) from behind a proxy server, you must configure it to know that it is being run in this configuration. In the case of IE, you can select Tools and then Internet Options to do this. From the resulting menu, select Connections and then choose the LAN Settings button. A screen similar to the one in Figure 1.1 will appear. This screen shows you how to configure IE for the correct proxy settings.

NOTE	This book assumes that you have a working Internet connection. You will need the information presented here to allow Java to use your proxy server. Just having the settings in IE does not configure every network service on your computer to use the proxy server. Each application must generally be configured separately.

FIGURE 1.1:

Proxy settings in
Internet Explorer

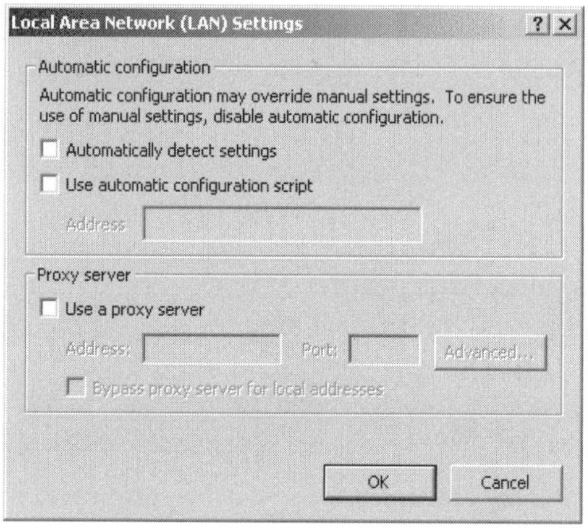

Configuring Java to Use a Proxy Server

There are two ways to configure Java to use a proxy server. The proxy configuration can be either set by the Java code itself, or it can be set as parameters to the Java Virtual Machine (JVM) when the application is first started. The proxy settings for Java are contained in system properties and can be specified from the command line or can be set by the program. Table 1.3 shows a list of some of the more common proxy-related system properties. Like any system property, proxy-related properties can be set in two different ways. The first is by specifying them on the command line to the JVM. For example, to execute a program called UseProxy .class, you could use the following command:

```
java -Dhttp.ProxyHost=socks.myhost.com -Dhttp.ProxyPort=1080 UseProxy
```

If you would prefer to set the proxy information programmatically from your program, you can use the following section of code to accomplish the same thing. You do not need to use both methods—one will suffice.

```
public class UseProxy
{
  public static void main(String args[])
  {
   System.setProperty("http.proxySet",true);
   System.setProperty("http.proxyHost","socks.myhost.com");
   System.setProperty("http.proxyPort","1080");
    // program continues here
  }
}
```

WARNING   If you are connecting to the Internet through a proxy server, you *must* use one of the above methods to let Java know about your proxy settings. If you fail to do this, the programs in this book will not be able to connect to the Internet.

TABLE 1.3: Common Command Line Proxy Settings in Java

System Property	Values	Purpose
FtpProxySet	true/false	Set to true if a proxy is to be used for FTP connections.
FtpProxyHost	hostname	The host address for a proxy server to be used for FTP connections.
FtpProxyPort	port number	The port to be used on the specified hostname to be used for FTP connections.
gopherProxySet	true/false	Set to true if a proxy is to be used for Gopher connections.
gopherProxyHost	hostname	The host address for a proxy server to be used for Gopher connections.
gopherProxyPort	port number	The port to be used on the specified hostname to be used for Gopher connections.
http.proxySet	true/false	Set to true if a proxy is to be used for HTTP connections.
http.proxyHost	hostname	The host address for a proxy server to be used for HTTP connections.
http.proxyPort	port number	The port to be used on the specified hostname to be used for HTTP connections.
https.proxySet	true/false	Set to true if a proxy is to be used for HTTPS connections.
https.proxyHost	hostname	The host address for a proxy server to be used for HTTPS connections.
https.proxyPort	port number	The port to be used on the specified hostname to be used for HTTPS connections.

Socket Programming in Java

Java has greatly simplified socket programming, especially when compared to the requirements and constructs of many other programming languages. Java defines two classes that are of particular importance to socket programming: Socket and ServerSocket. If the program you are writing is to play the role of server, it should use ServerSocket. If the program is to connect to a server, and thus play the role of client, it should use the Socket class.

The Socket class, whether server (when done through the child class ServerSocket) or client, is only used to initially start the connection. Once the connection is established, input and output streams are used to actually facilitate the communication between the client and server. Once the connection is made, the distinction between client and server is purely arbitrary. Either side may read from or write to the socket.

All socket reading is done through a Java InputStream class, and all socket writing is done through a Java OutputStream class. These are low-level streams provide only the most rudimentary input methods. All communication with the InputStream and the OutputStream must be done with bytes—bytes are the only data type recognized by these classes. Because of this, the InputStream and OutputStream classes are often paired with higher-level Java input classes. Two such classes for InputStream are the DataInputStream and the Buffered-Reader. The DataInputStream allows your program to read binary elements, such as 16- or 32-bit integers from the socket stream. The BufferedReader allows you to read lines of text from the socket. For OutputStream, the two possible classes are DataOutputStream and the PrintWriter. The DataOutputStream allows your program to write binary elements, such as 16- or 32-bit integers from the socket stream. The PrintWriter allows you to write lines of text from the socket.

As mentioned earlier, sockets form the lowest-level protocol that most programmers ever deal with. Layered on top of sockets are a host of other protocols used to implement Internet standards. These socket protocols are documented in RFCs. You will now learn about RFCs and how they document socket protocols.

Socket Protocols and RFCs

Sockets merely define a way to have a two-way communication between programs. These two programs can write any sort of data, be it binary or textual, to/from each other. If there is to be any order to this, though, there must be an established protocol. Any protocol will define how each side should communicate and what is to be accomplished by this communication.

Every Internet protocol is documented in a RFC—RFCs will be quoted as sources of information throughout this book. RFCs are numbered; for example, HTTP is documented in RFC1945. A complete set of RFCs can be found at http://www.rfc-editor.org.

RFC numbers are never reused or edited. Once an RFC is published, it will not be modified. The only way to effectively modify an RFC is to publish a new RFC that makes the old RFC obsolete.

NOTE To see which RFC number applies to protocols such as HTTP, SMTP, FTP, and other Internet protocols, refer back to Table 1.1.

For the remainder of the chapter, we will be examining client sockets and server sockets. These will be described in detail through the use of two RFCs. First, you'll look at RFC821, which defines SMTP and shows a client implementation. Second, you will examine RFC1945, which defines HTTP and shows a simple web server implementation.

Client Sockets

Client sockets are used to establish a connection to server sockets, and they are the type of sockets that will be used for the majority of socket examples throughout this book. To demonstrate client sockets, we will look at an example of SMTP. You will be shown SMTP through the use of an example program that sends an e-mail.

The Simple Mail Transfer Protocol

The *Simple Mail Transfer Protocol (SMTP)* forms the foundation of all e-mail delivery by the Internet. As you can see from Table 1.1, SMTP uses port 25 and is documented by RFC821.

When you install an Internet e-mail program, such as Microsoft Outlook Express or Eudora Mail, you must specify a SMTP server to process outgoing mail. This SMTP server is set up to receive mail messages formatted by Eudora or similar programs. When an SMTP server receives an e-mail, it first examines the message to determine who it is for. If the SMTP server controls the mailbox of the receiver, then the message is delivered. If the message is for someone on another SMTP server, then the message is forwarded to that SMTP server.

NOTE For the purposes of this chapter, you do not care whether the SMTP server is going to forward the e-mail or handle the e-mail itself. Your only concern is that you have handed the e-mail off to an SMTP server, and you assume that the server will handle it appropriately. You will not be aware of it if the e-mail needs to be forwarded or processed.

The SMTP protocol that RFC821 defines is nothing more than a series of requests and responses. The SMTP client opens a connection to the server. Once the connection is established, the client can issue any of the commands shown in Table 1.4.

NOTE Table 1.4 does not show a complete set of SMTP commands, just the commands needed for this chapter. For a complete list of commands refer to RFC821.

TABLE 1.4: Selected SMTP Commands

Command	Purpose
HELO [*client name*]	Should be the first command, and should identify the client computer.
MAIL FROM [*user name*]	Should specify who the message is from, and should be a valid e-mail address.
RCPT TO [*user name*]	Should specify the receiver of this message, and should be a valid e-mail address.
DATA	Should be sent just before the body of the e-mail message. To end this command, you must send a period (".") as a single line.

Here, you can see a typical communication session, including the commands discussed in Table 1.4, between an RFC client and the RFC server:

1. The client opens the connection. The server responds with

   ```
   220 heat-on.com ESMTP Sendmail 8.11.0/8.11.0; Mon, 28 May 2001 15:41:26
   -0500 (CDT)
   ```

2. The client sends its first command (the HELO command) to identify itself, followed by the hostname:

   ```
   HELO JeffSComputer
   ```

   Sometimes the hostname is used for security purposes, but generally it is just logged. By convention, the hostname of the client computer should be displayed after the HELO command as seen here.

3. The server responds with

   ```
   250 heat-on.com Hello SC1-178.charter-stl.com [24.217.160.175], pleased to
   meet you
   ```

4. The client sends its second command:

   ```
   MAIL FROM: thesender@senderhost.com
   ```

   It is here that the e-mail sender is specified. Some SMTP severs will verify that the person the e-mail is from is a valid user for this system. This is to prevent certain bulk e-mailers from fraudulently sending large quantities of unwanted e-mail from an unsuspecting SMTP server.

5. The server responds with

   ```
   250 2.1.0 thesenderj@senderhost.com... Sender ok
   ```

6. The client sends its third command:

   ```
   RCPT TO: touser@tohost.com
   ```

This command specifies to whom the e-mail is being sent. The SMTP server looks at this command to determine what to do with the e-mail. If the user specified here is in the same domain handled by the SMTP server, then it sends the message to the correct mailbox. If the user specified here is elsewhere, then it forwards the mail message to the server that handles mail for that user.

7. The server responds with:

```
250 2.1.5 touserj@tohost.com... Recipient ok
```

8. The client now begins to send data:

```
DATA
```

9. The server responds with

```
354 Enter mail, end with "." on a line by itself
```

10. The client sends its data and ends it with a single "." on a line by itself:

```
This is a test message.
.
```

11. Finally, the server responds with

```
250 2.0.0 f4SKfQH59504 Message accepted for delivery
```

12. The session is complete and the connection is closed.

From this description, it should be obvious that security is at a minimum with SMTP. You can specify essentially any address you wish with the MAIL FROM command. This makes it very easy to forge an e-mail. Of course, a savvy Internet user can spot a forgery by comparing the e-mail headers to a known valid e-mail from that person. SMTP servers will always show the path that the e-mail went through in the headers. But to an unsuspecting user, such e-mails can be very confusing and misleading. Bulk e-mailers, who seek to hide their true e-mail addresses, often use such tactics. This is why when you attempt to reply to a bulk e-mail, the message usually bounces.

Using SMTP

Now that we have reviewed SMTP, we will create an example program that implements an SMTP client. This example program will allow the user to send an e-mail using SMTP. This program is shown running in Figure 1.2, and its source code is show in Listing 1.2. The source code is rather extensive; we'll review it in detail following the code listing.

FIGURE 1.2:

SMTP example
program

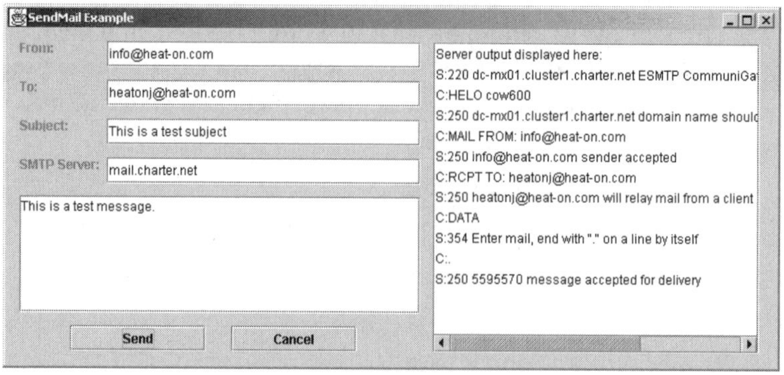

Listing 1.2   A Client to Send SMTP Mail (SendMail.java)

```java
import java.awt.*;
import javax.swing.*;

/**
 * Example program from Chapter 1
 * Programming Spiders, Bots and Aggregators in Java
 * Copyright 2001 by Jeff Heaton
 *
 * SendMail is an example of client sockets.  This program
 * presents a simple dialog box that prompts the user for
 * information about how to send a mail.
 *
 * @author Jeff Heaton
 * @version 1.0
 */
public class SendMail extends javax.swing.JFrame {

  /**
   * The constructor.  Do all basic setup for this
   * application.
   */
  public SendMail()
  {
    //{{INIT_CONTROLS
    setTitle("SendMail Example");
    getContentPane().setLayout(null);
    setSize(736,312);
    setVisible(false);
    JLabel1.setText("From: ");
    getContentPane().add(JLabel1);
    JLabel1.setBounds(12,12,36,12);
    JLabel2.setText("To: ");
    getContentPane().add(JLabel2);
```

```
        JLabel2.setBounds(12,48,36,12);
        JLabel3.setText("Subject:");
        getContentPane().add(JLabel3);
        JLabel3.setBounds(12,84,48,12);
        JLabel4.setText("SMTP Server:");
        getContentPane().add(JLabel4);
        JLabel4.setBounds(12,120,84,12);
        getContentPane().add(_from);
        _from.setBounds(96,12,300,24);
        getContentPane().add(_to);
        _to.setBounds(96,48,300,24);
        getContentPane().add(_subject);
        _subject.setBounds(96,84,300,24);
        getContentPane().add(_smtp);
        _smtp.setBounds(96,120,300,24);
        getContentPane().add(_scrollPane2);
        _scrollPane2.setBounds(12,156,384,108);
        _body.setText("Enter your message here.");
        _scrollPane2.getViewport().add(_body);
        _body.setBounds(0,0,381,105);
        Send.setText("Send");
        Send.setActionCommand("Send");
        getContentPane().add(Send);
        Send.setBounds(60,276,132,24);
        Cancel.setText("Cancel");
        Cancel.setActionCommand("Cancel");
        getContentPane().add(Cancel);
        Cancel.setBounds(216,276,120,24);
        getContentPane().add(_scrollPane);
        _scrollPane.setBounds(408,12,312,288);
        getContentPane().add(_output);
        _output.setBounds(408,12,309,285);
        //}}


        //{{INIT_MENUS
        //}}

        //{{REGISTER_LISTENERS
        SymAction lSymAction = new SymAction();
        Send.addActionListener(lSymAction);
        Cancel.addActionListener(lSymAction);
        //}}

        _output.setModel(_model);
        _model.addElement("Server output displayed here:");
        _scrollPane.getViewport().setView(_output);
        _scrollPane2.getViewport().setView(_body);
    }

/**
 * Moves the app to the correct position
```

```
 * when it is made visible.
 *
 * @param b True to make visible, false to make
 * invisible.
 */
public void setVisible(boolean b)
{
  if ( b )
    setLocation(50, 50);
  super.setVisible(b);
}

/**
 * The main function basically just creates a new object,
 * then shows it.
 *
 * @param args Command line arguments.
 * Not used in this application.
 */
static public void main(String args[])
{
  (new SendMail()).show();
}

/**
 * Created by VisualCafe.  Sets the window size.
 */
public void addNotify()
{
  // Record the size of the window prior to
  // calling parents addNotify.
  Dimension size = getSize();

  super.addNotify();

  if ( frameSizeAdjusted )
    return;
  frameSizeAdjusted = true;

  // Adjust size of frame according to the
  // insets and menu bar
  Insets insets = getInsets();
  javax.swing.JMenuBar menuBar =
    getRootPane().getJMenuBar();
  int menuBarHeight = 0;
  if ( menuBar != null )
    menuBarHeight = menuBar.getPreferredSize().height;
  setSize(insets.left
          + insets.right
          + size.width,
          insets.top
          + insets.bottom
```

```
                    + size.height
                    + menuBarHeight);
}

// Used by addNotify
boolean frameSizeAdjusted = false;

//{{DECLARE_CONTROLS

/**
 * A label.
 */
javax.swing.JLabel JLabel1 =
  new javax.swing.JLabel();

/**
 * A label.
 */
javax.swing.JLabel JLabel2 =
  new javax.swing.JLabel();

/**
 * A label.
 */
javax.swing.JLabel JLabel3 =
  new javax.swing.JLabel();

/**
 * A label.
 */
javax.swing.JLabel JLabel4 =
  new javax.swing.JLabel();

/**
 * Who this message is from.
 */
javax.swing.JTextField _from =
  new javax.swing.JTextField();

/**
 * Who this message is to.
 */
javax.swing.JTextField _to =
  new javax.swing.JTextField();

/**
 * The subject of this message.
 */
javax.swing.JTextField _subject =
  new javax.swing.JTextField();

/**
```

```
 * The SMTP server to use to send this message.
 */
javax.swing.JTextField _smtp =
  new javax.swing.JTextField();

/**
 * A scroll pane.
 */
javax.swing.JScrollPane _scrollPane2 =
  new javax.swing.JScrollPane();

/**
 * The body of this email message.
 */
javax.swing.JTextArea _body =
  new javax.swing.JTextArea();

/**
 * The send button.
 */
javax.swing.JButton Send =
  new javax.swing.JButton();

/**
 * The cancel button.
 */
javax.swing.JButton Cancel =
  new javax.swing.JButton();

/**
 * A scroll pain.
 */
javax.swing.JScrollPane _scrollPane
= new javax.swing.JScrollPane();

/**
 * The output area.  Server messages
 * are displayed here.
 */
javax.swing.JList _output =
  new javax.swing.JList();
//}}

/**
 * The list of items added to the output
 * list box.
 */
javax.swing.DefaultListModel _model
= new javax.swing.DefaultListModel();

/**
 * Input from the socket.
```

```
   */
java.io.BufferedReader _in;

/**
 * Output to the socket.
 */
java.io.PrintWriter _out;

//{{DECLARE_MENUS
//}}


/**
 * Internal class created by VisualCafe to
 * route the events to the correct functions.
 *
 * @author VisualCafe
 * @version 1.0
 */
class SymAction
  implements java.awt.event.ActionListener {

  /**
   * Route the event to the correction method.
   *
   * @param event The event.
   */
  public void actionPerformed
    (java.awt.event.ActionEvent event)
  {
    Object object = event.getSource();
    if ( object == Send )
      Send_actionPerformed(event);
    else if ( object == Cancel )
      Cancel_actionPerformed(event);
  }
}

/**
 * Called to actually send a string of text to the
 * socket.  This method makes note of the text sent
 * and the response in the JList output box.  Pass a
 * null value to simply wait for a response.
 *
 * @param s A string to be sent to the socket.
 * null to just wait for a response.
 * @exception java.io.IOException
 */
protected void send(String s) throws java.io.IOException
{
  // Send the SMTP command
  if ( s!=null ) {
```

```
      _model.addElement("C:"+s);
      _out.println(s);
      _out.flush();
    }
    // Wait for the response
    String line = _in.readLine();
    if ( line!=null ) {
      _model.addElement("S:"+line);
    }
}

/**
 * Called when the send button is clicked.  Actually
 * sends the mail message.
 *
 * @param event The event.
 */
void Send_actionPerformed(java.awt.event.ActionEvent event)
{
  try {

    java.net.Socket s
    = new java.net.Socket( _smtp.getText(),25 );
    _out = new java.io.PrintWriter(s.getOutputStream());
    _in = new java.io.BufferedReader(
      new java.io.InputStreamReader(s.getInputStream()));

    send(null);
    send("HELO " +
        java.net.InetAddress.getLocalHost().getHostName() );
    send("MAIL FROM: " + _from.getText() );
    send("RCPT TO: " + _to.getText() );
    send("DATA");
    _out.println("Subject:" + _subject.getText());
    _out.println( _body.getText() );
    send(".");
    s.close();

  } catch ( Exception e ) {
    _model.addElement("Error: " + e );
  }

}

/**
 * Called when cancel is clicked.  End the application.
 *
 * @param event The event.
 */
void Cancel_actionPerformed(java.awt.event.ActionEvent event)
{
```

```
    System.exit(0);

  }
}
```

Using the SMTP Program

To use the program in Listing 1.2, you must know the address of an SMTP server—usually provided by your ISP. If you are unsure of your SMTP server, you should contact your ISP's customer service. In order for outbound e-mail messages to be sent, your e-mail program must have this address. Once it does, you can enter who is sending the e-mail (if you are sending it, you would type your e-mail address in) and who will be on the receiving end. This is usually entered under the Reply To field of your e-mail program. Both of these addresses *must* be valid. If they are invalid, the e-mail may not be sent. After you have entered these addresses, you should continue by entering the subject, writing the actual message, and then clicking send.

NOTE   For more information on how to compile examples in this book, see Appendix E "How to Compile Examples Under Windows."

As stated earlier, to send an e-mail with this program, you must enter who is sending the message. You may be thinking that you could enter any e-mail address you want here, right? Yes, this is true; as long as the SMTP server allows it, this program will allow you to impersonate anyone you enter into the To address field. However, as previously stated, a savvy Internet user can tell whether the e-mail address is fake.

After the mention of possible misrepresentation of identity on the sender's end, you may now be asking yourself, "Is this program dangerous?" This program is no more dangerous than any e-mail client (such as Microsoft Outlook Express or Eudora) that also requires you to tell it who you are. In general, all e-mail programs must request both your identity and that of the SMTP server.

Examining the SMTP Server

You will now be shown how this program works. We will begin by looking at how a client socket is created. When the client socket is first instantiated, you must specify two parameters. First, you must specify the host to connect to; second, you must specify the port number (e.g., 80) you would like to connect on. These two items are generally passed into the constructor. The following line of code (from Listing 1.2) accomplishes this:

```
java.net.Socket s =new java.net.Socket( _smtp.getText(),25 );
```

This line of code creates a new socket, named s. The first parameter to the constructor, _smtp .getText(), specifies the address to connect to. Here it is being read directly from a text field. The second parameter specifies the port to connect to. (The port for SMTP is 25.) Table 1.1

shows a listing of the ports associated with most Internet services. The hostname is retrieved from the _smtp class level variable, which is the JTextField control that the SMTP hostname is entered into.

If any errors occur while you are making the connection to the specified host, the Socket constructor will throw an IOException. Once this connection is made, input and output streams are obtained from the Socket.getInputStream and Socket.getOutputStream methods. This is done with the following lines of code from Listing 1.2:

```
_out = new java.io.PrintWriter(s.getOutputStream());
_in = new java.io.BufferedReader(new
    java.io.InputStreamReader(s.getInputStream()));
```

These low-level stream types are only capable of reading binary data. Because this data is needed in text format, filters are used to wrap the lower-level input and output streams obtained from the socket.

In the code above, the output stream has been wrapped in a PrintWriter object. This is because PrintWriter allows the program to output text to the socket in a similar manner to the way an application would write data to the System.out object—by using the print and println methods. The application presented here uses the println method to send commands to the SMTP server. As you can see in the code, the InputStream object has also been wrapped; in this case, it has been wrapped in a BufferedReader. Before this could happen, however, this object must first have been wrapped in an InputStreamReader object as shown here:

```
_in = new java.io.BufferedReader(new
    java.io.InputStreamReader(s.getInputStream()));
```

This is done because the BufferedReader object provides reads that are made up of lines of text instead of individual bytes. This way, the program can read text up to a carriage return without having to parse the individual characters. This is done with the readLine method.

You will now be shown how each command is sent to the SMTP server. Each of these commands that is sent results in a response being issued from the SMTP server. For the protocol to work correctly, each response must be read by the SMTP client program. These responses start with a number and then they give a textual description of what the result was. A full-featured SMTP client should examine these codes and ensure that no error has occurred.

For the purposes of the SendMail example, we will simple ignore these responses because most are informational and not needed. Instead, for our purposes, the response will be read in and displayed to the _output list box. Commands that have been sent to the server are displayed in this list with a C: prefix to indicate that they are from the client. Responses returned from the SMTP server will be displayed with the S: prefix.

To accomplish this, the example program will use the send method. The send method accepts a single String parameter to indicate the SMTP command to be issued. Once this command is sent, the send method awaits a response from the SMTP host. The portion of Listing 1.2 that contains the send method is displayed here:

```
protected void send(String s) throws java.io.IOException
{
  // Send the SMTP command
  if(s!=null)
  {
    _model.addElement("C:"+s);
    _out.println(s);
    _out.flush();
  }
  // Wait for the response
  String line = _in.readLine();
  if(line!=null)
  {
    _model.addElement("S:"+line);
  }
}
```

As you can see, the send method does not handle the exceptions that might occur from its commands. Instead, they are thrown to the calling method as indicated by the throws clause of the function declaration. The variable s is checked to see if it is null. If s is null, then no command is to be sent and only a response is sought. If s is *not* null, then the value of s is logged and then sent to the socket. After this happens, the flush command is given to the socket to ensure that the command was actually sent and not just buffered. Once the command is sent, the readLine method is called to await the response from the server. If a response is sent, then it is logged.

Once the socket is created and the input and output objects are created, the SMTP session can begin. The following commands manage the entire SMTP session:

```
send(null);
send("HELO " +
  java.net.InetAddress.getLocalHost().getHostName() );
send("MAIL FROM: " + _from.getText() );
send("RCPT TO: " + _to.getText() );
send("DATA");
_out.println("Subject:" + _subject.getText());
_out.println( _body.getText() );
send(".");
s.close();
```

TIP   Refer to Table 1.4 in the preceding section to review the details of what each of the SMTP commands actually means.

The rest of the SendMail program (as seen in Listing 1.2) is a typical Swing application. The graphical user interface (GUI) layout for this application was created using VisualCafé. The VisualCafé comments have been left in to allow the form's GUI layout to be edited by VisualCafé if you are using it. If you are using an environment other than VisualCafé, you may safely delete the VisualCafé comments (lines starting in //). The VisualCafé code only consists of comments and does not need to be deleted to run on other platforms.

Server Sockets

Server sockets form the side of the TCP/IP connection to which client sockets connect. Once the connection is established, there is little distinction between the server sockets and client sockets. Both use exactly the same commands to send and retrieve data. Server sockets are represented by the ServerSocket class, which is a specialized version of the Socket class. The Socket class is the same class that was discussed in the earlier section about client sockets.

The Hypertext Transfer Protocol

Unlike SMTP, which is used to send e-mail messages, HTTP forms the foundation of all web browsing on the Internet. HTTP differs from SMTP in one very important way: SMTP is made up of a series of single-line packets (or communications) between the client and server, but the typical HTTP request has only two packets—the request and the response. In HTTP, the client sends a series of lines that specify what the client is requesting, and the server then responds with the response as one single packet. Listed below, you can see a typical HTTP client request for the page http://www.heat-on.com,

```
GET / HTTP/1.0
Accept: image/gif, image/x-xbitmap, image/jpeg, image/pjpeg, application/vnd.ms-
excel, application/msword, application/vnd.ms-powerpoint, */*
Accept-Language: en-us
Accept-Encoding: gzip, deflate
User-Agent: Mozilla/4.0
Host: WWW.HEAT-ON.COM
```

which is followed by the corresponding server response:

```
HTTP/1.1 200 OK
Server: Microsoft-IIS/4.0
Date: Thu, 02 Nov 2000 02:30:16 GMT
Content-Type: text/html
Set-Cookie: ASPSESSIONIDGGGGQRZC=KCGDKDABODIEPLJPHAMBMOFB; path=/
Cache-control: private

<!DOCTYPE HTML PUBLIC "-//W3C//DTD HTML 3.2//EN">

<HTML>
```

```
<HEAD>
   <TITLE>Jeff Heaton</TITLE>
.... The rest of the HTML document .....
```

The request and response packets shown here have similar formats. Each one has two areas: the header and the body. The first blank line is the border between the header area and the body area. Usually requests will not have a body, so they end with the first blank line. The body portion of the response is generally the only portion that is actually seen by the user. The headers control information that the client and server send to each other. The body contains the actual HTML code that will be displayed, and it begins immediately after the first blank line.

NOTE   The meanings of the headers in HTTP are important. We will discuss them in greater detail in Chapter 2. The section in Appendix B, "HTTP Headers," lists most of the HTTP headers that will be used throughout this book.

The first line of the request is the most important because it specifies the document that is being requested. In the previous example, the server assumes that the browser has been asked to retrieve the URL http://www.heat-on.com. The first line GET / HTTP/1.0 says three important things about this request: what type of request it is, what document is being requested, and what version of HTTP is needed. This line will usually be either GET, POST, or HEAD; in this case, this is a GET request. GET simply requests a document and sends a little information to the server. This request is mostly used when you click any link you may find on a web page. The POST request is used when you submit a form, but this rule does not always apply because JavaScript can alter this behavior (JavaScript can allow POSTs to be linked to nearly any user event, such as clicking a hyperlink). The / indicates the document that being requested. Specifying / means that the root document is being requested, not a specific document. Finally HTTP/1.0 just specifies the HTTP version that is needed.

NOTE   For more information on the HEAD request, refer to Chapter 2.

After the GET or POST request is received by the web server, a response is sent back. A sample response is shown in the second part of the previous example. There are two parts to this response. The first is the mention of HTTP headers, with the first line of the HTTP headers specifying the status of the request. The second part of the response is the body, the HTML returned from the server to the browser. The status is shown here:

```
HTTP/1.1 200 OK
```

This first line of the HTTP headers starts with a numeric error code; some of the common ones are listed here. (The section in Appendix B, "HTTP Status Codes," lists the standard meanings of each of these responses.)

100-199   Is an informational message and is not generally used.

200-299   Means a successful request.

300-399   Indicates that the requested resource has been moved. These are often used for redirection.

400-499   Indicates client errors.

500-599   Indicates server errors.

The remaining lines of the header, repeated here, comprise the actual message.

```
Server: Microsoft-IIS/4.0
Date: Thu, 02 Nov 2000 02:30:16 GMT
Content-Type: text/html
Set-Cookie: ASPSESSIONIDGGGGQRZC=KCGDKDABODIEPLJPHAMBMOFB; path=/
Cache-control: private

... message continues here ...
```

Using HTTP

Listing 1.3 shows the example of server sockets for this chapter. In this listing, you are introduced to a very simple web server that would not be practical for any use because it only displays one page. This example does demonstrate the use of a server socket, however. It also shows a simple use of HTTP; more complex uses of HTTP will be discussed in Chapter 2.

Listing 1.3   **A Simple Web Server (WebServer.java)**

```java
import java.net.*;
import java.io.*;

/**
 * Example program from Chapter 1
 * Programming Spiders, Bots and Aggregators in Java
 * Copyright 2001 by Jeff Heaton
 *
 * WebServer is a very simple web-server.  Any request
 * is responded with a very simple web-page.
 *
 * @author Jeff Heaton
 * @version 1.0
 */
public class WebServer {

  /**
   * WebServer constructor.
   */
  protected void start()
  {
    ServerSocket s;
```

```java
      System.out.println("Webserver starting up on port 80");
      System.out.println("(press ctrl-c to exit)");
      try {
        // create the main server socket
        s = new ServerSocket(80);
      } catch ( Exception e ) {
        System.out.println("Error: " + e );
        return;
      }

      System.out.println("Waiting for connection");
      for ( ;; ) {
        try {
          // wait for a connection
          Socket remote = s.accept();
          // remote is now the connected socket
          System.out.println("Connection, sending data.");
          BufferedReader in = new BufferedReader(
            new InputStreamReader(remote.getInputStream()) );
          PrintWriter out
          = new PrintWriter(remote.getOutputStream());

          // read the data sent.  We basically ignore it,
          // stop reading once a blank line is hit.  This
          // blank line signals the end of the client HTTP
          // headers.
          String str=".";
          while ( !str.equals("") )
            str = in.readLine();

          // Send the response
          // Send the headers
          out.println("HTTP/1.0 200 OK");
          out.println("Content-Type: text/html");
          out.println("Server: Bot");
          // this blank line signals the end of the headers
          out.println("");
          // Send the HTML page
          out.println(
            "<H1>Welcome to the Ultra Mini-WebServer</H2>");
          out.flush();
          remote.close();
        } catch ( Exception e ) {
          System.out.println("Error: " + e );
        }
      }
    }

  /**
   * Start the application.
   *
```

```
 * @param args Command line parameters are not used.
 */
public static void main(String args[])
{
  WebServer ws = new WebServer();
  ws.start();
}
}
```

Listing 1.3 implements this very simple web server that is shown in Figure 1.3 below. This listing demonstrates how server sockets are used to listen for requests and then fulfill them.

TIP To use the program in Listing 1.3, you must execute it on a computer that does not already have a web server running. If there is already a web server running, an error will be displayed and the example program will terminate. For more information on how to compile and execute a program, see Appendix E.

Because a full-featured web server would be beyond the scope of this book, the program in Listing 1.3 will ignore any requests and simply respond with the page shown in Figure 1.3. Because this program is a web server, to see its output, you must access it with a browser. To access the server from the same machine that the server is running on, select http://127.0.0.1 as the address that the browser is to look at. The IP address 127.0.0.1 always specifies the local machine. Alternatively, you can view this page from another computer by pointing its browser at the IP address of the computer running the web server program.

FIGURE 1.3:

The mini web server

Examining the Mini Web Server

Server sockets use the ServerSocket object rather than the Socket object that client sockets use. There are several constructors available with the ServerSocket object. The simplest constructor accepts only the port number on which the program should be listening. *Listening* refers to the mode that a server is in while it waits for clients to connect. The following lines of code are used in Listing 1.3 to create a new ServerSocket object and reserve port 80 as the port number on which the web server should listen for connections:

```
try
{
    // create the main server socket
    s = new ServerSocket(80);
}
catch(Exception e)
{
    System.out.println("Error: " + e );
    return;
}
```

The try block is necessary because any number of errors could occur when the program attempts to register port 80. The most common error that would result is that there is already a server listening to port 80 on this machine.

Once the program has port 80 registered, it can begin listening for connections. The following line of code is used to wait for a connection:

```
Socket remote = s.accept();
```

The Socket object that is returned by accept is exactly the same class that is used for client sockets. Once the connection is established, the difference between client and server sockets fade. The primary difference between client and server sockets is the way in which they connect. A client sever connects to something. A server socket waits for something to connect to it.

The accept method is a *blocking* call, which means the current thread will wait for a connection. This can present problems for your program if there are other tasks it would like to accomplish while it is waiting for connections. Because of this, it is very common to see the accept method call placed in a worker thread. This allows the main thread to carry on other tasks, while the worker thread waits for connections to arrive.

Once a connection is made, the accept method will return a socket object for the new socket. After this point, reading and writing is the same between client and server sockets. Many client server programs would create a new thread to handle this new connection.

Now that a connection has been made, a new thread could be created to handle it. This new worker thread would process all the requests from this client in the background, which allows the ServerSocket object to wait for and service more connections. However, the example program in Listing 1.3 does not require such programming. As soon as the socket is accepted, input and output objects are created; this same process was used with the SMTP client. The following lines from Listing 1.3 show the process of preparing the newly accepted socket for input and output:

```
// remote is now the connected socket
System.out.println("Connection, sending data.");
BufferedReader in = new BufferedReader(
  new InputStreamReader(remote.getInputStream()) );
PrintWriter out = new PrintWriter(remote.getOutputStream());
```

Now that the program has input and output objects, it can process the HTTP request. It first reads the HTTP request lines. A full-featured server would parse each line and determine the exact nature of this request, however, our ultra-simple web server just reads in the request lines and ignores them, as shown here:

```
// read the data sent. We basically ignore it,
// stop reading once a blank line is hit. This
// blank line signals the end of the
// client HTTP headers.
String str=".";
while(!str.equals(""))
  str = in.readLine();
```

These lines cause the server to read in lines of text from the newly connected socket. Once a blank line (which indicates the end of the HTTP header) is reached, the loop stops, and the server stops reading. Now that the HTTP header has been retrieved, the server sends an HTTP response. The following lines of code accomplish this:

```
// Send the response
// Send the headers
out.println("HTTP/1.0 200 OK");
out.println("Content-Type: text/html");
out.println("Server: Bot");
// this blank line signals the end of the headers
out.println("");// Send the HTML page
out.println(
  "<H1>Welcome to the Ultra Mini-WebServer</H2>");
```

Status code 200, as shown on line 3 of the preceding code, is used to show that the page was properly transferred, and that the required HTTP headers were sent. (Refer to Chapter 2 for more information about HTTP headers.) Following the HTTP headers, the actual HTML page is transferred. Once the page is transferred, the following lines of code from Listing 1.3 are executed to clean up:

```
out.flush();
remote.close();
```

The flush method is necessary to ensure that all data is transferred, and the close method is necessary to close the socket. Although Java will discard the Socket object, it will not generally close the socket on most platforms. Because of this, you must close the socket or else you might eventually get an error indicating that there are no more file handles. This becomes very important for a program that opens up many connections, including one to a spider.

Summary

Socket programming is an area of Java that many programmers are unaware of. Sockets are used to implement bidirectional communication channels between programs that are typically running on different computers. All support for sockets is directly built into the JDK and does not require the use of third-party class libraries. Sockets are divided into two categories: client sockets and server sockets. Client sockets initiate the communication between programs; server sockets wait for clients to connect. Once the user has connected, both types function in the same manner and both can send and receive data packets.

Keep in mind that server sockets must specify a port on which to listen for connections. Each computer on the Internet has numeric ports assigned to it, and no two services on the same machine may share a port number. However, two clients may connect to the same port on the same machine.

The protocol by which a client and server communicate must also be well defined. The client and server programs are rarely made by the same vendor, so open standards are very important. Most Internet standards are documented in Request for Comments (RFCs). RFCs are never altered or removed once they have been published; instead, to change information in a RFC, a new one is published that is said to make the old one obsolete.

Now that you know the basics of socket communication, you can begin to explore HTTP. Chapter 2 focuses exclusively on implementing the routines necessary to communicate with a web server. (Web servers are also known as HTTP servers.) The GET and POST methods of the HTTP protocol will be examined in detail.

CHAPTER 2

Examining the Hypertext Transfer Protocol

- Understanding address formats

- Using HTTP through sockets

- Using the HTTP class

- How the HTTPSocket class works

Much goes on in the background while a computer user surfs from page to page when they are browsing the Internet. As the user surfs, lots of information is exchanged between their web browser and the site's web server. For instance, when the user points their web browser at a site, the web server responds by sending the Hypertext Markup Language (HTML) that makes up that site. The web browser then scans this HTML that was just downloaded and determines what additional information, such as images, applets, and multimedia files, it needs. If there are images to be displayed, the browser will display them incrementally as they are downloaded. This is all accomplished using the *Hypertext Transfer Protocol (HTTP)*—the protocol that web browsers use to transfer information on the Internet.

NOTE   HTTP is often confused with HTML. The difference between them is that HTML is a language for creating documents, and HTTP is the transport mechanism used to retrieve HTML (or other data) from a location on the Internet.

A *protocol* is a set of rules that governs a process. Many of these protocols can be used to programmatically access information using the Internet. Though there may be times when you must access information using other Internet protocols, such as FTP or Gopher, HTTP will be the one you use the most. As a result, this book focuses primarily on HTTP and HTTPS (the secure form of HTTP), which are examples of *communications protocols*. Communication protocols lay the groundwork for how two systems converse on a given topic.

An effective protocol must have well documented specifications. These specifications must state the exact format of the data that will be exchanged. The specifications for Internet communications protocols are called *Request for Comments (RFC)*. RFCs usually have a number associated with them; for example, the RFC associated with HTTP is RFC2616. This chapter presents how to implement the information contained in RFC2616 using Java.

NOTE   RFCs in general, which are freely available for download through the Internet (just go to http://www.rfc-editor.org for more information), are covered in greater detail in Chapter 1, "Java Socket Programming."

Address Formats

Before we can explain HTTP in greater detail, we must first examine *Internet addressing*. Internet addressing is a way of combining several component parts into one address that uniquely identifies a file on the Internet. Because information available on the Internet is so abundant, you must be able to specify exactly what piece of information you are seeking; Internet addressing helps you do this.

The most familiar Internet address format is the URL. The URL is actually a subclass of the URI, as is the URN (which is not used much on the Internet). But because the URL is the predominant format in use, after a brief introduction to URIs and a brief mention of URNs, we will spend the remainder of this section seeing how to take a URL and break it down into its component parts.

The URI Format

The *Uniform Resource Identifier (URI)* is the most basic form of address used by the Internet. URIs are the underlying format that the more commonly known URL format maps into. A URI is made up of two components: schemes and scheme specific addresses.

The format of a URI is

```
Scheme: scheme-specific-address
```

The first component of a URI, the scheme, is a short identifier that specifies the format of this protocol. For example, the URI `http://www.heat-on.com/java/intro` specifies that the scheme is HTTP. Assuming we knew nothing about the specifics of this protocol, we could not tell much just from the simple format of a URI, so we would still be left wondering what the `//www.heat-on.com/java/intro` component of the URI meant. The data contained after the scheme is dependent upon what scheme is being used. The scheme tells you how to figure out the rest of the address. You will now be shown some of the more common schemes and how they represent their addresses.

The two most common schemes are HTTP and HTTPS. In the future, it is likely that many other protocols will be added as schemes for use with URI addresses; in the meantime, refer to Table 2.1 to view many of the currently available schemes.

TABLE 2.1: Common Schemes

Scheme	Type of Data Represented by the Scheme
data	The data will be encoded using base64 encoding.
File	The data is a file stored on the local file system.
FTP	The data will be transferred using the file transfer (FTP) protocol.
HTTP	The data will be transferred using unsecured Hypertext Transfer Protocol (HTTP).
HTTPS	The data will be transferred using Hypertext Transfer Protocol Secure (HTTPS).
gopher	The data will be transferred using Gopher.
mailto	The data will be transferred using Simple Mail Transfer Protocol (SMTP).
news	The data will be transferred using a news server.
Telnet	The data will be transferred using a telnet connection.

The second component of the URI, the scheme specific address, does not have an official syntax. However, what most protocols use is

```
//host/path?query
```

Here, *host* generally specifies the entity that is responsible for resolving the rest of the address. In this case, if you refer back to the URI of `http://www.heat-on.com/java/intro`, the host is `www.heat-on.com`. In this example, the host is responsible for resolving the rest of the path—here, the *path* is represented by `/java/intro`.

By using this popular convention, in addition to specifying the host and the path, you can specify a query by concatenating a question mark and following it with a query. For example, take the URI `http://www1.fatbrain.com/asp/bookinfo/bookinfo.asp?theisbn=0672314045&vm=`, which specifies a path and a query. Here, the path is `/asp/bookinfo/bookinfo.asp`, and the query is `theisbn=0672314045&vm=`. In this example, the query information is not part of the path; instead, it is additional information that is sent to the resource specified by the path. The term *resource* is used to define any single item of data that can be requested using a URL. Resources are often files, but they can also be the output of a script.

Very often you are required to have a username and a password to access a specific resource, especially when you are accessing an FTP server. Here is the syntax for such a site:

```
ftp://username:password@ftpaddress/path/
```

Here, the *username* and *password* are used to specify the user and password information that is needed to access this site. Like FTP, other protocols such as HTTP allow for a username and password as well, but they use different conventions than this one. (Refer to Chapter 3, "Accessing Secure Sites with HTTPS," for a discussion of the convention that HTTP usually uses.)

WARNING   One of the biggest concerns with username and password specification is that it is not very secure. Most browsers display the URL/URI line that they are currently browsing. In this situation, the username and password would be clearly visible on the user's screen. Any person looking at the user's browser screen could easily see their password as part of the address line.

The URN Format

URNs are not widely used and are mentioned here only to give you a complete picture of the URI format. The general form of a URN is

```
urn:namespace:resource
```

URNs are intended to be used for resources that may have copies in many locations. URNs are also not limited to just Internet resources. Books are a great example of URNs. For instance, if you wanted to represent a book with the ISBN number of 0672314045, you would use the URN of `urn:isbn:0672314045`. This type of system might be used internally as part of a library or a large file archive that is available from many locations. In general, URNs are not used much on the Internet.

The URL Format

Locations on the Internet are specified using *Uniform Resource Locators (URLs)*. These are addresses that uniquely identify specific resources on the Internet. For example, `http://www.jeffheaton.com/images/jeffpic1.jpg` identifies an image stored on my web server. There are several parts to this URL, as we will see in "Breaking Down a URL."

A URL is a locator, or a pointer, to a resource on the World Wide Web. A resource can be something as simple as a file or a directory, or it can be a reference to a more complicated object, such as a query to a database or to a search engine, a CGI-BIN program, a servlet, or a JSP page.

Breaking Down a URL

A URL can be broken into several parts, as shown in Table 2.2. Before you look at the table, take a look at the general format of a URL, which is expressed in one of these two ways:

    scheme://hostname:port/path?query

or

    scheme://hostname:port/path#anchor

TABLE 2.2: The Makeup of a URL

Part of URL	Function
Scheme	This is the portion of the URL that specifies the protocol. This will usually be either HTTPS or HTTP, though others can be specified too. For a list, refer to Table 2.1.
Hostname	This is the actual server that this document is stored on. This can be a name, such as `www.yahoo.com`, or an IP address, such as `216.115.108.243`.
Port	A URL can optionally specify a port. The default port is 80 for HTTP and 443 for HTTPS. You can override the default by specifying a port.
Path	This specifies the actual file that is being requested from the server.
Anchor	This specifies a location within the document. This is just a short string and acts as a label.

Here are two example URLs and their meanings:

1. `http://www.ncsa.uiuc.edu:8080/demoweb/url-primer.html`

   In the URL above, here is the breakdown:

   - The scheme is `http`.
   - The hostname is `www.ncsa.uiuc.edu`.
   - The port is `8080`.
   - The path is `/demoweb/url-primer.html`.
   - There is no anchor.

2. `http://www.heat-on.com/links_jh.shtml#top`

Here is the breakdown of this URL:

- The scheme is `http`.
- The hostname is `www.heat-on.com`.
- The port is not specified, and because of this, it will default to 80.
- The path is `/links_jh.shtml`.
- The anchor is `top`.

Here is one more example; in this example, we will explore what the above part names mean. In the URL `http://www.jeffheaton.com/images/jeffpic1.jpg`, the protocol being used is HTTP and the information needed resides on a host machine named `www.jeffheaton.com`. The information on that host machine is named `/images/jeffpic1.jpg`.

NOTE   It is up to the web server to give meaning to path information. Usually this information maps to some physical subset of the file system on the server computer, but the path does not need to point to a physical file on the server. It is impossible to make a distinction between a physical file and the output of a program by looking at the path. It is the web server that makes this determination based upon how it was configured. The path can also specify that the browser should display the output of a program.

Relative URLs

Sometimes only part of a URL will be specified. Rather than seeing the full URL of `http://www.jeffheaton.com/images/logo.gif`, you will see `/images/logo.gif`, `images/logo.gif`, or perhaps just `logo.gif`. These are considered *relative URLs*.

A relative URL cannot be resolved by itself. It is always combined with the URL of the page that contains it. For example, if we were viewing the page `http://www.jeffheaton.com/index.html`, that address would be used to resolve each of the relative URLs.

If a relative address begins with a slash (/), it is taken to mean "directly from the host." This means that it will use the same hostname, but it will completely replace the path. For example, if `http://www.jeffheaton.com/index.html` contained a relative address of `/images/logo.gif`, the actual URL would be `http://www.jeffheaton.com/images/logo.gif`.

A relative address that does not begin with a slash is simply concatenated to the directory containing the page being viewed. For example, if `http://www.jeffheaton.com/java/index.html` contained a relative address of `intro/index.shtml`, the actual URL would be `http://www.jeffheaton.com/java/intro/index.shtml`.

Using Sockets to Program HTTP

Before you can understand how HTTP works, you must refer back to the discussion of TCP/IP sockets, the basic transport mechanism of the Internet (see Chapter 1). Once you have reviewed this information, you are ready to move forward.

You will now be shown how to use sockets to handle HTTP requests. This will be done using a client socket to connect to a web server. Because a bot must be able to retrieve information from a web server, it typically uses a client socket to do so, which is where this chapter's coverage begins. The bot will access this data using HTTP, and you will see how to examine these requests. After you have done this, you will be shown how to use the URL class to construct the exact address of the document you are requesting.

HTTP Requests

The most basic function of any spider or bot is to retrieve web pages using HTTP. Usually a spider or bot only needs to retrieve the HTML pages on a site, and it can skip the time-consuming process of downloading the images. Though the HTTP class will support the download of such data, we will be primarily focused on the download of HTML documents. Like all Internet protocols, HTTP is defined by an RFC, which is documented in RFC2616. This RFC documents the structure of an HTTP session. In this section, you will begin examining this structure.

An HTTP request starts on the browser. The browser sends a request to a web server; the web server responds. (As mentioned earlier, this is nothing more than a socket connection to port 80.) Once the connection is established, some text, which describes the request, is transmitted to the server. The server answers back with a few *headers* followed by the requested data. These HTTP headers contain useful information, such as the last modified date of the page and the type of web server that is being run. An example of HTTP server headers is shown here.

```
HTTP/1.1 200 OK
Connection: Keep-Alive
Server: Microsoft-IIS/4.0
Content-Type: text/html
Cache-control: private
Transfer-Encoding: chunked
Via: 1.1 c760 (NetCache 4.1R4D1)
Date: Tue, 13 Mar 2001 03:55:05 GMT
```

TIP   What do these requests look like? To see them, you will need a spy utility, like the Trace-Plus 32/Web Detective. This is a commercial product available from SST Incorporated at http://www.sstinc.com. By using this utility, you can watch all of the HTTP transactions that occur as you use a browser to access the Internet.

Now that you have seen the structure of an HTTP request, you must see what is actually transferred between the web browser and server. To see what transpires, you can use a simple trick to allow an HTTP response to be viewed. The TELNET protocol can be used to simulate the web browser's end of an HTTP connection.

To see this, open a telnet connection to any web server. To open a connection on a Win32 system, open Run under the Start menu, and type in **Telnet**. A telnet session command prompt window opens. Type **?** for instructions to connect to a site, print, or end the session. To connect to a site, type **open <url_name>**. Now type the following and press enter twice:

```
GET / HTTP/1.0 <enter><enter>
```

You will not be able to see the above command as you type it. This applies to both UNIX and Windows systems. On a Windows system, telnet will appear in a separate window; under UNIX the session will be displayed in your terminal window. By typing the line mentioned above and pressing enter twice, you have completed the request. The web server should respond by sending several lines of headers and then a stream of HTML. This allows you to quickly determine if the web server is listening/responding to the specified port. This example demonstrates a GET HTTP request. You will now be shown the GET request, as well as two other HTTP requests:

The GET request   Requests a page and sends only a limited amount of data to a web server. The complete resource that was requested is then transferred. This is usually the HTML data of the page.

The POST request   Sends data to the web server and then allows the web server to send data back.

The HEAD request   Works just like the GET request, except the resource itself is not sent back. This request is sent just to verify the existence of a resource without actually downloading it.

In a moment, we will examine each of these request types in detail.

When a typical web page is requested, many requests go back and fourth to accomplish the page's display. Listing 2.1 shows the necessary requests that you would need to use to produce the page at http://www.heat-on.com (shown in Figure 2.1). As you can see in Listing 2.1, first the root document ("/") is requested, and then all of the requests that bring up the images that make up this page follow.

Listing 2.1   **Conversation between Web Server and Browser**

```
1. Client: GET / HTTP/1.1
2. Server: HTTP/1.1 200 OK
3. Client: GET /heaton.css HTTP/1.1
```

```
 4. Client: GET /images/jhlogo.gif HTTP/1.1
 5. Server: HTTP/1.1 200 OK
 6. Server: HTTP/1.1 200 OK
 7. Client: GET /images/blank.gif HTTP/1.1
 8. Client: GET /images/greenfade.gif HTTP/1.1
 9. Server: HTTP/1.1 200 OK
10. Client: GET /images/white.gif HTTP/1.1
11. Server: HTTP/1.1 200 OK
12. Server: HTTP/1.1 200 OK
```

F I G U R E   2.1:

How www.heat-on
.com is displayed

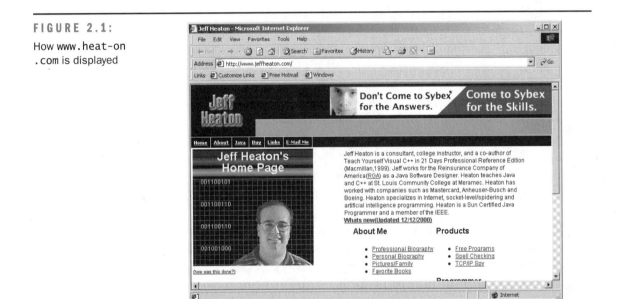

The HTTP *GET* Request

GET is the most common of the HTTP requests. Nearly every Internet web traffic request is a GET. Generally, any page retrieved that is not a result of a form submission is sent as an HTTP GET. The client must initiate the request by sending a request packet, a packet similar to the one shown below. The first line contains the most important information. The first word, GET, states that this is a GET request. A space separates the request type from the next field, which is the requested resource. The requested resource is usually a path name starting with a "/", which specifies the root. For instance, to specify a file named file.html located in the site virtual directory, you would send the request /site/file.html.

A typical browser GET request is shown here:

```
GET /grindex.asp HTTP/1.1
Accept: image/gif, image/x-xbitmap, image/jpeg, image/pjpeg,
```

```
application/vnd.ms-powerpoint, application/vnd.ms-excel,
application/msword, */*
Accept-Language: en-us
Accept-Encoding: gzip, deflate
User-Agent: Mozilla/4.0 (compatible; MSIE 5.5; Windows NT 5.0)
Host: www.classinfo.net
Connection: Keep-Alive
Cookie: ASPSESSIONIDGGGGQHPK=BHLGFGOCHAPALILEEMNIMAFG
```

Here is how the server would respond to the browser's request:

```
HTTP/1.1 200 OK
Connection: Keep-Alive
Server: Microsoft-IIS/4.0
Content-Type: text/html
Cache-control: private
Transfer-Encoding: chunked
Via: 1.1 c760 (NetCache 4.1R4D1)
Date: Tue, 13 Mar 2001 03:55:05 GMT

<!DOCTYPE HTML PUBLIC "-//W3C//DTD HTML 3.2//EN">
<HTML>
... the rest of the HTML document ...
```

You will probably have noticed that there is considerable additional information transmitted by the server responding to the HTTP GET request. The first section of information in this response is referred to as *header* information, and all header information must occur before the first blank line. After the first blank line, the header section ends, and the *body* of the message begins. In this example, the actual HTML of the page requested begins just after the first blank line in the body of the response. Here, the HTML begins with the DOCTYPE tag.

The browser's GET request, on the other hand, is composed only of headers and no body. Only the response to a GET has a body. As a result, you didn't see any blank lines in the request.

The HTTP *POST* Request

HTTP POST requests usually result from a form being submitted. The request part of an HTTP POST, though similar to that of an HTTP GET request, must also carry the values entered into the fields of the form, as shown here:

```
POST /grlogin.asp HTTP/1.1
Accept: image/gif, image/x-xbitmap, image/jpeg, image/pjpeg,
application/vnd.ms-powerpoint, application/vnd.ms-excel,
application/msword, */*
Referer: http://www.classinfo.net/grindex.asp
Accept-Language: en-us
Content-Type: application/x-www-form-urlencoded
Accept-Encoding: gzip, deflate
```

```
User-Agent: Mozilla/4.0 (compatible; MSIE 5.5; Windows NT 5.0)
Host: www.classinfo.net
Content-Length: 46
Connection: Keep-Alive
Cookie: ASPSESSIONIDGGGGQHPK=BHLGFGOCHAPALILEEMNIMAFG

UID=jheaton&PWD=joshua&LOGIN.x=18&LOGIN.y=16
```

In this example, this POST request is sending the data UID=jheaton&PWD=joshua&LOGIN.x=18&LOGIN.y=16 as the body of its request (see the last line of the listing). This body is provided by the browser, from data filled in by the user. The browser must also inform the web server of the length of this body data. This information is shown in the Content-Length header, which provides the exact length, in bytes, of the posted data. The form that produced this data can be seen in Figure 2.2.

FIGURE 2.2:

A form used to produce a POST

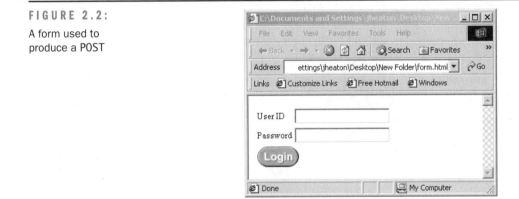

How did the browser determine the data to be posted to the web server? This data came directly from an HTML form. Take a look at the HTML code used to produce the display seen in Figure 2.2:

```
<table border="0">
<form method="post" action="postit.jsp">
<tr><td>User ID</td><td><input type="text" NAME ="UID"></td></tr>
<tr><td>Password</td><td><input type="password" NAME = "PWD"></td></tr>
<tr><td colspan="2"><INPUT TYPE="IMAGE" NAME="LOGIN"
SRC="BtnLogin.gif"></td></tr>
</form>
</table>
```

The form shown above contains three components that contribute to the data being posted. First, there is a User ID text box (referred to as UID in the HTML code) that allows the user to enter their user ID. Second, there is a Password box (named PWD in the HTML code) that allows the user to enter their password. Finally, there is a Login button (LOGIN in the HTML) that the user clicks to actually process the login. Each of these components is placed into the body of the POST request as part of a [name]=[value] pair. The name-value pairs are then separated by ampersands (&); there are no other formatting codes, such as quotes. This is easy to see for the UID and PWD controls in the body of the browser POST request shown earlier in this section. In this line,

```
UID=jheaton&PWD=joshua&LOGIN.x=18&LOGIN.y=16
```

the user typed in a UID of jheaton and a PWD of joshua. The login image is not nearly so simple to pick out. This is because image buttons also transfer the x and y coordinates that were clicked by the user. In the body code line above, the LOGIN button reveals its x position with the LOGIN.x=18 value and its y location with the LOGIN.y=16 value.

Now that we have discussed the POST request, let's take a look at the response the browser would get back from the web server. You will notice that it is identical to the response to the GET request from the previous section. GET and POST are different only in how they present data to the web server, but the end result is always the same—a page sent. This response is shown below:

```
HTTP/1.1 200 OK
Server: Microsoft-IIS/4.0
Content-Type: text/html
Cache-control: private
Transfer-Encoding: chunked
Via: 1.1 c760 (NetCache 4.1R4D1)
Date: Tue, 13 Mar 2001 03:56:43 GMT

<!DOCTYPE HTML PUBLIC "-//W3C//DTD HTML 3.2//EN">
<HTML>
... the rest of the HTML document ...
```

NOTE   Not all posted data is as simple as the values displayed in this example. For instance, what happens when the values include spaces, tabs, or carriage returns? For these cases, the values are *URL encoded*. URL coding transforms the string Hello World to Hello-%20World. The %20 indicates a special character, whose value is 20 hex, or 32 decimal, which is a space. Chapter 5, "Posting Forms," will cover posting and URL encoding in much greater detail.

The HTTP *HEAD* Request

The HTTP HEAD request is the least used of these requests. HTTP HEAD is usually only used by a browser to verify a document's existence without requesting for the document to be sent. This request is often sent by a search engine or web directory to verify that the page is still valid. HTTP HEAD requests do not take as much server overhead to process because no actual data is sent other than the header. Here is a simple HEAD request

```
HEAD / HTTP/1.0
```

and the server response:

```
HTTP/1.0 200 OK
Date: Thu, 28 Jun 2001 01:00:45 GMT
Content-Type: text/html
Server: Apache/1.3.12 (Unix) ApacheJServ/1.1.2
Via: 1.1 c760 (NetCache NetApp/5.0.1R2D6)
```

Using the *URL* Class

Java provides many classes that support Internet connections. In addition to the socket classes already discussed, the URL class is provided to work with URL addresses. The URL class is used extensively throughout this book. This class allows URLs to easily be *parsed*, or broken down into their component parts. Once a URL object has been created for a given URL, it is easy to break the URL down into the hostname and path. You will now be shown how to use this class.

The *URL* Constructor

Before a URL can be parsed, a URL object must be constructed. The usual form for creating a URL object is by using its constructor. Take a look at the following example:

```
URL url = new URL("http://www.jeffheaton.com");
```

This will create a new URL object that holds the URL of my home page.

The URL constructor is capable of throwing the MalformedURLException, which is a checked exception that must be dealt with. This exception is thrown when the URL class is unable to parse the URL that was sent to its constructor. For example, the URL http//www.jeffheaton.com would generate this exception because the colon after http was left out, which causes this URL to be malformed.

Because the URL object can throw a MalformedURLException when passed an invalid URL, this exception must be caught. (Java requires that all thrown exceptions be caught.) The usual syntax for constructing a URL and catching this exception is as follows:

```
try
{
  URL url = new URL("http://www.jeffheaton.com");
}
catch(MalformedURLException e)
{
  System.out.println("Error:" + e);
}
```

The constructor that was just demonstrated is not the only constructor; there are several others that provide for other cases in which only a partial URL is given. The following constructor combines the path name of the resource /java/intro with the completed URL of http://www.jeffheaton.com, which results in an effective URL of http://www.jeffheaton .com/java/intro/:

```
URL url = new URL( new URL("http://www.jeffheaton.com")
    "/java/intro/" );
```

Opening a Connection

The URL class also has the ability to open a connection to the URL address that it is pointing to and to retrieve information from that URL. This is a very powerful feature of Java, and it makes it easy to create Java programs that require reasonably simple access to websites. Listing 2.2 shows a program that retrieves information from a web page using the URL object. This program is a Java application that is designed to be called from the command line. It should be passed one argument that specifies the URL it should retrieve. For example, to retrieve the page sitting at http://www.yahoo.com you would pass it the command java GetURL http://www.yahoo.com.

Listing 2.2   **Using the *URL* Class (GetURL.java)**

```java
import java.io.*;
import java.net.*;

/**
 * Chapter 2 Example
 *
 * This program uses the standard Java URL class to open a
 * connection to a web page and download the contents.
 *
 * @author Jeff Heaton
 * @version 1.0
 */
class GetURL
{

  /**
   * This method will display the URL specified by the parameter.
   *
   * @param u The URL to display.
   */
  static protected void getURL(String u)
  {
    URL url;
    InputStream is;
```

```
    InputStreamReader isr;
    BufferedReader r;
    String str;

    try
    {
      System.out.println("Reading URL: " + u );
      url = new URL(u);
      is = url.openStream();
      isr = new InputStreamReader(is);
      r = new BufferedReader(isr);
      do
      {
        str = r.readLine();
        if(str!=null)
          System.out.println( str );
      } while( str!= null );
    }
    catch(MalformedURLException e)
    {
      System.out.println("Must enter a valid URL");
    }
    catch(IOException e)
    {
      System.out.println("Can't connect");
    }
  }

  /**
   * Program entry point.
   *
   * @param args Command line arguments. Specified the URL to download.
   */
  static public void main(String args[])
  {
    if( args.length<1)
      System.out.println("Usage: GetURL ");
    else
      getURL( args[0] );
  }
}
```

This application first checks to see if it was provided with an argument. If it wasn't, then it displays proper usage instructions. These instructions simply state that the application is to be called with a single parameter specifying the URL to be downloaded. If a URL was provided by the command-line arguments, then the application passes the URL to the getURL method in this class. This method then opens a connection to the specified URL, and then it downloads and displays the contents of that page.

To complete this task, the getURL method starts up by declaring the variables that it will need:

```
URL url;
InputStream is;
InputStreamReader isr;
BufferedReader r;
String str;
```

The variable url is needed to hold the URL class. An InputStream (is), InputStreamReader (isr), and BufferedReader (r) are all declared to read the stream. These are used later to hold the stream and buffers that are used to read from the URL.

The openStream method of the URL class opens the connection to the specified URL and returns an InputStream to the caller. This InputStream is assigned to the is variable. This InputStream (is) is used with a BufferedReader (r) to read in the data from the URL (as shown here):

```
try
{
  System.out.println("Reading URL: " + u );
  url = new URL(u);
  is = url.openStream();
  isr = new InputStreamReader(is);
  r = new BufferedReader(isr);
```

The BufferedReader class allows the stream to read line-by-line. (The technique of using buffers was covered in Chapter 1.) The following loop will read lines of text from the reader until there is no more data:

```
do
{
  str = r.readLine();
  if(str!=null)
    System.out.println( str );
} while( str!= null );
```

The result is that the document that is stored at the specified URL will be downloaded and then displayed to the screen line-by-line. The readLine method will return null when there is no more data to read.

There are several exceptions than can be thrown during this operation, which are shown here:

```
catch(MalformedURLException e)
{
  System.out.println("Must enter a valid URL");
}
catch(IOException e)
{
  System.out.println("Can't connect");
}
```

A MalformedURLException is thrown when an invalid URL is provided. An IOException will be thrown if an error occurs while connecting to the site, or while transferring data.

The connection provided by the URL class provides easy access to web information from inside a Java program. Although you might think that this class would provide the foundation for building spiders, bots, and aggregators, this is not the case. Though both the URL class and the URLConnection class (which is accessed through the URL class and provides for greater control than the URL class) do provide for simple access to the Web, they do not provide the advanced functionality that is required to produce the majority of these programs.

Bot Package Classes for HTTP

This book will present many reusable classes. These classes are grouped together into a Java package called the Bot package, which can be imported using the com.heaton.bot identifier. Most chapters will examine a particular part of this package, and as the book progresses, these classes will be explained in detail. This section discusses the HTTP class that is provided by the Bot package.

WARNING   The HTTP class and others are stored in the bot.jar file contained on the companion CD-ROM. If the bot.jar file is not properly installed, none of the examples contained in this book will function properly. Appendix E "How to Compile Examples Under Windows" covers the proper installation of this file. You may also refer to Appendix C, "Troubleshooting," if you have problems executing example programs.

We will now examine the classes of the Bot package that are used to implement HTTP. The HTTP class and the classes that inherit directly from it are the most basic of those included in the Bot package, and they form the foundation for the other classes in the package.

NOTE   The book's author wrote the Bot package provided for this book. It provides many reusable classes that can be used to construct bots. The internal workings of this package will be explained in each of the chapters of this book, and the components of this package may be freely used in any program.

Using the *HTTP* Class

The HTTP class specifically handles cookies, the referrer tag, user authentication, automatic redirection, and HTTP headers. The HTTPSocket class is derived from the HTTP class. The HTTPSocket class is the class that the Bot package will use to communicate with web servers using HTTP. Because the HTTP class is the parent class of HTTPSocket, all of its methods are also available to the HTTPSocket class.

The *HTTP* Class versus the *URLConnection* Class

Java already contains the URLConnection class (mentioned in the previous section), which does many of the same things done by the HTTP class presented here. You may now be asking why a new class should be created when Java already contains a similar implementation. The answer is that the URLConnection class falls short in the following ways:

The URLConnection object does not support the referrer tag.   As the user moves from page to page, the web browser transmits a referrer tag. This allows the web server to know what page the user was on before. Some interactive websites depend on this value being set. In order for the spiders and bots to properly use this header, it must be set. Unlike the HTTP class presented here, which automatically tracks this tag and properly transmits it, the URLConnection object does not support this header.

The URLConnection object does not support cookies.   Cookies are an important part of the interactive websites that are often the target of spiders and bots. The URLConnection object does not support cookies. The HTTP class, on the other hand, automatically tracks the values of cookies that are assigned by the web server.

The URLConnection object does not support user authentication.   User authentication allows the web browser to submit an ID and password for the current user. The web browser then decides if the user should be allowed to proceed. The HTTP class presented here supports user authentication, but the URLConnection object doesn't.

Because of these limitations, I decided to create a more advanced replacement for the URLConnection object. The HTTP and HTTPSocket classes provide this functionality to the other classes that will be created through this book.

The Methods of the *HTTP* Class

The following methods briefly show the public interface of the HTTP class provided by the Bot package. These methods can be used in any program that needs to communicate using HTTP, and they will be used by other classes (presented later) that must also use HTTP. In the following list of methods, each method is followed by a short description and then an example of how this method might appear in code.

TIP   For more information about the HTTP class, or any other class in the Bot package, refer to Appendix A, "The Bot Package," which contains an abbreviated outline of the JavaDoc style documentation for this package. The complete JavaDoc documentation can be found on the companion CD-ROM.

The clearCookies method   This method will clear out the cookie store for the HTTP object. Cookies are objects that the web server stores in the browser to maintain state. When a browser maintains state, it allows a user to remain logged in to the website. Usually, you can remain unaware of cookies. But if you're writing a Bot program, you may need to support cookies to allow logins by users. By enabling cookie support in the HTTP object, most, if not all, of the cookie processing will be handled by the Bot package. Chapter 7, "Cookies," goes into much greater detail about how cookies are processed.

```
public void clearCookies()
```

The getAgent method   The browser normally transmits an agent HTTP header when pages are requested from the server. By default, the Bot class sets this value to Mozilla/4.0. When you call this method, you can determine what the agent header will be set to.

```
public String getAgent()
```

The getBody method   This method will retrieve the actual text that was transmitted as a result of the HTTP request. If the result of this request was binary, then the bytes will be packed into this string.

```
public String getBody()
```

The getClientHeaders() method   This method will return an AttributeList that contains all *client headers*. Client headers are the HTTP headers that are normally transmitted by a web browser.

```
public AttributeList getClientHeaders()
```

The getCookie method   Cookies allow the web server to store state in the web browser. The topic of storing state using cookies will be discussed in Chapter 7. Call this method to retrieve an individual cookie by name.

```
public CookieParse getCookie(String name)
```

The getCookies method   This method will return an AttributeList that contains all the cookies currently held by this HTTP session.

```
public AttributeList getCookies()
```

The getPassword method   HTTP allows a user and a password to be transmitted as part of the HTTP headers. This method allows you to determine the password that was last set.

```
public String getPassword()
```

The getPerminantCookies method   This method returns true if the HTTP object should use permanent cookies.

```
public boolean getPerminantCookies()
```

The getReferrer method   This method will return the HTTP referrer. This value is the last page that was visited. This value is sent to the web server to allow the web server to know where the user came from.

```
public String getReferrer()
```

The `getServerHeaders` method   This method will return an `AttributeList` that contains all *server headers*. Server headers are the HTTP headers that are normally transmitted to a web browser by the server.

```
public AttributeList getServerHeaders()
```

The `getTimeout` method   This method gets the current timeout specified for this HTTP object. The timeout value is stored in milliseconds.

```
public int getTimeout()
```

The `getURL` method   This method returns the URL that was requested by the last call to the send method. This is not necessarily the URL that was passed to the send method. If redirection is enabled, the send method will seamlessly request the URL that it was redirected to. Calling getURL will allow you to determine the URL that was ultimately requested.

```
public String getURL()
```

The `getUseCookies` method   This method returns true if the HTTP object should use cookies.

```
public boolean getUseCookies()
```

The `getUser` method   HTTP allows a user and password to be transmitted as part of the HTTP headers. This method allows you to determine the user ID that was last set.

```
public String getUser()
```

The send method   The send method is used to transmit an HTTP request and retrieve the result from the web server. This method can be called repeatedly on the same HTTP object to move through pages in succession. By calling this object rapidly on the same HTTP object, you will allow the referrer header to be properly sent as well as cookies to be processed.

If redirection is enabled, the send method will seamlessly request the redirected URL. To find the URL that was ultimately requested as a result of the send method, call the getURL method.

```
public void send(String url,String post)
    throws java.net.UnknownHostException,java.io.IOException
```

The `setAgent` method   The browser normally transmits an agent HTTP header when pages are requested from the server. By default, the Bot class sets this value to Mozilla/4.0. Calling this method allows you to set what the agent header will be.

```
public void setAgent(String a)
```

The `setAutoRedirect` method   No specific action is taken by calling this function. It sets the automatic redirection attribute that will be used when a HTTP request is initiated by calling the send method. A web server can choose to redirect the browser to a totally different page. If `setAutoRedirect` is set to true, these redirections will be transparent. You will only be given the page that you were redirected to. In certain rare circumstances, you may not want to automatically follow the redirection. If you would prefer to be given the redirect packet as presented by the web server, set this property to false. Cases in which you might want to set this property to false include certain diagnostic operations where you want to trace the redirection used by a site.

```
public void setAutoRedirect(boolean b)
```

The setPassword method   HTTP allows a user and password to be transmitted as part of the HTTP headers. This method allows you to set the password to be transmitted.

```
public void setPassword(String p)
```

The setReferrer method   This method allows the referrer to be set. This value is the last page that was visited. This value is then available to be sent to the web server to allow the web server to know where the user came from.

```
public void setReferrer(String referrer)
```

The setTimeout method   This method sets the timeout for an HTTP request. The timeout is specified in milliseconds.

```
public void setTimeout(int i)
```

The setURL method   This method sets the URL property. Setting the URL property is generally of little value. To move to a specific URL, you should call the `send` method with that URL.

```
public void setURL(String u)
```

The setUseCookies method   Cookies allow the web server to store state in the web browser. Call this method to control which types of cookies, if any, this HTTP instance will support.

For this to work, two parameters must be provided. The first parameter enables session cookies. Session cookies have a lifespan as long as the current user remains connected. The second parameter specifies if permanent cookies should be stored. Permanent cookies will remain until their expiration date.

```
public void setUseCookies(boolean session,boolean perm)
```

The setUser method   HTTP allows a user and password to be transmitted as part of the HTTP headers. This method allows you to set the user ID to be transmitted.

```
public void setUser(String u)
```

Using the *HTTPSocket* Class

The HTTP class contains all of the properties and methods needed to actually facilitate an HTTP connection. Yet it is abstract and does not specify exactly how these HTTP requests are carried out. The class that you will use when you actually instantiate an HTTP reference is the HTTPSocket class. This class communicates with a web server using sockets. Currently, this is the only mode of communication supported by the Bot package, but other methods of accessing pages could be added later. For example, you could use the URLConnection object provided by Java rather than sockets.

The usual way in which you will instantiate an HTTP object using HTTPSocket is as follows:

```
HTTP http = new HTTPSocket();
```

You will see this line of code used in nearly all of the examples. Though it may seem redundant to separate all socket specific programming into the HTTPSocket class, this would allow the Bot package to take advantage of other protocols. For now, HTTPSocket is the only option.

Using the *Attribute* Class

The Bot package provides several classes that are used to represent HTTP headers and cookies, including the Attribute class. This class stores a name-value pair, which works much like a dictionary. The name specifies an entry that can be looked up; this in turn reveals some value. Only one value per name is allowed. The Attribute class is stored in an Attribute list, which is maintained by the AttributeList class. When you request a list of HTTP headers or cookies, you will be given an Attribute list. The following list gives a brief description of the constructors and methods used for the public interface to the Attribute class followed by an example of how they might appear in code. The AttributeList class is described in the next section.

The Attribute constructor   This constructor constructs a new Attribute object having an empty string name and value.

```
public Attribute()
```

The name, value constructor   This constructor constructs a new Attribute object having the specified name and value.

```
public Attribute(String name,String value)
```

The clone method   This method creates a new copy of this object.

```
public Object clone()
```

The getName method   This method retrieves the name of this Attribute object.

```
public String getName()
```

The getValue method   This method retrieves the value of this Attribute object.

```
public String getValue()
```

The setName method   This method sets the name of this Attribute object.

```
public void setName(String name)
```

The setValue method   This method sets the value of this Attribute object.

```
public void setValue(String value)
```

Using the *AttributeList* Class

The AttributeList class is another of the classes used to represent HTTP headers and cookies that the Bot package provides. This class also maintains a list of Attribute objects. When you request a list of HTTP headers or cookies, you will be given this list. This list is in the form of Attribute objects (the Attribute class was described in the previous section). The following list gives a brief description of the constructors and methods for the public interface to the AttributeList class followed by an example of how they might appear in code.

> **TIP**   For more information about the AttributeList class, or any other class in the Bot package, refer to Appendix A, which contains the complete JavaDoc style documentation for the package.

The AttributeList constructor   This constructor creates a new object with an empty list.

```
public AttributeList()
```

The add method   This method will add the specified Attribute object to the list. Attributes with duplicate names are allowed.

```
synchronized public void add(Attribute a)
```

The clear method   This method will clear all Attribute objects from the list.

```
synchronized public void clear()
```

The clone method   This method creates a new exact copy of this object.

```
public Object clone()
```

The get(int id) method   This method will return the Attribute object specified by the index held in the ID variable. Attribute lists are zero based and will return null if an out-of-bound Attribute index is requested.

```
synchronized public Attribute get(int id)
```

The get(String id) method   This method will return the Attribute object specified by the name held in the ID variable. Attribute names are case insensitive and will return null if the specified name is not found in the list.

```
synchronized public Attribute get(String id)
```

The isEmpty method   This method returns true if no Attribute objects exist in this list.

```
synchronized public boolean isEmpty()
```

The length method   This method will return the number of Attribute objects contained in this list.

```
synchronized public int length()
```

The set method   This method will set the Attribute object specified by the parameter name's case-insensitive value to the value contained in the value parameter. If there is no such attribute, one will be created. This method will never cause a duplicate attribute to be created.

```
synchronized public void set(String name,String value)
```

Putting the *HTTP*, *Attribute*, and *AttributeList* Classes to Work

The HTTP class can be used to communicate with a web server and retrieve files. When this is done, overhead is kept to a minimum, and few methods are called to retrieve a document.

In Listing 2.3, a simple example is provided to show how to retrieve documents from a web server. This simple program uses the HTTPSocket class to display a window, as seen in Figure 2.3. To use this program, you would enter a URL and press the Go button. The program would then display all the data it retrieved from the web server. As you can see in Figure 2.3, the top portion of the window displays the HTTP headers, and the bottom portion displays the actual data that was retrieved. This data will generally be in the form of an HTML document. If the web server redirects to a new page instead of sending the HTML document, that page's URL will be displayed in the URL line. After this happens, the user can enter another URL and repeat the process.

FIGURE 2.3:

Viewing a URL

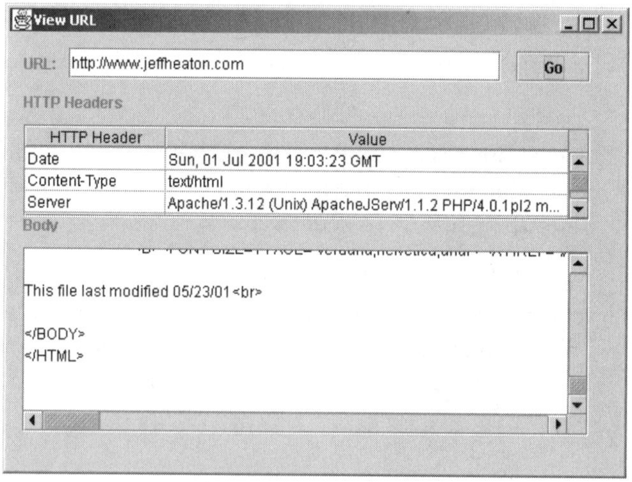

NOTE   The example program was created using VisualCafé. The comments left by VisualCafé to allow visual editing of the elements have been left in for those of you who might use VisualCafé. This program will compile with JDK.

Listing 2.3   **View URL (ViewURL.java)**

```java
import java.awt.*;
import javax.swing.*;
import javax.swing.table.*;
import com.heaton.bot.*;

/**
 * Example program from Chapter 2
 * Programming Spiders, Bots and Aggregators in Java
 * Copyright 2001 by Jeff Heaton
 *
 *
 * This application displays a dialog box that allows
 * the user to specify any URL. This URL is requested,
 * using the Bot package, and displayed in the dialog box.
 * Both the body and HTTP headers are displayed.
 *
 * @author Jeff Heaton
 * @version 1.0
 */
public class ViewURL extends javax.swing.JFrame {

  /**
   * The HTTP connection used by this application.
   */
  HTTP _http;

  /**
   * The constructor.  This method sets up all the
   *    * components needed by this class.
   * A new HTTPSocket object is also constructed to
   *    * mananage the connection.
   */
  public ViewURL()
  {
    _http = new HTTPSocket();
    //{{INIT_CONTROLS
    setTitle("View URL");
    getContentPane().setLayout(null);
    setSize(495,341);
    setVisible(false);
    getContentPane().add(_pane2);
    _pane2.setBounds(12,168,456,144);
    _body.setEditable(false);
```

```
_pane2.getViewport().add(_body);
_body.setBounds(0,0,453,141);
getContentPane().add(_pane1);
_pane1.setBounds(12,72,456,72);
_pane1.getViewport().add(_headers);
_headers.setBounds(0,0,453,0);
_label3.setText("Body");
getContentPane().add(_label3);
_label3.setBounds(12,144,456,12);
_label1.setText("URL:");
getContentPane().add(_label1);
_label1.setBounds(12,12,36,24);
_url.setText("http://www.jeffheaton.com");
getContentPane().add(_url);
_url.setBounds(48,12,348,24);
_go.setText("Go");
_go.setActionCommand("Go");
getContentPane().add(_go);
_go.setBounds(408,12,60,24);
_label2.setText("HTTP Headers");
getContentPane().add(_label2);
_label2.setBounds(12,48,384,12);
//}}

//{{REGISTER_LISTENERS
SymWindow aSymWindow = new SymWindow();
this.addWindowListener(aSymWindow);
SymAction lSymAction = new SymAction();
_go.addActionListener(lSymAction);
//}}
}

/**
 * Set the visibility of this window.
 *
 * @param b true for visible, false for invisible
 */
public void setVisible(boolean b)
{
  if (b)
    setLocation(50, 50);
  super.setVisible(b);
}

/**
 * The entry point for this application.
 *
 * @param args Arguments are not used by this program.
 *        * Required for proper main signature.
 */
static public void main(String args[])
{
```

```java
    (new ViewURL()).setVisible(true);
}

/**
 * Called to add notification handlers.
 */
public void addNotify()
{
  // Record the size of the window prior to
  // calling parents addNotify.
  Dimension size = getSize();

  super.addNotify();

  if (frameSizeAdjusted)
    return;
  frameSizeAdjusted = true;

  // Adjust size of frame according to the insets
  Insets insets = getInsets();
  setSize(insets.left +
          insets.right +
          size.width,
          insets.top +
          insets.bottom +
          size.height);
}

/**
 * Put here by VisualCafe.
 */
// Used by addNotify
boolean frameSizeAdjusted = false;

//{{DECLARE_CONTROLS

/**
 * The bottom scroll pane.
 */
javax.swing.JScrollPane _pane2 = new javax.swing.JScrollPane();

/**
 * The area that the body of this HTTP request will be displayed.
 */
javax.swing.JTextArea _body = new javax.swing.JTextArea();

/**
 * The top scroll pane.
 */
javax.swing.JScrollPane _pane1 = new javax.swing.JScrollPane();

/**
```

```
 * The area that the HTTP headers will be stored.
 */
javax.swing.JTable _headers = new javax.swing.JTable();

/**
 * A static label.
 */
javax.swing.JLabel _label3 = new javax.swing.JLabel();

/**
 * A static label.
 */
javax.swing.JLabel _label1 = new javax.swing.JLabel();

/**
 * The URL requested by the user.
 */
javax.swing.JTextField _url = new javax.swing.JTextField();

/**
 * The GO button.
 */
javax.swing.JButton _go = new javax.swing.JButton();

/**
 * A static label.
 */
javax.swing.JLabel _label2 = new javax.swing.JLabel();
//}}

/**
 * Class created by VisualCafe
 */
class SymWindow extends java.awt.event.WindowAdapter {
  public void windowClosed(java.awt.event.WindowEvent event)
  {
    Object object = event.getSource();
    if (object == ViewURL.this)
      ViewURL_windowClosed(event);
  }

  public void windowClosing(java.awt.event.WindowEvent event)
  {
    Object object = event.getSource();
    if (object == ViewURL.this)
      ViewURL_WindowClosing(event);
  }
}

/**
 * Called when the window closes.
 *
```

```
    * @param event The event.
    */
   void ViewURL_WindowClosing(java.awt.event.WindowEvent event)
   {
     // Hide the Frame
     setVisible(false);

     // Free the system resources
     dispose();
   }
   //{{DECLARE_MENUS
   //}}

   /**
    * Class created by VisualCafe
    */
   class SymAction implements java.awt.event.ActionListener {
     public void actionPerformed(java.awt.event.ActionEvent event)
     {
       Object object = event.getSource();
       if (object == _go)
         Go_actionPerformed(event);
     }
   }

   /**
    * Called when the GO button is clicked.
    *
    * @param event The event.
    */
   void Go_actionPerformed(java.awt.event.ActionEvent event)
   {
     try {
       _http.send(_url.getText(),null);
       _body.setText(_http.getBody());
       _url.setText(_http.getURL());

       TableModel dataModel = new AbstractTableModel()
       {
         public int getColumnCount() { return 2;}
         public int getRowCount() { return _http.getServerHeaders().length();}
         public String getColumnName(int columnIndex)
         {
           switch (columnIndex) {
           case 0:return "HTTP Header";
           case 1:return "Value";
           }
           return "";
         }
         public Object getValueAt(int row, int col)
         {
           if (col==0)
```

```
              return _http.getServerHeaders().get(row).getName();
            else
              return _http.getServerHeaders().get(row).getValue();
          }
        };
        _headers.setModel(dataModel);
        _headers.sizeColumnsToFit(0);
      } catch (Exception e) {
        _body.setText(e.toString());
      }
    }

    /**
     * Called once the window closes.
     *
     * @param event The event.
     */
    void ViewURL_windowClosed(java.awt.event.WindowEvent event)
    {
      System.exit(0);

    }
  }
```

Under the Hood

In this final section of each chapter, we will continue to explore how to use the new classes (from the Bot package) to which you have been introduced. Because this is the first chapter in which we examined the Bot package, this is the first chapter that includes such a section.

Though this section provides much lower-level information that you might not be concerned with initially, it also provides insights into exactly how the Bot package was constructed. If you are content to just use the Bot package without understanding exactly how the underlying technology works, you can safely skip these sections.

We will now examine the classes used to work directly with HTTP, and the other supporting classes, such as the Log class. Finally, we will proceed through the HTTP send method to see how the HTTP request is actually constructed and transmitted.

The *Log* Class

All logging performed by the Bot package is done through the Log class. Logging is particularly important for unattended Internet clients, such as spiders, bots, and aggregators. But because spiders and bots usually run unattended, though some record of what was done is often needed to diagnose problems, problem diagnosis usually occurs after the program has finished executing.

The Log class is completely static and is never meant to be instantiated. By calling its static members, you are defining logging operations for the entire application.

There are already many logging calls built into the Bot package. Many of these helped debug this package while this version was under development. If you examine the program source code, you will see log calls placed sporadically about in the code. Log calls generally take the following form:

```
Log.log(Log.LOG_LEVEL_NORMAL,"HTTP GET " + url );
```

The above log command would log the text HTTP GET (without quotes, space, followed by the URL) to the log with NORMAL listing priority.

The Log class defines several constants that allow log messages to be grouped. These different levels are meant to indicate the importance, or severity, of the message. This allows the application to choose what level of messages they would like to receive. The lower the level you request, the more messages you will receive. For instance, take a look at the following:

```
public final static int LOG_LEVEL_DUMP = 1;
public final static int LOG_LEVEL_TRACE = 2;
public final static int LOG_LEVEL_NORMAL= 3;
public final static int LOG_LEVEL_ERROR = 4;
public final static int LOG_LEVEL_NONE = 5;
```

These levels are specifically defined as follows:

Log.LOG_LEVEL_DUMP   This is the most verbose of all modes. All data packets will be dumped to the log as well as every other log entry available.

Log.LOG_LEVEL_TRACE   This mode gives information to indicate program flow but does not display much actual data-packet information. URLs are displayed.

Log.LOG_LEVEL_NORMAL   This mode gives general program-flow information and lists most major URLs that are hit by the program.

Log.LOG_LEVEL_ERROR   This mode only displays actual errors.

Log.LOG_LEVEL_NONE   This mode shows no logging requested.

There are two types of logging that are supported: file based and console based (see the getFile method, below). Console-based logging writes log information to the system console (stdout). File-based logging writes log information to a file. It is possible to use both file- and console-based logging at the same time. This would both display the log and save it to a file.

The Log class also contains several methods (shown below) that are used both to log information and to determine how much of the log should be displayed. To select file- or console-based logging, the setConsole and setFile methods are used. It is possible to use both console and file logging by passing true to both setConsole and setFile.

The getConsole method   This method determines whether console-based logging is enabled or not.

```
static public boolean getConsole()
```

The getFile method   This method determines if file-based logging is enabled or not.

```
static public boolean getFile()
```

The getLevel method   This method allows you to determine the logging level. This method will return the level constants that were discussed earlier.

```
static public int getLevel()
```

The log method   This method is the main worker method for this class. The log method is called to actually make log entries. The level (see setLevel) that this message refers to should be specified using one of the level constants so that this entry can properly be categorized.

```
synchronized static public void log(int level,String event)
```

The logException method   The logException method is responsible for logging errors. The parameter event specifies the text to describe this log event. The e parameter specifies the exception.

```
static public void logException(String event,Exception e)
```

The getPath method   If file-based logging is enabled, this method allows you to retrieve the path that the log file should be written to. This is a fully qualified filename. If the path is omitted, the log file will be stored in the current directory.

```
static public String getPath()
```

The setConsole method   This method sets whether console-based logging is enabled or not.

```
static public void setConsole(boolean b)
```

The setFile method   This method sets whether file-based logging is enabled or not.

```
static public void setFile(boolean b)
```

The setLevel method   This method should be called by the main application to determine what level of logging is desired. This parameter should be one of the level constants that are discussed earlier in this section.

```
static public void setLevel(int l)
```

The setPath method   If file-based logging is enabled, this method allows you to define the path that the log file should be written to. This should be a fully qualified filename. If the path is omitted, the log file will be stored in the current directory.

```
static public void setPath(String s)
```

The *HTTPSocket* Class

The HTTPSocket class is the primary interface to HTTP servers. This class is used by many of the examples that will be shown in many of the chapters of this book. The HTTPSocket class descends from the HTTP class that was described earlier. We will now examine the methods that make up the HTTPSocket class.

The *send* Method

The send method is the main entry point to the HTTP class from programs that make use of the Bot package. By using the send method, you can request that data be sent and retrieved from web servers, but this does not result in any direct communications to the web server. The send command hands off to another send command called lowLevelSend. The lowLevelSend method is covered in the next section.

The send method is primarily responsible for managing cookies and auto-redirects. The method declaration, local variables, and opening lines for this method are as follows:

```
public void send(String url,String post)
  throws java.net.UnknownHostException,java.io.IOException
{
  int rtn; // the return value

  if( post==null )
    Log.log(Log.LOG_LEVEL_NORMAL,"HTTP GET " + url );
  else
    Log.log(Log.LOG_LEVEL_NORMAL,"HTTP POST " + url );
```

The method begins by checking to see if this is a POST or a GET request and then logs it accordingly. The method then continues with

```
setURL(url);
if(_referrer!=null)
  _clientHeaders.set("referrer",_referrer.toString());

_clientHeaders.set("Accept","image/gif,"
   + "image/x-xbitmap,image/jpeg, "
   + "image/pjpeg, application/vnd.ms-excel,"
   + "application/msword,"
   + "application/vnd.ms-powerpoint, */*");
_clientHeaders.set("Accept-Language","en-us");
_clientHeaders.set("User-Agent",_agent);
```

First, the above code records the URL by calling setURL. This may change, if a redirect is encountered and auto-redirection is occurring. Next, all of the standard HTTP headers are added, and the referrer lists the previous page visited (for a list of common HTTP headers, see Appendix B, "HTTP Headers"). After this, a seemingly endless loop is entered:

```
while(true)
{
  if(_useCookies )
    addCookieHeader();
  addAuthHeader();
  lowLevelSend(_url,post);

  if(_useCookies)
    parseCookies();
  Attribute a = _serverHeaders.get("Location");

  if((a==null) || !_autoRedirect )
  {
    _referrer = getURL();
    return;
  }

  URL u = new URL(new URL(_url),a.getValue());
  Log.log(Log.LOG_LEVEL_NORMAL,"HTTP REDIRECT to " + u.toString() );
  post=null;// don't redirect as a post
  setURL(u.toString());
}
```

This loop will continue until the final redirection is resolved. For instance, if the page contains a location HTTP header, a browser would normally redirect itself to the page specified in the header. In order for this to happen, the cookies must first be added to the header (if there are cookies). If the cookies are added, the user could be inadvertently logged out of a site. (Cookies will be covered in Chapter 7.). However, if user authentication is used, the user authentication header will be added. (User authentication is covered in Chapter 3.) Once this is complete, the request is actually made by calling lowLevelSend. Finally, if auto-redirection is called for, the method will automatically continue to look for and seek out the redirected page. Cookies are carried to a redirected page, but any posted data is not.

This while loop continues to search until no more redirections are encountered. Multiple redirections occur when a page redirects to a page that has a redirection itself.

The *lowLevelSend* Method

The HTTPSocket class is the part of the Bot package that facilitates the actual connections to web servers using HTTP. The HTTP class provides an abstract method called lowLevelSend. Because this method must be implemented by any *derived class*, the HTTPSocket class actually implements it. A derived, or child class, is one that inherits functionality from a parent. When an application is using the HTTPSocket class (a child class), many of the methods from the HTTP class (the parent) are actually being used.

We will now examine the lowLevelSend method and see exactly how it establishes a connection. The method declaration and local variables for the lowLevelSend method are listed here:

```
public void lowLevelSend(String url,String post)
  throws java.net.UnknownHostException, java.io.IOException
{
  String command;// What kind of send POST or GET
  StringBuffer headers;// Used to hold outgoing client headers
  byte buffer[]=new byte[1024];//A buffer for reading
  int l,i;// Counters
  Attribute a;// Used to process incoming attributes
  int port=80;// What port, default to 80
  boolean https = false;// Are we using HTTPS?
  URL u;// Used to help parse the url parameter
```

The first thing that must be done to establish a connection is the URL must be processed. This is done mostly with the URL class provided by Java. There is one problem with the URL class, however; it will throw an exception if it does not recognize the specified scheme. Because of this, we will use the secure HTTPS scheme, which is one it will recognize. Another reason for using HTTPS is that it is needed to communicate with any site that uses a secure connection, and many sites that bots may need information from often use a secured connection. The HTTPS scheme can be problematic, though, because it can cause the URL class to throw a MalformedURLException. Because of this, we must first check to see if this URL starts with HTTPS. If HTTPS support is detected, the URL is given a HTTP scheme so that the URL class can be used to parse the rest of the URL. The default port for HTTPS is 443. The following code determines if the HTTPS scheme is being used:

```
// parse the URL

  if(url.toLowerCase().startsWith("https"))
  {
    url = "http" + url.substring(5);// so it can be parsed
    u = new URL(url);
    if( u.getPort()==-1 )
      port=443;
    https = true;
  }
  else
    u = new URL(url);

  if(u.getPort()!=-1)
    port = u.getPort();
```

After the URL has been processed and parsed, a connection must be established. If an HTTPS connection is needed, we use the SSL class provided by the Bot package to open the connection. For a normal HTTP connection, a new socket is simply created. Once the socket is opened, input and output streams are established. If HTTPS is being used, the following code acquires a secure socket layer (SSL) socket with which to communicate:

NOTE   More information about HTTPS and SSL processing can be found in Chapter 3.

```
// connect
  if(https)
    _socket = SSL.getSSLSocket(u.getHost(),port);
  else
    _socket = new Socket(u.getHost(),port);

  _socket.setSoTimeout(_timeout);
  _socketOut = _socket.getOutputStream();
  _socketIn = _socket.getInputStream();
```

After this, the following if statement must determine if this is a GET or a POST request; this knowledge is necessary in order for the HTTP command to be built. The HTTP command is made up from the command type, the file requested, and the HTTP version number. The following code makes this determination and builds a request:

```
// send command, i.e. GET or POST
  if( post == null )
    command = "GET ";
  else
    command = "POST ";

  command = command + u.getFile() + " HTTP/1.0";
  writeString(command);
```

Next, any client headers must be processed, so if this is a POST command, the Content-Length header is sent. (Remember, the Content-Length header only has meaning in a POST where it reports the length of the posted data.) An HTTP GET request does not contain any posted data, and therefore, it has no need of a Content-Length header.

The host header is also prepared. Web servers have the option of attaching more than one hostname to a single IP address. The host header is sent by the browser to let the web server know which host the browser meant. For example, if www.hosta.com and www.hostb.com were both attached to 192.168.1.1, the web sever needs to know if it was www.hosta.com or www.hostb.com that initiated the request. The host header allows this determination to be made.

All of the client headers are copied to a buffer. Each client header is assumed to be of the form "name:value"—HTTP headers always start with the header name, followed by a colon, which is in turn followed by the data. Finally, all client headers are transmitted as a block. The following code shows how to setup the headers.

```
// Process client headers

  if(post!=null)
    writeString("Content-Length: " + post.length());

  writeString("Host: " + u.getHost() );

  i=0;
  headers = new StringBuffer();
  do
  {
    a = _clientHeaders.get(i++);
    if(a!=null)
    {
      headers.append(a.getName());
      headers.append(':');
      headers.append(a.getValue());
      headers.append("\r\n");
      Log.log(Log.LOG_LEVEL_TRACE,"Client Header:" + a.getName() + "=" +
a.getValue() );
    }
  } while(a!=null);

  if(headers.length()>=0)
    _socketOut.write( headers.toString().getBytes() );
```

If this is a POST, any post data is now transmitted. A blank line is transmitted to delineate the headers from body.

```
// Send a blank line to signal end of HTTP headers
  writeString("");
// transmit a blank line
  if( post!=null )
  {
    Log.log(Log.LOG_LEVEL_TRACE,"Socket Post(" + post.length() + " bytes):" +
new String(post) );
    _socketOut.write( post.getBytes() );
  }
```

Once the complete request has been transmitted, the result must be read back. The header is read into the _header variable, which is done by the while loop seen below. The while loop keeps track of carriage returns and waits for a blank line to indicate completion of the headers. Once the while loop terminates, the headers will have been read into the _headers variable.

```
/* Read the result */
```

```
/* First read HTTP headers */

_header.setLength(0);
int chars = 0;
boolean done = false;

while(!done)
{
  int ch;

  ch = _socketIn.read();
  if(ch==-1)
    done=true;

  switch(ch)
  {
    case '\r':
      break;
    case '\n':
      if(chars==0)
        done =true;
      chars=0;
      break;
    default:
      chars++;
      break;
  }

  _header.append((char)ch);
}
```

Once the headers are read, they must be parsed, and then the actual body must be read in. It is important to parse the headers first so that the content length can be determined. If no content length is specified, the socket is read until there is no more data. Otherwise, the number of bytes, specified by content length, is read in. The following code processes the data that was returned from the request:

```
// now parse the headers and get content length
parseHeaders();
Attribute acl = _serverHeaders.get("Content-length");
int contentLength=0;
try
{
  if(acl!=null)
    contentLength = Integer.parseInt(acl.getValue());
}
catch(Exception e)
```

```
{
  Log.log(Log.LOG_LEVEL_ERROR,"Bad value for content-length");
}

 _body.setLength(0);

if(contentLength!=0)
{
// read in using content length
  while((contentLength-)>0)
  {
    l = _socketIn.read(buffer);
    if(l<0)
      break;
    _body.append(new String(buffer,0,l));
  }
}
else
{
  // read in with no content length
  do
  {
    l = _socketIn.read(buffer);
    if(l<0)
      break;
    _body.append(new String(buffer,0,l));
  } while(l!=0);
}

Log.log(Log.LOG_LEVEL_DUMP,"Socket Page Back:" + _body + "\r\n" );
```

At this point, all that's left to do is the cleanup. The input and output streams are closed, as is the socket itself.

```
// Cleanup

_socketOut.close();
_socketIn.close();
_socket.close();
_socketOut = null;
_socketIn = null;
_socket = null;
```

Summary

All data transmitted between a web browser and web server is transmitted using HTTP. The spiders, bots, and aggregators that will be built in later chapters will rely heavily on this protocol.

The HTTP GET request is the most common of the HTTP request types. GET requests ask that a single web resource be transmitted to the web browser, but the GET request does not allow the web browser to transmit much data back to the web server.

When a large amount of data must be sent back, the HTTP POST request type should be used. The usual sources of HTTP POST requests are forms. When the user fills out a form and clicks the submit button, a POST is generated.

The HTTP HEAD request allows a client to query the status of a single web page, but it doesn't ask for content data to be sent about this web page. This is a quick, low-overhead way to determine if a web page is still valid. This is the least used of the HTTP request types.

The HTTP and HTTPSocket classes are provided in the Bot package. By using these two classes, you can form HTTP requests that support cookies and use the referrer tag and user authentication.

Spiders and bots often run unattended; because of this, logging is of particular importance. The Bot package contains a class named Log that allows events to be logged. This log supports several detail levels and can be written to a file or streamed to stdout. While you are debugging, it is often convenient to display log information by writing it to stdout, as well as writing it to a file. The Log class supports several detail levels, and it independently supports both logging to a file or to stdout.

HTTP forms the foundation of the Web. Now that we have learned how HTTP functions, we will see how another scheme works. In the next chapter, we will examine the HTTPS scheme and how secure web communication works.

CHAPTER 3

Accessing Secure Sites with HTTPS

- HTTPS compared to HTTP

- Using JSSE to implement HTTPS

- The RSA patent

S ecurity was not a major concern when the early Internet protocols, such as HTTP, were drafted. This was because the Internet was never really intended to be the huge global network that it is today. But as the Internet becomes more and more common in the daily lives of people around the world, security becomes much more of an issue.

E-commerce in particular has become a major component of the Internet. E-commerce allows merchants to set up virtual storefronts from which they can sell goods and services to users of the Internet. In addition, banking customers can check their balances and transfer funds using their bank's website. Similarly, brokerage customers can check stock positions, view portfolio holdings, and even buy and sell equities online.

These and other actions performed by today's users require that they trust the systems they used. Users want to be sure that only the intended party receives the confidential information they transmit. Many users fear that a third party will intercept their transactions before they reach the intended site, even though most confidential information is not stolen off the wire as it is transmitted from browser to server. Instead, most information is stolen from the internal company databases where the web servers store it.

This chapter will show you how to access sites that use security. You will see how to access sites using the Hypertext Transfer Protocol Secure (HTTPS). You will also see how sites authenticate the identity of the user using HTTP authentication. You will begin by seeing the difference between HTTP and HTTPS.

HTTP versus HTTPS

You may be wondering how different HTTP is from HTTPS. After all, their names are only different by one letter, and at first glance, the two don't appear very different. In fact, the small lock symbol that appears in the bottom of the status bar in the browser window is the only visual clue that something is different. Other than this lock symbol, a secure document looks exactly the same as an unsecured one.

The average user is barely aware of browser security if they are aware of it at all. Many users don't notice the HTTP or HTTPS specification at the top of their browser, and the typical user just looks to see if the safe-lock symbol is present at the bottom of the browser— some users are not even familiar with that. In reality, there is considerable work going on that remains unnoticed to a naive user and the apparent simplicity of HTTPS is deceiving.

In fact, HTTP and HTTPS are radically different in their low-level implementation. For instance, unlike HTTP, HTTPS is encrypted between the browser and server. A complex series of validations ensure that the data being transmitted by the web server cannot be intercepted. HTTPS also allows you to be sure that you are actually connected to the domain name you expect. It does this by causing the browser to warn you if it fails to authenticate that the site you are communicating with is the correct one.

In most respects, HTTP is very similar to HTTPS. Once the HTTPS packets are decrypted, most elements of the protocol are the same. The HTTP headers that we learned about in the previous chapter are all the same; both protocols have GET, POST, and HEAD requests.

A protocol called *Secure Socket Layer (SSL)* is what provides the low-level encryption that makes HTTPS different. From Java's standpoint, SSL is just a special type of socket. When you create a SSL-based socket you communicate with it just as you would with any ordinary socket. However, this socket is doing a great deal of behind-the-scenes work. Every piece of information that you transmit is automatically encoded, and incoming data is decoded.

Security-oriented Internet protocols, such as HTTPS, protect information as it is transmitted between the web server and web browser. Using these protocols, a web server can be sure that the data is not being intercepted. But these protocols provide no support to allow the web server to determine *who* is actually accessing the server. Determining who is connecting to the web server will be discussed in the later section entitled "HTTP User Authentication."

First we will examine how to use HTTPS with Java.

NOTE   HTTPS is not directly built into JDK V1.3 and lower. This is due to patent restrictions that are discussed in the side bar "The RSA Patent" that appears later in this chapter.

NOTE   Because HTTPS is not directly supported by the JDK, some additional class package must be included. JSSE, or Java Secure Socket Extension, is Sun's solution to implementing the SSL and HTTPS protocols.

Using HTTPS with Java

If you have ever tried to use Java's URL class to open a URLConnection to an address that starts with HTTPS://, you've probably noticed that the standard java.net.URL class doesn't support HTTPS. This lack of support is due to patent restrictions that were in force when Java was created. (Most other web servers support the HTTPS protocol.) Many sites do take advantage of HTTPS. Because of this, it is very likely that you will need to create a bot to access such a site. You will now be shown how to enable support of HTTPS and SSL in the Java programming language.

As mentioned earlier, HTTPS and SSL are not supported directly by the Java programming language. This is because the HTTPS protocol uses an encryption algorithm that was originally patented by RSA Security. Though this patent has since expired, it has left a legacy that will continue for some time. This is because prior to the patent's expiration, companies were required to pay royalties to RSA in order to use this algorithm. Browser manufacturers licensed the algorithm but Sun Microsystems refused to license it, so it wasn't included in the standard Java URL class implementation. This is evident when you attempt to construct a URL object with a string specifying HTTPS as the protocol. When you try this, a `MalformedURL-Exception` will be thrown. Fortunately, the Java specification provides an alternative so that you are able to select an alternate stream handler for the URL class.

The RSA Patent

The implementation of any system that uses HTTPS has been affected by the fact that HTTPS uses patented technology assigned to RSA. There are many misconceptions that surround this patent, but most are now moot because RSA has waived its rights to this infamous patent.

Here is some history about this technology, which was assigned U.S. patent number 4,405,829. This patent began being enforced on September 20, 1983. With funding from the United States government (because of this monetary contribution, the U.S. government has rights to this invention; see Contract No. N00014-67-A-0204, awarded by the Department of the Navy, and Grant No. MCS76-14249, awarded by the National Science Foundation [NSF]), RSA and the Massachusetts Institute of Technology (MIT) developed the invention covered by this patent. The patent was actually assigned to MIT, not RSA, but because of their involvement in this project, RSA had MIT contractually assign them an exclusive license to this technology.

Patent 4,405,829 is commonly referred to by its most basic formula, c=m(e) mod n. This technique has proven both effective and enduring for the encryption of data. It is this technology, which is part of the HTTPS and SSL protocols, that previously required patent licensing from RSA. Though RSA did not own a patent on HTTPS, SSL, or even c = m(e) mod n, their exclusive agreement with MIT granted them a legal stranglehold over Internet security.

The fact that c = m(e) mod n was used as the default security method by the Internet attests to its suitability to this need. If other nonpatented algorithms existed, surely they would have been used in place of the patented c = m(e) mod n.

If you are using a version of the JDK prior to 1.4 you must install the JSSE add-on from Sun in order to use HTTPS and SSL.

Installing JSSE for JDK1.3 and Lower

Though installation of JSSE is meant to be a relatively straightforward process, it has generated a great deal of confusion. If you read Java newsgroups or the Sun Java developer forum messages, you will find many questions from users about how to correctly install this package. There are a number of steps that must be followed, and many users fail to correctly follow these installation instructions and end up with incomplete installations.

Installing JSSE is generally no more difficult than installing any other third-party Java package. In this section, we will attempt to remove some of the confusion and show you how to correctly obtain, install, and use JSSE

1. Download the JSSE package.

   The first step is to acquire the JSSE package and install it. JSSE can be downloaded from the Sun site at the URL http://java.sun.com/products/jsse/. In order to download JSSE, you must first certify that you are from within the United States. This is because the U.S. has certain laws that restrict the export of software with certain kinds of encryption.

WARNING   Even though the patent covering HTTPS has expired, there are still national laws affecting encryption technology. Export of software from the U.S. containing certain encryption technology is regulated. Certain countries have laws that make it illegal for a private citizen to own encryption technology.

2. Extract JSSE from its archive (i.e., ZIP or UNIX tar).

   Once JSSE is downloaded, you will have a ZIP file that contains the complete distribution. JSSE should be unzipped to the default directory that your ZIP program will specify. This directory is usually c:\jsse1.0.2\ on the Windows platform or /usr/local/jsse1.0.2/ on a UNIX platform.

3. Set the CLASSPATH.

   Inside of your JSSE directory, there should be a lib directory that contains three JAR files. The files, jsse.jar, jcert.jar, and jnet.jar, must be added to your CLASSPATH in order for you to be able to use JSSE. For more information about using the CLASSPATH, refer to the section in Appendix E "Adding to the CLASSPATH and System Path." Though the locations of these three files differ depending on where they are installed, on a Windows system they are usually predictably located in one of these locations:

   - c:\jsse1.0.2\lib\jsse.jar
   - c:\jsse1.0.2\lib\jcert.jar
   - c:\jsse1.0.2\lib\jnet.jar

   On a UNIX system their locations can vary depending on platform and installation options, but generally, they appear in the following locations:

   - /usr/local/jsse1.0.2/lib\jsse.jar
   - /usr/local/jsse1.0.2/jcert.jar
   - /usr/local/jsse1.0.2/jnet.jar

TIP   If you are unfamiliar with how to unzip files, the site `http://www.winzip.com` contains all of the software and information you need.

TIP   The CLASSPATH addition that I use on my Windows machine is `C:\jdk1.3\jre\lib\ ext\bot.jar;c:\jsse1.0.2\lib\jsse.jar;c:\jsse1.0.2\lib\jcert.jar;c:\ jsse1.0.2\lib\jnet.jar`. If you have installed these files to a different location, yours will be different.

The aforementioned steps will install JSSE so that it is available to the command line version of JDK. If you would like to use JDK with one of the IDEs, such as VisualCafé or Jbuilder, you must complete the steps described in the next section as well.

Installing JSSE for IDEs

Installing JSSE for use with one of the IDEs involves a few additional steps. As with the JDK, the three files `jsse.jar`, `jcert.jar`, and `jnet.jar` must be installed into the CLASSPATH of the IDE.

1. Add the JSSE JAR files to the class directories.

   Most IDEs do not read the operating system environmental variable CLASSPATH because most IDEs have their own configuration options that specify the CLASSPATH.

   VisualCafé has an option to set the CLASSPATH under the Directories tab of the Project Options dialog box. To bring up this dialog box, select project and then options. This will bring up the Project Options dialog box. From here select the Directories tab. Figure 3.1 shows this screen and the settings necessary to properly configure VisualCafé. In this figure, you should also note that a path to the Bot package is provided.

2. Install the correct `cacerts` file.

   Java provides a file named `cacerts` that maps encryption algorithms to their correct implementation. The `cacerts` file provided with VisualCafé is incompatible with JSSE. (This was true for Version 4 of VisualCafé. Future versions may correct this.) You should try to compile programs without this step and see if it works and only fix the `cacerts` file if necessary. To fix the `cacerts` file, copy the `cacerts` file specified by the path `<JAVA-HOME>\ lib\security\cacerts` to `<VC-HOME>\lib\security`, or in the case of my own installation, copy `C:\jdk1.3\jre\lib\security\cacerts` to `C:\VisualCafe\Java2\lib\security`.

WARNING   Some IDEs contain an invalid `cacerts` file for use with JSSE. To obtain one that works, you may need to copy the `cacerts` file from JDK to your IDE. This may also be true if you are using a version of the Java compiler (javac) other than the one that is provided by Sun.

3. Enable JSSE debugging (optional).

If you encounter other configuration problems, you may want to enable JSSE debugging. To do so, add this command to the beginning of your Java program.

```
setProperty("javax.net.debug", "all");
```

This will cause JSSE to display considerably more debugging information than would be displayed without this command.

FIGURE 3.1:

Using JSSE with
VisualCafé

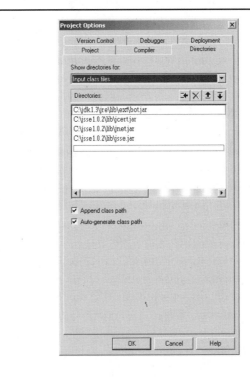

Using JSSE

Just installing JSSE does not mean your programs will automatically make use of it. Once JSSE has been installed, you must set a system property to communicate to Java that JSSE has been installed. By placing the following lines near the beginning of a Java program, you will enable it to use JSSE:

```
System.setProperty(
  "java.protocol.handler.pkgs",
  "com.sun.net.ssl.internal.www.protocol");
  Security.addProvider(
    new com.sun.net.ssl.internal.ssl.Provider());
```

These lines of code allow Java to recognize HTTPS as a valid protocol type for a URL. It is now legal to construct a URL that contains HTTPS, as follows.

```
URL url = new URL("https://[specify a server]");
```

By default, HTTPS uses port 443 instead of the standard port 80 used by HTTP. An HTTPS connection is not required to use this standard port. Just like an HTTP connection, an HTTPS connection can specify any desired port. This is done by placing a colon (:) just after the server name and then following it with a port. For example, the following would specify an HTTPS connection over port 8080.

```
URL url = new URL("https://[specify a server]:8080");
```

This section presented the basics of how to use JSSE with Java. The next section will show you how to use JSSE through the Bot package.

HTTPS with the Bot Package

Unfortunately, using URLConnection to communicate using HTTPS has all of the same limitations as communicating using HTTP over the URLConnection object. For a discussion of the weaknesses present in the URLConnection object, refer to the section entitled "The HTTP Class versus the URLConnection Class" in Chapter 2, "Examining the Hypertext Transfer Protocol." Once JSSE is installed, using HTTPS with the Bot package is very easy.

Using HTTPS from within the Bot package is just like using HTTP. All you need to do is pass a URL that specified an HTTPS scheme to the send method of the HTTPSocket method, and it is done. Whenever HTTPSocket detects that it is being directed to an HTTPS site, it automatically switches classes so that it is using secure sockets. More information about how this switch actually occurs is presented in the "The SSL Class" section of this chapter.

To open an HTTPS connection with the Bot package, use the following lines of code:

```
HTTPSocket http = new HTTPSocket();
http.send("[https or http url]",null);
```

Of course, fill in [https or http url] with a URL of your choice that supports HTTPS. This URL must start with the HTTPS scheme. As you can see, using HTTPS with the Bot package is exactly the same as using it with HTTP (as seen in "The URL Format" section of Chapter 2). All that needs to change is the HTTPS scheme specified in the URL.

HTTP User Authentication

Up until now, we've talked just about how to secure the connection between the client and the server. The true benefit to technologies such as HTTPS and SSL are twofold. First, they allow us to ensure that no third party is intercepting sensitive data. Second, they allow us to be sure that the server we are reaching out to is indeed the server we think it is. But how does the web server know that we are who we say we are? This is the job of user authentication.

There are two primary ways in which users are authenticated, both of which are used extensively throughout the Internet; this book will cover both of these methods. This first method, that of HTTP header user authentication, will be covered in this chapter. When you use HTTP header user authentication, an encrypted HTTP header is sent to the server, along with the rest of the GET, POST, or HEAD HTTP requests so that the user's identity can be validated. During this approach, the user is presented with a small dialog box that requests them to enter their user ID and password.

If they fail to enter the correct login information, they will not be allowed access and will see something similar the screen shown here.

The second approach is more complex and far less standardized. This approach uses cookies and/or query strings to maintain state as the user logs into the system. The cookie or query string allows the server to remember which session the user is attached to. The user is prompted for their login information by an HTML form, and a back-end server program, such as a JSP page, authenticates the user and sets the cookie/session information accordingly. An example of this can be seen in Figure 3.2.

FIGURE 3.2:

Non-HTTP user authentication

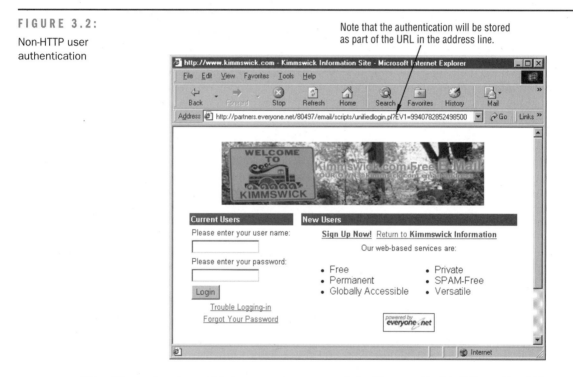

We will examine the cookie/query string approach in Chapter 10, "Building a Bot." For now, while we are still learning HTTPS, we will examine how to use the HTTP user authentication method.

Server Setup for HTTP User Authentication

First we will examine how to set up user authentication from the server side. When you are writing bots, you will most often be using HTTP user authentication from the client side, but nevertheless, it is good to know how this is configured from a typical web server point of view.

Apache web server is the most widely used web server on the Internet (and it happens to be the one I use), so we will examine how to configure HTTP user authentication for Apache. Other web servers follow similar approaches, with the exception of Microsoft IIS, which integrates user authentication with the Windows NT/2000 user manager. If you are using IIS, consult your documentation because the procedure is very different than the one presented here.

First, you must choose the directory that you want secured. (Access is restricted by directory, so all files in the same directory will be protected.) This directory must be HTTP accessible; that is, files placed in the directory must be visible to visiting web browsers. In the case of Apache, this means any directory that is a child of the `htdocs` directory. For the purposes of this example, the directory that I am securing on my site is `http://www.jeffheaton.com/secure/` from the Web, and from UNIX it is `/usr/local/www/vhosts/heat-on.com/htdocs/secure/`. This directory fits the criteria because it is a child of the `htdocs` directory, and therefore, it is HTTP accessible.

In order to secure this directory, you must create several files. One of these files is named `.htaccess`, and it must be created to specify the restrictions. Another file is a `.htpasswd` file, and it must be created to hold user information. You will now be shown how to create these files.

Apache uses the `.htaccess` file to restrict access to web documents. You can place this file in any directory that Apache exposes to HTTP. After you have placed this file in such a directory, your web browser will prompt you for a username and password when a user next browses this page. The change is immediate because the web server searches for the `.htaccess` file with each web browser request. This password prompt will only be shown to the web browser once per session, however. A user ID and password specified for one resource from a protected directory are valid for any others in that same directory. So, as the web browser moves from page to page, the user is not prompted again for a password. But this specified password is not stored in the user's browser between uses. Once you close the browser, all user IDs and passwords are forgotten. If you try to reconnect to a site that you had previously entered a user ID and password for, the web browser will prompt you to enter the user id and password again.

WARNING Please make sure you are creating these files in the directory that you want password protected. If you do not, the `.htpasswd` file will end up in the wrong directory.

To actually create these files you should open a connection (e.g., telnet) to the host you wish to configure and move to the directory to secure. The first step is to create the `.htaccess` file. (Again, make sure you are creating it in the directory that contains the documents you wish to restrict access to.) The contents of this `.htaccess` file specify the name of the password file. For example, if you were user jheaton with Web documents in the local directory `/usr/local/www/vhosts/heat-on.com/htdocs/secure/` that you wanted to restrict access to, your `.htaccess` might look like this:

```
AuthUserFile /usr/local/www/vhosts/heat-on.com/htdocs/secure/.htpasswd
AuthName secure_area
AuthType Basic
```

```
<Limit GET>
require valid-user
</Limit>
```

WARNING The `.htaccess` will not work if there are extra spaces after `AuthUserFile`. There should be only one space between the `AuthUserFile` command and the path that it specifies.

Next, you will need to create a `.htpasswd` file in the same directory. This file contains the user IDs and passwords for the users. To create the `.htpasswd` file, log into this server again using telnet, move to the directory that you want to restrict access to, and issue the following command

```
htpasswd -c .htpasswd jheaton
```

for the first user (where `jheaton` is the username). You will then be prompted twice for the user's password. The `-c` option causes the `.htpasswd` file to be created. For each additional user, type

```
htpasswd .htpasswd otheruser
```

NOTE There is no correspondence between the usernames and passwords used for accounts on this server and usernames and passwords in any specific `.htpasswd` file. A user doesn't need to have an account on this system in order to be validated for access to files protected by HTTP-based authentication.

Because the passwords are encrypted, you must use the `.htpasswd` utility to generate your user information. The contents of the `.htpasswd` are shown below. As you can see, the password is encrypted. The password, by the way, is the classic *War Games* password of `joshua`.

```
jheaton:TSyqGXEftppw.
```

For more information about how user authentication is set up, you can refer to the NCSA document stored at `http://hoohoo.ncsa.uiuc.edu/docs/tutorials/user.html`.

NOTE There are two filenames that we discuss in this section, both named `htpasswd`. If specified without a dot as `htpasswd`, this refers to the Apache utility used to create the `.htpasswd` file. When the dot is specified, this is the password file created by the aforementioned utility.

How HTTP User Authentication Works on the Client

On the client, HTTP user authentication works by simply adding one header to the HTTP request. (For more information on HTTP requests, refer to Chapter 2, "Examining the Hypertext Transfer Protocol.") To see how this works, we will examine the same HTTP session we examined previously. This time, however, we will examine the HTTP requests actually being sent by the browser.

First, the user requests the document `http://www.jeffheaton.com/secure`.

```
GET /secure HTTP/1.1
Accept: application/vnd.ms-powerpoint, application/vnd.ms-excel,
application/msword, image/gif, image/x-xbitmap, image/jpeg, image/pjpeg, */*
Accept-Language: en-us
Accept-Encoding: gzip, deflate
User-Agent: Mozilla/4.0 (compatible; MSIE 5.5; Windows NT 4.0)
Host: www.jeffheaton.com
Connection: Keep-Alive
```

The web server sees the `.htaccess` file sitting in this directory and responds with an error. This error is not really an error; it just prompts the browser to request login information. The error response is shown here.

```
HTTP/1.1 401 Authorization Required
Date: Mon, 02 Jul 2001 13:53:22 GMT
Server: Apache/1.3.12 (Unix) ApacheJServ/1.1.2 PHP/4.0.1pl2 mod_perl/1.24
FrontPage/4.0.4.3 AuthMySQL/2.20 mod_ssl/2.6.4 OpenSSL/0.9.5a
WWW-Authenticate: Basic realm="secure_area"
Connection: close
Transfer-Encoding: chunked
Content-Type: text/html; charset=iso-8859-1
```

Once the web browser receives this message back, it prompts the user for login information. The user enters this information, which causes the browser to respond to the web server with the user ID and password contained in an Authorization header. The user ID and password contained in this header are encrypted so that they cannot be seen by someone who may be observing the packets being transferred. (The exact details of how this data gets encrypted are covered in the last section of this chapter, "The `Base64OutputStream` Class.") This browser's response to the server is shown here:

```
GET /secure HTTP/1.1
Accept: application/vnd.ms-powerpoint, application/vnd.ms-excel,
application/msword, image/gif, image/x-xbitmap, image/jpeg, image/pjpeg, */*
Accept-Language: en-us
Accept-Encoding: gzip, deflate
User-Agent: Mozilla/4.0 (compatible; MSIE 5.5; Windows NT 4.0)
Host: www.jeffheaton.com
Connection: Keep-Alive
Authorization: Basic amhlYXRvbjpqb3NodWE=
```

Once the web server receives the correct Authorization header, it sends back a normal response for that document, as if no authentication had been requested. The web browser will continue to send this Authorization header for the duration of the session with that website.

This final acceptance response is shown below; it is a normal HTTP response as seen in Chapter 2.

```
HTTP/1.1 200 OK
Date: Mon, 02 Jul 2001 13:53:47 GMT
Server: Apache/1.3.12 (Unix) ApacheJServ/1.1.2 PHP/4.0.1pl2 mod_perl/1.24
FrontPage/4.0.4.3 AuthMySQL/2.20 mod_ssl/2.6.4 OpenSSL/0.9.5a
Last-Modified: Mon, 02 Jul 2001 13:53:07 GMT
ETag: "b50a-7b-3b407cc3"
Accept-Ranges: bytes
Content-Length: 123
Connection: close
Content-Type: text/html
```

User Authentication with the Bot Package

The HTTP class, discussed in Chapter 2, handles all of the details of user authentication. All you have to do is call the setUser and setPassword methods to define the user ID and password. Once you instantiate an HTTP object, the user ID and password are set, and all pages requested by that HTTP object would contain a valid Authorization header containing the specified user ID and password. The following code shows an example of this:

```
HTTPSocket http = new HTTPSocket();
http.setUser("user here");
http.setPassword("password here")
http.send("[https or http url]",null);
```

Once the user ID and password are set, they will remain set in this HTTP object. In the next section, we will examine an example program that makes use of this technique.

Securing Access

The example in this section, which functions like a very simple browser, illustrates both HTTPS and user authentication. Figure 3.3 shows this program running. To use this program, enter a URL to browse to and press the Go button. For the URL, you may enter any address, either HTTP or HTTPS. If the program detects that the requested page is requesting user authentication, a small input dialog box is displayed to allow you to enter your user ID and password.

This program is shown below as two listings. First, Listing 3.1 shows the source code needed to produce SecurePrompt.java. The SecurePrompt class is used to prompt the user for their ID and password. The main class for this program is given as Listing 3.2. If you choose to test these two examples with the URL of http://www.jeffheaton.com/secure/, the password you should use is "Joshua".

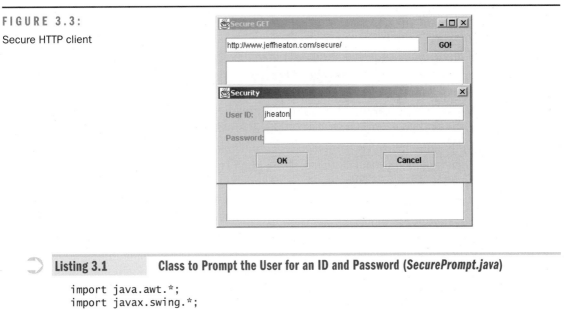

FIGURE 3.3:

Secure HTTP client

Listing 3.1   Class to Prompt the User for an ID and Password (*SecurePrompt.java*)

```java
import java.awt.*;
import javax.swing.*;

/**
 * Example from Chapter 3
 *
 * Simple object to prompt for user id/password.
 *
 * @author Jeff Heaton
 * @version 1.0
 */
public class SecurePrompt extends javax.swing.JDialog
{
    public SecurePrompt(Frame parent)
    {
        super(parent,true);

        //{{INIT_CONTROLS
        setTitle("Security");
        getContentPane().setLayout(null);
        setSize(403,129);
        setVisible(false);
        JLabel1.setText("User ID:");
        getContentPane().add(JLabel1);
        JLabel1.setBounds(12,12,48,24);
        JLabel2.setText("Password:");
        getContentPane().add(JLabel2);
        JLabel2.setBounds(12,48,72,24);
        _uid.setText("jheaton");
        getContentPane().add(_uid);
```

```java
      _uid.setBounds(72,12,324,24);
      _ok.setText("OK");
      getContentPane().add(_ok);
      _ok.setBounds(60,84,84,24);
      getContentPane().add(_pwd);
      _pwd.setBounds(72,48,324,24);
      _cancel.setText("Cancel");
      getContentPane().add(_cancel);
      _cancel.setBounds(264,84,84,24);
      //}}

      //{{REGISTER_LISTENERS
      SymAction lSymAction = new SymAction();
      _ok.addActionListener(lSymAction);
      _cancel.addActionListener(lSymAction);
      //}}
   }

   public void setVisible(boolean b)
   {
      if (b)
         setLocation(50, 50);
      super.setVisible(b);
   }

   public void addNotify()
   {
      // Record the size of the window prior to calling parents addNotify.
      Dimension size = getSize();

      super.addNotify();

      if (frameSizeAdjusted)
         return;
      frameSizeAdjusted = true;

      // Adjust size of frame according to the insets
      Insets insets = getInsets();
      setSize(insets.left +
        insets.right +
        size.width,
        insets.top +
        insets.bottom +
        size.height);
   }

   // Used by addNotify
   boolean frameSizeAdjusted = false;

   //{{DECLARE_CONTROLS
   javax.swing.JLabel JLabel1 = new javax.swing.JLabel();
   javax.swing.JLabel JLabel2 = new javax.swing.JLabel();
```

```java
/**
 * The user ID entered.
 */
javax.swing.JTextField _uid = new javax.swing.JTextField();

/**
 */
javax.swing.JButton _ok = new javax.swing.JButton();

/**
 * The password is entered.
 */
javax.swing.JPasswordField _pwd = new javax.swing.JPasswordField();
javax.swing.JButton _cancel = new javax.swing.JButton();
//}}


class SymAction implements java.awt.event.ActionListener
{
    public void actionPerformed(java.awt.event.ActionEvent event)
    {
        Object object = event.getSource();
        if (object == _ok)
            Ok_actionPerformed(event);
        else if (object == _cancel)
            Cancel_actionPerformed(event);
    }
}

/**
 * Called when ok is clicked.
 *
 * @param event
 */
void Ok_actionPerformed(java.awt.event.ActionEvent event)
{
    setVisible(false);
}

/**
 * Called when cancel is clicked.
 *
 * @param event
 */
void Cancel_actionPerformed(java.awt.event.ActionEvent event)
{
  _uid.setText("");
  _pwd.setText("");
    setVisible(false);
}
}
```

Listing 3.2   **Get a HTTP file (*SecureGET.java*)**

```java
import java.awt.*;
import javax.swing.*;
import com.heaton.bot.*;

/**
 * Example program from Chapter 3
 * Programming Spiders, Bots and Aggregators in Java
 * Copyright 2001 by Jeff Heaton
 *
 *
 * This example displays a mini-browser, similar to
 * chapter 3. This browser supports HTTPS(through
 * JSSE) and also allows access to HTTP password
 * protected sites.
 *
 * @author Jeff Heaton
 * @version 1.0
 */
public class SecureGET extends javax.swing.JFrame {

  /**
   * Constructor
   */
  public SecureGET()
  {
    //{{INIT_CONTROLS
    setTitle("Secure GET");
    getContentPane().setLayout(null);
    setSize(405,305);
    setVisible(false);
    _url.setText("http://www.jeffheaton.com/secure/");
    getContentPane().add(_url);
    _url.setBounds(12,12,312,24);
    _go.setText("GO!");
    _go.setActionCommand("GO!");
    getContentPane().add(_go);
    _go.setBounds(336,12,60,24);
    JScrollPane1.setOpaque(true);
    getContentPane().add(JScrollPane1);
    JScrollPane1.setBounds(12,48,384,252);
    _body.setEditable(false);
    JScrollPane1.getViewport().add(_body);
    _body.setBounds(0,0,381,249);
    //}}

    //{{INIT_MENUS
    //}}

    //{{REGISTER_LISTENERS
```

```java
    SymAction lSymAction = new SymAction();
    _go.addActionListener(lSymAction);
    //}}
  }

/**
 * Constructor with a title.
 *
 * @param sTitle The title.
 */
public SecureGET(String sTitle)
{
   this();
   setTitle(sTitle);
}

/**
 * Added by VisualCafe.
 *
 * @param b display or not.
 */
public void setVisible(boolean b)
{
   if ( b )
     setLocation(50, 50);
   super.setVisible(b);
}

/**
 * The main function.  Program starts
 * here.
 *
 * @param args Command line arguments not used.
 */
static public void main(String args[])
{
   (new SecureGET()).setVisible(true);
}

/**
 * Added by VisualCafe.
 */
public void addNotify()
{
   // Record the size of the window prior to calling parents addNotify.
   Dimension size = getSize();

   super.addNotify();

   if ( frameSizeAdjusted )
     return;
```

```
      frameSizeAdjusted = true;

      // Adjust size of frame according to the insets and menu bar
      Insets insets = getInsets();
      javax.swing.JMenuBar menuBar = getRootPane().getJMenuBar();
      int menuBarHeight = 0;
      if ( menuBar != null )
        menuBarHeight = menuBar.getPreferredSize().height;
      setSize(insets.left +
              insets.right +
              size.width,
              insets.top +
              insets.bottom +
              size.height +
              menuBarHeight);
    }

    /**
     * Added by VisualCafe
     */
    // Used by addNotify
    boolean frameSizeAdjusted = false;

    //{{DECLARE_CONTROLS
    javax.swing.JTextField _url = new javax.swing.JTextField();
    javax.swing.JButton _go = new javax.swing.JButton();
    javax.swing.JScrollPane JScrollPane1 = new javax.swing.JScrollPane();
    javax.swing.JTextArea _body = new javax.swing.JTextArea();
    //}}

    //{{DECLARE_MENUS
    //}}


    class SymAction implements java.awt.event.ActionListener {
      public void actionPerformed(java.awt.event.ActionEvent event)
      {
        Object object = event.getSource();
        if ( object == _go )
          Go_actionPerformed(event);
      }
    }

    /**
     * This method is where most of the action happens.
     * When the user clicks GO, this method is executed.
     *
     * @param event The event.
     */
    void Go_actionPerformed(java.awt.event.ActionEvent event)
    {
```

```
      boolean done = false;

      // create a HTTP object outside the loop
      HTTPSocket http = new HTTPSocket();

      // loop until non-security error or success
      while ( !done ) {
        // Attempt to connect to the URL with no id/password
        // the first time, then with an id/password on
        // subsequent trys.
        try {
          http.send(_url.getText(),null);
          _body.setText(http.getBody());
          done = true;
        } catch ( Exception e ) {
          // was it a security error?
          if ( e.getMessage().indexOf("401")!=-1 ) {
            // did we already try an id/password
            // if so display error
            if ( (http.getUser().length()!=0) ||
                 (http.getPassword().length()!=0) ) {
              JOptionPane.showMessageDialog(this,
                                        "Invalid user id/password.",
                                        "Security Error",
                                        JOptionPane.OK_CANCEL_OPTION,
                                        null );
            }
            // prompt the user for id/password
            SecurePrompt prompt = new SecurePrompt(this);
            prompt.show();
            if ( (prompt._uid.getText().length()!=0) ||
                 (prompt._pwd.getText().length()!=0) ) {
              // set the id/password for next try
              http.setUser( prompt._uid.getText() );
              http.setPassword( prompt._pwd.getText() );
            } else
              done = true;
          } else
            // something else bad happened, so give up
            done=true;
          _body.setText(e.getMessage());
        }
      }
```
```
  }
}
```

This program works by allowing the user to enter a URL that they want to retrieve. If the URL is HTTPS, the Bot package automatically routes the socket creation call to JSSE so that a SSL socket can be created. The program waits for a security exception to be thrown. When it is, the user is prompted for a user ID and password.

The main processing loop for the program is contained in the method Go_actionPerformed, which can be seen in Listing 3.2. This method must set up a loop that will continue until either a non-security exception is thrown, or until the page is read correctly. The Go_action-Performed method is called when the user presses the Go button. After this method is called, the program begins by setting a done flag to false and creating a new HTTPSocket class, as shown here:

```
boolean done = false;

// create a HTTP object outside the loop
HTTPSocket http = new HTTPSocket();
```

Because a new HTTPSocket class is created each time the method is called, user IDs and passwords are not carried over from previous clicks of the Go button. With the newly created HTTPSocket object, the program begins a loop and attempts to read in the specified URL by calling the send method of the HTTPSocket object. If no exception is thrown, the body text received is copied to the _body control and done is set to true to exit the loop:

```
// loop until non-security error or success
  while(!done)
  {
    // Attempt to connect to the URL with no id/password
    // the first time, then with an id/password on
    // subsequent trys.
    try
    {
      http.send(_url.getText(),null);
      _body.setText(http.getBody());
      done = true;
    }
```

If no security or other exceptions occur, the above portion is the only part of the Go_action-Performed method that is executed. If an exception is thrown, the catch statement shown in Listing 3.2 is executed. The catch statement evaluates to see if this was a security exception. A user authentication error will always be a 401 error, like the one shown here:

```
if( e.getMessage().indexOf("401")!=-1 )
```

If the error code is 401, then the method must determine if this error is the result of a bad user ID or a secured page being entered for the first time. If there is already a user ID and password stored in the HTTP object, then we know the user already made at least one attempt on this page. If this is the case, we display an error message. The code that accomplishes this is shown here:

```
// did we already try an id/password?
// if so display error
```

```
if( (http.getUser().length()!=0) ||
    (http.getPassword().length()!=0) )
{
  JOptionPane.showMessageDialog(this,
    "Invalid user id/password.",
    "Security Error",
    JOptionPane.OK_CANCEL_OPTION,
    null );
}
```

If this is the first time the user has entered this page and the user ID and password properties are empty, then the user will be prompted to enter a user ID and password. The user is also prompted for a user ID and password if the error message was just displayed as a result of a bad user ID and password. This allows the user to retry the access attempt:

```
SecurePrompt prompt = new SecurePrompt(this);
prompt.show();
if( (prompt._uid.getText().length()!=0) ||
    (prompt._pwd.getText().length()!=0) )
{
  // set the id/password for next try
  http.setUser( prompt._uid.getText() );
  http.setPassword( prompt._pwd.getText() );
}
else
  done = true;
```

If the user clicks cancel, the `else` clause will be executed and a security fault will be displayed on the application. Finally, if some other non-security related fault occurs, the error is displayed with the following code:

```
// something else bad happened, so give up
  done=true;
_body.setText(e.getMessage());
```

NOTE   For a complete list of error codes, refer to the section in Appendix B, "HTTP Status Codes."

Under the Hood

The code you would use to support and initiate the security features talked about in this chapter is not confined easily to just one class. Much of this necessary code is contained in the HTTP class that was already discussed in Chapter 2. Here we will examine the code that is added to the HTTP class as well as the two security specific classes that are part of the Bot package.

SSL and Base64OutputStream are the two security specific classes contained in the Bot package. The SSL class allows all JSSE specific code to be isolated to one class. This is done by making sure no JSSE-dependent code is introduced into classes other than the SSL class. The advantage of such isolation is that if JSSE cannot be found, only one class will fail, and the program can generally continue without error. Of course, it will fail if an HTTPS site is accessed.

The `Base64OutputStream` class implements an output stream that accepts data and filters it to base64-encoded form. Base64-encoded form is used by the user authentication header. In order to provide some very limited security, the user authentication header is scrambled with base64 encoding.

The *Base64OutputStream* Class

Base64 encoding is a method for encoding binary data to a pure ASCII form, which allows it to be transferred more easily over the Internet. Base64 is also useful because it encrypts the data, making it harder to understand. HTTP user authentication uses base64 encoding to obscure the user ID and password. Unfortunately, this method does not really conceal any information because if someone intercepted the packet, they could easily run a base64 decoder on the data.

This is why HTTP user authentication is particularly effective when it is combined with HTTPS. The HTTPS security prevents someone from intercepting the packet, conceals the inner workings of the HTTP user authentication headers, and allows the authentication to effectively restrict access to a particular Internet resource.

But what is the algorithm for base64 encoding? Base64 encoding is defined by RFC1341. This RFC is about MIME types, but part of it defines base64 encoding. This portion of RFC1341 is discussed in the sidebar called "Understanding Base64 Encoding" later in this chapter.

Listing 3.3 shows a class that can be used to perform this encoding. This is a simple Java class that implements base64 encoding as a Java output filter. This typical Java filter can be used just like any other filter. Any other class that will use the `Base64OutputStream` class should use the method called `base64Encode` that is contained in the `URLUtility` class of the Bot package. This method can be seen below.

NOTE   The Bot package does not directly use the `Base64OutputStream`; instead, the `base64Encode` method of `URLUtility` is used.

```
static public String base64Encode(String s)
{
  ByteArrayOutputStream bout = new ByteArrayOutputStream();

  Base64OutputStream out = new Base64OutputStream(bout);
  try
  {
```

```
    out.write(s.getBytes());
    out.flush();
  }
  catch(IOException e)
  {}

  return bout.toString();
}
```

To use this method, you simply call it as follows:

```
String base64 = URLUtility.base64Encode("text to encode");
```

Understanding Base64 Encoding

Base64 is an encoding method that will transform text into a form that is not easily read by humans. To see how to convert something into base64, we will walk through how the word "Spider" would be converted to base64. First we must look at the ASCII values of each (for further ASCII values, see Appendix B, "Various HTTP Related Charts"):

S = 83

p = 112

i = 105

d = 100

e = 101

r = 114

Therefore, the word "Spider" is 83 112 105 100 101 114 in decimal form, which we must now convert to binary:

83 = 01010011

112 = 01110000

105 = 01101001

100 = 01100100

101 = 01100101

114 = 01110010

These binary numbers must then be concatenated into one long string, as shown here:

010100110111000001101001011001000110010101110010

This string of bits must now be broken into 6-bit words

010100 110111 000001 101001 011001 000110 010101 110010

Continued on next page

which are then converted back into decimal.

010100 = 20

110111 = 55

000001 = 1

101001 = 41

011001 = 25

000110 = 6

010101 = 21

110010 = 50

Each of these decimal numbers must now be converted to a base64 character. (The table to do this is shown at the end of this sidebar.) This process is shown here.

20 = U

55 = 3

1 = B

41 = p

25 = Z

6 = G

21 = V

50 = y

This all results in the word "Spider" becoming "U3BpZGVy" when it is encoded to base64.

The following is an excerpt from RFC1341 by N. Borenstein, Bellcore, and N. Freed (Innosoft, June 1992).

Value	Encoding	Value	Encoding	Value	Encoding	Value	Encoding
0	A	18	S	36	k	54	2
1	B	19	T	37	l	55	3
2	C	20	U	38	m	56	4
3	D	21	V	39	n	57	5
4	E	22	W	40	o	58	6
5	F	23	X	41	p	59	7
6	G	24	Y	42	q	60	8
7	H	25	Z	43	r	61	9
8	I	26	a	51	z	62	+
9	J	34	i	52	0	63	/
17	R	35	j	53	1	(pad)	=

Continued on next page

Listing 3.3   **Base64 Encoding (*Base64OutputStream.java*)**

```java
package com.heaton.bot;

import java.io.*;

/**
 * This filter is used to 64-bit encode the specified string.  This allows a
string to be displayed with only ASCII characters.  It is also used to provide
HTTP authorization.
 *
 * @author Jeff Heaton
 * @version 1.0
 */
class Base64OutputStream extends FilterOutputStream
{

  /**
   * The constructor.
   *
   * @param out The stream used to write to.
   */
  public Base64OutputStream(OutputStream out)
  {
    super(out);
  }

  /**
   * Write a byte to be encoded.
   *
   * @param c The character to be written.
   * @exception java.io.IOException
   */
  public void write(int c) throws IOException
  {
    _buffer[_index] = c;
    _index++;
    if(_index==3)
```

```
    {
      super.write(toBase64[(_buffer[0]&0xfc)>>2]);
      super.write(toBase64[((_buffer[0] &0x03)<<4) |
        ((_buffer[1]&0xf0)>>4)]);
      super.write(toBase64[((_buffer[1]&0x0f)<<2) |
        ((_buffer[2]&0xc0)>>6)]);
      super.write(toBase64[_buffer[2]&0x3f]);
      _column+=4;
      _index=0;
      if(_column>=76)
      {
        super.write('\n');
        _column = 0;
      }
    }
  }

  /**
   * Ensure all bytes are written.
   *
   * @exception java.io.IOException
   */
  public void flush()
    throws IOException
  {
    if(_index==1)
    {
      super.write(toBase64[(_buffer[2]&0x3f) >> 2]);
      super.write(toBase64[(_buffer[0]&0x03) << 4]);
      super.write('=');
      super.write('=');
    }
    else if(_index==2)
    {
      super.write(toBase64[(_buffer[0]&0xfc) >> 2]);
      super.write(toBase64[((_buffer[0]&0x03)<<4)|
        ((_buffer[1]&0xf0)>>4)]);
      super.write(toBase64[(_buffer[1]&0x0f)<<2]);
      super.write('=');
    }
  }

  /**
   * Allowsable characters for base-64.
   */
  private static char[] toBase64 =
  { 'A','B','C','D','E','F','G','H',
    'I','J','K','L','M','N','O','P',
    'Q','R','S','T','U','V','W','X',
    'Y','Z','a','b','c','d','e','f',
    'g','h','i','j','k','l','m','n',
```

```
   'o','p','q','r','s','t','u','v',
   'w','x','y','z','0','1','2','3',
   '4','5','6','7','8','9','+','/'};

/**
 * Current column.
 */
private int _column=0;

/**
 * Current index.
 */
private int _index=0;

/**
 * Outbound buffer.
 */
private int _buffer[] = new int[3];

}
```

The above listing is used to do base64 encoding. Now that a class has been created to allow base64 encoding, the HTTP class must be extended to accommodate user authentication. This extension to the HTTP class will make use of the base64 class just described.

Implementing User Authentication in the *HTTP* Class

The HTTP class also needs to be extended to support user authentication. The necessary additions to the HTTP class to provide user authentication is relatively simple. All you need to do to use user authentication is specify a user ID and password using the setUser and setPassword methods of the HTTP class. To do this, you send these two properties as part of an HTTP header, which is created by the addAuthHeader method of HTTP. The addAuthHeader is called inside of the send method of HTTP.

```
while(true)
{
  if(_useCookies )
    addCookieHeader();
  addAuthHeader();
  lowLevelSend(_url,post);
```

The addAuthHeader method itself is also relatively simple. The format of an HTTP user authorization header is Authorization:Basic userid:password. The last part, beyond the word Basic, is base64 encoded. This base64 encoding is accomplished with the addAuthHeader method of the HTTP class. The following code shows how this user authentication header is constructed.

```
/**
 * This method is called to add the user authorization headers
 * to the HTTP request.
 */
protected void addAuthHeader()
{
  if( (_user.length()==0) || (_password.length()==0) )
    return;
  String hdr = _user + ":" + _password;
  String encode = URLUtility.base64Encode(hdr);
  _clientHeaders.set("Authorization","Basic " + encode );
}
```

So far you have seen how the Bot package sends the identity and password of the user. The Bot package must also implement HTTPS and send requests to the web server in an encrypted form. To implement HTTPS, the Bot package must use SSL. You will now see how the Bot package implements HTTPS using the SSL classes provided by JSSE.

The *SSL* Class

Using methods from JSSE can be somewhat tricky. Because we do not want to cause the Bot package to be dependent on JSSE being installed because JSSE is not legally available in all parts of the world, we limit all JSSE access to the SSL class. No other class in the Bot package makes use of JSSE. Any access that the Bot package must have with JSSE will be through this SSL class. That way, if JSSE is not present, any problems will be contained within the SSL class.

This allows both compile-time and runtime errors related to the absence of JSSE to be isolated to just the SSL class, which makes it much easier to trap these errors. In order for the SSL class to be properly created, JSSE needs to be present when the Bot package is recompiled, but it is not necessary for JSSE to be present for the Bot package to work.

NOTE   Recompiling the Bot package is discussed in Appendix G.

Listing 3.4 shows the SSL class. This class is meant to be a static class, and it contains a private constructor to prevent instantiation.

Listing 3.4   **Accessing JSSE (*SSL.java*)**

```
package com.heaton.bot;

import java.io.*;
import java.net.*;
import javax.net.ssl.*;
import java.security.*;

/**
```

```
   * The SSL class is used to provide an interface to JSSE without
   * making the entire package dependant on JSSE being installed.
   *
   * @author Jeff Heaton
   * @version 1.0
   */
class SSL
{

  /**
   * This is a static class, so it has a private constructor.
   */
  private SSL()
  {
  }

  /**
   * A factory used to create SSL sockets from. This
   * factory is created when the class is first loaded
   * and reused for each new socket.
   */
  protected static SSLSocketFactory _factory = null;

  /**
   * This method is called to get an SSL client socket
   * for the specified host and port.
   *
   * @param host The host to connect to.
   * @param port The port to connect to.
   * @return A SSL socket.
   * @exception java.net.UnknownHostException
   * @exception java.io.IOException
   */
  static public Socket getSSLSocket(String host,int port)
    throws UnknownHostException,IOException
  {
    if(_factory==null)
    {
      java.security.Security.addProvider(new
com.sun.net.ssl.internal.ssl.Provider());

System.setProperty("java.protocol.handler.pkgs","com.sun.net.ssl.internal.www.pr
otocol");
      _factory = (SSLSocketFactory)SSLSocketFactory.getDefault();
    }

    SSLSocket socket = (SSLSocket) _factory.createSocket(host,port);
    return socket;
  }

}
```

Listing 3.4 showed all of the necessary calls to JSSE to implement HTTPS. You will now be shown how this SSL class works. This very simple class contains only one method, getSSLSocket. You will now be shown how to use this method.

By using this method, the HTTPSocket class is able to obtain an SSL socket when needed. The getSSLSocket method is called using

```
Socket sock = SSL.getSSLSocket("address",443);
```

Before a SSL socket can be created, a socket factory must be obtained from JSSE. Because it is very likely that additional SSL sockets will be needed, the socket factory is stored in a protected property named _factory, as is shown here:

```
protected static SSLSocketFactory _factory = null;
```

NOTE   A factory is an object used to create other objects of a specific type. A factory is used when additional operations must occur beyond the simple constructor invocation (that results from a new operator being called). The use of SSLSocketFactory allows the new SSL socket to be created and at the same time be properly bound to the internal JSSE classes that implement the SSL protocol.

Once the getSSLSocket method is called, a new factory is obtained if this is the first call. If it is the first call, we also added JSSE to the Java security provider and specify which handler to use as a system property. The JSSE installation instructions recommend adding these two lines to every program that uses JSSE. We internalize them here.

```
if(_factory==null)
{
    java.security.Security.addProvider(new
com.sun.net.ssl.internal.ssl.Provider());

System.setProperty("java.protocol.handler.pkgs","com.sun.net.ssl.internal.www.pr
otocol");
    _factory = (SSLSocketFactory)SSLSocketFactory.getDefault();
}
```

Finally, with the one-time configuration out of the way, we can actually obtain a SSL socket. Calling the createSocket method of the secure socket factory does this. The following lines of code create a secure socket using the secure socket factory.

```
SSLSocket socket = (SSLSocket) _factory.createSocket(host,port);
return socket;
```

Interfacing the *HTTP* Class to JSSE

The interface from the HTTP class to the SSL class for HTTPS handling is very simple. It occurs inside the lowLevelSend method of the HTTPSocket class. About 10 lines in to the lowLevelSend method, after the scheme is determined, the lowLevelSend method determines which scheme is being used. If this is the HTTPS scheme, the socket is created using the `SSL.getSSLSocket` method. If this is not an HTTPS scheme, the socket is created using Java's standard `Socket` constructor (using the new operator). This is shown here:

```
// connect
  if(https)
    _socket = SSL.getSSLSocket(u.getHost(),port);
  else
    _socket = new Socket(u.getHost(),port);
```

This allows a normal `Socket` class to be used if the connection is not HTTPS. The `SSL` class was discussed previously in the preceding section earlier in the chapter.

Summary

HTTPS is a protocol that allows secure transmission of Web documents. This security is two-fold. First HTTPS encodes the document so that your data cannot be intercepted. Second, HTTPS ensures that you are actually connected to the site that you believe you are.

HTTPS makes use of the RSA encryption algorithm. This algorithm was patented, but the patent expired September 20, 2000. Though the patent is no longer a consideration, it has left a legacy of HTTPS separation that still exists today. This legacy separates HTTPS from many products. This is because these products implemented HTTPS as add-ons so they would be able to limit the amount of licensing required. Java does not have HTTPS support due to these patent restrictions, and it also makes HTTPS available as an add-on.

In order to get the security of HTTPS with Java, you must use the JSSE package. This package can be downloaded, without charge, from the Sun website. Once this package is installed, Java programs can make use of HTTPS and SSL.

HTTP and HTTPS both contain built-in user authentication, which allows the browser to transmit an ID and password for the user as part of the HTTP or HTTPS request. This allows the web server to determine the identity of the user. HTTPS is not directly supported by Java. To use HTTPS the JSSE package (obtainable from Sun) must be installed.

The Bot package contains several classes that enable the use of JSSE, which is necessary to perform HTTPS transfers. This use of JSSE is transparent to the programmer. Once JSSE is installed, the `HTTPSocket` method should be able to access the JSSE package, which will allow you to access sites using HTTPS.

Up until this point, the book has focused primarily on the protocols used to transfer data between a web browser and web server. Now the book begins to focus more on processing the data retrieved from the web server. The next chapter shows how to parse the HTML documents that will be downloaded from web servers.

CHAPTER 4

HTML Parsing

- Understanding HTML

- Using Swing to parse HTML

- Using the HTMLParse class to gain access to Java's HTML parser

- Downloading the images from a site

- Translating a site into another language

U p until this point, we have only been concerned with how to retrieve pages from a web server. The actual data retrieved has generally been displayed to a window. Because spiders, bots, and aggregators will run into many kinds of data on the Internet, when you create them, you will need to make sure that they can not only retrieve this data but that they can understand it as well. The type of data we are concerned with here is Hypertext Markup Language (HTML). In this chapter, you will learn how to *parse*, or interpret, this data.

Programs that interpret text data are called *parsers*. Writing an HTML parser can be a challenging task. This is because the *syntax* of HTML is not terribly consistent. For instance, in any one document, you may find a mix of beginning tags, ending tags, simple tags, and text. On top of this, adherence to what syntactical rules HTML does have is not strictly enforced. Fortunately, there is a complete HTML parser built into Java. This chapter will not show how to create a parser, but rather how to use it.

Working with HTML

Most of the data found on websites is stored in HTML. You must understand the structure of these HTML documents in order to create a spider, bot, or aggregator. Before you are shown how to use the built-in Java HTML parser, however, you must first review some basic HTML. Readers who are already familiar with HTML will likely need to only lightly skim this section.

An HTML document has five well-defined components:

- Text
- Comments
- Simple tags
- Beginning tags
- Ending tags

These are described in more detail in the following pages. We will see how to parse each.

Text

Text is the wording that you see on an HTML page. Except for the case of script code, any data in an HTML document that is not part of a tag is considered text. This text is formatted and controlled by the tags that enclose it. For example, the following HTML contains two tags and the text "Hello World!"

```
<h1>Hello World!</h1>
```

As mentioned, there is one time when the data located outside of tags is not considered text; in this case, it is script code. The most likely script code that will be encountered is *JavaScript*.

JavaScript is a small program contained inside of an HTML document. A JavaScript program is contained between the tags <script> and </script>. It is important that a bot program not confuse JavaScript code for text data. The following is an example of a JavaScript block of code:

```
<script>
var wpop_;
function myfunct(para)
{
  if(wpop_&&!wpop_.closed)
  {
    wpop_.location.href=para;
  }
  wpop_.focus();
}
</script>
```

In the above example, a browser executes this code, and it is not displayed as text would be.

Comments

Comments represent portions of the HTML document that are not displayed to the user. They are usually notes that are left behind by the HTML programmer. Because comments are not displayed, the programs presented in this book are not terribly concerned with them because the user never sees them.

HTML comments begin with <!- and end with ->; Here is an example of an HTML comment:

```
<!-- This is a comment -->
```

Comments can also be used to hide JavaScript from browsers that do not support it. JavaScript is usually used to provide animations and to validate forms. The bot does not usually have much need of such data because the bot is likely just harvesting textual data from the site. Enclosing JavaScript in comments is very useful for bots because this automatically hides the JavaScript from a bot that is already ignoring comments. The following code uses this technique:

```
<script>
<!--
var wpop_;
function myfunct(para)
{
  if(wpop_&&!wpop_.closed)
  {
    wpop_.location.href=para;
  }
  wpop_.focus();
}
//--></script>
```

Here the JavaScript is between the `<script>` and `</script>` tags, and comment tags enclose all of the text in this area. This would cause a bot to completely ignore this JavaScript area because, to the bot, it is just a large comment.

Simple Tags

Simple tags are HTML tags that are completely represented by a single tag. Perhaps the most common simple tags are the break (`<br>`) and image (`<img>`) tags, which have no corresponding ending (`</br>` or `</img>`) tags because they are not required. Simple tags appear like this in HTML:

```
First line of text<br>
Second line of text<br>
Third line of text<br>
```

Beginning and Ending Tags

Most HTML tags consist of beginning and ending tags. Beginning tags start out much like simple tags; the only difference between a simple tag and a beginning tag is that the beginning tag has a corresponding ending tag that occurs later. The following code shows beginning and ending tags. The `form` tag is a beginning tag, and the `/form` tag is an ending tag.

```
<form method="post">
<input type=submit>
</form>
```

Beginning and ending tags are used to control the functionality of the HTML code that is enclosed by them.

NOTE   The above example also contains a simple tag, the `input` tag.

Tags a Bot Cares About

The preceding material showed you the five major categories of HTML data. Now you will see how to process individual HTML tags.

HTML includes many different tag types, and not all of these are of concern to a spider or bot. A bot will go about its business scanning pages until it finds the page that it is interested in. The code in the Bot package on the companion CD-ROM will also navigate through such pages. But in order to perform this navigation, the Bot package must pay attention to certain HTML tags that define the structure of the website.

The HTML tags found in a document can be fundamentally grouped into two categories. First are the tags that convey data; these are the tables and paragraphs that display the information contained in the website. This category is the one that the user is most directly aware of. Infrastructure tags are the second type of tag. These tags tell the browser how to get from this web page to other web pages.

This chapter is primarily concerned with the infrastructure tags, which are the tags that allow the Bot package to locate other pages, as long as the page has been parsed. Infrastructure tags are those that form hyperlinks, image maps, and any other information used to navigate to a new page.

Navigating with Hyperlinks

Hyperlinks, or links, are the defining features of the World Wide Web that connect documents through the Internet. As a result, they are the first type of HTML tag that we will look at in depth. Because their primary purpose is to allow the user to move to a new page and travel easily between documents, links fit in to the category of infrastructure tags. You will now be shown how a bot uses links to navigate.

The Format of a Link

The bot usually enters a website from its homepage. From this homepage, the bot must navigate to the information that it was sent to retrieve. To find this information, the bot must examine and follow links. Here is the general form of a link:

```
<a href="linked page" alt="Go Here">Click Here</a>
```

Very little data from the above code is actually displayed to the user. The only words that would appear on the browser page would be "Click Here."

The text "Go Here," contained in the `alt` attribute, would be displayed in a small popup if the user hovered the mouse over the link. The `alt` attribute is not required, but if it is included, it can provide an excellent marker for the bot. This is because the bot can use this `alt` attribute marker as a quick way to identify a link.

The `href` attribute, also present in the code line shown here, defines the target of this link. The `href` attribute of a link contains the URL to which the user should be taken if the link is clicked.

Absolute and Relative URLs

Such URLs can be either *absolute* or *relative*. An *absolute URL* specifies the exact, unambiguous location of a resource on the Internet. An absolute URL will contain the hostname and the filename. For example, `http://www.jeffheaton.com/myfile.html`, would be an absolute URL—`www.jeffheaton.com` is the hostname and `myfile.html` is the filename.

A *relative URL* specifies only part of the absolute URL. Very often, a relative URL will be nothing more than a filename. For example, if the file stored at `http://www.jeffheaton.com/myfile.html` contained a file named simply `myotherfile.html`, this would be considered a relative URL. The browser would use both the *base URL* (`http://www.jeffheaton.com/myfile.html`) and the relative URL (`myotherfile.html`) to retrieve the file stored at `http://www.jeffheaton.com/myotherfile.shtml`.

> **TIP**   A relative URL never specifies the `http://` prefix.

Relative URLs can also specify child and parent directories. To specify a child directory using a relative URL, you will need to specify the directory name with no leading /, for example, `images/myimage.gif`. To specify the parent directory, use the "`..`" directory name. Table 4.1 shows some relative URLs and their corresponding absolute URLs.

TABLE 4.1:   Resolving Relative URLs (Base Is `http://www.jeffheaton.com/site/index.html`)

Relative URL	URL Resolved To
`images/myimage.gif`	`http://www.jeffheaton.com/site/images/myimage.gif`
`../test.html`	`http://www.jeffheaton.com/test.html`
`/test.html`	`http://www.jeffheaton.com/test.html`

Relative URLs are frequently used on the Internet. Because of this, the bots that we create must be aware of them. But some classes, including the `HTTP` class (discussed in Chapter 2, "Examining the Hypertext Transfer Protocol"), are not aware of relative URLs. Therefore, relative URLs must be resolved before they are passed to the `HTTP` class.

The `java.net.URL` class provides an easy mechanism for resolving relative URLs. There are several constructors provided for this class. One of these constructors accepts two `String` objects as parameters and can be used to resolve a relative URL. For this to occur, the base URL should be passed as the first String parameter, and the relative URL should be passed as the second. For example, the following command would resolve the `myfile.html` URL to `http://www.jeffheaton.com/site/myfile.html`.

```
URL u = new
URL("http://www.jeffheaton.com/site/index.html","myfile.html");
```

Image Maps

Links are not the only infrastructure tag that takes the user to a totally different page when they are clicked. The website can also establish image maps that will take the user to new pages based on what image they click. Image maps consist of client and server side image maps, but server-side image maps have been almost completely replaced by client-side ones. This is because server-side images require a server component to register the region where the user clicked, where as client-side image maps are contained completely in the HTML file. Because they are much more prevalent, this book discusses only client-side image maps.

Client-side image maps do not require the presence of a server-side script in order to interpret the coordinates of the "hot" regions of a multiclickable image. In fact, the client-side image map is much more efficient than the server-side image map, and it allows the visitor to see the actual URL associated with the mapped regions in the status bar of their web browser. This status text appears as the user hovers the mouse of over each section of the image map.

A client-side image map will include a map, as seen below, that links each image area to a URL:

```
<map name="sample">
<area shape="rect" coords="20,27,82,111" href="hotspot1.html">
<area shape="circle" coords="129,113,29" href="hotspot2.html">
<area shape="rect" coords="21,158,170,211" href="hotspot3.html">
<area shape="default" nohref>
</map>
```

Then later on in the HTML file, the map will be used with a command like the following:

```
<img border="0" src="image.gif" usemap="#sample">
```

NOTE   The Bot package does not contain any code to make it inherently aware of image maps. Image maps, however, can easily be handled just like any other HTML tag.

Parsing Forms

Many web pages contain elements called forms into which you can enter data. For example, many websites will prompt the user to enter an ID and password. The user fills in the requested data and clicks one of the buttons on the form. This information is then sent to the web server for processing. The web server responds by sending back a page. The data on this page usually is some sort of status information about the data that the user had entered.

Because forms are heavily used by interactive websites, it is very likely that you will have to use them in your bot programs. Because this chapter is only about HTML parsing, it only lightly touches on forms. Chapter 5, "Posting Forms," is dedicated exclusively to form handling and it will show you how to interact with them.

A form is completely enclosed by a beginning <form> tag and an ending </form> tag. Inside this form, there will be several <input> tags that specify the components that should be available on the form. The following code shows a very simple form that could be used to prompt the user to enter an ID and password:

```
<table border="0">
<form method="post" action="target.jsp">
<tr><td>User ID</td><td><input type="text" name="id"></td></tr>
<tr><td>Password</td><td><input type="password" name="pw"></td></tr>
<tr><td colspan="2"><input type="submit" value="Login"></td></tr>
</form>
</table>
```

This form, which can be seen in Figure 4.1, will transmit the data entered into it, via a POST request, to the file target.jsp. This form will collect two pieces of information. First, the user ID will be collected and returned under the name id. Second, the password will be collected and returned under the name of pw. A Login button is provided to allow the user to perform the POST. This is an example of the structure of an HTML form. As you can see, a form is parsed just like any other HTML segment. Chapter 5 will show how to respond back the web server based on a form.

An HTML form

Deciphering Tables

Tables are HTML constructs that are commonly used to hold data that can be clearly represented in a tabular form. A table is a complex HTML structure that consists of the <table>, <tr>, <th>, and <td> tags. By using these tags, you can define the tabular layout of a table. The specific duties of each of these tag types are shown here:

The <table> tag   This delineates a table. A <table> tag is placed at the beginning of the table information, and a </table> tag is placed at the end. An attribute named width can be specified within this tag to specify the width of the border lines that should be drawn around the table cells; specifying zero means no boundary lines will be drawn. For example, to specify a width of 1, you would specify the tag <table width="1">.

The <th> tag   The table header tag delineates a table header. A <th> tag is placed at the beginning of a column or row header. A corresponding </th> tag is placed at the end. For example, to specify a row or column head with the text "header," you would use the following: <th>header</th>.

The <td> tag   The table definition tag delineates a table element. A <td> tag is placed at the beginning of an individual table cell. A corresponding </td> tag is placed at the end. For example, to specify an individual table cell with the text "Table Cell," you would use the following: <td>Table Cell</td>.

The `<tr>` tag   The table row tag organizes `<td>` and `<th>` tags into a table row. A `<tr>` tag is placed at the beginning of the table information, and a `</tr>` tag is placed at the end. For example, to specify a table row with the cells "Cell 1," "Cell 2," and "Cell3," you would use the following: `<tr><td>Cell 1</td><td>Cell 2</td><td>Cell 3</td></tr>`

Figure 4.2 shows what an example of a more complex table that combines all of these tags looks like in the browser. The following code shows the HTML that is necessary to create this table.

```
<table border="1">
<tr><th>Header 1</th><th>Header 2</th><th>Header 3</th></tr>
<tr><td>col1,row1</td><td>col2,row1</td><td>col3,row1</td></tr>
<tr><td>col1,row2</td><td>col2,row2</td><td>col3,row2</td></tr>
<tr><td>col1,row3</td><td>col2,row3</td><td>col3,row3</td></tr>
</table>
```

FIGURE 4.2:

An HTML table

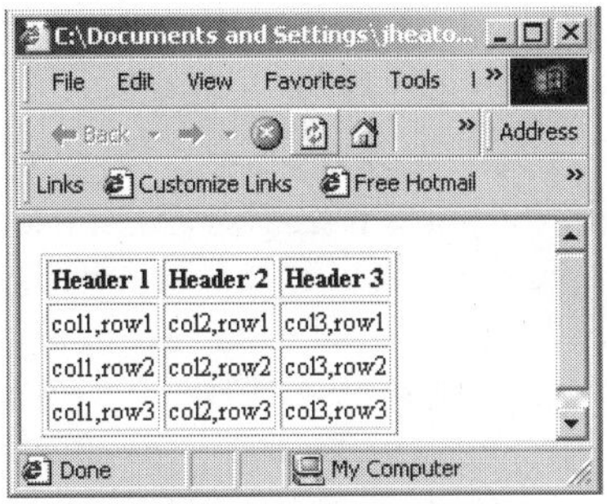

The HTML code shown above is completely enclosed by `<table>` and `</table>` tags. The first row of the table shown in Figure 4.2 contains the column headings. This first row, delimitated by `<tr>` and `</tr>` tags in the code, contains three column headings. Each of these column headings is delineated by the header tags `<th>` and `</th>`. The remaining rows contain normal table cells, which are delineated by `<td>` and `</td>`.

HTML That Requires Special Handling

Most HTML constructs are very easy to parse and their start and end tags are easy to see. However, there are several HTML constructs that can be particularly challenging to bot programs. We will discuss them here and examine ways that they might be dealt with.

Dealing with JavaScript

The challenges presented to a bot program by JavaScript are twofold. The first challenge is that the bot must not mistake JavaScript code for actual displayed text. The second is that sometimes JavaScript is used in an infrastructure capacity to take the user to different pages. The bot must know how to differentiate between these two challenges.

Because JavaScript usually falls between HTML comments, as was previously discussed, the bot program usually simply filters JavaScript out and does not deal with it; this process is relatively easy. To accomplish this, your bot program must be aware of the structure of HTML comments in order to recognize them, and it must know not to process data inside these comments. Because JavaScript is also always contained between the `<script>` beginning HTML tag and the `</script>` ending HTML tag, your program can avoid these sections with little effort by learning how to recognize these tags and to skip them when it encounters them. Both of these methods of screening can be accomplished with little effort if you are using the Swing HTML parser. The Swing HTML parser is discussed later in the section entitled "Using Swing Classes for HTML Parsing."

Dealing with JavaScript code that is being used in an infrastructure capacity can be particularly troublesome to bots. This is when JavaScript is used to create a link that will move from one page to the next. The following code shows an example of what this looks like:

```
<a href="javascript:openHelp(helpMenuValue,'personal')">Help</a>
```

In this example, the bot will see this line and attempt to follow the `href` attribute. However, the `href` attribute specifies a JavaScript function and not a true URL. The JavaScript function being called will likely take the user to a new window, but there is no way for the bot to follow this link. To follow the link, the bot would have to be able to interpret JavaScript.

There are two ways to tackle this ambiguous link issue. The first is for you, as a programmer, to resolve where the link goes. After you do, you should include this destination as part of your program code. Unfortunately, this method of solving the problem is inflexible; this is because if the link is ever changed on the website, your bot will still be using the old link, and therefore, it won't be able to find the new destination. But in the case of JavaScript links, you often have no choice.

Here is an example of how this works. If you know, for instance, that when you click a link, you will just be sent to a file named `target.jsp`, then you can build that fact into your program. When it is time to follow the link, your program just inserts the `target.jsp` link rather than trying to resolve the JavaScript. The following function, which looks for any link that starts with "javacript:" (which designates a JavaScript link), shows how this might be done:

```
String resolveLink(String url)
{
// check to see if its a Javascript link
  if(url.beginsWith("javascript:"))
    return "target.jsp";
  else
    return url;
}
```

The other way to solve this ambiguous link problem is much more complex. Basically, by using Rhino, an open-source implementation of JavaScript that is written entirely in Java, your bot program could be extended so that it could recognize JavaScript. Rhino is typically embedded into Java applications to provide scripting to end users, and from what I have heard, this open source library could be included in your bot to allow the bot to understand JavaScript.

NOTE   Because of its complexity, and because resolving the link yourself rarely fails, this implementation method will not be discussed in this book. If you are interested in Rhino or this method, however, more information can be found at `http://www.mozilla.org/rhino/`, and a complete, open source implementation of JavaScript can be downloaded from the Rhino project, at `http://www.mozilla.org/rhino/`.

Avoiding Frames

Frames have also long been an enemy of bots and spiders. This is because a frame conceals much of the information contained on a site.

An HTML file from a site that has frames will look similar to the following:

```
<!DOCTYPE HTML PUBLIC "-//W3C//DTD HTML 3.2 Final//EN">
<HTML>
<HEAD>
    <TITLE>Untitled</TITLE>
</HEAD>
<frameset cols="130,*" frameborder="1" border=0 framespacing="0">
<!-- company logo -->
<frameset rows="65,*">
  <frame name="logo" src="logo.htm" FRAMEBORDER="0" marginheight="0"
  marginwidth="0"></frame>
  <frame name="sidenav" src="nav.htm" FRAMEBORDER="0" marginheight="0"
  marginwidth="0"></frame>
</frameset>
  <frame name="clsmain" src="profile.htm" frameborder="1"></frame>
</frameset>
</HTML>
```

The above HTML could represent a site that is rich in content, but none of this content is seen because it is hidden behind the frames. Basically, frames display a composite view of HTML, which means that a framed website may show several HTML files simultaneously. This is usually done to create a consistent header, footer, or side navigation area for the web site. To the typical user, this appears as a single document.

However, a site that uses frames is often visually indistinguishable from a non-framed site. For instance, the above frameset creates a view composed of the following HTML files: `logo.htm`, `nav.htm`, and `profile.htm`. The use of these three files complicates the bot's job because it prevents the bot from finding all of its data on one page. Instead, the bot must now look at all three HTML files to find the complete contents of this page.

WARNING   Because search engines typically use spiders to track down sites to list in their index, and because frames may prevent the visiting search engine spider from being able to properly determine the content of your site, the use of frames on your home page may really limit your search engine's listing possibilities. In other words, don't use frames on your home page, although you may use them throughout the less important pages on your site.

The spider provided in the Bot package does its best to handle frames. As it encounters framed documents, each of the compound elements is remembered for later processing. This is covered in greater detail in Chapter 8, "Building a Spider."

Understanding Embedded Objects

HTML documents allow objects to be embedded directly into them. Two of the most common forms of these objects are Shockwave files and Java applets.

Macromedia Flash is used to produce multimedia presentations in the form of Shockwave files. Shockwave objects will generally look something like this:

```
<object classid="clsid:D27CDB6E-AE6D-11cf-96B8-444553540000"  loop="false"
    width="453" height="340" id=ShockwaveFlash1>
<param name=movie value="splash.swf">
<param name=quality value=high>
<PARAM NAME="LOOP" VALUE="false"></object>
```

Java applets are classes written in Java that extend from the `Applet` class and can display graphical information directly onto the browser screen. Applets will generally look something like this:

```
<applet code=TheApplet.class
   width=250
   height=237 >
</applet>
```

Neither a Shockwave file nor a Java applet is particularly useful to a bot. This is because a bot cannot probe the Shockwave file or Java applet and extract data from them, which means that there is no effective way for the bot to get to this data.

Unfortunately, there is little that can be done about the Shockwave file or Java applet. They must simply be avoided. If the data that your bot seeks is contained in one of these, then it is unlikely that your bot will be able access this data.

Now that you are aware of some of the common problems a bot can encounter while it is examining the structure of an HTML file, you are almost ready to see the code that actually parses these files. But first, you will be introduced to the Bot package classes used for HTML parsing.

Using Bot Classes for HTML Parsing

The classes the Bot package contains for parsing retrieve many of the more common data elements that are often parsed from HTML documents. In this section, you will be shown how to use these HTML classes.

Using the *HTMLPage* Class

The Bot package's HTMLPage class is used to read the HTML from a specified URL and extract useful information from it. This class is particularly useful for extracting links, images, and forms from a web page that contains HTML data. You can also use this class with your own, more customized parsing class, which you have developed so that it can look for other tags as well. You will now be shown the methods that make up the HTMLPage class, starting with the constructor. The brief descriptions of what these are for are followed by a line that demonstrates how they might appear in code.

The HTMLPage constructor   Constructs the object and defines the HTTP object that should be used for all communication.

```
public HTMLPage(HTTP http)
```

The getForms method   Gets a list of all of the forms that were retrieved from the last call to the open method. If this method is called before the open method is called, an empty list will be returned. If this method is to be used, then null must have been passed as the callback object to the open method. For more information about the callback object, refer to the open method.

```
public Vector getForms()
```

The getHTTP method   Gets the underlying HTTP object that was sent to the constructor.

```
public HTTP getHTTP()
```

The getImages method   Gets a list of all of the images from this page. If this method is to be used, then null must have been passed as the callback object to the open method.

```
public Vector getImages()
```

The getLinks method   Gets a list of all of the links from the specified page. If this method is to be used, then null must have been passed as the callback object to the open method.

```
public Vector getLinks()
```

The getURL method   Gets the URL that is represented by the specified page.

```
public String getURL()
```

The open method   Called to open a page and read it in. If null is specified for the callback, then the other methods in this class may be used to look at images, links, and forms. Once this method has been called, the getForms, getImages, and getLinks methods can be used.

If a callback is specified, then the callback is given information about the tags and data contained in the HTML document. The use of callback objects is discussed shortly in the section entitled "Using Bot Classes for HTML Parsing."

```
public void open(String url,HTMLEditorKit.ParserCallback callback)
```

The post method   Called to perform a POST request for the specified form. See Chapter 6, "Interpreting Data," for specific examples of how to use this method.

```
public void post(HTMLForm form)
```

Using the *Link* Class

The Bot package's Link class is a very simple data class that holds HTML links. This class holds both the actual link URL, as well as the alt attribute. The Link class is the class that is held by the vector that is returned by calling the HTMLPage.getLinks() method.

The Link class contains methods that allow you to access its contents. You will now be shown how to use these methods, starting with the constructor. Each of these descriptions will be followed be a brief example of how they might appear in code.

The Link constructor   Constructs the object with the specified alt attribute and link.

```
public Link(String alt,String href)
```

The getALT method   Calls the alt attribute for the specified link.

```
public String getALT()
```

The getHREF method   Calls the href attribute for the specified link.

```
public String getHREF()
```

The toString method   Calls the href attribute for the specified link.

```
public String toString()
```

The HTMLPage and Link classes both rely on using the underlying Swing HTML parser, which is discussed next.

Using Swing Classes for HTML Parsing

The previous section mentioned that you can pass a callback to the HTMLPage object's open method for even more control. This section will explain the Swing classes, and ultimately how to use a callback method.

JDK version 1.2 and higher contains a complete HTML parser. In this version of Java, there is a new feature that allows most text-based Swing components (which are buttons, labels, menu items, and tabbed panes) to incorporate HTML for display. For example, the following button uses bold and italics:

```
JButton b = new JButton(
  "<html><b><I>Press Me</I></b></html>");
```

For the purposes of spiders and bots, we are less interested in the display of HTML, but we must be able to parse it. Because of the integration of HTML into Swing, HTML parsing support is already built in to Java. We will use these classes to parse HTML in this chapter.

NOTE Swing was added to Java with version 1.2. Swing allows Java to display elements that are normally associated with dialog boxes. When you use Swing, you can develop Java programs that take advantage of buttons, radio buttons, check boxes, and other dialog box type elements.

Creating Callback Methods for HTML Parsing

You can use the JDK `ParserCallback` class to create your own custom parser. The `HTMLPage` class provided by the Bot package contains a generic callback class that is able to retrieve forms, images, and links. For the simple image and link gathering, the built in callback file will suffice. If you need more information than this, you must create your own callback object. By using your own callback method you will have access to all data contained in the HTML file. Your callback class will be sent data corresponding to every tag and text element encountered in the HTML document. This section shows how to construct your own callback class. The translation example shown later in the section entitled "Providing Website Translations" will use this same method.

To use the callback class from the Bot package, you must override the methods that correspond to the types of information you are interested in. By overriding the `handleComment`, `handleEndTag`, `handleError`, `handleSimpleTag`, `handleStartTag` and `handleText` methods, you can handle each of these types of information from your callback object.

When your callback class is passed to the open method of the `HTMLPage` object (described in the earlier section "Using the `HTMLPage` Class,") the callback object will be notified as the Swing parser finds tags and text in the HTML file. For each type of data that the parser finds, a `handler` method is called in the callback object. Each of these handler methods is described in detail here. They are followed by examples of how they might appear in code.

The `handleComment` method Called by the Swing parser when an HTML comment is located. The text of the comment is contained in data. The pos parameter gives the current position.

```
public void handleComment(char[] data,int pos)
```

The `handleEndTag` method Called by the Swing parser when an ending HTML tag is located. The tag is contained in the `t` parameter. The `pos` parameter gives the current position.

```
public void handleEndTag(HTML.Tag t,int pos)
```

The `handleError` method Called by the Swing parser when an error occurs. The error message text is contained in `errorMsg`. The `pos` parameter gives the current position.

```
public void handleError(String errorMsg,int pos)
```

The `handleSimpleTag` method Called by the Swing parser when a simple tag is located. The tag is contained in `t`, and the list of attributes is contained in `a`. The `pos` parameter gives the current position.

```
public void handleSimpleTag(HTML.Tag t,MutableAttributeSet a,int pos)
```

WARNING Simple tags are sometimes ending tags. If the Swing parser encounters an ending tag for a tag type that it considers either simple or unknown, `handleSimpleTag` will be called for the ending tag. The only way to detect whether this is an ending tag or a true simple tag is to check for the occurrence of the `HTML.Attribute.ENDTAG` attribute. Only ending tags will contain this attribute.

The `handleStartTag` method Called by the Swing parser when a starting HTML tag is located. The tag is contained in the parameter `t`. The `pos` parameter gives the current position.

```
public void handleStartTag(HTML.Tag t,MutableAttributeSet a,int pos)
```

The `handleText` method Called by the Swing parser when text is located in the HTML document. The text is contained in the `data` parameter. The `pos` parameter gives the current position.

```
public void handleText(char[] data,int pos)
```

Using the *HTML.Tag* Class

The `HTML.Tag` class of the `javax.swing.text.html` package is used to represent an HTML tag. It is used by the callback class to hold a single HTML tag, and it is passed into many of the methods provided by the `ParserCallback` class. The `HTML.Tag` class provides four methods that provide basic information about the tag. Each of these methods is described here and is followed by an example of how it might appear in code.

The `breaksFlow` method Returns true if this tag should cause a single line break.

```
public boolean breaksFlow()
```

The isBlock method   Returns true if this tag should cause a double line break.

```
public boolean isBlock()
```

The isPreformatted method   Returns true if white space should be preserved by this tag.

```
public boolean isPreformatted()
```

The toString method   Converts the tag name to a string so that it can be handled as a string. This method only converts the name, it does not add the attributes or the delimiting < and >.

```
public String toString()
```

The aforementioned methods are useful for getting basic information about the type of tag you're dealing with. Usually, you will just want to know what type of tag the Swing parser encountered. To discover this, you should use the predefined tag constants in HTML.Tag. For example, to see if the tag stored in the variable t is an H1 tag, use the following code:

```
if( t==HTML.Tag.H1 )
```

The following is a list of the 75 HTML tags recognized by the Swing HTML parser. All are public static final fields of HTML.Tag.

HTML.Tag.A	HTML.Tag.ADDRESS
HTML.Tag.APPLET	HTML.Tag.AREA
HTML.Tag.B	HTML.Tag.BASE
HTML.Tag.BASEFONT	HTML.Tag.BIG
HTML.Tag.BLOCKQUOTE	HTML.Tag.BODY
HTML.Tag.BR	HTML.Tag.CAPTION
HTML.Tag.CENTER	HTML.Tag.CITE
HTML.Tag.CODE	HTML.Tag.COMMENT
HTML.Tag.CONTENT	HTML.Tag.DD
HTML.Tag.DFN	HTML.Tag.DIR
HTML.Tag.DIV	HTML.Tag.DL
HTML.Tag.DT	HTML.Tag.EM
HTML.Tag.FONT	HTML.Tag.FORM
HTML.Tag.FRAME	HTML.Tag.FRAMESET
HTML.Tag.H1	HTML.Tag.H2
HTML.Tag.H3	HTML.Tag.H4

HTML.Tag.H5	HTML.Tag.H6
HTML.Tag.HEAD	HTML.Tag.HR
HTML.Tag.HTML	HTML.Tag.I
HTML.Tag.IMG	HTML.Tag.IMPLIED
HTML.Tag.INPUT	HTML.Tag.ISINDEX
HTML.Tag.KBD	HTML.Tag.LI
HTML.Tag.LINK	HTML.Tag.MAP
HTML.Tag.MENU	HTML.Tag.META
HTML.Tag.NOFRAMES	HTML.Tag.OBJECT
HTML.Tag.OL	HTML.Tag.OPTION
HTML.Tag.P	HTML.Tag.PARAM
HTML.Tag.PRE	HTML.Tag.S
HTML.Tag.SAMP	HTML.Tag.SCRIPT
HTML.Tag.SELECT	HTML.Tag.SMALL
HTML.Tag.STRIKE	HTML.Tag.STRONG
HTML.Tag.STYLE	HTML.Tag.SUB
HTML.Tag.SUP	HTML.Tag.TABLE
HTML.Tag.TD	HTML.Tag.TEXTAREA
HTML.Tag.TH	HTML.Tag.TITLE
HTML.Tag.TR	HTML.Tag.TT
HTML.Tag.U	HTML.Tag.UL
HTML.Tag.VAR	

These tags act as constants that should be used to compare against an unknown tag. For example, the following method would return true if passed an `applet` tag.

```
boolean checkApplet(HTML.Tag tag)
{
  if( tag == HTML.Tag.APPLET )
    return true;
  return false;
}
```

Using the *HTML.Attribute* Class

Often, you will need to look at the attributes of a particular HTML tag to obtain useful information such as the filename of an image to display, or the name of a button. The

`HTML.Attribute` class is used to represent an HTML tag. When you request an attribute from one of the Swing parser objects, you will be given an `HTML.Attribute` object. The 80 HTML attributes recognized by the Swing HTML parser are listed here.

`HTML.Attribute.ACTION`	`HTML.Attribute.ALIGN`
`HTML.Attribute.ALINK`	`HTML.Attribute.ALT`
`HTML.Attribute.ARCHIVE`	`HTML.Attribute.BACKGROUND`
`HTML.Attribute.BGCOLOR`	`HTML.Attribute.BORDER`
`HTML.Attribute.CELLPADDING`	`HTML.Attribute.CELLSPACING`
`HTML.Attribute.CHECKED`	`HTML.Attribute.CLASS`
`HTML.Attribute.CLASSID`	`HTML.Attribute.CLEAR`
`HTML.Attribute.CODE`	`HTML.Attribute.CODEBASE`
`HTML.Attribute.CODETYPE`	`HTML.Attribute.COLOR`
`HTML.Attribute.COLS`	`HTML.Attribute.COLSPAN`
`HTML.Attribute.COMMENT`	`HTML.Attribute.COMPACT`
`HTML.Attribute.CONTENT`	`HTML.Attribute.COORDS`
`HTML.Attribute.DATA`	`HTML.Attribute.DECLARE`
`HTML.Attribute.DIR`	`HTML.Attribute.DUMMY`
`HTML.Attribute.ENCTYPE`	`HTML.Attribute.ENDTAG`
`HTML.Attribute.FACE`	`HTML.Attribute.FRAMEBORDER`
`HTML.Attribute.HALIGN`	`HTML.Attribute.HEIGHT`
`HTML.Attribute.HREF`	`HTML.Attribute.HSPACE`
`HTML.Attribute.HTTPEQUIV`	`HTML.Attribute.ID`
`HTML.Attribute.ISMAP`	`HTML.Attribute.LANG`
`HTML.Attribute.LANGUAGE`	`HTML.Attribute.LINK`
`HTML.Attribute.LOWSRC`	`HTML.Attribute.MARGINHEIGHT`
`HTML.Attribute.MARGINWIDTH`	`HTML.Attribute.MAXLENGTH`
`HTML.Attribute.METHOD`	`HTML.Attribute.MULTIPLE`
`HTML.Attribute.N`	`HTML.Attribute.NAME`
`HTML.Attribute.NOHREF`	`HTML.Attribute.NORESIZE`
`HTML.Attribute.NOSHADE`	`HTML.Attribute.NOWRAP`
`HTML.Attribute.PROMPT`	`HTML.Attribute.REL`
`HTML.Attribute.REV`	`HTML.Attribute.ROWS`

```
HTML.Attribute.ROWSPAN              HTML.Attribute.SCROLLING

HTML.Attribute.SELECTED             HTML.Attribute.SHAPE

HTML.Attribute.SHAPES               HTML.Attribute.SIZE

HTML.Attribute.SRC                  HTML.Attribute.STANDBY

HTML.Attribute.START                HTML.Attribute.STYLE

HTML.Attribute.TARGET               HTML.Attribute.TEXT

HTML.Attribute.TITLE                HTML.Attribute.TYPE

HTML.Attribute.USEMAP               HTML.Attribute.VALIGN

HTML.Attribute.VALUE                HTML.Attribute.VALUETYPE

HTML.Attribute.VERSION              HTML.Attribute.VLINK

HTML.Attribute.VSPACE               HTML.Attribute.WIDTH
```

Attributes and tags from the above lists will be passed into the methods of the callback class. The handleSimpleTag and handleStartTag methods are passed in a MutableAttributeSet that contains a list of attributes. The MutableAttributeSet object can be used to gain access to any of the attributes of the tag that was just found. For example, to retrieve the href attribute from a MutableAttributeSet named a, use the following commands:

```
public void handleStartTag(HTML.Tag t,
  MutableAttributeSet attributes,int pos)
{
  Enumeration e = attributes.getAttributeNames();
  Object name = e.nextElement();
  String value = (String)attributes.getAttribute("href");
```

The above code shows the beginning of a typical handleStartTag method. This typical method begins by retrieving the href attribute from the tag that was passed in. The attributes for this tag are passed in as a MutableAttributeSet. From the MutableAttributeSet object, an enumeration object is returned that is used to access any of the attributes. The above code looks for an attribute named href.

Bot Package HTML Parsing Examples

Now that you know how to parse HTML, you will be shown two examples that show this process in detail. These examples will further demonstrate how to use the HTMLPage class (discussed earlier) with or without a callback method. The first example, which does not use callback, uses the HTMLPage class (which is built into the Bot package) to retrieve all images that are stored on a particular web page. The second example uses a custom callback method to translate a site, in real time, to another language.

Extracting Images from an HTML Page

First you will be shown an example that does not use a callback file. This example simply reads a specified HTML page and extracts all of the images from that page. The images are then downloaded and stored at the specified local directory. Figure 4.3 shows this program running, and Listing 4.1 shows the source code used to create this example. This code will be discussed immediately following the listing.

FIGURE 4.3:

The Get Images example

Listing 4.1   **Extracting Images from a Web Page (GetImage.java)**

```java
import java.awt.*;
import java.util.*;
import javax.swing.*;
import java.io.*;

import com.heaton.bot.*;

/**
 * Example program from Chapter 4
 *
 * This program accepts a URL as input and then scans all images
 * from that one page. These images are saved to the specified
 * directory.
 *
 * @author Jeff Heaton
 * @version 1.0
 */
public class GetImage extends javax.swing.JFrame
{

    /**
```

```java
 * The constructor.
 */
public GetImage()
{
    //{{INIT_CONTROLS
    setTitle("Download Images");
    getContentPane().setLayout(null);
    setSize(405,305);
    setVisible(false);
    JLabel1.setHorizontalTextPosition(javax.swing.SwingConstants.LEFT);
    JLabel1.setVerticalTextPosition(javax.swing.SwingConstants.TOP);
    JLabel1.setVerticalAlignment(javax.swing.SwingConstants.TOP);
    JLabel1.setText("Download images from(one page only):");
    getContentPane().add(JLabel1);
    JLabel1.setBounds(12,12,384,24);
    JLabel2.setText("URL:");
    getContentPane().add(JLabel2);
    JLabel2.setBounds(12,36,36,24);
    getContentPane().add(_url);
    _url.setBounds(48,36,348,24);
    JLabel3.setText("Select local path to download images to:");
    getContentPane().add(JLabel3);
    JLabel3.setBounds(12,72,384,24);
    getContentPane().add(_save);
    _save.setBounds(12,96,384,24);
    JScrollPane1.setOpaque(true);
    getContentPane().add(JScrollPane1);
    JScrollPane1.setBounds(12,168,384,132);
    JScrollPane1.getViewport().add(_log);
    _log.setBounds(0,0,381,129);
    _go.setText("GO!");
    getContentPane().add(_go);
    _go.setBounds(84,132,216,24);
    _go.setActionCommand("jbutton");
    //}}

    //{{INIT_MENUS
    //}}

    //{{REGISTER_LISTENERS
    SymAction lSymAction = new SymAction();
    _go.addActionListener(lSymAction);
    //}}
}

/**
 * Added by VisualCafe.
 *
 * @param b
 */
public void setVisible(boolean b)
{
```

```java
    if (b)
        setLocation(50, 50);
    super.setVisible(b);
}

/**
 * Program entry point.
 *
 * @param args
 */
static public void main(String args[])
{
    (new GetImage()).setVisible(true);
}

/**
 * Added by VisualCafe.
 */
public void addNotify()
{
    // Record the size of the window prior to calling parents addNotify.
    Dimension size = getSize();

    super.addNotify();

    if (frameSizeAdjusted)
        return;
    frameSizeAdjusted = true;

    // Adjust size of frame according to the insets and menu bar
    Insets insets = getInsets();
    javax.swing.JMenuBar menuBar = getRootPane().getJMenuBar();
    int menuBarHeight = 0;
    if (menuBar != null)
        menuBarHeight = menuBar.getPreferredSize().height;
    setSize(insets.left +
      insets.right +
      size.width,
      insets.top +
      insets.bottom +
      size.height + menuBarHeight);
}

// Used by addNotify
boolean frameSizeAdjusted = false;

//{{DECLARE_CONTROLS
javax.swing.JLabel JLabel1 = new javax.swing.JLabel();
javax.swing.JLabel JLabel2 = new javax.swing.JLabel();

/**
```

```
 * The URL to be scanned for images.
 */
javax.swing.JTextField _url = new javax.swing.JTextField();
javax.swing.JLabel JLabel3 = new javax.swing.JLabel();

/**
 * The directory that these images are to be saved in.
 */
javax.swing.JTextField _save = new javax.swing.JTextField();
javax.swing.JScrollPane JScrollPane1 = new javax.swing.JScrollPane();

/**
 * Progress display.
 */
javax.swing.JList _log = new javax.swing.JList();

/**
 * Button to be pressed to start the scan.
 */
javax.swing.JButton _go = new javax.swing.JButton();
//}}

//{{DECLARE_MENUS
//}}


class SymAction implements java.awt.event.ActionListener
{
    public void actionPerformed(java.awt.event.ActionEvent event)
    {
        Object object = event.getSource();
        if (object == _go)
            Go_actionPerformed(event);
    }
}

/**
 * Called for each image. The name(URL) of each image
 * is passed to this method so that it can be retrieved and
 * saved.
 *
 * @param name The complete URL of the image to save.
 */
protected void processImage(String name)
{
  try
  {
    if(_save.getText().length()>0)
    {
      int i = name.lastIndexOf('/');
      if(i!=-1)
      {
```

```
        FileOutputStream fso
          = new FileOutputStream(
          new File(_save.getText(),name.substring(i)) );
        HTTPSocket http = new HTTPSocket();
        http.send(name,null);
        fso.write( http.getBody().getBytes("8859_1") );
        fso.close();
      }
    }
  }
  catch(Exception e)
  {
    JOptionPane.showMessageDialog(this,
      e,
      "Error",
      JOptionPane.OK_CANCEL_OPTION,
      null );
  }
}

/**
 * This is where most of the action takes place. This
 * method is called when the GO! button is pressed.
 *
 * @param event The event
 */
void Go_actionPerformed(java.awt.event.ActionEvent event)
{
  try
  {
    // open the connection and get the page.
    HTTPSocket http = new HTTPSocket();
    HTMLPage page = new HTMLPage(http);
    page.open(_url.getText(),null);

    // look at the images.
    Vector vec = page.getImages();
    if(vec.size()>0)
    {
      // copy the images to an array for display
      String array[] = new String[vec.size()];
      vec.copyInto(array);
      _log.setListData( array );
      // loop through and process each image
      for(int i=0;i<vec.size();i++)
        processImage((String)vec.elementAt(i));
    }
  }
  catch(Exception e)
  {
    String s[] = new String[1];
    s[0] = "Error: " + e;
```

```
            _log.setListData( s );
        }
    }
}
```

The preceding code listing shows a class that will download all images from an individual web page. You will now be shown exactly how this example works.

Handling the Image List

Nearly all of the work that was performed by the GetImage example is handled by the Go_actionPerformed method, near the end of the listing. This method is called when the user clicks the Go button. The Go_actionPerformed method begins by using HTTPSocket to open a connection to the web page that was specified by the user, as shown here:

```
// open the connection and get the page.
HTTPSocket http = new HTTPSocket();
HTMLPage page = new HTMLPage(http);
page.open(_url.getText(),null);
```

In this segment, the HTMLPage object is used to read and then parse the user specified web page. This begins when the open method is called and the user specified URL of the web page to download from is passed. After the page is retrieved, the HTMLPage object parses out all the links, images, and forms from the specified URL. For our purposes in this example, you will only need to be concerned with the images.

As the HTMLPage's open method parses the page, a list of images is built. A vector containing these images is retrieved form the getImages method, as shown here:

```
// look at the images.
Vector vec = page.getImages();
```

If there are any images listed in this vector, they are copied to an array so that they may then be copied to the list box. Each image is then passed to the processImage method so that it can be downloaded. (The processImage method is described later in this section.) This process is shown here:

```
if(vec.size()>0)
{
    // copy the images to an array for display
    String array[] = new String[vec.size()];
    vec.copyInto(array);
    _log.setListData( array );
    // loop through and process each image
    for(int i=0;i<vec.size();i++)
        processImage((String)vec.elementAt(i));
}
```

At this point, the listing uses the following lines to request that any errors that might occur be displayed and then logged:

```
catch(Exception e)
{
  String s[] = new String[1];
  s[0] = "Error: " + e;
  _log.setListData( s );
}
```

The above code handed off each image to the processImage method. You will now be shown how the processImage method was constructed.

Downloading Individual Images

The processImage method, provided in Listing 4.1, causes each image to be downloaded and then stored. First, the processImage method checks to make sure that a path to store the images to was specified. The following code checks to see if a path was specified. If no path was specified, the image will not be saved.

```
if(_save.getText().length()>0)
{
```

Next, the image name must be stripped from the path so that a filename for this image can be determined. This name is easily determined because it is assumed to be the part of the URL that is just beyond the final "/". The code that allows this to be decided is shown here:

```
int i = name.lastIndexOf('/');
if(i!=-1)
{
```

If a valid filename is found in this manner, a FileOutputStream is created to accept the data for that image. This file will be stored in the directory specified by the _save component.

```
FileOutputStream fso
  = new FileOutputStream(
  new File(_save.getText(),name.substring(i)) );
```

A FileOutputStream object, name fso, is created. This prepares an empty file to retrieve the contents of the image as it is downloaded. To download the image, an HTTPSocket connection is established to retrieve the data for this image. The data is written with the 8859_1 option to ensure that the bytes are not translated to Unicode, which would distort the image.

```
HTTPSocket http = new HTTPSocket();
http.send(name,null);
fso.write( http.getBody().getBytes("8859_1") );
fso.close();
```

Once the file is written, it is closed.

NOTE   This example only retrieves images from a single page. Spiders allow us to find other pages on a website by examining hyperlinks. Chapter 8 will introduce spiders, and it will show a more advanced version of this example that can be used to retrieve all of the images from a website.

Providing Website Translations

The users of the Internet are people of many different nationalities. When they interact online, they share pieces of various cultures and a wide array of languages. As a result, there are many non-English websites throughout the Internet, and there are many non-English speakers who can't read the English-based websites. This presents the need for there to be a way to translate websites from one language to another.

If you look at the URL http://world.altavista.com you will see just such a utility, called Babel Fish. When you use this utility, you can enter in any URL and get the utility to translate that site to/from a selected language. Once you enter a URL and choose the language you want it translated into, you will see a completely translated representation of that website. Not only is that page translated, but any links that you follow will be captured and translated as well.

Babel Fish is an excellent example of a bot in action. This real-time bot retrieves pages as the user browses, and then it displays them already translated. The translation example provided in this section shows how this seemingly complex task can be accomplished.

Introducing a Simple Translation

Now that you have seen what a real-world example of a translation service can do, you are ready to be introduced to what is required to make a similar (though not quite as high tech) translation example. Unlike the example described in the previous section, however, this example does require a callback file.

Making a translation program involves two major components. First a bot-based infrastructure must be created that can retrieve the URLs as the user requests them. This same infrastructure must also be able to modify links so that they come back to the translation web site. This first major component is what the example program, presented here, focuses on. The second component is the actual language translation algorithm and dictionary, but this component will not be discussed in detail because it is beyond the scope of this book.

Instead, this example will focus on the two parts of the HTML file that are to be translated. First, this example will translate the text of the HTML page into Pig Latin, which is described momentarily. Second, this example will change all link URLs so that they point back to the translator program. This action will cause subsequent pages viewed by the user to be translated as well.

Translating English to Pig Latin

Pig Latin is more of a form of cryptology than an actual language. It is most commonly used on English text, but I have seen it applied to Spanish and other languages as well.

Here, a simple translation algorithm for Pig Latin is described. This will give you an idea of how the translation algorithm for the AltaVista Babel Fish translation utility might work.

To translate English into Pig Latin, you must keep three rules in mind.

1. If a word starts with a consonant and ends with a vowel, put the first letter of the word at the end and add "ay."

   Noise =Oisenay

2. If a word starts with two consonants, move them to the end of the word and add "ay."

   Check = Eckchay

3. If a word starts with a vowel, add the word "way" to the end of the word.

   Apple = Appleway

   These rules make up a simple translation algorithm for converting English to Pig Latin. As you might imagine, the rules needed to translate French to English would be much more complex. Because the purpose of this example is to show the bot portion of the technology, the simple Pig Latin algorithm is used. The techniques used to translate human languages could easily fill several books.

Exploring the Translation Code

Now let's take a look at the actual code for this example, which is composed of two parts (Listing 4.2 and 4.3). First, in Listing 4.2, a JSP page is used to work with the web server to gather the pages to be translated and display the results. Second, in Listing 4.3, an object that can be instantiated by the JSP page is provided; this object will perform the actual translation.

TIP

In Listing 4.2 (`translate.jsp`), the JSP page has been designed so that it can be called with the website to be translated as part of the query string. For example, to translate the website www.kimmswick.com, you would call `translate.jsp` with a query string of url=www.kimmswick.com/. This would result in the URL of `translate.jsp?url=` www.kimmswick.com/.

Listing 4.2   **Translation JSP Page (translate.jsp)**

```jsp
<%@page import="com.heaton.bot.translate.*" %>
<%
if(request.getParameter("url")==null)
{%>
<html>
<head>
<title>Translate</title>
</head>
<body>
<h1>Translate to Pig Latin</h1>
<form method="get">
Select a URL to translate to Pig Latin:<input type=text name=url
value="http://www.kimmswick.com/" size="50">
<input type="submit" value="Translate">
</form>
</body>
</html>
<%
}
else
{
  try
  {
    String str = Translate.translate(
      request.getParameter("url"),"translate.jsp?url=");
    out.println( str );
  }
  catch(Exception e)
  {
    out.println("Error:" + e );
  }
}
%>
```

The first thing that `translate.jsp` must do is determine if the query string contains a valid URL to translate. If no valid URL is provided, the JSP page assumes that this is the first time it is being called, and it displays a form to allow the user to enter such a URL. This determination is made by the following if statement:

```jsp
if(request.getParameter("url")==null)
```

If a URL is provided, the JSP page will then pass that URL off to the class provided by `Translate.java` (shown in Listing 4.3). This is a relatively simple procedure and is accomplished by the following two lines:

```jsp
String str = Translate.translate(
  request.getParameter("url"),"translate.jsp?url=");
out.println( str );
```

The translate method shown in the previous code lines requires two parameters. The first parameter tells the translation e object which URL should be translated. The second parameter tells this object which URL it should redirect any links back to.

At this point, the translate object shown in Listing 4.3 does the actual translation. This object is actually a ParserCallback descendant used for HTML parsing—the HTMLPage object handles the actual parsing and relays the information back to the ParserCallback object. The translate method called by the JSP is a static method that instantiates the translate object and uses HTMLPage to translate it. What happens in this listing will be discussed in more detail momentarily.

Listing 4.3   Translation Routines (translate.java)

```java
package com.heaton.bot.translate;
import java.util.*;
import javax.swing.text.*;
import javax.swing.text.html.*;
import com.heaton.bot.*;


/**
 * Example program from chapter 4
 *
 * This class is used to translate web sites into Pig Latin.
 * This class does three main things.
 *
 * 1. Resolves all image URLs
 * 2. Resolves all links and points them back to the translator
 * 3. Translates actual text into Pig Latin
 *
 * @author Jeff Heaton
 * @version 1.0
 */
public class Translate extends HTMLEditorKit.ParserCallback
{

  /**
   * Used to hold the page as it is translated.
   */
  protected String _buffer = "";

  /**
   * The base URL, which is the page being translated.
   * This is used to resolve relative links.
   */
  protected String _base;

  /**
   * This is the name of the URL that pages should be reflected
   * back to for further translation. This allows links to be
   * translated too.
```

```
 */
protected String _reflect;

/**
 * The constructor.
 *
 * @param t The URL to translate.
 * @param reflect The page to reflect back to.
 * @see _reflect
 */
Translate(String t,String reflect)
{
  _base = t;
  _reflect = reflect;
}

/**
 * Get the translated page.
 *
 * @return The translated page.
 */
public String getBuffer()
{
  return _buffer;
}

/**
 * Called by the parser whenever an HTML comment is found.
 *
 * @param data The actual comment.
 * @param pos The position.
 */
public void handleComment(char[] data,int pos)
{
  _buffer+="<!-- ";
  _buffer+= new String(data);;
  _buffer+=" -->";
}

/**
 * A method used to handle HTML attributes. This is called
 * by most tag types.
 *
 * @param attributes The attributes.
 */
protected void attributes(AttributeSet attributes)
{
  Enumeration e = attributes.getAttributeNames();
  while(e.hasMoreElements())
  {
    Object name = e.nextElement();
    String value = (String)attributes.getAttribute(name);
```

```java
      if(name == HTML.Attribute.HREF )
        value = _reflect + URLUtility.resolveBase(_base,value);
      else
      if( name == HTML.Attribute.SRC ||
          name == HTML.Attribute.LOWSRC )
        value = URLUtility.resolveBase(_base,value);

      _buffer+= " " + name + "=\"" + value + "\" ";
    }
  }

  /**
   * Handle an HTML start tag.
   *
   * @param t The tag encountered.
   * @param a The attributes for that tag.
   * @param pos The position.
   */
  public void handleStartTag(HTML.Tag t,MutableAttributeSet a,int pos)
  {
    _buffer+="<" + t;
    attributes(a);
    if( t == HTML.Tag.APPLET &&
      a.getAttribute(HTML.Attribute.CODEBASE)==null )
    {
      String codebase = _base;
      if( codebase.toUpperCase().endsWith(".HTM") ||
          codebase.toUpperCase().endsWith(".HTML") )
        codebase = codebase.substring(0,codebase.lastIndexOf('/'));

      _buffer+=" codebase=\"" + codebase + "\"";
    }
    _buffer+=">";
  }

  /**
   * Handle an HTML end tag.
   *
   * @param t The tag encountered.
   * @param pos The position.
   */
  public void handleEndTag(HTML.Tag t,int pos)
  {
    _buffer+="</" + t + ">";
  }

  /**
   * Handle a simple tag(one without an end tag)
   *
   * @param t The tag encountered.
   * @param a The attributes for that tag.
```

```
   * @param pos The position.
   */
  public void handleSimpleTag(HTML.Tag t,MutableAttributeSet a,int pos)
  {
    if( (t.toString()).startsWith("__"))
      return;
    _buffer+="<";
    if(a.getAttribute(HTML.Attribute.ENDTAG)!=null)
    {
      _buffer+="/"+t;
    }
    else
    {
      _buffer+=t;
      attributes(a);
    }
    _buffer+=">";
  }

  /**
   * Handle text.
   *
   * @param data
   * @param pos
   */
  public void handleText(char[] data,int pos)
  {
    _buffer+=pigLatin(new String(data));
  }

  /**
   * Translate a string to Pig Latin.
   *
   * @param english The English string.
   * @return A Pig Latin string.
   */
  protected String pigLatin( String english )
  {
    String pigWord; //an array of
    String pigLatin;
    String temp;
    int mode;// 0=lower,1=cap,2=upper

    StringTokenizer englishWords = new StringTokenizer( english );
    //StringTokenizer is used to parse a string
      //creates an emptry string
      pigLatin = "";
      //checks for the next word
    while ( englishWords.hasMoreTokens() )
    {
      //puts the next word into temp
```

```
      temp = new String (englishWords.nextToken() );

      if( (temp.charAt(0)>='A' && temp.charAt(0)<='Z') &&
          (temp.charAt(1)>='A' && temp.charAt(1)<='Z') )
        mode=2;
      else if( (temp.charAt(0)>='A' && temp.charAt(0)<='Z') &&
          (temp.charAt(1)>='a' && temp.charAt(1)<='z') )
        mode=1;
      else
        mode=0;

      //if the word is more than one char long
      if ( temp.length() > 1 )
      {
        //calls function to rearrange word
        String start = new String(firstVowel(temp));
        pigWord = new String ( start + "ay" );
//takes the first letter of the word, concatenates it and "ay" to the end
//of the word and puts it in the array
      }
      else
      {
        pigWord = temp + "ay"; //add "ay" to a one letter word
      }
      if(pigWord.trim().length()>0)
      {
        if(pigLatin.length()>0)
          pigLatin+=" ";
        switch(mode)
        {
          case 0:
            pigLatin+=pigWord.toLowerCase();
            break;
          case 1:
            pigLatin+=pigWord.substring(0,1).toUpperCase();
            pigLatin+=pigWord.substring(1).toLowerCase();
            break;
          case 2:
            pigLatin+=pigWord.toUpperCase();
            break;
        }
      }
    }

    return pigLatin;
  }

  /**
   * Find the first vowel in a string, used by the pigLatin
   * method.
   *
```

```
 * @param s A string.
 * @return The location of the first vowel.
 */
protected String firstVowel(String s)
{
  String consonants = new String();
  String remain = new String();
  String newWord = "";
  int letterIndex = 0;   //The index of a letter in the word

  //checks each letter in the word for a vowel
  while(letterIndex < s.length())
  {
    if((s.charAt(letterIndex) != 'a') &&
       (s.charAt(letterIndex) != 'A') &&
      (s.charAt(letterIndex) != 'e') &&
      (s.charAt(letterIndex) != 'E') &&
      (s.charAt(letterIndex) != 'i') &&
      (s.charAt(letterIndex) != 'I') &&
      (s.charAt(letterIndex) != 'o') &&
      (s.charAt(letterIndex) != 'O') &&
      (s.charAt(letterIndex) != 'u') &&
      (s.charAt(letterIndex) != 'U'))
    {
      consonants += s.substring(letterIndex,(letterIndex + 1));
      letterIndex++;  //concatenats the consonants into a string
    }
    else
    {
      //puts the rest of the word into a string
      remain += s.substring(letterIndex,s.length());
      letterIndex = s.length();  //ends the loop
    }
  }
  if(consonants != "")
  {
    //concatenates the consonants onto the end of the word
    newWord = remain + consonants;
  }
  else
  {
    newWord = remain;
  }
return newWord;
}


/**
 * Static method that should be called to actually translate
 * a URL. This is the main entry point.
 *
```

```
 * @param url The URL to translate.
 * @param callback The URL that all links should be redirected through for
 * further translation.
 * @return The text of this page translated.
 * @exception java.io.IOException
 * @exception javax.swing.text.BadLocationException
 */
public static String translate(String url,String callback)
  throws java.io.IOException,javax.swing.text.BadLocationException
{
  Translate trans = new Translate(url,callback);
  HTMLPage page = new HTMLPage(new HTTPSocket());
  page.open(url,trans);
  return trans.getBuffer();
}
}
```

In Listing 4.3, the translate method first creates a new translate and HTMLPage object. Then the open method is called on the HTMLPage object so that the page can be translated with this translation object. Calling the open method like this retrieves the data from the page. This data is then passed on to the page variable so that it can be parsed. As the HTML is parsed, it will be relayed to the Translate callback object. The following code illustrates this process:

```
Translate trans = new Translate(url,callback);
HTMLPage page = new HTMLPage(new HTTPSocket());
page.open(url,trans);
return trans.getBuffer();
```

After this, the Translate callback provides the methods handleComment, handleEndTag, handleError, handleSimpleTag, handleStartTag and handleText to handle each type of tag encountered. Each time one of these types of tags is found, the tag will be routed to the appropriate callback method for proper handling. As each of these tag types are encountered, the HTML is reconstructed into the _buffer property. For most of the handlers, this simply means that the HTML will need to be reconstructed. However, certain attributes must be changed. These include attributes that contain links to other HTML pages, which will have to be modified so that the links first pass through the translated page.

For example, if the site being translated has an image referenced, the image tag might look something like this:

```
<IMG WIDTH="134" HEIGHT="106" SRC="/images/kwlogo.gif" BORDER=0
  ALT="Kimmswick.com">
```

Here, the image URL is given as /images/kwlogo.gif. This relative URL will resolve to http://www.kimmswick.com/images/kwlogo.gif when the image is being displayed at kimmwsick.com, but for it to work from another site, this relative URL must be resolved.

Because the JSP page doing the translation will not reside at the address `kimmswick.com`, it will not be able to resolve this relative URL. Instead, the `attributes` method will accomplish this because this is one of its main functions.

In order for this resolution to happen, the `attributes` method is called by several of the handler methods so that they can process the attributes for that tag. First, the `attributes` method obtains an enumeration of all of the attributes for the tag being processed, as shown here:

```
Enumeration e = attributes.getAttributeNames();
while(e.hasMoreElements())
{
```

Next, the attribute name is determined so that any special handling can be performed:

```
Object name = e.nextElement();
String value = (String)attributes.getAttribute(name);
```

If the attributes are determined to be of the type `HREF`, their absolute URL is then determined and inserted so that the URL has meaning outside of the website. At this point, the callback specified by `_reflect`, is attached at the beginning of the URL of the tag being converted so that any link pointed to by this tag will also be translated once the user clicks it. This process is shown here:

```
if(name == HTML.Attribute.HREF )
  value = _reflect + URLUtility.resolveBase(_base,value);
else
```

In the case of `SRC` attributes such as images, the URL is completely resolved before it is attached to the HTML being generated.

```
if( name == HTML.Attribute.SRC ||
    name == HTML.Attribute.LOWSRC )
  value = URLUtility.resolveBase(_base,value);

_buffer+= " " + name + "=\"" + value + "\" ";
}
```

In addition to tags, text must also be handled. As text is retrieved by the `handleText` method, it is sent off to the `pigLatin` method to be translated. The `pigLatin` method is a relatively simple implementation of the Pig Latin algorithm mentioned earlier.

By using this JSP page, a site can provide a fairly advanced translation service. Figure 4.4 shows the `kmmswick.com` site before translation, and Figure 4.5 shows the `kimmswick.com` site after translation.

FIGURE 4.4:

Kimmswick.com in
English

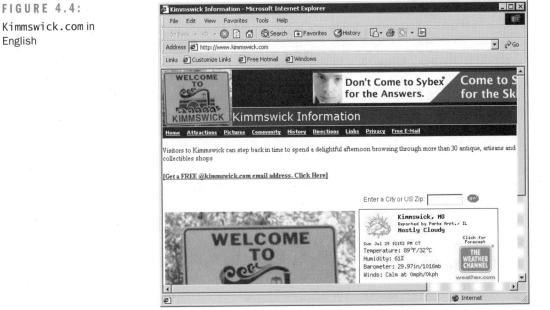

FIGURE 4.5:

Kimmswick.com in
Pig Latin

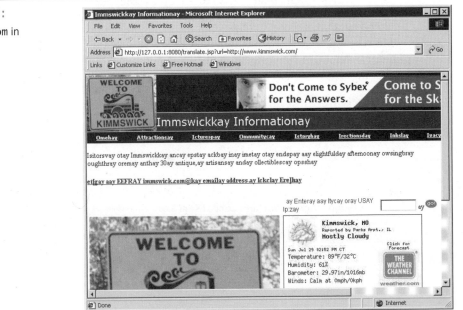

Under the Hood

The HTML Swing classes mentioned earlier in this chapter handle most of the low-level details of HTML parsing. The Bot package provides the HTMLParse, HTMLPage, and Link classes to augment these services.

Constructing the *HTMLParse* Class

The HTMLParse class is one of the simplest classes in the Bot package. Its complete listing is shown in Listing 4.4. The entire purpose of this class is to create a public version of the get-Parser method because the HTMLEditorKit provided by Swing does not make the getParser method public. Without a public getParser method, you will be unable to parse HTML using the Swing classes. The HTMLParse class overrides the getParser method provided by HTMLEditorKit in order to make the getParser method public. This allows you to instantiate a parser with the HTMLPage class.

Listing 4.4   A Simple Class to Get an HTML Parser (HTMLParse.java)

```
package com.heaton.bot;
import javax.swing.text.html.*;

/**
 * A VERY simple class meant only to subclass the
 * HTMLEditorKit class to make the getParser method
 * public so that we can gain access to an
 * HTMLEditorKit.Parser object.
 *
 * @author Jeff Heaton
 * @version 1.0
 */
public class HTMLParse extends HTMLEditorKit
{

  /**
   * Call to obtain a HTMLEditorKit.Parser object.
   *
   * @return A new HTMLEditorKit.Parser object.
   */
  public HTMLEditorKit.Parser getParser()
  {
    return super.getParser();
  }
}
```

Constructing the *HTMLPage* Class

The HTMLPage class is shown in Listing 4.5. We've already demonstrated how to use this class in the section entitled "Using the HTMLPage Class," earlier in this chapter; now, we will describe how it was created. First we will examine the source code for this page.

Listing 4.5   **Parsing an HTML Page (HTMLPage.java)**

```java
package com.heaton.bot;
import java.util.*;
import com.heaton.bot.*;
import java.net.*;
import java.io.*;
import javax.swing.text.*;
import javax.swing.text.html.*;

/**
 * The HTMLPage class is used to parse an HTML page and store
 * that page, in a parsed form, in memory.
 *
 * Copyright 2001 by Jeff Heaton
 *
 * @author Jeff Heaton
 * @version 1.0
 */
public class HTMLPage
{

  /**
   * A list of images on this page.
   */
  protected Vector _images = new Vector();

  /**
   * A list of links on this page.
   */
  protected Vector _links = new Vector();

  /**
   * A list of forms on this page.
   */
  protected Vector _forms = new Vector();

  /**
   * The underlying HTTP object for this page.
   */
  protected HTTP _http;

  /**
   * The base URL to resolve relative URLs.
```

```
  */
protected String _base;

/**
 * Construct an HTMLPage object.
 *
 * @param http The HTTP object(or subclass) to use to
 * download pages.
 */
public HTMLPage(HTTP http)
{
  _http = http;
}


/**
 * Called to open a page and read it in. If null
 * is specified for the callback, then the other
 * methods in this class may be used to look at
 * images, links, and forms.
 *
 * @param url The URL to read.
 * @param callback A callback class to handle the parse, or null
 * to use the built-in one.
 * @exception java.io.IOException
 * @exception javax.swing.text.BadLocationException
 */
public void open(String url,HTMLEditorKit.ParserCallback callback)
throws IOException,BadLocationException
{
  _http.send(url,null);
  _base = url;
  processPage(callback);
}

/**
 * Internal function called to start the parse.
 *
 * @param callback The callback object to use.
 * @exception java.io.IOException
 */
protected void processPage(HTMLEditorKit.ParserCallback callback)
throws IOException
{
  StringReader r = new StringReader(_http.getBody());
  HTMLEditorKit.Parser parse = new
  HTMLParse().getParser();

  if(callback==null)
  {
    HTMLPage.Parser p=new HTMLPage.Parser();
    parse.parse(r,p,true);
```

```
    }
    else
      parse.parse(r,callback,false);

}

/**
 * Get the underlying HTTP object that was
 * sent to the constructor.
 *
 * @return The underlying HTTP object.
 */
public HTTP getHTTP()
{
  return _http;
}

/**
 * Get a list of all of the links from this page.
 * If this is to be used, then null must have been
 * passed as the callback object to the open method.
 *
 * @return All links on this page.
 */
public Vector getLinks()
{
  return _links;
}

/**
 * Get a list of all of the images from this page.
 * If this is to be used, then null must have been
 * passed as the callback object to the open method.
 *
 * @return A list of all of the images on this page.
 */
public Vector getImages()
{
  return _images;
}

/**
 * Get a list of all of the forms from this page.
 * If this is to be used, then null must have been
 * passed as the callback object to the open method.
 *
 * @return A list of forms.
 */
public Vector getForms()
{
  return _forms;
}
```

```
/**
 * Called to perform a post for the specified form.
 *
 * @param form The form object to post.
 * @exception java.io.IOException
 */
public void post(HTMLForm form)
throws IOException
{
  _http.getClientHeaders().set("Content-Type","application/x-www-form-
  urlencoded");
  _http.send(form.getAction(),form.toString());
  processPage(null);
}

/**
 * Get the URL that is represented by this page.
 *
 * @return The URL that is represented by this page.
 */
public String getURL()
{
  return _http.getURL();
}

/**
 * Called internally to add an image to the list.
 *
 * @param img The image to add.
 */
protected void addImage(String img)
{
  img = URLUtility.resolveBase(_base,img);
  for(int i=0;i<_images.size();i++)
  {
    String s = (String)_images.elementAt(i);
    if(s.equalsIgnoreCase(img))
      return;
  }
  _images.addElement(img);
}

/**
 * A HTML parser callback used by this class to
 * detect links, images, and forms.
 *
 * @author Jeff Heaton
 * @version 1.0
 */
protected class Parser extends HTMLEditorKit.ParserCallback
{
```

```java
/**
 * Used to build up data for an HTML form.
 */
protected HTMLForm _tempForm;

/**
 * Called to handle comments.
 *
 * @param data The comment.
 * @param pos The position.
 */
public void handleComment(char[] data,int pos)
{
}

/**
 * Called to handle an ending tag.
 *
 * @param t The ending tag.
 * @param pos The position.
 */
public void handleEndTag(HTML.Tag t,int pos)
{
  if(t==HTML.Tag.FORM)
  {
    if(_tempForm!=null)
      _forms.addElement(_tempForm);
  }
}

/**
 * Called to handle an error. Not used.
 *
 * @param errorMsg The error.
 * @param pos The position.
 */
public void handleError(String errorMsg,int pos)
{
}

/**
 * Called to handle a simple tag.
 *
 * @param t The simple tag.
 * @param a The attribute list.
 * @param pos The position.
 */
public void handleSimpleTag(HTML.Tag t,MutableAttributeSet a,int pos)
{
  if(t==HTML.Tag.INPUT)
  {
```

```
      if(_tempForm==null)
        return;

      String type = (String)a.getAttribute(HTML.Attribute.TYPE);
      if(type==null)
        return;

      if(type.equalsIgnoreCase("text") ||
        type.equalsIgnoreCase("edit") ||
        type.equalsIgnoreCase("password") ||
        type.equalsIgnoreCase("hidden") )
      {
        _tempForm.addInput(
          (String)a.getAttribute(HTML.Attribute.NAME),
          (String)a.getAttribute(HTML.Attribute.VALUE),
          (String)a.getAttribute(HTML.Attribute.TYPE));
      }
    }
    else if(t==HTML.Tag.BASE)
    {
      String href = (String)a.getAttribute(HTML.Attribute.HREF);
      if(href!=null)
        _base = href;
    }
    else if(t==HTML.Tag.IMG)
    {
      String src = (String)a.getAttribute(HTML.Attribute.SRC);
      if(src!=null)
        addImage(src);
    }
  }

  /**
   * Called to handle a starting tag.
   *
   * @param t The starting tag.
   * @param a The attribute list.
   * @param pos The position.
   */
  public void handleStartTag(HTML.Tag t,MutableAttributeSet a,int pos)
  {
    if(t==HTML.Tag.A)
    {
      String href = (String)a.getAttribute(HTML.Attribute.HREF);

      if(href!=null)
      {
        Link link = new Link(
          (String)a.getAttribute(HTML.Attribute.ALT),
          URLUtility.resolveBase(_base,href) );
        _links.addElement(link);
      }
```

```
    }
    else if(t==HTML.Tag.FORM)
    {
      if(_tempForm!=null)
        _forms.addElement(_tempForm);

      String action =
        (String)a.getAttribute(HTML.Attribute.ACTION);
      if(action!=null)
      {
        try
        {
          URL aurl = new URL(new URL(_http.getURL()),action);
          action = aurl.toString();
        }
        catch(MalformedURLException e)
        {
          action = null;
        }
      }

      _tempForm = new HTMLForm(
        (String)a.getAttribute(HTML.Attribute.METHOD),
        action );
    }
  }

  /**
   * Called to handle text.
   *
   * @param data The text.
   * @param pos The position.
   */
  public void handleText(char[] data,int pos)
  {
  }
 }
}
```

The HTMLPage class contains an inner class, named Parser, that implements a specialized parser callback that can be used to track images, hyperlinks, and forms. The open method is the usual entry point into the HTMLPage class. The open method accepts two parameters that tell it, the URL, to process and which parser to callback. The open method uses the URL parameter to call the send method and passes the callback parameter to the processPage method (shown here):

```
_http.send(url,null);
_base = url;
processPage(callback);
```

First, the open method requests the URL from the _http object, and then it calls the processPage method, where the data is actually parsed. The processPage method begins by first creating a string reader to encapsulate the page that was just loaded. Then the HTML-Parse class, described in the previous section, is called to create a new HTML parser:

```
StringReader r = new StringReader(_http.getBody());
HTMLEditorKit.Parser parse = new HTMLParse().getParser();
```

Next, the code determines if a custom callback class was provided. If a custom callback was provided, it is used, and this essentially ends the work done by the HTMLPage class. If no callback was provided, then HTMLPage will use its built-in callback. The built-in callback class, called Parser, is designed to track images, hyperlinks, and forms. The following lines of code determine if an external callback class has been provided. If the callback variable is null, then HTML-Page's internal parser, named Parser is used. If callback is not null, then it specifies a callback object to use.

```
if(callback==null)
    {
        HTMLPage.Parser p=new HTMLPage.Parser();
        parse.parse(r,p,true);
    }
    else
        parse.parse(r,callback,false);
```

Once the parsing begins, the real work is done by the various handler methods, which are provided by callback methods. The exact structure of these handler functions is mentioned earlier in this chapter under the "Using Bot Classes for HTML Parsing" section. For the call-back class provided here, most work is done by the handleSimpleTag and handleStartTag methods.

Constructing the *Link* Class

The Link class is a simple data container class that is used to hold the href and alt attributes for a hyperlink. There is no code other than the get/set methods for these attributes. Listing 4.6 shows this object.

Listing 4.6   **A Class to Store Links(Link.java)**

```
package com.heaton.bot;

/**
 * Very simple data class to hold HTML links.
 * This class holds both the actual link URL,
 * as well as the alt attribute.
 *
 * @author Jeff Heaton
```

```
 * @version 1.0
 */
public class Link
{

  /**
   * The alt attribute.
   */
  protected String _alt;

  /**
   * The href (link) attribute.
   */
  protected String _href;
  /**
   * The constructor.
   *
   * @param alt The alt attribute for this link.
   * @param href The URL this link goes to.
   */

  public Link(String alt,String href)
  {
    _alt = alt;
    _href = href;
  }

  /**
   * Returns the alt attribute.
   *
   * @return The alt attribute.
   */
  public String getALT()
  {
    return _alt;
  }

  /**
   * Returns the href (link) attribute.
   *
   * @return The href (link) attribute.
   */
  public String getHREF()
  {
    return _href;
  }

  /**
   * Returns the link URL.
   *
   * @return The link URL.
```

```
    */
    public String toString()
    {
      return _href;
    }
  }
}
```

Summary

This chapter focused on how to parse HTML. HTML is not easily parsed, and the rules governing the structure of HTML documents are not strict. As a result, there can be a potentially unlimited number of HTML files that could all produce the same final output.

Swing gives Java an HTML parser that can be used to parse the HTML files commonly found on web pages. Swing examines such files, and it also provides extensive resources for HTML parsing. HTML parsers work with five components of an HTML document: text, comments, simple tags, beginning tags, and ending tags. To parse an HTML file, a program simply constructs a callback object that contains handler methods for these components. The parser provides all the data contained in the HTML document. Your program must determine what data it needs.

There is a great deal of data contained in HTML documents that is of no direct concern to the Bot package. The HTML tags that the Bot package is the most concerned with are links, forms, and base URL tags. In addition, JavaScript, embedded objects, and frames can complicate the life of a bot by concealing data that the bot might be after.

There are many different kinds of programs that can take advantage of HTML parsing. If you wished to create a program that can download every image on a site, you will find it necessary to parse out every image URL. If you were to create a program that translates a web page into an alternate language, you will find it necessary to parse the HTML in order to determine where translatable text falls.

Now that you can parse HTML, you can learn to process and react to the HTML. Chapter 5 will show you how to process HTML forms and respond to them. You will also see how to use a program to fill out the form fields and then submit the form.

CHAPTER 5

Posting Forms

- Evaluating forms

- Posting form data from forms

- Posting non-form (raw) data

- Using the HTMLPage and HTMLForm classes

The HTTP POST request is one of the most common ways to exchange information on the Internet. When you use a POST, you can potentially send large amounts of data from a web browser back to the server. The forms that users fill out from web servers are one of the most common sources of HTTP POST requests. As a result, virtually any time you fill out a website's form and click one of the submit buttons, you are invoking an HTTP POST.

A bot program will most likely need to be able to post as well. This is because one of the primary goals of a bot is to be able to emulate a user and directly interact with the web server. Because forms are such a ubiquitous part of websites today, handling them is a very important component of bot programming. Just as a user types data into a form and clicks the submit button, an automated bot must send the same information without human intervention. This chapter focuses exclusively on HTTP POST requests, as well as the forms that generate them.

In the process of discussing POST requests and forms, we will cover the following two classes from the Bot package on the companion CD: HTMLForm and HTMLPage. HTMLForm is used to read and then post an HTML form. HTMLPage is used to locate forms on an HTML page (though this was discussed briefly in Chapter 4, "HTML Parsing," it will be covered in more detail here).

Before we get into the details of these forms, we will learn how to use them.

Using Forms

Forms are very important components of the user interface that is provided by most web applications. These forms allow the user to enter information into various controls and then submit the result to the web server. Other than the information the web application gains from the simple browsing practices of the user as they are following hyperlinks from page to page, forms are the primary way that a web application collects real data from the user.

Because forms are so popular, a bot must often imitate a user entering data on a form. In fact, to the web server, the bot must be indistinguishable from a human user filling out the same form. This section will show you how this can be done by showing you the structure of a form and how to evaluate it and then showing you how to send data back to the web sever. This entire process of evaluating and responding to forms is called form emulation.

Emulating Forms

As just mentioned, bots must be capable of communicating with a web server and submitting data to a web server just as a human user would.

This process is called *emulation*. Emulation allows a bot program to present data in exactly the same format that another program would. When the bot program encounters a form, it does not display any sort of GUI-based form in response. Instead, it simply looks at the form and then produces a response that matches what the browser would have submitted had a real user completed all of the data requested by the form.

You should know exactly how the bot examines and then emulates these forms. In the process of presenting this information, this chapter produces a reusable object for the purpose of posting HTML forms. This class is called HTMLForm, and it is included as part of the Bot package and will be discussed in more detail later in this chapter. (This class will also be used in more advanced bots in Chapter 10, "Building a Bot.")

The first step in emulation is evaluation. Before a POST request can be sent, its underlying form must first be evaluated.

Evaluating a Form

HTTP POST requests originate from forms stored in HTML. Before any data can be posted, however, these forms must be evaluated to reveal the structure of the data to be posted.

Figure 5.1 shows a typical web form that was created in HTML. This figure shows a login form from a web-based e-mail system, and a simplified version of the HTML required to produce this form can be seen in Listing 5.1.

Listing 5.1   A typical HTML form (*form.html*)

```
<form name="myForm" method="post" action="loginuser.pl">
Login Name: <input type="text" name="loginName" size="15" value=""
maxlength="32"><br>
Password: <input type="password" name="user_pwd" size="15" maxlength="32"><br>
<input type="submit" value="Login" name="login"><br>
<input type="hidden" name="redir" value="">
<input type="hidden" name="cho" value="cv">
</form>
```

By examining the HTML code above, you can gain some insight into how this form operates. The first tag you should examine is the <form> tag, which has two main attributes: the method attribute and the action attribute. The method attribute specifies the method by which the form data should be sent back to the web server. This is usually part of a POST, but it may sometimes be part of a GET. The next attribute, action, specifies the URL to which the data from this form should be posted.

Between the beginning <form> tag and the ending </form> tag there is additional HTML code. Though nearly any HTML can be inserted between form tags, the <input> HTML tags that appear here are what the browser is particularly interested in because these items directly control the data that is posted back to the web server. Most <input> tags allow the user to enter information, like the information seen here:

```
loginName=jheaton&user_pwd=joshua&login=Login&redir=&cho=cv
```

FIGURE 5.1:

An HTML form

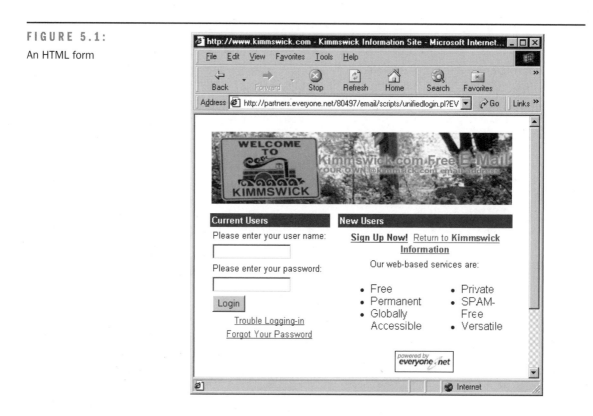

Using HTTP to Post

In order for the form seen in Listing 5.1 to be emulated, the bot must reproduce this line of text and post it to the web server. This is a relatively easy process. Most bots would submit this form using code very similar to the following:

```
String uid = ...// Insert the desired user ID
String pwd = ...// Insert the desired password
String postdata="loginName=";
postdata += uid;
postdata += "&user_pwd=";
postdata += pwd;
postdata += "&login=Login&redir=&cho=cv";

// ... post data to web server
```

To use this method of emulation, the programmer simply examines the HTML source code that was used to produce the form. The programmer then *hard codes* the specifics of the form into the Java source code. The process of hard coding refers to putting literal values right into the program code. This prevents the program itself from changing these values. For example, the above code would work if the user ID field was named `loginName`, but it would fail on any other value.

This approach will produce a program that correctly emulates this particular form, but it will not have much flexibility. A more flexible approach would be to gather the field names directly from the form. This is the approach that will be used when you are using the `HTMLForm` object. This is described in the "Using the `HTMLForm` Class" section later in this chapter.

The form being emulated here contains two hidden variables (`redir` and `cho`). Though the user does not see these variables, they do appear to the web server just like any visible component. They allow extra information to be sent back to the web server. The exact meaning of this information is dependent on the underlying website.

What if a new hidden variable were added, however? Websites do change quite frequently because their programmers are given new features to add. If a new hidden variable were to be introduced, this would break the bot program. Again, responding to changes in the underlying form will be addressed by using the `HTMLForm` object.

WARNING   Changes to the underlying site are one of the biggest issues that face bot programmers. Even minor changes to the site being accessed can break a bot program if precautions are not taken. Chapter 10 will show how to make your bots as resistant as possible to changes in the underlying site.

Forms Revealed

A *form* is nothing more than a section of the HTML document containing normal content and markup. A form, however, also includes special elements called *controls*; some examples of controls include check boxes, radio buttons, menus, and so on. Users generally complete a form by first modifying its controls (entering text, selecting menu items, etc.) and then submitting the form to the web server by clicking one of the button controls.

To complete a form, users interact with named controls. A control's control name is given by its `name` attribute. The scope of the `name` attribute for a control appears between the beginning `<form>` tag and ending `</form>` tag.

A control starts with an *initial value* that is specified by the `value` attribute. The *current value* of a component is the value that the control has after the user has changed whatever initial value was set. Of course, the user can choose not to modify the control. In this case, the current value remains the same as the initial value.

Both the initial value and the current value are character strings. The interpretation of the initial and current values of some controls differ slightly from the norm, which is the `value` attribute followed by an equal sign (=), followed by the control's initial value between quotes. The following is a typical example:

```
<input type="text" value="initial value">
```

The most notable exception to this is the TEXTAREA control. The initial value of a TEXTAREA tag is given by its contents (i.e., <TEXTAREA>initial value</TEXTAREA>), and the initial value of an OBJECT tag in a form is determined by the object implementation. This is the general format of the controls that bots will need to deal with.

Bots cannot generally interact with object type controls. You will now be shown the form of each of these control types.

TIP   The initial value of a control does not change. You can perform a reset on the form by clicking a reset button (if one is provided by the form), which will restore all controls to their initial values.

Control Types

The HTML controls are what determine how much data and what kind of data a form will collect. HTML forms support several types of controls, specified through <input> tags. You will now be shown each type of control supported by HTML.

Buttons   There are three types of buttons that can appear inside of a form, and all three are similar in appearance.

Submit buttons   *Submit buttons* are used to request that the data from the form be posted back to the web server. A form may have several submit buttons; if this is the case, then the buttons are differentiated by their names.

The typical HTML code for a submit button is as follows:

```
<input type="submit" name="thename" value="Log In">
```

This button would produce the name-value pair thename=Log In if it were selected.

Reset buttons   Clicking a *reset button* will reset all of the form controls to their initial values. Bots are not concerned with reset buttons because they don't interact with the server; they simply reset all controls to their initial values.

The typical HTML code for a reset button is as follows:

```
<input type="reset">
```

The above button would not produce a name-value pair when selected because it sends nothing to the server.

Push buttons   A *push button* is a button that does not automatically submit the form the way a submit button would. Push buttons are used to execute client-side JavaScript, and they contain an `onclick` attribute that usually specifies a JavaScript method to run. Push buttons are difficult for bots to work with because the bots can't resolve the JavaScript code to any meaningful URL.

The typical HTML code for a push button is as follows:

```
<input type="button" value="Update Screen" onclick="buttonSubmit()">
```

This button would not produce a name-value pair; it would simply execute the JavaScript method `buttonSubmit` on the client side.

Check boxes   A *check box* is a control that can be either selected or not. If the user selects a check box, it will produce a name-value pair when the form is submitted. If the check box is not selected, then no name-value pair will be generated.

The typical HTML code for a check box is as follows:

```
<input type="checkbox" name="thename" value="Yes">
```

This check box would produce the name-value pair `thename=Yes` if it were selected.

NOTE   Several check boxes in a form may share the same control name. Thus, for example, check boxes allow users to select several values for the same property. The `input` tag is used to create a check box control.

Radio buttons   A *radio button* is very similar to a check box in that it is either selected or not. However, radio buttons are typically grouped. If one radio button in a group is selected, then the other radio buttons are not. The group is established by creating several radio button controls that have the same name.

The typical HTML code for a radio button group is as follows:

```
<input type="radio" name="radioname" value="OptionA">Option A<br>
<input type="radio" name="radioname" value="OptionB">Option B<br>
<input type="radio" name="radioname" value="OptionC">Option C<br>
```

This code would produce the name-value pair `radioname=OptionB` if the second radio button were chosen.

Menus   A *menu* is a list of values that a user can select. These options will be displayed to the user as a list from which they can select.

Typical HTML code for a menu is as follows:

```
<select name="selectname">
  <option Value="OptA">Option A</option>
```

```
    <option Value="OptB">Option B</option>
    <option Value="OptC">Option C</option>
</select>
```

This code would produce the name-value pair `selectname=OptB` if the second menu item were chosen.

Text input   *Text input controls* allow the user to enter text. There are two types of text input controls. The `text` control allows the user to enter just one line of text. The `textarea` control allows the user to enter many lines of text.

The typical HTML code for text input is as follows:

```
<input type="text" name="textfield">
<textarea name="textfield">initial value</textarea>
```

The above two components would each produce a name-value pair, when taken separately, of `textfield=the text the user typed`.

Hidden controls   *Hidden controls* allow the web programmer to introduce values into the HTML form that will be posted back to the web server with the other controls. These controls are typically used to allow the web programmer to store read-only values that a user should not be able to change.

The typical HTML code for a hidden control is as follows:

```
<input type="hidden" name="CustomerNumber" value="123">
```

The above hidden control would produce the name-value pair `CustomerNumber=123` when the form was submitted.

The tags that are used to create the controls displayed on a form should appear between `<FORM>` and `</FORM>` tags.

NOTE   Though form control tags almost always fall between the `<FORM>` and `</FORM>` tags, these control tags can also appear outside of the bounding form tags. If a control is placed outside of a form, it will have to be processed by a JavaScript event, however. This practice is somewhat rare, and it is generally incompatible with bots. In order to process such tags, the bot programmer must examine the JavaScript code and determine how to correctly process it.

All of the form controls send their data back to the web server using the same format. As the form is processed, each control contributes to an ever-increasing line of text that is posted back to the web server. Each control represents a name-value pair. For example, if the name of the control is `id` and the final value of the control is `jheaton`, then the name-value pair could be said to be `id=jheaton`. If there is more than one control, and there usually is, the controls are separated by the ampersand (&) sign. For example, if the name-value pairs of id=jheaton and pwd=joshua were combined, the result would be id=jheaton&pwd=joshua.

From the perspective of a bot, the individual types of controls that appear on a form are far less important than the final product. The HTMLForm class does track the type of each component, but this value is for reference only. The HTMLForm method is primarily concerned with tracking the name-value pairs that make up the form.

Bot Classes for a Generic Post

The Bot package contains classes designed to make working with HTML forms easier. By using the Bot package, you can quickly load a form template from a website. Your program can then fill in the needed fields and request that the form be posted back to the web server. This eliminates the need for manually constructing the string of name-value pairs that will need to be posted back to the web server. Instead, this process will be performed by the HTML-Form class. You will be shown how to use this class later in this section. HTML forms are always contained on HTML pages. You will get HTMLForm objects from the HTMLPage class. You will now be shown how to use the HTMLPage class.

Using the *HTMLPage* Class

The HTMLPage class was first introduced in Chapter 4, "HTML Parsing," but it is also used in conjunction with the HTMLForm class presented in this chapter. For a complete discussion of the HTML parsing features of the HTMLPage class, refer back to Chapter 4.

The HTMLForm class is related to the HTMLPage class in that it is the HTMLPage class that actually creates HTMLForm objects. As Chapter 4 demonstrated, it is the HTMLPage class that is used for parsing an HTML page. As an HTMLPage object parses through an HTML page, it looks for certain HTML constructs. In addition to the links and images you saw it searching for in Chapter 4, the HTMLPage object is also looking for forms. Each time that an HTMLPage object finds a form, an HTMLForm object is instantiated to hold the structure of that form.

You will now be shown an example of how an HTMLPage object is used to access HTMLForm objects. First, an HTMLPage object must be instantiated and then an HTML page needs to be located for the HTMLPage object to parse. The following code instantiates a new HTMLPage object and then downloads a form from http://www.yahoo.com.

```
HTMLPage page = new HTMLPage(new HTTPSocket());
page.open(_"http://www.yahoo.com/",null);
```

With the first page from Yahoo! now downloaded and parsed, you must obtain an HTML-Form object that corresponds to the search form that is contained on the first page of Yahoo!. This is done using the getForms method, which returns a Vector object that contains a list of all forms found on this page. To use the `HTMLForm Vector` object, the `getForms` method of an `HTMLPage` object should be called. The following code accesses the first `HTMLForm` object contained on an `HTMLPage` object.

```
HTMLForm form = (HTMLForm)page.getForms().elementAt(0);
```

Of course, you could access a page that contains no forms at all. If this is the case, the `Vector` object returned by `getForms` will contain no elements. Now that you have seen how to acquire an `HTMLForm` object, the next section will show you what can be done with that `HTMLForm` object.

Using the *HTMLForm* Class

The `HTMLForm` object, which is usually obtained from an `HTMLPage` object, holds the contents of an HTML form. You can use the `HTMLForm` object to parse and then fill in values for an HTML form. This data can then be posted to the web server.

The `HTMLForm` object also contains an embedded object named `HTMLForm.FormElement`. This object is used to represent individual controls on the HTML form. `HTMLForm` is a descendant of `AttributeList` and `HTMLForm.FormElement` is a descendant of `Attribute`.

TIP   Refer back to Chapter 2, "Examining the Hypertext Transfer Protocol," to review all of the specifics of the `Attribute` and `AttributeList` commands.

The `HTMLForm` class contains the following constructor and methods. Here, each method will be described and then it will be followed by a short example of how it might appear in code.

The `HTMLForm` constructor   Creates a new `HTMLForm` object with the specified method and action. The method is either a GET or POST, the action is the URL that the GET or POST will be performed on.

```
public HTMLForm(String method,String action)
```

The `addInput` method   Adds input items encountered in the form while this `HTMLForm` object is being constructed. The `name` parameter specifies the name of the control. The `value` parameter indicates the initial value of the control. The `type` parameter indicates the type of control.

```
public void addInput(String name,String value,String type)
```

The `getAction` method   Returns the URL to which the form will be posted.

```
public String getAction()
```

The `getMethod` method   Retrieves the method specified for this object.

```
public String getMethod()
```

The toString method   Converts this form object into the data that would be posted to a web server.

```
public String toString()
```

Using the *HTMLForm.FormElement* Class

The FormElement object is used to hold the controls that make up the HTML form. The FormElement class is a very simple class, a descendant of the Attribute class, which adds a single String attribute named type. The FormElement class contains the following methods:

The getType method   Returns the value stored in the type attribute.

```
public String getType()
```

The setType method   Sets the type attribute to the value specified by the t parameter.

```
public void setType(String t)
```

An Example: Submit to Search Engines

One very common way to use bots is to use them to submit your site to multiple search engines. Some services claim to submit your site to over 5,000 such search engines. Surely human workers do not complete such tasks, so you can bet that they are done by bots. Examining such a submission process, and a bot's role in it, is a good example for this chapter. This will teach you to write a bot that can submit to several different websites.

Search engines are sites that keep lists of URLs that can be scanned by keyword, or a similar search mechanism. A search engine usually does not review or categorize its contents—examples of such search engines include Google and AltaVista. A site such as Yahoo!, which does categorize its content, would generally be considered a directory instead of a search engine, though Yahoo! currently defaults to a Google search if no suitable content is found in the Yahoo! directory.

Most search engines allow URLs to be submitted to their databases. For example, if you would like to add your site to the Google search engine, you must visit http://www.google.com/addurl.html. Here you will find an HTML form that allows you to enter the specifics of your site so that it may be included. Since Google uses an HTML form, you can submit data to it using the HTMLForm object discussed earlier in the chapter.

The example for this chapter will collect information about a site and then submit it to five search engines. This program (see Listing 5.2, which follows the "Sites That Prohibit Automated Submission" sidebar) results in the form shown in Figure 5.2.

FIGURE 5.2:

Site submit example

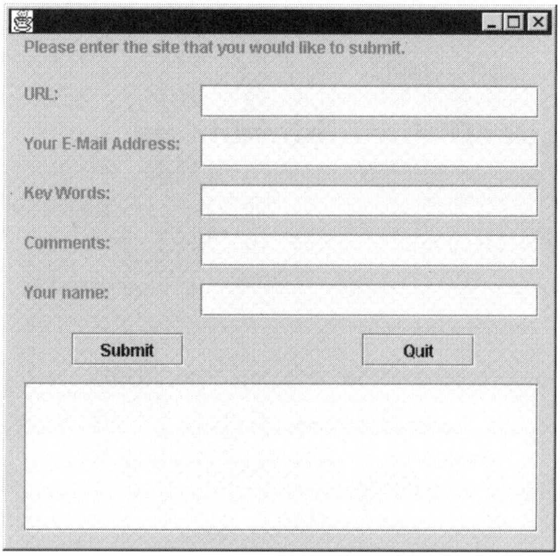

Sites That Prohibit Automated Submission

Though automatic site submission is a common practice, some search engines prohibit this practice. AltaVista is one such example. Because AltaVista has one of the largest site databases and can be an excellent resource for searches, it is important that you do get your site submitted to it, so you will just have to do it manually.

If you want to know how AltaVista prevents automatic site submission, visit the URL `http://add-url.altavista.com/cgi-bin/newurl?`. You will find yourself at the AltaVista URL submission page. This page uses a typical form to allow you to submit your site.

On this form, AltaVista asks for the usual information about a site, but it also includes one extra piece of information; this takes the form of a large image that displays a relatively short code in a strange font. You will need to retype this code into the HTML form provided by AltaVista. This action, which is relatively easy for a human user, makes automated access nearly impossible. A program that accesses this site is incapable of retyping the code because it cannot interpret the image that contains the code. There are possible ways around this, such as Optical Character Recognition (OCR), which would allow the computer to read the image as text. But the strange use of fonts on this page would hinder any OCR attempts.

Continued on next page

To think of ways around such sites is pointless. Such automated attempts can be detected and all that will happen is that security will be increased to thwart new automated submission attempts. Plus, the sites that do not encourage automated submission are relatively few, and their wishes should be respected. If a site is taking steps to prevent automated submission, it is probably a violation of that site's terms of service to try to go around such measures anyway.

You must always be sure that you are complying with site agreements and copyright law when you are using automated submission techniques. Whenever you feel that your practices are in question, you should always consult an attorney.

Listing 5.2 is a Swing application similar to examples presented in previous chapters. The majority of the work is done when the submit button is clicked by the user.

Listing 5.2   Submitting Your Site to Multiple Search Engines (*SiteSubmit.java*)

```java
import java.io.*;
import java.awt.*;
import javax.swing.*;
import com.heaton.bot.*;


/**
 * Example program from Chapter 5
 * Programming Spiders, Bots, and Aggregators in Java
 * Copyright 2001 by Jeff Heaton
 *
 *
 * This is an example program that submits your site
 * to five popular search engines. This shows you how to
 * use the HTMLForm object.
 *
 * @author Jeff Heaton
 * @version 1.0
 */
public class SiteSubmit extends javax.swing.JFrame {

  /**
   * A list of search engines to submit to.
   */
  protected Site _list[] = {
    new Site("Lycos(tm)", // engine name
            "http://home.lycos.com/addasite.html",
            "query",// url
            "email",// email
            null,// keys
            null,// comments
```

```
                  null,// user name
                  null),// submit

          new Site("HotBot(tm)", // engine name
                  "http://hotbot.lycos.com/addurl.asp",
                  "newurl",// url
                  "email",// email
                  null,// keys
                  null,// comments
                  null,// user name
                  null),// submit

          new Site("Direct Hit(tm)",
                  "http://www.directhit.com/util/addurl.html",
                  "URL",// url
                  "email",// email
                  "keys",// keys
                  null,// comments
                  null,// user name
                  null),// submit

          new Site("Northern Light(tm)",
                  "http://www.northernlight.com/docs/regurl_help.html",
                  "page",// url
                  "EMAIL",// email
                  null,// keys
                  null,// comments
                  "contact",// user name
                  null),// submit

          new Site("Google(tm)", // engine name
                  "http://www.google.com/addurl.html",// post
                  "q",// url
                  null,// email
                  null,// keys
                  "dq",// comments
                  null,// user name
                  null)// submit
      };

      /**
       * The constructor. Sets up all the controls.
       */
      public SiteSubmit()
      {
        //{{INIT_CONTROLS
        getContentPane().setLayout(null);
        setSize(405,370);
        setVisible(false);
        JLabel1.setVerticalTextPosition(
          javax.swing.SwingConstants.TOP);
```

```
JLabel1.setVerticalAlignment(
  javax.swing.SwingConstants.TOP);
JLabel1.setText(
  "Please enter the site that you would like to submit.");
getContentPane().add(JLabel1);
JLabel1.setBounds(12,0,360,24);
JLabel2.setText("URL:");
getContentPane().add(JLabel2);
JLabel2.setBounds(12,36,36,12);
JLabel3.setText("Your E-Mail Address:");
getContentPane().add(JLabel3);
JLabel3.setBounds(12,72,120,12);
JLabel4.setText("Key Words:");
getContentPane().add(JLabel4);
JLabel4.setBounds(12,108,108,12);
JLabel5.setText("Comments:");
getContentPane().add(JLabel5);
JLabel5.setBounds(12,144,96,12);
JLabel6.setText("Your name:");
getContentPane().add(JLabel6);
JLabel6.setBounds(12,180,108,12);
getContentPane().add(_url);
_url.setBounds(144,36,252,24);
getContentPane().add(_email);
_email.setBounds(144,72,252,24);
getContentPane().add(_keys);
_keys.setBounds(144,108,252,24);
getContentPane().add(_keys);
getContentPane().add(_comments);
_comments.setBounds(144,144,252,24);
getContentPane().add(_username);
_username.setBounds(144,180,252,24);
JButton1.setText("Submit");
JButton1.setActionCommand("Submit");
getContentPane().add(JButton1);
JButton1.setBounds(48,216,84,24);
JButton2.setText("Quit");
JButton2.setActionCommand("Quit");
getContentPane().add(JButton2);
JButton2.setBounds(264,216,84,24);
JScrollPane1.setOpaque(true);
getContentPane().add(JScrollPane1);
JScrollPane1.setBounds(12,252,384,108);
JScrollPane1.getViewport().add(_output);
_output.setBounds(0,0,381,105);
//}}

//{{INIT_MENUS
//}}

//{{REGISTER_LISTENERS
SymAction lSymAction = new SymAction();
```

```java
    JButton2.addActionListener(lSymAction);
    JButton1.addActionListener(lSymAction);
    //}}
}

/**
 * Generated by VisualCafe.
 *
 * @param b True/false to set the visiblity of the window.
 */
public void setVisible(boolean b)
{
  if ( b )
    setLocation(50, 50);
  super.setVisible(b);
}

/**
 * The main entry point of the program.
 *
 * @param args No program arguments are used.
 */
static public void main(String args[])
{
  (new SiteSubmit()).setVisible(true);
}
/**
 * Generated by VisualCafe to setup all
 * notifications.
 */

public void addNotify()
{
  // Record the size of the window prior to
  // calling parents addNotify.
  Dimension size = getSize();

  super.addNotify();

  if ( frameSizeAdjusted )
    return;
  frameSizeAdjusted = true;

  // Adjust size of frame according to the insets and menu bar
  Insets insets = getInsets();
  javax.swing.JMenuBar menuBar = getRootPane().getJMenuBar();
  int menuBarHeight = 0;
  if ( menuBar != null )
    menuBarHeight = menuBar.getPreferredSize().height;
  setSize(insets.left +
          insets.right +
          size.width, insets.top +
```

```
            insets.bottom + size.height +
            menuBarHeight);
}

// Used by addNotify
boolean frameSizeAdjusted = false;

//{{DECLARE_CONTROLS
javax.swing.JLabel JLabel1
= new javax.swing.JLabel();
javax.swing.JLabel JLabel2
= new javax.swing.JLabel();
javax.swing.JLabel JLabel3
= new javax.swing.JLabel();
javax.swing.JLabel JLabel4
= new javax.swing.JLabel();
javax.swing.JLabel JLabel5
= new javax.swing.JLabel();
javax.swing.JLabel JLabel6
= new javax.swing.JLabel();
javax.swing.JTextField _url
= new javax.swing.JTextField();
javax.swing.JTextField _email
= new javax.swing.JTextField();
javax.swing.JTextField _keys
= new javax.swing.JTextField();
javax.swing.JTextField _comments
= new javax.swing.JTextField();
javax.swing.JTextField _username
= new javax.swing.JTextField();
javax.swing.JButton JButton1
= new javax.swing.JButton();
javax.swing.JButton JButton2
= new javax.swing.JButton();
javax.swing.JScrollPane JScrollPane1
= new javax.swing.JScrollPane();
javax.swing.JTextArea _output
= new javax.swing.JTextArea();
//}}

//{{DECLARE_MENUS
//}}

/**
 * This internal class is used to hold information
 * about an individual search engine.
 *
 * @author Jeff Heaton
 */
class Site {

  /**
```

```
 * The constructor. Used to create a site.
 *
 * @param name The name of the person submitting.
 * @param post The page that contains the submit form.
 * @param url Field name: the URL being submitted
 * @param email Field name: the email address of the
 * person submitting.
 * @param keys Field name: keywords for this site
 * @param comments Field name: comments for this site
 * @param username Field name: who is submitting
 * @param submit Field name: the name of the submit button
 */
public Site(
           String name,
           String post,
           String url,
           String email,
           String keys,
           String comments,
           String username,
           String submit )
{
  _name = name;
  _post = post;
  _url = url;
  _email = email;
  _keys = keys;
  _comments = comments;
  _username = username;
  _submit = submit;
}

/**
 * The name of this search engine.
 */
public String _name;

/**
 * The page used to post a new site form.
 * This is the page that contains the form.
 */
public String _post;

/**
 * The name of the <input> tag used to
 * specify the URL to be submitted.
 */
public String _url;

/**
 * The name of the <input> tag used to
 * specify the e-mail address of the
```

```
    * person submitting.
    */
   public String _email;

   /**
    * The name of the <input> tag used to
    * specify the keywords of the site.
    */
   public String _keys;

   /**
    * The name of the <input> tag used to
    * specify comments about the site.
    */
   public String _comments;

   /**
    * The name of the <input> tag used to
    * specify the username of the person
    * submitting the site.
    */
   public String _username;

   /**
    * The name of the <input> tag used to
    * specify the name of the submit control.
    */
   public String _submit;
}


/**
 * This internal class is used by VisualCafe
 *-generated code to dispatch events.
 */
class SymAction implements java.awt.event.ActionListener {
  public void actionPerformed(java.awt.event.ActionEvent event)
  {
    Object object = event.getSource();
    if ( object == JButton2 )
      JButton2_actionPerformed(event);
    else if ( object == JButton1 )
      JButton1_actionPerformed(event);
  }
}

/**
 * Quit the program.
 *
 * @param event The button event.
 */
void JButton2_actionPerformed(java.awt.event.ActionEvent event)
```

```
{
  System.exit(0);

}

/**
 * Called to write a line of text to the edit control.
 * This lets the user review the outcome.
 *
 * @param text
 */
protected void log(String text)
{
  _output.insert(text + "\n",_output.getText().length());
}

/**
 * Main function that does the submitting. Triggered
 * by the submit button being clicked.
 *
 * @param event The button event.
 */
void JButton1_actionPerformed(java.awt.event.ActionEvent event)
{
  FileOutputStream fw = null;
  PrintStream ps = null;

  log("-----------------------------");
  log("Submit: " + _url.getText() );
  try {
    fw = new FileOutputStream("result.log",false);
    ps = new PrintStream(fw);
  } catch ( Exception e ) {
    log("Can't write to log file: " + e );
  }
  for ( int i=0;i<_list.length;i++ ) {
    try {
      // download and parse the submit page form
      // the search engine.
      HTMLPage page = new HTMLPage(new HTTPSocket());
      page.open(_list[i]._post,null);

      // Some of these pages have more than one
      // form. Find the correct form.
      // The one that contains a control with a
      // name matching the one that we plan to
      // copy the URL into will signify the correct
      // form.
      int j=0;
      HTMLForm found = null;
      while ( j<page.getForms().size() ) {
        HTMLForm form = (HTMLForm)page.getForms().elementAt(j);
```

```
                if ( form.get( _list[i]._url ) !=null ) {
                  found = form;
                  break;
                }
                j++;
              }

              if ( found==null ) {
                log("**Submit to: " + _list[i]._name + " Failed: No form" );
                continue;
              }

              // fill in all form elements that are required
              // for this search engine.

              if ( _list[i]._url!=null )
                found.set(_list[i]._url,_url.getText());

              if ( _list[i]._keys!=null )
                found.set(_list[i]._keys,_keys.getText());

              if ( _list[i]._email!=null )
                found.set(_list[i]._email,_email.getText());

              if ( _list[i]._comments!=null )
                found.set(_list[i]._comments,_comments.getText());

              if ( _list[i]._username!=null )
                found.set(_list[i]._username,_username.getText());

              // now attempt to post(or get) the form
              page.post(found);
              if ( ps!=null ) {
                ps.println("*******************************************");
                ps.println(page.getHTTP().getBody());
              }

              log("Submit to: " + _list[i]._name );

            } catch ( Exception e ) {
              log("**Submit to: " + _list[i]._name + "(" + _list[i]._post +")" + "
    Failed:" + e );
            }
          }
        }
        try {
          ps.close();
          fw.close();
        } catch ( Exception e ) {
        }
      }
```

The most important part of this example is the `Jbutton1_actionPerformed` event handler. This method begins by opening an output file into which it will record log information. Then it enters its main loop that will submit the site specified on the form to every site in the _site array. This is done with the following loop:

```
for(int i=0;i<_list.length;i++)
{
```

For each site in the list of search engines, you must read in and parse that search engine's submit page. You will then be able to fill out the form and retrieve the data. The following code opens a connection to the search engine site and downloads the form:

```
// download and parse the submit page from
// the search engine.
HTMLPage page = new HTMLPage(new HTTPSocket());
page.open(_list[i]._post,null);
```

Once a page is loaded in, the correct form must be found. A loop is constructed that loops through each of the forms found on the page. Once you locate the input field of the URL of the site being submitted, you can assume that the correct form has been found. The following lines of code locate this form:

```
int j=0;
HTMLForm found = null;
while( j<page.getForms().size() )
{
  HTMLForm form = (HTMLForm)page.getForms().elementAt(j);
  if( form.get( _list[i]._url ) !=null )
  {
    found = form;
    break;
  }
  j++;
}
```

Once the correct form is found, it will be copied to the found variable. If no suitable form is found, an error will be generated.

Next, a series of `if` statements fills in each of the form elements as they are needed. The `if` statements are necessary because not every search engine requires every attribute. Some search engines want keywords; others want an e-mail address. Some want both. The following lines of code fill in the appropriate fields on the search engine submit form:

```
if(_list[i]._url!=null)
  found.set(_list[i]._url,_url.getText());

if(_list[i]._keys!=null)
```

```
found.set(_list[i]._keys,_keys.getText());

if(_list[i]._email!=null)
  found.set(_list[i]._email,_email.getText());

if(_list[i]._comments!=null)
  found.set(_list[i]._comments,_comments.getText());

if(_list[i]._username!=null)
  found.set(_list[i]._username,_username.getText());
```

Now that the form has properly been filled out, the page will be posted back to the web server, as shown here:

```
// now attempt to post(or get) the form
page.post(found);
```

Raw Posting

On certain occasions, you may want to post data directly to an HTTP resource. For instance, you may want to just post raw binary data and forgo the name-value–pair formatting of the standard HTML form. This is called *raw posting*, and it allows you to send any sort of data to the web server. Cases where it is desirable to do this are rare, however. Also, posting data that is not compatible with the HTML form is not standard and will not work with all software.

If you do decided that you want to try raw posting, here is how you would proceed. To post raw data directly to an HTTP resource, you do not need to use the HTMLForm object. The HTTPSocket class, first discussed in Chapter 2, is all that is required to post raw data to a form. This is accomplished by feeding binary data to the second parameter of the HTTPSocket.send method. For example, to post the raw binary string "Hello World" to http://www.jeffheaton.com, you would use the following code.

```
HTTPSocket http = new HTTPSocket();
String str = "Hello World";
http.send("http://www.jeffheaton.com",str);
```

Under the Hood

This chapter showed you how to process HTML forms using the HTMLForm class. You will now be shown how this class was constructed.

NOTE   If you are interested in seeing how the HTMLPage class was constructed, refer back to the section in Chapter 4 called "Constructing the HTMLPage Class."

The HTMLForm object is relatively simple. It is primarily a container class for HTML forms. The HTMLForm class holds the data form controls that were located as the form was parsed. The HTMLForm class does not actually parse the HTML forms; it is actually the HTMLPage class that parses the forms.

In this section, we will see how the data is sent to the web server. (For more information about this process, see Chapter 4.) The complete listing for HTMLForm.java can be seen in Listing 5.3. After this listing, we will see how the HTMLForm class actually works.

Listing 5.3   Processing an HTML Form (*HTMLForm.java*)

```java
package com.heaton.bot;
import com.heaton.bot.*;
import java.net.*;

/**
 * The HTMLForm class is used to create a response to an HTML form
 * and then transmit it to a web server.
 *
 * @author Jeff Heaton
 * @version 1.0
 */
public class HTMLForm extends com.heaton.bot.AttributeList
{

  /**
   * The method(i.e., GET or POST)
   */
  protected String _method;

  /**
   * The action or the site to post the form to.
   */
  protected String _action;

  /**
   * Construct an HTMLForm object.
   *
   * @param method The method(i.e., GET or POST)
   * @param action The action or the site that the result should be posted to.
   */
  public HTMLForm(String method,String action)
  {
    _method = method;
    _action = action;
  }
  /**
   * Call to get the URL to post to.
   *
```

```
 * @return The URL to post to.
 */

public String getAction()
{
  return _action;
}

/**
 * @return The method(GET or POST)
 */
public String getMethod()
{
  return _method;
}

/**
 * Add an HTML input item to this form.
 *
 * @param name The name of the input item.
 * @param value The value of the input item.
 * @param type The type of input item.
 */
public void addInput(String name,String value,String type)
{
  FormElement e = new FormElement();
  e.setName(name);
  e.setValue(value);
  e.setType(type.toUpperCase());
  add(e);
}

/**
 * Convert this form into the string that would be posted
 * for it.
 */
public String toString()
{
  String postdata;

  postdata = "";
  int i=0;
  while( get(i)!=null )
  {
    Attribute a = get(i);
    if(postdata.length()>0)
      postdata+="&";
    postdata+=a.getName();
    postdata+="=";
    postdata+=URLEncoder.encode(a.getValue());
    i++;
```

```
    }
    return postdata;
  }

  public class FormElement extends Attribute
  {
    protected String _type;
    public void setType(String t)
    {
        _type = t;
    }

    public String getType()
    {
      return _type;
    }
  }
}
```

The `HTMLForm` object shown here contains the `action` and `method` attributes of the `<form>` tag that created it. These two attributes, stored in `_method` and `_action`, are used when the form must later be submitted.

The `HTMLForm` object also maintains a list of form elements, stored as `FormElement` objects. As the form is parsed, the `HTMLPage` object calls the `addInput` method for each form input item encountered. Each form input item is stored in the forms list of controls with the following code:

```
FormElement e = new FormElement();
e.setName(name);
e.setValue(value);
e.setType(type.toUpperCase());
add(e);
```

The other primary responsibility of the `HTMLForm` class is to construct the actual data to be posted back to the website. This is done with the `toString` method. This method begins by creating an empty string named `postdata`, shown here:

```
String postdata;

postdata = "";
int i=0;
```

The method will now loop through all the controls on the form so that their name and value can be copied to the `postdata` variable.

```
while( get(i)!=null )
{
  Attribute a = get(i);
```

Each attribute will be attached to `postdata` if its length is greater than zero. Ampersands (&) are also added to separate name-value pairs.

```
if(postdata.length()>0)
  postdata+="&";
```

The name is added first, followed by the value. The value must be URL encoded, which allows special characters to be included. The following code adds the data from each individual form control to the data to be posted:

```
postdata+=a.getName();
postdata+="=";
postdata+=URLEncoder.encode(a.getValue());
i++;
}
```

Finally the result is returned from the `toString` method.

```
return postdata;
```

Unsafe Characters and URL Encoding

URL encoding is necessary so that certain character types can safely be included as part of a URL or HTTP POST. Some of the characters presented here are either unsafe on one operating system or another, or they are reserved by the HTML or URL specification. To be assured of cross-platform compatibility and functionality, you will need to use the hexadecimal encoding shown below when these characters appear in URLs. For the reserved characters, do not encode them when they appear in their conventional meaning for a URL; for example, do not encode the slash (/) when using it as part of the URL syntax. Always encode the unsafe characters in URLs.

The following characters are reserved and must be encoded:

- ; semicolon encodes to %2B

- / slash encodes to %2F

- ? question mark encodes to %3F

- : colon encodes to %3A

- @ at sign encodes to %40

- = equals sign encodes to %3D

- & ampersand encodes to %26

  The ampersand is a special case because it has a special meaning in HTML. In this book, the examples that show URLs being written into files are almost always HTML, so the ampersand should be encoded as an entity rather than as a hexadecimal code.

Summary

Forms are an important part of most interactive websites. To create effective bots, you must be able to parse and interact with forms exactly as a user does. The Bot package on the companion CD provides the HTMLForm class for exactly this purpose.

Forms are nothing more than blocks of components stored in HTML forms. These blocks are made up of <input> tags enclosed by <form> and </form> tags. Components of these forms can include buttons, radio buttons, menus, text input, and hidden controls.

Though bots can interact with most of these components, sometimes they encounter problems. For instance, both embedding objects and using scripts from buttons are problematic to bots. Retrieving data from these component types is also very difficult for them. Another challenge is faced once data is collected from all of the components on a form and it must be transmitted (posted) back to the web server.

Forms are always embedded in the HTML code found on web pages. The HTMLPage class, provided by the Bot package, allows you to process a page of HTML. The HTMLPage class returns HTMLForm objects to represent any forms that were encountered on the HTML page.

The HTMLForm class allows you to process a form found on an HTML page. This class will seek out form elements and prepare a name-value pair list that represents these components. When you are ready, the HTMLForm object will then post the contents of the form, that you specify, back to the web server. The Bot package gives you the HTMLForm class to locate and then submit these name-value pairs.

Up to this point, the only data that we have extracted from websites is in the form of images and URLs. But the data found on websites can be stored in a variety of other formats as well. The next chapter will show how to interpret some of these formats.

CHAPTER 6

Interpreting Data

- Understanding data formats

- Processing CSV files

- Decoding QIF files

- Accessing XML files

In past chapters, we focused primarily on how to retrieve pages from a website. We examined how to parse HTML and how to obtain data that was stored as HTML. HTML is not the only format for data that we will find on a website, however. This chapter explores some of the other types of data that you might find, and it explains how to parse them.

In particular, this chapter will explore the QIF, CSV, and XML data formats. Intuit Quicken's QIF format can be used to gather financial information from the websites that support it, and comma-separated value (CSV) file formats are commonly produced by spreadsheets. Finally, we will examine the Extensible Markup Language (XML), which can store a variety of hierarchical formats, and we will learn how to parse documents that contain it.

The Structure of the CSV File

The CSV file is commonly used to store tabular data, such as the data you might see in a spreadsheet or a database. This file format is very common and it has been around for a long time. In fact, nearly every database and spreadsheet program supports this format. Often, tabular data in this type of format may be stored on websites. Because of this, a bot program must be aware of the CSV format.

The CSV File Format

The format of a CSV file is mostly self-explanatory. This is because it is structured with ASCII text, in which the format is obvious to a typical user examining the file. If you export a file from a database in CSV format and look at it, you will find each record on a separate row. As each row is examined, you will see that they are a list of fields separated by commas. A sample CSV file is shown here.

```
1,"Doe","John","01/12/1972"
2,"Doe","Jane","01/24/1974"
```

NOTE   Variants of this format use different separators—the semicolon (;) or pipe (|) are common. These variants are particularly likely to appear if the data is of European origin and contains decimal points; this is because much of Europe uses a comma as a decimal point.

You will notice that some of the fields above appear with quotes. If a field is text, and therefore it is likely to contain an embedded comma, the entire field is enclosed in quotes. If a quote (") is to be stored as part of a text field, two quotes ("") should be inserted. For example, take the following text:

```
Jim said, "Hello how are you?"
```

To store this text as a CSV, you would encode it as follows:

```
"Jim said, ""Hello how are you?"""
```

CSV Parsing Example

The Java classes used to perform advanced string parsing on CSV classes include the String, StringBuffer, StringTokenizer, and StreamTokenizer classes. Unfortunately, none of these classes directly support parsing CSV files. Instead, such parsing has to be done manually.

Listing 6.1 shows a command-line invoked Java program, ParseCSV.java, which shows how a CSV file can be parsed. This process begins when ParseCSV.java is given either a file-name or URL as its single command-line parameter. This example program will read the CSV so that it can be parsed from either the specified file or URL. Once this file is read, it will be parsed according to the CSV file format.

A sample CSV file is provided with the example program on the companion CD. The file testfile.csv, shown here, allows you to see the example program in action.

```
1,"This is Field 2,Row 1","This is Field 3, Row 1"
1,"This is Field 2,Row 2","This is Field 3, Row 2"
1,"This is Field 2,Row 3","This is Field 3, Row 3"
1,"This is Field ""2"",Row 4","This is Field 3, Row 4"
```

When the example program is executed and given testfile.csv as its parameter, you will see the following output:

```
Field #0:1
Field #1:This is Field 2,Row 1
Field #2:This is Field 3, Row 1
-------------
Field #0:1
Field #1:This is Field 2,Row 2
Field #2:This is Field 3, Row 2
-------------
Field #0:1
Field #1:This is Field 2,Row 3
Field #2:This is Field 3, Row 3
-------------
Field #0:1
Field #1:This is Field "2",Row 4
Field #2:This is Field 3, Row 4
-------------
-------------
```

In this code, each line of dashes represents the end of one row and the beginning of the next. The individual fields are read between the rows. Some of the fields contain embedded quotes ("), mentioned earlier, which are processed correctly.

Listing 6.1   **Parsing a CSV file(*ParseCSV.java*)**

```java
import java.io.*;
import java.net.*;
import java.util.*;
import com.heaton.bot.*;

/**
 * Example from Chapter 6
 *
 * This example program parses a CSV file. This file
 * may come from either the Internet or a local drive.
 *
 * @author Jeff Heaton
 * @version 1.0
 */
public class ParseCSV
{

  /**
   * This method will read lines from a CSV file, line by line.
   * Each time that this method is called, an array of strings
   * is returned that contains all of the fields read from * that line.
   *
   * @param  A BufferedReader to read the CSV from, line
   * by line.
   * @return An array of fields read from one line of the CSV file.
   */
  public static String []parseCSVLine(BufferedReader r)
  {
   //variable to hold the contents
   //from the readLine method call
    String str;
   //variable into which we'll build the
   //text of a field, character by character.
    String rtn;
    boolean quote = false;
    int i;
    Vector vec = new Vector();

    // first read in a line
    try
    {
      str = r.readLine();
    }
    catch(Exception e)
    {
      return null;
    }
```

```
    /* if the readLine method returns a null, we have reached the end of the
file, so we'll quit this method.
    */
    if(str==null)
      return null;

    // now loop through this line
    rtn = "";
    for(i=0;i<str.length();i++)
    {
      if(str.charAt(i)=='\"')
      {
        // found a ", check to see if
        // there is a second one
        if( (i+1)<str.length()&&
          (str.charAt(i+1)=='\"') )
        {
          // found a "" so just insert a single "
          rtn+="\"";
          i++;
          continue;
        }
        // toggle quote mode
        quote=!quote;
      }
      else if( (str.charAt(i)==',') &&
        (!quote) )


      {
        /* found a comma and we're not in quote mode, so we're at the delimiter
for the field and have finished building up the field contents into our rtn
variable. Add the field to the vector, and then reset the holding variable.
    */
        vec.addElement(rtn);
        rtn = "";
      }
      else
      {
        // we're not at the end of the field, so append the character to our rtn
variable.
        rtn+=str.charAt(i);
      }


    }

    // there isn't a delimiter character after the last field, so we have to
separately add in the last element, if present
    if(rtn.length()>0)
      vec.addElement(rtn);
```

```
    // create a String array and return it
    String arr[] = new String[vec.size()];
    vec.copyInto(arr);
    return arr;
}

/**
 * Main entry point.
 *
 * @param args The first command line parameter specifies the URL or filename.
 */
public static void main(String args[])
{
  FileReader f=null;
  BufferedReader r=null;

  if(args.length!=1)
  {
    // display usage
    System.out.println("Usage:");
    System.out.println("javac ParseCSV [csv file or URL to parse]");
    System.exit(0);
  }
  try
  {
    // first try and open it as a file
    f = new FileReader( new File(args[0]) );
      r = new BufferedReader(f);
  }
  catch(FileNotFoundException e)
  {
    // if it fails as a file, try as a URL
    try
    {
      HTTPSocket http = new HTTPSocket();
      http.send(args[0],null);
      StringReader sr = new StringReader(http.getBody());
      r = new BufferedReader(sr);
    }
    catch(UnknownHostException ee)
    {
      // if it fails as a URL too, give up
      System.out.println(
        "Can't open file or URL named: "
        + args[0] + "(" + ee + ")");
      System.exit(0);
    }
    catch(IOException ee)
    {
      System.out.println( e );
      System.exit(0);
```

```
      }
    }

    // loop through each line and display
    String a[];
    while( (a=parseCSVLine(r)) != null )
    {
      for(int i=0;i<a.length;i++)
      {
        System.out.println("Field #"
          + i + ":" + a[i] );
      }
      System.out.println("-------------");
    }

    // close out the file
    try
    {
      if(r!=null)
        r.close();
      if(f!=null)
        f.close();
    }
    catch(IOException e)
    {
      System.out.println("Error:" + e );
      System.exit(0);
    }
  }
}
```

TIP   The most important method in this example is `parseCSVLine`. This method will parse a
CSV file one line at a time; it will also loop through the characters of each line and look
for the comma delimiters. The method then breaks the individual fields up into strings
and returns them as an array.

The Structure of a QIF File

A QIF (Quicken Interchange Format) file is a specially formatted ASCII text file that is used to
transfer data between different Quicken applications and other competing applications, such as
Microsoft Money. Many financial institutions that allow web access to accounts have the option
of exporting QIF data. Because of this, bot programs designed to interact with financial institutions can benefit from using the QIF format.

You need to keep a few points in mind if you want your program to stay compliant with the QIF standard. First, the QIF file must have a name between three and eight characters long followed by the `.qif` extension (for example, `Business.qif`) in order for Quicken to recognize it. Also, a QIF file is a standard text file, and it can be edited in any text-editing program—Microsoft Notepad, for instance.

The Format of a QIF File

QIF files follow a relatively simple format that can be easily parsed by a program.

In general, QIF files must adhere to the following rules:

- Each transaction must end with a ^ symbol.
- Each item in the transaction must appear on a separate line.
- When Quicken exports an account register, it adds one of the following lines at the beginning of the file to identify the type of account.

File Line	**Description**
`!Type:Bank`	Bank account
`!Type:Invst`	Investment account
`!Type:Cash`	Cash account
`!Type:Oth A`	Other asset account
`!Type:Ccard`	Credit card account
`!Type:Oth L`	Other liability account

The other lines of the QIF file specify individual values. For example, the value D specifies that the date of a transaction will follow. For information about other possible field meanings, refer to the description column of Table 6.1, which gives you some typical examples.

A sample QIF file is shown here. The meaning of each line is shown in Table 6.1.

```
!Type:Bank
D8/12/01
U-1,200.00
N1002
Pcable TV Bill
Amy Cable Company
A257 Fresno Street
Ast. Louis, MO 63125
Lutility
^
D6/13/01
```

```
T-80.24
CR
N1003
Pcomputer Store
Lcomputer Stuff
Ssupplies
Eoffice
$-40.00
Ssupplies
$-40.24
^
```

TABLE 6.1: A QIF File

File Line	Description
!Type:Bank	Header line
D8/12/01	Date of first transaction
U-1,200.00	Amount of first transaction
N1002	Check number
Pcable TV Bill	Payee
Amy Cable Company	Address (first line)
A257 Fresno Street	Address (second line)
Ast. Louis, MO 63125	Address (third line)
Lutility	Category/Transfer/Class
^	Ends first transaction
D6/13/01	Date (second transaction)
T-80.24	Amount (second transaction)
CR	Status in Cleared column
N1003	Check number
Pcomputer Store	Payee
Lcomputer Stuff	Category/Transfer/Class
Ssupplies	First category in split
Eoffice	Supplies first memo in split
$-40.00	First amount in split
Ssupplies	Second memo in split
$-40.24	Second amount in split
^	Ends second transaction

You will now be shown an example of a Java program reading a QIF file.

QIF Parsing Example

An example of QIF parsing can be seen in Listing 6.2. This program works in a manner that is very similar to the CSV parsing example in that it takes a URL or a filename as a source from which to parse. Like in the CSV discussion, there is an example QIF file, named test-file.qif, which is provided on the companion CD. To execute the example program with this QIF file, the command java ParseQIF testfile.qif should be used. If the above QIF file is run through the ParseQIF example program in Listing 6.2, it will produce the following output.

```
Date:8/12/01
Amount:-1,200.00
Number:1002
Payee:cable TV
Address Line 1:My Cable Company
Address Line 2:257 Fresno Street
Address Line 3:St. Louis, MO 63125
Category:null
-------------
Date:6/13/01
Amount:-80.24
Number:1003
Payee:Computer Store
Address Line 1:null
Address Line 2:null
Address Line 3:null
Category:null
-------------
```

Listing 6.2   Parsing a QIF file (*ParseQIF.java*)

```java
import java.io.*;
import java.net.*;
import java.util.*;
import com.heaton.bot.*;

/**
 * Example from Chapter 6
 *
 * This example program parses a QIF file. This file
 * may come from either the Internet or a local drive.
 *
 * @author Jeff Heaton
 * @version 1.0
 */
public class ParseQIF
{
```

```java
/**
 * This method will read lines from a QIF file, line by line.
 * Each time that this method is called a new QIFElement
 * is returned that contains all of the fields read from that
 * entry.
 *
 * @param r A BufferedReader to read the QIF from, line by line.
 * @return An array of fields read from one line of the QIF file.
 */
public static QIFElement parseQIFLine(BufferedReader r)
{
  boolean done=false;
  QIFElement rtn = new QIFElement();

  try
  {
    while(!done)
    {
      String str = r.readLine();
      if(str==null)
        return null;
      switch(str.charAt(0))
      {
        case '^':
          return rtn;
        case 'P':
          rtn.payee = str.substring(1);
          break;
        case 'D':
          rtn.date = str.substring(1);
          break;
        case 'U':
          rtn.amount = str.substring(1);
          break;
        case 'N':
          rtn.number = str.substring(1);
          break;
        case 'A':
          int i=0;
          for(i=0;i<3;i++)
          {
            if(rtn.address[i]==null)
              break;
          }
          if(i<3)
            rtn.address[i] = str.substring(1);
          break;
      }
    }
  }
  catch(IOException e)
```

```
    {
      return null;
    }
    return null;
}

/**
 * Main entry point.
 *
 * @param args The first command line parameter specifies the URL or filename.
 */
public static void main(String args[])
{
  FileReader f=null;
  BufferedReader r=null;

  if(args.length!=1)
  {
    // display usage
    System.out.println("Usage:");
    System.out.println("javac ParseQIF [qif file or URL to parse]");
    System.exit(0);
  }
  try
  {
    // first try to open it as a file
    f = new FileReader( new File(args[0]) );
      r = new BufferedReader(f);
  }
  catch(FileNotFoundException e)
  {
    // if it fails as a file, try as a URL
    try
    {
      HTTPSocket http = new HTTPSocket();
      http.send(args[0],null);
      StringReader sr = new StringReader(http.getBody());
      r = new BufferedReader(sr);
    }
    catch(UnknownHostException ee)
    {
      // if it fails as a URL too, give up
      System.out.println("Can't open file or URL named: "
        + args[0] + "(" + ee + ")");
      System.exit(0);
    }
    catch(IOException ee)
    {
      System.out.println( e );
      System.exit(0);
    }
```

```java
    }

    // loop through each line and display
    QIFElement a;
    while( (a=parseQIFLine(r)) != null )
    {
     System.out.println("Date:" + a.date );
      System.out.println("Amount:" + a.amount );
      System.out.println("Number:" + a.number );
      System.out.println("Payee:" + a.payee );
      System.out.println("Address Line 1:" + a.address[0] );
      System.out.println("Address Line 2:" + a.address[1] );
      System.out.println("Address Line 3:" + a.address[2] );
      System.out.println("Category:" + a.category );

      System.out.println("------------");
    }

   // close out the file
    try
    {
      if(r!=null)
        r.close();
      if(f!=null)
        f.close();
    }
    catch(IOException e)
    {
      System.out.println("Error:" + e );
      System.exit(0);
    }
  }
}

/**
 * Used to hold one element from a QIF file.
 *
 * @author Jeff Heaton
 * @version 1.0
 */
class QIFElement
{
  public String date;
  public String amount;
  public String number;
  public String payee;
  public String address[] = new String[3];
  public String category;
}
```

The XML File Format

The XML file format is a complex, all encompassing file format that can store nearly any type of data. XML is a standard that is governed by the World Wide Web Consortium (W3C). The complete XML specification can be found at `http://www.w3c.com`, the W3C website.

XML has two advantages over standard text files. First, XML can store hierarchical data, unlike a CSV file, which is a flat file and does not contain any depth to its data. In fact, a CSV file is simply row after row of the same type of data. XML, on the other hand, can support very complex hierarchies. Second, XML is a widely accepted standard, and because of this, there are many third-party tools that are designed to work with it.

XML is very important to bot programs because it is specifically designed to facilitate the transfer of data. As a result, it is much easier for a bot program to glean information from an XML document than from the usual HTML documents that bots must work with. In the future, most information that will be available on the Internet should also be available in the XML format. Currently, however, XML is a new standard, so only a fraction of the Internet is available in XML form. But as the Internet further embraces XML, it will be much easier for bots to access Internet data.

Examining the XML File Format

First, we will examine the format of an XML file. The example file shown below, `testfile.xml`, contains an XML file that stores bank account information. This XML file is arbitrary in that it does not represent any standard. Such files are usually what must be parsed when you are dealing with the Internet. This sample XML file can be seen here:

```
<?xml version="1.0"?>
<BankAccount>
  <Transaction>
    <Date>8/12/01</Date>
    <Amount>-1,200.00</Amount>
    <Number>1002</Number>
    <Payee>Cable TV</Payee>
    <Address1>My Cable Company</Address1>
    <Address2>257 Fresno Street</Address2>
    <Address3>St. Louis, MO 63125</Address3>
    <Category>utility</Category>
  </Transaction>
  <Transaction>
    <Date>6/13/01</Date>
    <Amount>-80.24</Amount>
    <Number>1003</Number>
    <Payee>Computer Store</Payee>
    <Category>Computer Stuff</Category>
  </Transaction>
</BankAccount>
```

Many programs can recognize XML documents. Internet Explorer is one such program. If you were to double-click the `testfile.xml` document, Internet Explorer would be launched to view it. Figure 6.1 shows the `testfile.xml` document being viewed by Internet Explorer.

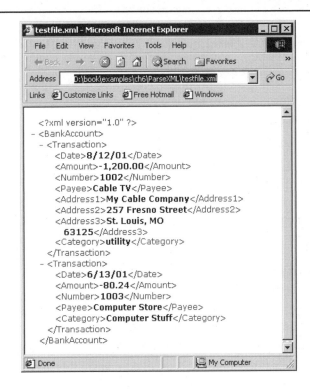

Understanding an XML File

XML looks very similar to HTML. These similarities can be misleading, however. XML and HTML are actually two very different formats. In this section, you will be shown the important elements of an XML file and how they differ from HTML.

XML use a tag structure just like HTML. Tags contain a tag name enclosed by less than (<) and greater than (>) signs. Just as <p> would be a valid HTML tag, it would also be a valid XML tag. However, with XML, there is one very important distinction to be made—it is case sensitive. HTML is not case sensitive, so under HTML, the tags <p> and <P> would mean the same thing. Under XML, however the tags <p> and <P> would have no relationship to each other.

Another similarity between the two languages is that both HTML and XML have ending tags. In both HTML and XML, these ending tags begin with a slash (/). For example, the ending tag to a <p> tag would be a </p> tag in both languages. As you may recall, though, HTML does not require that each beginning tag have a corresponding ending tag. In XML, this ending tag is absolutely required. Another difference is that XML allows you to combine starting and ending tags into one compound tag. Consider the HTML break tag (<br>). There is never an ending </br> because there is no reason to enclose data inside of break tags—a break simply means that a new line should be started. This same tag in XML would then have to be
</br> because every tag must end in XML. XML allows you to combine the beginning and ending tag by putting the slash on the end of the tag name. In this case
</br> would become <br/>; this means that the break tag should be started and stopped at once.

Now that you have beginning and ending tags, a hierarchy of tags can be built. Though HTML tags are slightly hierarchical, XML tags require a strict hierarchy. Under HTML, the following code would be perfectly legal (though perhaps a bit sloppy):

```
<p><b>Hello!</p></b>
```

The above code causes the <p> and <b> tags to overlap. This is not valid in XML. The correct XML would be as follows:

```
<p><b>Hello!</b></p>
```

Another significant difference between the two languages is apparent when you look at the relationship between the tags and their meanings. HTML contains many tags that have an implied meaning. For instance, the <p> tag begins a paragraph, the <img> tag inserts an image, and there are many other tags that perform other formatting tasks. XML, on the other hand, contains no reserved tag names. The meanings of the XML tags that are used are left up to the programmer to decide.

Tags are not the only level at which data can be stored. XML and HTML both allow attributes as well. Attributes are additional values that are stored within a tag. For example, the following tag contains two attributes:

```
<president first="George" last="Washington"/>
```

Each attribute consists of a name, followed by an equal sign (=), and then the quote enclosed value. Though XML requires that all of values be enclosed in quotes, HTML does not. The use of attributes means that there are several different ways to store the same data. For example, the XML shown above could just as easily be written as follows:

```
<president>
  <first>George</first>
  <last>Washington</last>
</president>
```

The choice of which method to employ depends upon the lengths of the fields. The above code has no limit on how long the data stored by the first and last tags can be. Entire paragraphs of information could be stored between the <first> and </first> tags.

As this section shows, HTML and XML are similar in appearance, but quite different in terms of use. The following list summarizes the differences between XML and HTML.

• XML is case sensitive; HTML is not.

- XML requires a strict hierarchy; HTML does not.

- XML allows a single tag to act as both a beginning and ending tag; HTML does not.

- XML requires all attribute values to be enclosed in quotes ("); HTML does not.

XML Parsing Example

Before you proceed, you need to know that if you are using JDK 1.4 or higher, this example should run as is because JDK 1.4 now has built-in XML parsing. If you are using a version of the JDK prior to 1.4, however, you will have to download and install a third party XML parser. This process is described in the "Installing JAXP" sidebar.

Most XML parsers, including the one built into JDK 1.4, follow a common interface, which makes them easily interchangeable. In fact, Sun and Apache make the two most common XML parsers available at no cost. Apache's Xerces is free and is distributed under the GNU license; it can be downloaded from `http://xml.apache.org/xerces-j/index.html`. Sun's JAXP (which can be downloaded from `http://java.sun.com/xml/download.html`) is now included in the reference implementation of the Java API for XML Parsing software, which can be downloaded for free commercial use.

Installing JAXP (Necessary for JDK 1.3 and Lower)

In order to use the `ParseXML.java` example in Listing 6.3, you will need to obtain and install an XML parser. This process is very similar to the one required to install any third-party Java package, such as the Bot package or HTTPS support. If you need more specific information about adding packages/JAR files to the CLASSPATH, please refer to Appendix E, "How to Compile Examples Under Windows" or Appendix F, "How to Compile Examples Under UNIX."

Before you can begin working with JAXP, you must first download it. As mentioned earlier, JAXP can be downloaded from `http://java.sun.com/xml/download.html`. JAXP will be downloaded to a ZIP file that must be extracted to your computer. When you extract it, JAXP will likely install to a directory named `c:\jaxp-1.1`. When you examine this directory you will see three JAR files:

- `crimson.jar`

- `jaxp.jar`

- `xalan.jar`

Remember, you must make these three files be part of the CLASSPATH in order to allow any of the XML examples in this book to run.

If you are using an IDE, such as VisualCafé, you must also configure the IDE to include the three JAR files in the CLASSPATH. You can usually configure this under the project settings.

The example program for this section, ParseXML.java, can be seen in Listing 6.3. This program works in a similar manner to the CSV/QIF parsing examples in that it takes a URL or a filename as a source from which to parse. This program will then display the hierarchy of the XML document being parsed; it is this action that represents an important difference between the XML example and the QIF and CSV examples. Where the QIF and CSV examples have no depth and only present a single level of data, the XML document can embed an unlimited number of layers by using enclosing tags.

The output that results from this program, when you use testfile.xml from the companion CD, is as follows.

```
DOC: nodeName="#document"
  ELEM: nodeName="BankAccount" local="BankAccount"
    TEXT: nodeName="#text" nodeValue=[WS]
    ELEM: nodeName="Transaction" local="Transaction"
      TEXT: nodeName="#text" nodeValue=[WS]
      ELEM: nodeName="Date" local="Date"
        TEXT: nodeName="#text" nodeValue="8/12/01"
      TEXT: nodeName="#text" nodeValue=[WS]
      ELEM: nodeName="Amount" local="Amount"
        TEXT: nodeName="#text" nodeValue="-1,200.00"
      TEXT: nodeName="#text" nodeValue=[WS]
      ELEM: nodeName="Number" local="Number"
        TEXT: nodeName="#text" nodeValue="1002"
      TEXT: nodeName="#text" nodeValue=[WS]
      ELEM: nodeName="Payee" local="Payee"
        TEXT: nodeName="#text" nodeValue="Cable TV"
      TEXT: nodeName="#text" nodeValue=[WS]
      ELEM: nodeName="Address1" local="Address1"
        TEXT: nodeName="#text" nodeValue="My Cable Company"
      TEXT: nodeName="#text" nodeValue=[WS]
      ELEM: nodeName="Address2" local="Address2"
        TEXT: nodeName="#text" nodeValue="257 Fresno Street"
      TEXT: nodeName="#text" nodeValue=[WS]
      ELEM: nodeName="Address3" local="Address3"
        TEXT: nodeName="#text" nodeValue="St. Louis, MO 63125"
      TEXT: nodeName="#text" nodeValue=[WS]
      ELEM: nodeName="Category" local="Category"
        TEXT: nodeName="#text" nodeValue="utility"
      TEXT: nodeName="#text" nodeValue=[WS]
    TEXT: nodeName="#text" nodeValue=[WS]
    ELEM: nodeName="Transaction" local="Transaction"
      TEXT: nodeName="#text" nodeValue=[WS]
      ELEM: nodeName="Date" local="Date"
        TEXT: nodeName="#text" nodeValue="6/13/01"
      TEXT: nodeName="#text" nodeValue=[WS]
```

```
ELEM: nodeName="Amount" local="Amount"
  TEXT: nodeName="#text" nodeValue="-80.24"
TEXT: nodeName="#text" nodeValue=[WS]
ELEM: nodeName="Number" local="Number"
  TEXT: nodeName="#text" nodeValue="1003"
TEXT: nodeName="#text" nodeValue=[WS]
ELEM: nodeName="Payee" local="Payee"
  TEXT: nodeName="#text" nodeValue="Computer Store"
TEXT: nodeName="#text" nodeValue=[WS]
ELEM: nodeName="Category" local="Category"
  TEXT: nodeName="#text" nodeValue="Computer Stuff"
TEXT: nodeName="#text" nodeValue=[WS]
TEXT: nodeName="#text" nodeValue=[WS]
```

The following code shows how to produce the previously mentioned output. By using the DOM a relatively simple program can parse the complex XML format.

Listing 6.3   **Parsing XML (*ParseXML.java*)**

```java
import java.net.*;
import javax.xml.parsers.*;
import org.xml.sax.*;
import org.xml.sax.helpers.*;
import org.w3c.dom.*;
import com.heaton.bot.*;
import java.io.*;

/**
 * Example from Chapter 6
 *
 * This example program parses an XML file. This file
 * may come from either the Internet or a local drive.
 *
 * @author Jeff Heaton
 * @version 1.0
 */
public class ParseXML
{
  /** Current indentation */
  static private int _indent = 0;

  /**
   * Display common data for every type of element.
   *
   * @param n The node.
   */
  static private void printlnCommon(Node n)
  {
    System.out.print(" nodeName=\"" + n.getNodeName() + "\"");
```

```java
      String val = n.getNamespaceURI();
      if (val != null)
        System.out.print(" uri=\"" + val + "\"");

      val = n.getPrefix();
      if (val != null)
        System.out.print(" pre=\"" + val + "\"");

      val = n.getLocalName();
      if (val != null)
        System.out.print(" local=\"" + val + "\"");

      val = n.getNodeValue();
      if (val != null)
      {
        System.out.print(" nodeValue=");
        if (val.trim().equals(""))
        {
        // Whitespace
          System.out.print("[WS]");
        }
        else
        {
          System.out.print("\"" + n.getNodeValue() + "\"");
        }
      }
      System.out.println();
    }

    /**
     * Indent the proper number of spaces for the display.
     */
    static private void doIndentation()
    {
      for (int i = 0; i < _indent; i++)
        System.out.print("  ");
    }

    /**
     * Display an idividual node. Called recursively.
     *
     * @param n
     */
    static private void display(Node n)
    {
      // Indent to the current level before printing anything
      doIndentation();

      int type = n.getNodeType();
      switch (type)
      {
        case Node.ATTRIBUTE_NODE:
```

```
      System.out.print("ATTR:");
      printlnCommon(n);
      break;
  case Node.CDATA_SECTION_NODE:
      System.out.print("CDATA:");
      printlnCommon(n);
      break;
  case Node.COMMENT_NODE:
      System.out.print("COMM:");
      printlnCommon(n);
      break;
  case Node.DOCUMENT_FRAGMENT_NODE:
      System.out.print("DOC_FRAG:");
      printlnCommon(n);
      break;
  case Node.DOCUMENT_NODE:
      System.out.print("DOC:");
      printlnCommon(n);
      break;
  case Node.DOCUMENT_TYPE_NODE:
      System.out.print("DOC_TYPE:");
      printlnCommon(n);

      // Print entities if any
      NamedNodeMap nodeMap = ((DocumentType)n).getEntities();
      _indent += 2;
      for (int i = 0; i < nodeMap.getLength(); i++)
        display((Entity)nodeMap.item(i));

      _indent -= 2;
      break;
  case Node.ELEMENT_NODE:
      System.out.print("ELEM:");
      printlnCommon(n);
      NamedNodeMap atts = n.getAttributes();
      _indent += 2;
      for (int i = 0; i < atts.getLength(); i++)
        display( (Node) atts.item(i) );
      _indent -= 2;
      break;
  case Node.ENTITY_NODE:
      System.out.print("ENT:");
      printlnCommon(n);
      break;
  case Node.ENTITY_REFERENCE_NODE:
      System.out.print("ENT_REF:");
      printlnCommon(n);
      break;
  case Node.NOTATION_NODE:
      System.out.print("NOTATION:");
      printlnCommon(n);
      break;
```

```java
        case Node.PROCESSING_INSTRUCTION_NODE:
          System.out.print("PROC_INST:");
          printlnCommon(n);
          break;
        case Node.TEXT_NODE:
          System.out.print("TEXT:");
          printlnCommon(n);
          break;
        default:
          System.out.print("UNSUPPORTED NODE: " + type);
          printlnCommon(n);
          break;
        }

    // Print children if any
    _indent++;
    for (Node child = n.getFirstChild(); child != null;
      child = child.getNextSibling())
      display(child);

    _indent--;
}


/**
 * Main entry point.
 *
 * @param args The first command line parameter specifies the URL or filename.
 */
public static void main(String args[])
{
  InputStream f=null;

  if(args.length!=1)
  {
    // display usage
    System.out.println("Usage:");
    System.out.println("javac ParseXML [qif file or URL to parse]");
    System.exit(0);
  }
  try
  {
    // first try and open it as a file
    f = new FileInputStream( new File(args[0]) );
  }
  catch(FileNotFoundException e)
  {
    // if it fails as a file, try as a URL
    try
    {
      HTTPSocket http = new HTTPSocket();
      http.send(args[0],null);
```

```
      f = new StringBufferInputStream(http.getBody());
    }
    catch(UnknownHostException ee)
    {
      // if it fails as a URL too, give up
      System.out.println("Can't open file or URL named: "
        + args[0] + "(" + ee + ")");
      System.exit(0);
    }
    catch(IOException ee)
    {
      System.out.println( e );
      System.exit(0);
    }
  }

  // parse the XML
  try
  {
    DocumentBuilderFactory dbf =
      DocumentBuilderFactory.newInstance();

    DocumentBuilder db = null;
    db = dbf.newDocumentBuilder();

    Document doc = null;
    doc = db.parse(f);

    // Parse the document
    display(doc);
  }
  catch(Exception e)
  {
    System.out.println("Error: " + e );
  }

  // close out the file
  try
  {
    if(f!=null)
      f.close();
  }
  catch(IOException e)
  {
    System.out.println("Error:" + e );
    System.exit(0);
  }
}

}
```

NOTE   Because there aren't any individual classes to handle each of these formats that are part of the Bot package, this chapter doesn't introduce any new functionality in the Bot package, nor are the contents of this chapter directly tied to the implementation of a bot. Because of this, this chapter contains no "Under the Hood" section. The CSV, QIF, and XML parsing classes were already explained earlier in this chapter, under their respective sections.

Summary

Bot programs will encounter a wide array of data formats including CSV, QIF, and XML, which were covered in this chapter, and the HTML format, which was covered in Chapter 4, "HTML Parsing." This chapter showed you how to parse CSV, QIF and XML formatted data.

The CSV file format is a common file format for storing spreadsheet or database information. CSV files are simple flat text files that can be easily parsed by a Java program.

The QIF file format was introduced by Quicken as a standard way to export data from the Quicken product. Many financial websites give you the option of downloading online statements in QIF format. If you are writing a bot that deals with financial sites, you will likely encounter the QIF file format.

XML is a relatively new file format to be used on the Internet, but it is becoming more and more popular. This file format allows for hierarchical files to be stored in a form that is widely accessible, thus, more Internet data is becoming available as XML. In order to support XML, you usually need to have a document object model (DOM) package installed.

As we move forward, we will continue to explore the technologies that we will eventually need to construct a bot program. The last of these prerequisite technologies, cookies, are the focus of the next chapter.

CHAPTER 7

Exploring Cookies

- What are cookies used for?

- The format of a cookie

- Parsing cookies

- Using session cookies

- Using persistent cookies

In the early days of the Web, sites merely presented information and were not interactive—they were just static collections of documents for users to view. For these non-interactive websites, a completely stateless connection to the web server was all that was required. Even now, as a web server goes through the process of receiving and returning requests, it retains no knowledge of which client requested what, which means that it is still completely stateless. As a result, the web server can't distinguish between a series of incoming requests from several different users. All that the web server sees is a string of incoming requests that must be filled. However, with the advent of online transactions and web server security, the ability to store the current state became required.

Before we see how a web server maintains state, we should first discuss what exactly is meant by state. A system that is *stateless* keeps no memory of the prior request. Each request is treated as a completely new request and it will be filled in exactly the same manner as any other identical request. *State*, on the other hand, means that the server maintains a memory from previous requests. As a result, initial requests can greatly affect subsequent requests. For example, when the user logs on, the rest of the site becomes available. The change in state from "no known user" to a "known user" affects how the rest of the site will respond.

Web servers maintain such state through the use of *cookies*. A cookie is a small amount of information that a web server sends back to the web browser. The web browser then retransmits that information as part of each subsequent request to that web server. In this manner, cookies allow the web server to tag incoming users so that subsequent requests from that same user will be recognized. This process allows the state to be stored primarily in the web browser. Permanent cookies can be useful because they allow the web browser to remember certain values that the user has entered. For example, if a site always prompts a user for their user ID, that user ID can be stored in a permanent cookie so that when the user returns, the user ID can automatically be filled in.

In this chapter, you will learn how cookies are used and what functionality is provided by the Bot package to facilitate their handling. You will find that cookies are easy to use, especially if you only want to know how to use the bot classes and you aren't interested in understanding their inner workings. If this is the case, you simply instruct the Bot package to begin processing cookies, and that is all that is required. However, if you are interested in how cookies work, continue reading, because this chapter will not only show you how to enable cookie processing, it will also discuss the more complex details of how the cookie processing was implemented in the Bot package.

Examining Cookies

It is a web browser's job to maintain cookies. As you move through different websites, you accumulate these small packets of information that the web server instructs your browser to keep. In fact, most users will find that they have many cookies stored in a web browser such as Internet Explorer.

Cookies and Internet Explorer

Internet Explorer gives you several tools to help you manage your cookies (as do other browsers). If you are like the majority of users, up until this point, you probably never looked at these cookies or knew about these tools. You probably just allowed the cookies to silently do their job.

The Bot package will allow you to follow this same usage pattern. If you do not want to learn about how cookies work, you only need to call the setUseCookies method of the HTTPSocket class. By default, the Bot package does not use cookies, but by calling setUseCookies with the parameter of true, you enable cookie processing. In addition, to create an HTTPSocket object that support cookies, you would just use the following code.

```
_http = new HTTPSocket();
_http.setUseCookies(true,true);
```

If you are curious about these cookies, though, start by exploring how they are used and where they are stored in Internet Explorer. In Internet Explorer, you can view the stored cookies by selecting the Tools menu item, and then choosing Internet Options. You will be presented with a tabbed dialog box that displays configuration settings. Click the General tag, and then click the Settings button in the Temporary Internet Files section. This will give you a screen that allows you to manage your cookies and cached files. If you click the View Files button, you will see a list of all your cached files and cookies. Figure 7.1 shows some of the cookies on my system.

FIGURE 7.1:

Cookies in Internet Explorer

The data stored in individual cookies can also be viewed through Internet Explorer. By right clicking a cookie and choosing the View option, you can see its contents. Figure 7.2 shows the contents of one of my cookies.

All of these cookies contain information that various websites store on your computer. These sites store cookies for a variety of reasons; for instance, some store cookies so that they can remember your e-mail or login when you return to the site, and some use cookies to assist banner advertising.

NOTE   Cookie support is one feature that is noticeably absent from Java's `URLConnection` object. As a result, all cookie support must be provided by the program and not by the Java classes. The Bot package contains routines to do this.

The Cookie RFC

Like most Internet standards, cookies are defined in an RFC document (RFC 2109). Before this RFC was made official in 1997, other methods were used to store cookies. Most of these other methods are no longer used, however, and all modern browsers support RFC 2109 cookies.

Receiving Cookies from the Web Server

To create a cookie, the web server must send the `Set-Cookie` command as part of its HTTP header. A web browser receiving this command will then begin returning this cookie as part of all future requests to this server.

The following shows the syntax for `Set-Cookie` command sent by the web server:

```
Set-Cookie: name=value;Version = "1"; ...other values, more cookies...
```

The above Set-Cookie server header begins with the Set-Cookie header followed by a comma-separated list of one or more cookies. The definition of each actual cookie begins with a name-value pair.

Immediately after this main name-value pair appears, a zero, or more semicolon-separated name-value pairs, appears; these make up the attributes of the cookie. The `name=value` attribute-value pair must come first in each cookie because this is what is required by the RFC. The other pairs, if present, can occur in any order. It is important, however, that the same attribute not occur more than once in the same cookie.

The following are the required standard attributes for a Set-Cookie header:

name=value (required)   The cookie's name, which is specified by the value. Names that begin with $ are reserved for other uses and should not be used. The value of the cookie can be anything of meaning to the server. This name is not normally seen by the user.

Version=version (required)   The Version attribute, which is a decimal integer. This version identifies the version of cookie being used. This chapter is describing the current version 1, Version=1, cookies. Vesion 1 cookies are the type that is recognized by all current web browsers.

In addition to these required attributes, there are also some optional attributes that can be specified for the cookie. They provide additional information for the web browser.

Comment=comment (optional)   The Cookie attribute lets original servers document their intended use of a cookie because these cookies can contain private information about users. The users can then examine this information to decide whether they want to initiate or continue a session with this cookie.

Domain=domain (optional)   The Domain attribute specifies to which URL the cookie belongs. For example, specifying the value of .mysite.com would specify the entire site mysite.com. This would mean that the cookie would be valid for any address that ends in mysite.com, whether it http://www.mysite.com or http://www3.mysite.com, for example.

Max-Age=seconds (optional)   The Max-Age attribute defines how long a cookie lasts; the units of measure are seconds. The number that represents these seconds must be a decimal non-negative integer. The web browser should get rid of the cookie after this amount of time elapses. If zero is given as this value, the browser discards the cookie right away.

Path=path (optional)   This attribute represents the subset of URLs to which the specified cookie belongs.

Secure (optional)   When the secure attribute is specified with no value, it tells the web browser that it should use only secure ways of contacting the server whenever it returns the specified cookie. The web browser may decide what security level is appropriate for cookies it considers secure; the user's input may be what determines this. The Secure attribute only specifies that reasonable attempts should be made to keep this cookie secure.

Returning Cookies to the Web Server

When a web browser sends a request to a web server, it also sends a Cookie request header at the same time if it has cookies that it received from that server. The format of this request is:

```
Cookie: NAME=VALUE;PATH=[path];DOMAIN=[domain];version=1
```

The above line specifies a typical version 1 cookie. The values that are actually specified are taken from the Set-Cookie header that originally created this cookie (described in the previous section). The values for the PATH and DOMAIN attributes are taken directly from the path and domain that were specified by the Set-Cookie command that the web server originally sent to create this cookie. If no path was specified, the PATH attribute should be omitted from the Cookie request header. Likewise, if no domain was specified, this attribute should also be omitted. Version 1 should be specified because it is the cookie version most widely used.

There is never a Comment attribute in the Cookie request header that corresponds to the one in the Set-Cookie response header. This is because the comment originated from the server, and the server has no reason to see this same comment back again from the browser. Also, the web browser never returns the comment information to the web server.

The following rules apply when you need to choose acceptable cookie values from among those cookies that the web browser has.

Domain   The web server's fully qualified hostname must start with the same address as the Domain attribute of the cookie. For example, the domain yahoo.com would match yahoo.com, mail.yahoo.com, and www.yahoo.com, but it would not match yahoo.net.

Path   The Path attribute of the cookie must match the prefix of the URI that was requested. For example, if the path /site/images were specified, this would include /site/images/gifs as well.

Max-Age   Expired cookies should be discarded. If this happens like it should, they won't be forwarded to a web server.

Multiple cookies could satisfy the criteria above. If this is the case, they are organized in the Cookie header so that the ones with the more specific Path attributes come before those with less specific ones.

> **NOTE**   To maintain backward compatibility with web browsers and servers that may support an older version of cookies, a semicolon (;) is always used as the separator in the Cookie header. However, web servers should also accept commas (,) that are functioning as separators between cookie values. By doing this, compatibility with future web servers and browsers will be ensured.

Appearance of a Cookie

We will now take a look at what an actual cookie looks like. To create a cookie, the web server will need to issue the set-cookie command. The set-cookie command is sent as part of the other HTTP headers. Here you can see such a request being fulfilled by a web server. JSP pages typically set a cookie to maintain state information. You can see the web server creating a cookie here:

```
HTTP/1.0 200 OK
Content-Type: text/html;charset=8859_1
Set-Cookie: JSESSIONID=7f7s2tif51;Path=/
Servlet-Engine: Tomcat Web Server/3.2.1 (JSP 1.1; Servlet 2.2; Java
```

Once the above response has been received from the web server, all future requests to the web server will contain the newly created cookie. The web browser responds with the following POST when a form is completed and sent back to the web server:

```
POST /index.jsp HTTP/1.1
Accept: image/gif, image/x-xbitmap, image/jpeg, image/pjpeg, application/vnd.ms-
    powerpoint, application/vnd.ms-excel, application/msword, */*
Referer: http://127.0.0.1:8080/index.jsp
Accept-Language: en-us
Content-Type: application/x-www-form-urlencoded
Accept-Encoding: gzip, deflate
User-Agent: Mozilla/4.0 (compatible; MSIE 5.01; Windows NT 5.0)
Host: 127.0.0.1:8080
Content-Length: 22
Connection: Keep-Alive
Cookie: JSESSIONID=7f7s2tif51

UID=&PWD=&action=login
```

Any subsequent request will now carry the cookie header when it is sent back to this server (see the example below).

A Typical Cookie Exchange

Now that you are familiar with the cookie request/return process and you have seen what a cookie looks like, you will probably find a typical example of how cookies can be used helpful. In this example, most of the details of the request and response headers are not shown. You should just assume that the web browser didn't initially have any cookies stored.

1. Browser to server

```
POST /estore/login HTTP/1.1
[form data]
```

In this step, the user is responding to a web server form that allows the user to log in. The user posts back its identification information, such as user ID and password.

2. Server to browser

```
HTTP/1.1 200 OK
Set-Cookie: Customer="jsmith"; Version="1"; Path="/estore"
```

The user has been identified, so the web server sends back a cookie, which is used to identify the user to the web browser. There is now a cookie named `Customer` that contains the value of `jsmith`.

3. Browser to server

   ```
   POST /estore/pickitem HTTP/1.1
   Cookie: $Version="1"; Customer="jheaton"; $Path="/estore" [form data]
   ```

   The web browser has accepted the cookie that was set in step 2. This cookie will now be sent in all future requests. The user now selects an item to add to a shopping cart and posts to `/estore/pickitem`.

4. Server to browser

   ```
   HTTP/1.1 200 OK
   Set-Cookie: Part_Number="ITEM3030"; Version="1"; Path="/estore"
   ```

   The web server accepts the request to add an item 3030 to the shopping cart. The server sends a `Set-Cookie` command to the browser to request that the web browser adds this cookie.

5. Browser to server

   ```
   POST /estore/shipping HTTP/1.1
   Cookie: $Version="1";
   Customer="jsmith"; $Path="/estore";
   Part_Number="ITEM3030"; $Path="/estore" [form data]
   ```

   The web browser has accepted the `Part_Number` cookie and it now adds it to the list of cookies to be transmitted with each request. The user now proceeds to a new screen to select a shipping method.

6. Server to browser

   ```
   HTTP/1.1 200 OK
   Set-Cookie: Shipping="ShipExpress"; Version="1"; Path="/estore"
   ```

   The server sends a `Set-Cookie` request to ask that a cookie named `Shipping` be created and assigned the value of `ShipExpress`.

7. Browser to server

   ```
   POST /estore/process HTTP/1.1
   Cookie: $Version="1";
   Customer="SOME_USER"; $Path="/estore";
   Part_Number="Rocket_Launcher_0001"; $Path="/estore";
   Shipping="ShipExpress"; $Path="/estore"
   [form data]
   ```

   The server accepts the new `Shipping` cookie and adds it to the list of cookies that are being sent with each request. The user now proceeds to a screen to complete the order by requesting the `/estore/process` page.

8. Server to browser

```
HTTP/1.1 200 OK
```

The server sends an order complete screen, and the transaction is finished.

In this process, you saw the web browser make a series of requests to the web server. After each, the browser would receive a new cookie from the server. All of the cookies had the same Path and Domain attributes. And because all of these request URLs had a prefix of /estore, which matches the Path attribute, each request contained all the cookies received so far.

> **NOTE** Only the HTTP protocol remains completely stateless. In the previous examples, the web server is likely remembering information associated with that particular user. Though cookies are an attempt to keep the web server completely stateless, many web servers use cookies to refer to "session information" which is technically actual state information that is stored by the web server.

Handling Session and Persistent Cookies

There are two main types of cookies: *session cookies* last only as long as the browser is open; *persistent cookies* remain indefinitely. Most of the cookies that have been discussed so far are session cookies.

Bots are generally concerned with session cookies only. The bot does not generally care about persistent cookies, which keep cookie values from one session to the next. This is because of the way a bot functions; the bot needs to log in, get its data, and get back out. The next session will be a completely new session for the bot.

The Bot package provides the ability to process both session and persistent cookies through the use of the setUseCookie method, which is provided by the HTTP class. The setUseCookie method accepts two Boolean values. The first value determines if the Bot package should support session cookies. The second specifies if the bot should handle persistent cookies. The Bot package doesn't support either type of cookie by default.

Also, even if the Bot package is set to handle persistent cookies, it does not keep them after the program is terminated. This is a feature that could be added relatively easy, but it is not required for most bot operations.

> **WARNING** Bots that visit large numbers of sites should not usually enable cookie processing. This is because storing cookies from large numbers of sites can present an unneeded drag on system resources.

Examining Cookies with *ViewURLCookie*

In Chapter 2, "Examining the Hypertext Transfer Protocol," we looked at an example program called ViewURL, which displayed header and body information for a URL. This example program, shown in Listing 7.1, takes the ViewURL of Chapter 2 and extends it so that it is cookie aware. By using this new example, called ViewURLCookie, you can examine any cookies that are returned by a given URL.

This program prompts the user for a URL. The URL is then visited and all of the HTTP headers and cookies, as well as the body of the request, are displayed. You can see the results of this program in Figure 7.3.

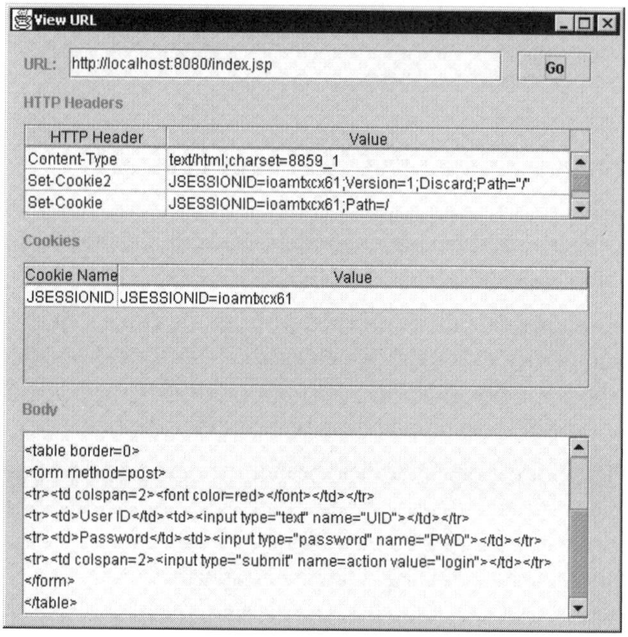

FIGURE 7.3:

The display of what results from the ViewURLCookie example program

Listing 7.1   **View Cookies (*ViewURLCookie.java*)**

```
import java.awt.*;
import javax.swing.*;
import javax.swing.table.*;
import com.heaton.bot.*;

/**
 * An example from Chapter 7.
 *
 * This application displays a dialog box that
```

```
 * allows the user to specify any URL. This URL
 * is requested, using the Bot package, and displayed
 * in the dialog box. Both the body and HTTP headers
 * are displayed, as well as the cookie information.
 * This example is very similar to the ViewURL example
 * from Chapter 2, except this version works with cookies.
 *
 * @author Jeff Heaton
 * @version 1.0
 */
public class ViewURLCookie extends javax.swing.JFrame
{

  /**
    * The HTTP connection used by this application.
    */
  HTTP _http;

    /**
      * The constructor. This method sets up all the components needed by this
class.
      * A new HTTPSocket object is also constructed to manange the connection.
      */
    public ViewURLCookie()
    {
      _http = new HTTPSocket();
      _http.setUseCookies(true,true);
      //{{INIT_CONTROLS
      setTitle("View URL");
      getContentPane().setLayout(null);
      setSize(490,462);
      setVisible(false);
      _pane2.setOpaque(true);
      getContentPane().add(_pane2);
      _pane2.setBounds(12,312,456,144);
      _body.setEditable(false);
      _pane2.getViewport().add(_body);
      _body.setBounds(0,0,453,141);
      _pane1.setOpaque(true);
      getContentPane().add(_pane1);
      _pane1.setBounds(12,72,456,72);
      _pane1.getViewport().add(_headers);
      _headers.setBounds(0,0,453,0);
      _label3.setText("Body");
      getContentPane().add(_label3);
      _label3.setBounds(12,288,456,12);
      _label1.setText("URL:");
      getContentPane().add(_label1);
      _label1.setBounds(12,12,36,24);
      _url.setText("http://www.jeffheaton.com");
      getContentPane().add(_url);
```

```
        _url.setBounds(48,12,348,24);
        _go.setText("Go");
        _go.setActionCommand("Go");
        getContentPane().add(_go);
        _go.setBounds(408,12,60,24);
        _label2.setText("HTTP Headers");
        getContentPane().add(_label2);
        _label2.setBounds(12,48,384,12);
        JLabel1.setText("Cookies");
        getContentPane().add(JLabel1);
        JLabel1.setBounds(12,156,456,12);
        JScrollPane1.setOpaque(true);
        getContentPane().add(JScrollPane1);
        JScrollPane1.setBounds(12,180,456,96);
        JScrollPane1.getViewport().add(_cookies);
        _cookies.setBounds(0,0,453,0);
        //}}

        //{{REGISTER_LISTENERS
        SymWindow aSymWindow = new SymWindow();
        this.addWindowListener(aSymWindow);
        SymAction lSymAction = new SymAction();
        _go.addActionListener(lSymAction);
        //}}
    }

    /**
     * Set the visibility of this window.
     *
     * @param b true for visible, false for invisible
     */
    public void setVisible(boolean b)
    {
        if (b)
            setLocation(50, 50);
        super.setVisible(b);
    }

    /**
     * The entry point for this application.
     *
     * @param args Arguments are not used by this program. Required for proper
    main signature.
     */
    static public void main(String args[])
    {
        (new ViewURLCookie()).setVisible(true);
    }

    /**
     * Called to add notification handlers.
```

```
     */
    public void addNotify()
    {
        // Record the size of the window prior to calling parents addNotify.
        Dimension size = getSize();

        super.addNotify();

        if (frameSizeAdjusted)
            return;
        frameSizeAdjusted = true;

        // Adjust size of frame according to the insets
        Insets insets = getInsets();
        setSize(insets.left + insets.right + size.width, insets.top +
insets.bottom + size.height);
    }

    /**
     * Put here by VisualCafe.
     */
    // Used by addNotify
    boolean frameSizeAdjusted = false;

    //{{DECLARE_CONTROLS
    javax.swing.JScrollPane _pane2 = new javax.swing.JScrollPane();
    javax.swing.JTextArea _body = new javax.swing.JTextArea();
    javax.swing.JScrollPane _pane1 = new javax.swing.JScrollPane();
    javax.swing.JTable _headers = new javax.swing.JTable();
    javax.swing.JLabel _label3 = new javax.swing.JLabel();
    javax.swing.JLabel _label1 = new javax.swing.JLabel();
    javax.swing.JTextField _url = new javax.swing.JTextField();
    javax.swing.JButton _go = new javax.swing.JButton();
    javax.swing.JLabel _label2 = new javax.swing.JLabel();
    javax.swing.JLabel JLabel1 = new javax.swing.JLabel();
    javax.swing.JScrollPane JScrollPane1 = new
javax.swing.JScrollPane();
    javax.swing.JTable _cookies = new javax.swing.JTable();
    //}}

    /**
     * Class created by VisualCafe
     */
    class SymWindow extends java.awt.event.WindowAdapter
    {
        public void windowClosed(java.awt.event.WindowEvent event)
        {
            Object object = event.getSource();
            if (object == ViewURLCookie.this)
                ViewURLCookie_windowClosed(event);
        }
```

```
        public void windowClosing(java.awt.event.WindowEvent event)
        {
            Object object = event.getSource();
            if (object == ViewURLCookie.this)
                ViewURLCookie_WindowClosing(event);
        }
    }

    /**
     * Called when the window closes.
     *
     * @param event The event.
     */
    void
    ViewURLCookie_WindowClosing(java.awt.event.WindowEvent event)
    {
        // Hide the Frame
        setVisible(false);

        // Free the system resources
        dispose();
    }
    //{{DECLARE_MENUS
    //}}

    /**
     * Class created by VisualCafe
     */
    class SymAction implements java.awt.event.ActionListener
    {
        public void actionPerformed(java.awt.event.ActionEvent event)
        {
            Object object = event.getSource();
            if (object == _go)
                Go_actionPerformed(event);
        }
    }

    /**
     * Called when the Go button is clicked.
     *
     * @param event The event.
     */
    void Go_actionPerformed(java.awt.event.ActionEvent event)
    {
        try
        {
            _http.send(_url.getText(),null);
            _body.setText(_http.getBody());
            _url.setText(_http.getURL());

            // handle the headers
```

```
TableModel dataModelHeader = new AbstractTableModel()
{
  public int getColumnCount() { return 2; }
  public int getRowCount() { return
_http.getServerHeaders().length();}
  public String getColumnName(int columnIndex)
  {
    switch(columnIndex)
    {
      case 0:return "HTTP Header";
      case 1:return "Value";
    }
    return "";
  }
  public Object getValueAt(int row, int col)
  {
    if(col==0)
      return
_http.getServerHeaders().get(row).getName();
    else
      return
_http.getServerHeaders().get(row).getValue();
  }
};
_headers.setModel(dataModelHeader);
_headers.sizeColumnsToFit(0);

  // handle the cookies
TableModel dataModelCookie = new AbstractTableModel()
{
  public int getColumnCount() { return 2; }
  public int getRowCount() { return
_http.getCookies().length();}
  public String getColumnName(int columnIndex)
  {
    switch(columnIndex)
    {
      case 0:return "Cookie Name";
      case 1:return "Value";
    }
    return "";
  }
  public Object getValueAt(int row, int col)
  {
    if(col==0)
      return _http.getCookies().get(row).getName();
    else
      return _http.getCookies().get(row).toString();
  }
};
_cookies.setModel(dataModelCookie);
_cookies.sizeColumnsToFit(0);
```

```
    }
    catch(Exception e)
    {
      _body.setText(e.toString());
    }
  }

  /**
   * Called once the window closes.
   *
   * @param event The event.
   */
  void ViewURLCookie_windowClosed(java.awt.event.WindowEvent event)
  {
      System.exit(0);

  }
}
```

As mentioned earlier, most of the code shown in Listing 7.1 is similar to the ViewURL example shown in Chapter 2. Only a few additional lines were added to support cookies; we will examine these new lines now.

The first two lines of the ViewURLCookie example create a new HTTPSocket object, and then they instruct it to use both persistent and session cookies.

```
_http = new HTTPSocket();
_http.setUseCookies(true,true);
```

The primary difference between the example Listing 7.1 and the ViewURL example of Chapter 2 is the addition of this setUseCookies method. By passing in both parameters as true, the program is instructed to track both session and persistent cookies. With the addition of this line, the program now supports cookies. The only additional code necessary for this program is the code used to display the cookies, shown here:

```
        // handle the cookies
        TableModel dataModelCookie = new AbstractTableModel()
        {
          public int getColumnCount() { return 2; }
          public int getRowCount() { return
        _http.getCookies().length();}
          public String getColumnName(int columnIndex)
          {
            switch(columnIndex)
            {
              case 0:return "Cookie Name";
              case 1:return "Value";
            }
            return "";
          }
```

```
        public Object getValueAt(int row, int col)
        {
          if(col==0)
            return _http.getCookies().get(row).getName();
          else
            return _http.getCookies().get(row).toString();
        }
      };
      _cookies.setModel(dataModelCookie);
      _cookies.sizeColumnsToFit(0);
```

This causes the cookies to be displayed in much the same manner as the HTTP headers in Chapter 2 would be. For example, an `AbstractTableModel` object is constructed that will feed values to a Swing `Jtable`, and the `getCookies` method is used to access a listing of cookies. This returns an `AttributeList` that allows you to retrieve the name and values of the cookies. Also, column 0 is used to store the names, while column 1 stores the values of the cookies.

This example shows the basics of how to use the Bot package's cookie handling capabilities. Now you will be shown the remaining cookie related classes provided by the Bot package.

Bot Classes for Cookie Processing

There are several classes provided in the Bot package that handle the low-level details of cookie processing. Generally, you will not need to be concerned with these classes unless you seek to extend the functionality of the Bot package's cookie handling. For example, you may want to store persistent cookies to disk so that they can be used when your Bot program is run again in the future.

Using the *Parse* Class

The `Parse` class is used to parse out name-value pairs. Name-value pairs were first introduced in Chapter 2, where they were used to store HTTP headers. The Bot package classes that Chapter 2 introduced to store these header were the `Attribute` and `AttributeList` classes. To store such headers, each name-value pair is stored in a single `Attribute` object, and a collection of these name-value pairings is stored in an `AttributeList` object. After these have been stored, in order to parse cookies into their name-value pairs, the `Parse` class will be used. It will examine the cookie and generate an `AttributeList` object that contains all of the attributes for a cookie.

This chapter uses the `Parse` class to parse cookies. Because a cookie is a collection of name-value pairs, the `Parse` class is particularly well suited for this purpose. As you will see in Chapter 8, "Building a Spider," the `Parse` class can also be used to parse HTML.

The following are the methods contained in this class, each of which is followed by an example of how it might appear in code:

The addAttribute method   Adds a newly parsed attribute (name-value pair) to the list.

```
public static boolean addAttribute(char ch)
```

The eatWhiteSpace method   Returns true if ch is either a tab carriage return, space, or line feed.

```
public static boolean eatWhiteSpace(char ch)
```

The eof method   Returns true if you have reached the end of the text to be parsed.

```
public static boolean eof()
```

The getParseDelim method   Gets the delimiter for the value just parsed. The *delimiter* is the character that encloses the value portion of a name-value pair. The delimiter is usually a quote (″) or an apostrophe (′). The name value pair a="value" uses the quote as a delimiter.

```
String getParseDelim()
```

The getParseName method   Returns the name just parsed.

```
String getParseName();
```

The getParseValue method   Returns the value just parsed.

```
String getParseValue()
```

The isWhiteSpace method   Returns true if ch is a tab carriage return, space, or line feed. Unlike the eatWhiteSpace method, this method only tests for the presence of white space; it does not actually delete white space.

```
public static boolean isWhiteSpace(char ch)
```

The parseAttributeName method   Parses the attribute name from a name-value pair.

```
public void parseAttributeName()
```

The parseAttributeValue method   Parses the attribute value from a name-value pair.

```
public void parseAttributeValue()
```

The setParseDelim method   Sets the delimiter for the value. This should usually not be set because the class will automatically determine this value.

```
void setParseDelim(String s)
```

The setParseName method   Sets the name portion of the most recently parsed name-value pair.

```
void setParseName(String s)
```

The `setParseValue` method   Sets the value portion of the most recently parsed name-value pair.

```
void setParseValue(String s)
```

Using the *CookieParse* Class

The `CookieParse` class is a descendant of the `Parse` class. The `CookieParse` class contains the entire cookie-specific code necessary to parse the name-value pairs associated with cookies. The following methods are included in the `CookieParse` class.

The get method   This method actually parses the cookie.

```
public boolean get()
```

The `parseAttributeValue` method   This method is a special version of the `parse-Attribute` method, which is used to parse the cookie. This method is not usually called directly.

```
public void parseAttributeValue()
```

The `toString` method   This method converts this cookie to a string to be sent as an HTTP header.

```
public String toString()
```

Under the Hood

This chapter showed you the format of cookies and how to use the Bot package to process them. Now you will be shown how the Bot package classes, used for cookie handling, were constructed. This discussion begins with how a cookie is parsed, and how the `Parse` class was constructed.

Constructing the *Parse* Class

The `Parse` class is a generic class that is meant to parse HTML as well as cookies. But because the Swing classes now handle HTML parsing, the `Parse` class only has to handle cookie parsing.

In order to parse, the `Parse` class must be provided with a `StringBuffer` object, which is stored in the _source property of this class. This `StringBuffer` object should contain the text of the cookie to be parsed. Once all of the parsing methods called in this class are loaded, they will operate on this `StringBuffer` object.

The `Parse` class, shown in Listing 7.2, class is a descendant of the `AttributeList` class, which was discussed in Chapter 2. As a result, each attribute that it encounters is stored into this list as an `Attribute` object. Because `AttributeList`, in turn, descends from the `Attribute` class, you can create lists of this class. This is useful because you may need to store lists of CookieParse objects. A list of cookies, stored as individual CookieParse classes, could be stored in a single AttributeList object. This is how the HTTP object stores collections of cookies. When you call the getCookiesMethod of the HTTP class, as shown in the ViewURL-Cookie example, you are returned an AttributeList object that contains any cookies that were retrieved by the last use of that HTTP object.

Though the Parse class is only used to parse cookies, it is designed to be able to parse any sort of attribute list of name-value pairs. The GET method of the Parse object is provided to parse out a list of name-value pairs. Calling the GET methods begins the parsing process.

Listing 7.2   **Parsing a name-value list (*Parse.java*)**

```java
/**
 * The Parse class is the low-level text parsing class
 * that all other parsing classes are based on.
 *
 * Copyright 2001 by Jeff Heaton
 *
 * @author Jeff Heaton
 * @version 1.0
 */
package com.heaton.bot;
import com.heaton.bot.*;

class Parse extends AttributeList {
  public StringBuffer _source;
  protected int _idx;
  protected char _parseDelim;
  protected String _parseName;
  protected String _parseValue;
  public String _tag;

  public static boolean isWhiteSpace(char ch)
  {
    return( "\t\n\r ".indexOf(ch) != -1 );
  }

  public void eatWhiteSpace()
  {
    while ( !eof() ) {
      if ( !isWhiteSpace(_source.charAt(_idx)) )
        return;
      _idx++;
    }
  }

  public boolean eof()
  {
```

```
    return(_idx>=_source.length() );
}

public void parseAttributeName()
{
  eatWhiteSpace();
  // get attribute name
  if ( (_source.charAt(_idx)=='\''
     || (_source.charAt(_idx)=='\"') ) {
    _parseDelim = _source.charAt(_idx);
    _idx++;
    while ( _source.charAt(_idx)!=_parseDelim ) {
      _parseName+=_source.charAt(_idx);
      _idx++;
    }
    _idx++;
  } else {
    while ( !eof() ) {
      if ( isWhiteSpace(_source.charAt(_idx)) ||
           (_source.charAt(_idx)=='=') ||
           (_source.charAt(_idx)=='>') )
        break;
      _parseName+=_source.charAt(_idx);
      _idx++;
    }
  }
  eatWhiteSpace();
}

public void parseAttributeValue()
{
  if ( _parseDelim!=0 )
    return;

  if ( _source.charAt(_idx)=='=' ) {
    _idx++;
    eatWhiteSpace();
    if ( (_source.charAt(_idx)=='\'') ||
         (_source.charAt(_idx)=='\"') ) {
      _parseDelim = _source.charAt(_idx);
      _idx++;
      while ( _source.charAt(_idx)!=_parseDelim ) {
        _parseValue+=_source.charAt(_idx);
        _idx++;
      }
      _idx++;
    } else {
      while ( !eof() &&
              !isWhiteSpace(_source.charAt(_idx)) &&
              (_source.charAt(_idx)!='>') ) {
        _parseValue+=_source.charAt(_idx);
        _idx++;
      }
```

```
      }
      eatWhiteSpace();
    }
  }


  void addAttribute()
  {
    Attribute a = new Attribute(_parseName,
      _parseValue,_parseDelim);
    add(a);
  }

  String getParseName()
  {
    return _parseName;
  }

  void setParseName(String s)
  {
    _parseName = s;
  }

  String getParseValue()
  {
    return _parseValue;
  }

  void setParseValue(String s)
  {
    _parseValue = s;
  }

  char getParseDelim()
  {
    return _parseDelim;
  }

  void setParseDelim(char s)
  {
    _parseDelim = s;
  }

}
```

Constructing the *CookieParse* Class

The CookieParse class is a special implementation of the Parse class, which is designed to handle cookies. This class not only parses cookies, but it also serves as the container for an individual cookie. The complete source code listing for CookieParse can be seen in Listing 7.3.

This class provides a special GET method that is designed to parse a cookie, and a toString method that is also used to transform the cookie back into text. This class is relatively simple and uses methods of Java's String class to parse the cookie.

Listing 7.3   **Parsing and storing a cookie (*CookieParse.java*)**

```
package com.heaton.bot;

/**
 * This class is used to parse cookies that are transmitted
 * with the HTTP headers.
 *
 * Copyright 2001 by Jeff Heaton
 *
 * @author Jeff Heaton
 * @version 1.0
 */
public class CookieParse extends Parse {

  /**
   * Special version of the parseAttribute method.
   */
  public void parseAttributeValue()
  {
    eatWhiteSpace();
    if ( _source.charAt(_idx)=='=' ) {
      _idx++;
      eatWhiteSpace();
      if ( (_source.charAt(_idx)=='\'') ||
           (_source.charAt(_idx)=='\"') ) {
        _parseDelim = _source.charAt(_idx);
        _idx++;
        while ( _source.charAt(_idx)!=_parseDelim ) {
          _parseValue+=_source.charAt(_idx);
          _idx++;
        }
        _idx++;
      } else {
        while ( !eof() && (_source.charAt(_idx)!=';') ) {
          _parseValue+=_source.charAt(_idx);
          _idx++;
        }
      }
      eatWhiteSpace();
    }
  }
}
/**
 * Called to parse this cookie.
 *
```

```java
     * @return The return value is unused.
     */

    public boolean get()
    {
      // get the attributes
      while ( !eof() ) {
        _parseName="";
        _parseValue="";

        parseAttributeName();

        if ( _source.charAt(_idx)==';' ) {
          addAttribute();
          break;
        }

        // get the value(if any)
        parseAttributeValue();
        addAttribute();

        // move forward to the ; if there is one
        eatWhiteSpace();
        while ( !eof() ) {
          if ( _source.charAt(_idx++)==';' )
            break;
        }
      }
      _idx++;
      return false;
    }

    /**
     * Convert this cookie to a string to be sent as
     * an HTTP header.
     *
     * @return This cookie as a string.
     */
    public String toString()
    {
      String str;
      str = get(0).getName();
      str+= "=";
      str+= get(0).getValue();
      return str;

    }
}
```

Summary

This chapter explained how to process and store cookies, which are units of data that a web server can store in a client browser. When these have been stored, the browser will then return them to the server whenever any request is made. This allows the web server to tag browser users so that they can be identified when they return.

The two types of cookies, session cookies and persistent cookies were also explored. The persistent cookie, which holds its value even after the user has closed the browser, is usually used to hold default values that a user would otherwise have to reenter each time they access the website. A session cookie, which only keeps its value until the user closes the browser or it times out, is typically used to store login information so that the web server can know who is logged into a particular session.

The `Parse` and `CookieParse` classes, which Bot package needs in order to enable cookies, were also detailed. The use of these additional classes is very simple. `HTTPSocket` supports a method called `setUseCookie`, which accepts two parameters that specify if session and persistent cookies are to be supported. Once cookie support is enabled, the `HTTPSocket` method will begin processing cookies.

We have now successfully laid out the low-level technologies needed to produce advanced spiders and bots. In the next several chapters, we will combine all of these technologies to build more advanced spiders, bots, and aggregators. The next chapter will begin with the process of building a spider.

CHAPTER 8

Building a Spider

- Structure of a website

- Examining the structure of a spider

- Following internal links

- Examining external links

This chapter demonstrates how to build a special type of bot called a spider. A *spider* is a type of bot that is capable of moving throughout the Web in order to search for new web pages, just as the arachnid moves about on the strands of its web looking for trapped food. The primary difference between a spider and a simple bot is that the spider is capable of moving to new pages not originally requested by its programmer.

Spiders proved to be very useful to one of the first utility sites to appear on the Web—the search engine. Search engines function as indexes to the content of the Web. As you know, you can type several keywords into a search engine, and it will provide you with links to sites on the Web that match your search criteria. It does this by drawing on its large databases, which contain the indexed content of the Web. But how is this data gathered and how do spiders fit into this?

It would be entirely too large a job for human workers to index and categorize the entire Web. This is a job that is almost always reserved for spiders, which scan websites and index their content. As the spider scans the site, it also looks at other pages to which the current site is linked. The spider keeps a list of these, and when it is finished scanning the current site, it visits these linked sites. Due to the widespread use of hyperlinking on the Web, it can be assumed that by following this pattern, a spider would eventually visit nearly every public page available on the Web. However, new sites are introduced daily, and it is unlikely that a spider would ever be able to visit every site on the Internet.

In addition to performing indexing functions for search engines, spiders can scan a website looking for broken links, they can download the entire contents of a website to your hard drive, and they can also create a visual map that shows the layout of a website. Spiders prove useful whenever data must be retrieved from a site whose structure is not known beforehand by the programmer.

The Bot package presented in this book contains several classes designed to implement a spider. These classes take care of the more routine issues a spider deals with, such as tracking links and avoiding repetition. After explaining spiders and their functions in more detail, this chapter will show how to uses these classes and how they were constructed.

Structure of Websites

A spider must travel from web page to web page. To accomplish this, a spider must be able to locate the links stored on each page that it visits. To do this, the spider examines the web page's HTML code and locates all the tags within it that facilitate some sort of link to another web page. Most tags that do link to other pages do this with a special type of attribute called a *hypertext reference (HREF)*. The different types of HREFs will be explored momentarily.

After discussing HREFs, but before we go on to examine the structure of a spider, we must first look at the structure of a site on which the spider may be used. We will do this by examining a small website that I created named `kimmswick.com`.

Types of Hypertext References (HREFs)

A spider must locate links to find other web pages. Web pages are linked together using HREFs, which are HTML attributes that specify links to other web pages.

All HTML links are contained in the `HREF` HTML attribute. `HREF` is not an HTML tag, it is just an attribute. As a result, you never see `HREF` as a tag on its own; instead, it is usually used in conjunction with an anchor tag. (Anchor tags and image maps were covered in Chapter 4, "HTML Parsing," under the section entitled "Tags a Bot Cares About.") For the purposes of a spider, anchor tags and image maps do the same thing—they function as pointers to some other page the spider should explore. The spider only looks at the `HREF` attributes contained as part of an anchor tag or image map, however. To a spider, the following anchor tag just means that there is another page named `nextpage.html` to be examined; all other data is ignored.

```
<a href="nextpage.html" alt="Go Here">Click Here</a>
```

Similarly, the following HTML image map means the same thing to the spider as the anchor tag above. This is because the spider only cares about `HREF` attributes.

```
<map name="sample">
<area shape="rect" coords="20,27,82,111" href="nextpage.html">
<area shape="default" nohref>
</map>
```

Depending on the data contained in the `HREF`, there are three kinds of links that the spider will encounter. *Internal links* point to pages that are a part of the same web server as the page that contains the link. *External links* refer to pages that are contained on different websites than the page that contained the link. There is also a third class of links, referred to as *other links*, which link to resources other than web pages. We will now explore each of these in more detail.

Internal Links

An internal link is one that connects a web page to another web page that is on the same site. For example, if the document stored at `http://www.kimmswick.com/index.shtml` is linked to `http://www.kimmswick.com/attractions.shtml`, this would be considered an internal link.

A simplified view of the structure of the Kimmswick website can be seen in Figure 8.1. This site, like many others, is made up of many interconnected web pages. The *root document*, called Kimmswick Information, is the page that is displayed when the user goes to the address `http://www.kimmswick.com`. From that root document, links are provided to other pages on the Kimmswick site. Figure 8.1 shows only some of the internal links found on this site.

FIGURE 8.1:

Structure of
`kimmswick.com`

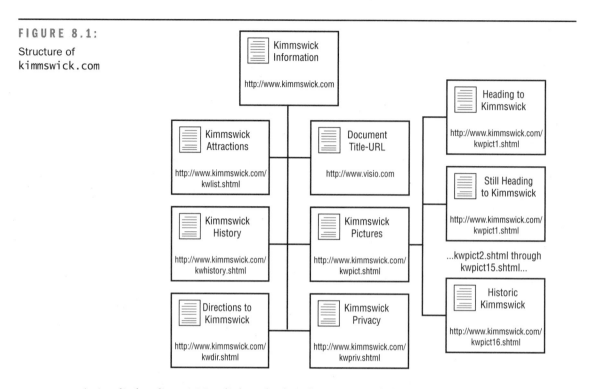

As implied earlier, visiting links, whether they are external or internal, is a recursive process. For instance, a spider visiting `kimmswick.com` would likely be given the URL of `http://www.kimmswick.com` as a starting point. This main page, as seen in Figure 8.1, contains internal links to six other pages. One of these six pages, Kimmswick Pictures, contains internal links to 16 pages. Thus, when the spider was sent to this URL, the Kimmswick Information page would be downloaded, the spider would encounter the first six links, and it would remember these for later exploration. When it visited each of these pages, the additional links that they contained would be found. This same process is replicated on a larger scale when a spider encounters external links.

External Links

To see how external links work, take a look at the following example. If you wanted to hyperlink the word Yahoo to `http://www.yahoo.com` in your HTML, you would use the following tag:

```
<a href="http://www.yahoo.com">Yahoo</a>
```

The above HTML anchor tag works because it specifies an HREF. The result of this tag would be a web browser that would display the word Yahoo underlined. When the user clicked this link, the web browser would take them to `http://www.yahoo.com`.

This is an example of an *external link*. This link is external because it points to a web page that is external to your website (unless your website happens to be Yahoo!). Spiders are frequently programmed not to follow external links to prevent them from the near-infinite process of visiting entirely new websites, which will in turn, cause them to visit every site on the Internet. Spiders that are not restricted in this manner are often referred to as *voyagers* or *world spiders*.

Other Links

A link does not have to point to a web page. It is just as valid when it points to an e-mail address or another resource. Links that specify a scheme other than HTTP or HTTPS fall into this category as well. For example, the mailto scheme can be used to specify an e-mail address. A mailto link such as the following would be used to specify the e-mail address `webmaster@kimmswick.com`:

```
<a href="mailto:webmaster@kimmswick.com">[Email WebMaster]</a>
```

Sources of Links

Links come from many sources. The most common form of a link is the anchor tag that we already examined. A spider should not restrict itself merely to anchor tags, however. Instead, the spider should examine any HREF attribute present in any HTML tag. Table 8.1 summaries a few of these tags.

TABLE 8.1: Some HTML Tags with HREFs

HTML Tag	Example	Purpose
Base	`<base href="http://www.yahoo.com/">`	Establishes a new base for the website. The base is usually the directory in which the HTML file is stored.
Area	`<area coords="0,0,52,52" href="page.html"/>`	Used to indicate a target for an image map.
A	`<a href="page.html">`	The anchor tag. This tag causes a portion of the HTML document to link to the specified page.

Structure of a Spider

There are two ways that a spider could be constructed. The first is by writing the spider as a recursive program. The second is by building a non-recursive spider that maintains a list of pages that it must ultimately visit. When you are trying to decide which approach to take, keep in mind that it must allow the spider to function properly with very large websites.

The Recursive Program

Recursion is the programming technique in which a method calls itself. For some projects, constructing your spider to use recursion seems like a logical choice. It is particularly useful whenever the same basic task must be done repeatedly or when the information for future tasks will be revealed as earlier tasks are processed. For instance, consider the following pseudocode:

```
void RecursiveSpider(String url)
{
   .... download URL ....
   .... parse URL ....
   for each URL found
     call RecursiveSpider(with found URL)
   end for
   .... process the page just downloaded...
}
```

In this piece of code, the task of looking at one single web page has been placed in a single method called `RecursiveSpider`. Here, the `RecursiveSpider` method is called to visit a URL. Instead, the method calls itself as it discovers links.

Though recursion seems like a logical choice for constructing a spider, it is not a suitable one unless there are relatively few pages to visit. This is because each iteration must be pushed onto the stack when a recursive program runs. (A *stack* is a basic programming construct in which return addresses are stored each time a method is called.) If the recursive program must run many times, the stack can grow very large, which can consume the entire stack memory and prevent the program from running.

Another problem with recursion is encountered when you want to use multithreading, which allows many tasks to run at once (see Chapter 9, "Building a High-Volume Spider"). Multithreading is not compatible with recursion because with this process, each thread has its own stack. As the methods called themselves, they would need to use the same stack. This means that a recursive spider could not be extended to include multithreading.

Examining Recursion

As stated previously, recursion is the process in which a method calls itself. The following code represents the simplest case of recursion.

```
void MyMethod
{
  MyMethod();
}
```

Continued on next page

Here, we have a method, named MyMethod, that calls itself. Though it looks harmless, this very simple method will result in a stack overflow, and the termination of your program.

In this case, in order to use recursion properly, you would need to make sure that the method ultimately stops calling itself and ends. To further explore this concept, consider calculating the factorial of a number. The factorial of n, denoted $n!$, is the product of all non-negative integers less than or equal to n. The factorial of n can be calculated as $n! = n \times (n-1) \times (n-2) .. \times 2 \times 1$. For example, the factorial of 5 (5!) would be equal to 5×4×3×2×1, or 24, which would allow the following examples to be true:

```
0! = 1
1! = 1
2! =2 × (2–1) = 2
3! = 3 × (3–1) × (3–2) =6
4! = 4 × (4–1) × (4–2) × (4–3) = 24
```

As you can see, each step in the factorial process depends on the step before it. The following method uses recursion to calculate the value of a factorial.

```
int fact(int n)
{
  if(n<=1)
     return 1;
  else
     return(fact(n-1)*n);
}
```

This represents a valid example of recursion because the process ultimately stops. The fact method is not called endlessly. Each time that the fact method is called, n decreases by one. Ultimately n will be less than one and the if(n<=1) statement will stop the recursion.

The Non-Recursive Construction

The second way to construct a spider, and the one that we will be using, is to approach the problem non-recursively. By doing this, you will be writing a spider that uses a method that does not call itself as each new page is found. Instead, this approach uses a *queue*. A queue is much like the roped line at an amusement park. Individuals must wait in line in order to ride the roller coaster. Likewise, the non-recursive spider uses queues in which the newly discovered pages must wait to be processed by the spider.

The Spider's Queues

When the non-recursive approach is followed, the spider will be given a page to visit, and it will add this page to a queue of sites it should visit. As the spider finds new links, they too will be added to the queue. Once the spider is finished with the current page, it will check the queue for the next page to process. (This differs from recursion, where a method to handle each page would immediately be called.)

Though only one queue was specified in this description, the spider will actually use a total of four queues, which are summarized below. Each of these queues will hold URLs that are in some stage of being processed.

Waiting queue   In this queue, URLs wait to be processed by the spider. New URLs are added to this queue as they are found.

Running queue   URLs are transferred to this queue once the spider begins processing them. It is very important that the same URL not be processed multiple times because this would be wasteful. Once the URL is processed, it moves either to the error queue or the complete queue.

Error queue   If an error occurs while the page is being downloaded, its URL is added to the error queue. The URL does not move into another queue after it lands here. Once moved to the error queue, a page will not be processed further by the spider.

Complete queue   If no error occurs while the page is being downloaded, the URL is added to the complete queue. The URL does not move into another queue after it has been assigned here.

An individual URL will only be in one queue at a time. This is also called the *state* of the URL because computer programs are often described by state diagrams in which the program flows from one state to the next. Figure 8.2 shows how these states interrelate and how a page flows from one queue to another.

FIGURE 8.2:

The flow of URL states

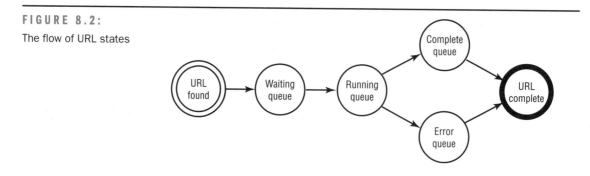

Figure 8.3 shows a simplification of what happens in one of the queues you saw in Figure 8.2. This figure only shows the flow of pages that did not result in an error. In this process, the spider is started when a single URL is added to the waiting queue. As long as there is a page in the waiting queue or the spider is processing a page, the spider will continue its job. When there is nothing in the waiting queue and no page is currently being processed, the spider will cease to function.

FIGURE 8.3:

Typical spider flowchart

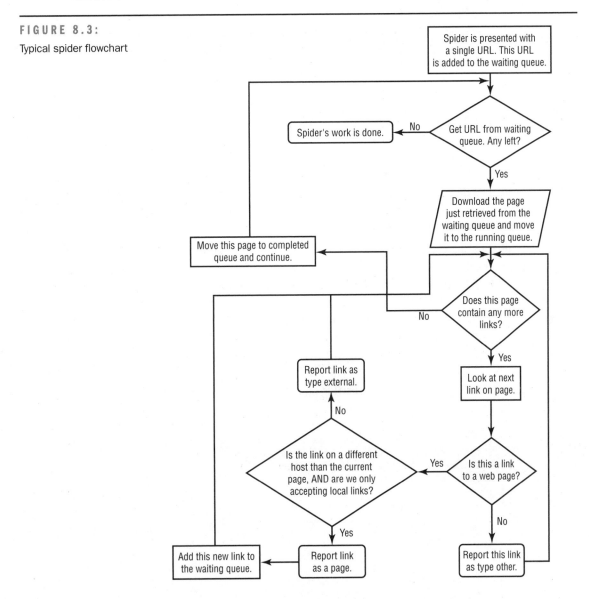

Now you will be shown how to construct a spider. You will see how the parts of a spider work together, and how you can extend the spider presented here. Then you will be shown how to put this spider to some practical use. The example presented later in this chapter uses the spider to save the contents of the website to a local disk.

Constructing a Spider

There are several classes and interfaces that you must be aware of in order to use the spider provided by the Bot package. First of all, there is an interface, named ISpiderReportable that you must implement. The Bot package spider will return all pages found to a class that implements this interface. In addition, there is a class called SpiderWorker that manages each of the spider's threads.

Before you start, make sure you have some reason for which you are creating a spider. For instance, perhaps you want to download all of the images from a site, or you want to see a specific piece of information. Whatever this purpose is, you must create a class that implements the ISpiderReportable interface to retrieve the pages found by the spider. This class that you create can then perform whatever tasks your application calls for on the pages.

The *ISpiderReportable* Interface

Implementing the ISpiderReportable interface allows a class, which you create, to receive the pages encountered by the spider. The next section will show you how to make the spider use your class. For now, you will be shown how to create a *spider manager*—a class that implements the ISpiderReportable interface. When this interface is used, your spider manager class can receive events from the spider as it visits the site that it was directed to visit. Listing 8.1 shows the ISpiderReportable interface and the methods that it supports; these methods will be discussed after the listing.

Listing 8.1   The Spider Reporting Interface (*ISpiderReportable.java*)

```
package com.heaton.bot;
/**
 * This interface represents a manager class that
 * the spider can report to. As the spider
 * does its job, events from this interface
 * will be called.
 *
 * Copyright 2001 by Jeff Heaton
 *
 * @author Jeff Heaton
 * @version 1.0
 */
```

```
public interface ISpiderReportable
{
    public boolean foundInternalLink(String url);
    public boolean foundExternalLink(String url);
    public boolean foundOtherLink(String url);
    public void processPage(HTTP page);
    public void completePage(HTTP page,boolean error);
    public boolean getRemoveQuery();
    public void spiderComplete();
}
```

The ISpiderReportable interface defines several events that the spider will send back to its controller. By providing handlers for each of these events, a wide variety of spiders can be created. The example program, shown later in this chapter, shows a spider that uses many of the methods described here. These methods are followed by a short description of their function and the code line in which they appear in Listing 8.1.

The completePage method   Called to request that a page be processed. This page was just downloaded by the spider. The parameter page contains the page contents. The parameter error is true if this page resulted in an HTTP error.

```
public void completePage(HTTP page, boolean error)
```

The getRemoveQuery method   Called by the spider to determine if query strings should be removed. If the query string is to be removed, this method should return true.

```
public boolean getRemoveQuery()
```

The foundExternalLink method   Called when the spider finds an external link. An external link does not share the same host address as the URL from which the spider started its search. The url parameter specifies the URL that was found by the spider. If this method returns true, the spider should add this URL to the workload. If this method returns false, the spider should not add this URL to the workload.

```
public boolean foundExternalLink(String url)
```

The foundInternalLink method   Called when the spider finds an internal link. An internal link shares the same host address as the URL that started the spider. The url parameter specifies the URL that was found by the spider. If this method returns true, the spider should add this URL to the workload. If this method returns false, the spider should not add this URL to the workload.

```
public boolean foundInternalLink(String url)
```

The foundOtherLink method   Called when the spider finds an other link. A link of type other does not point to an HTML page. Links of this type generally refer to e-mail address links. The url parameter specifies the URL that was found by the spider. If this method returns true, the spider should add this URL to the workload. If this method returns false, the spider should not add this URL to the workload.

```
public boolean foundOtherLink(String url)
```

The `processPage` method   Called to process a page. This is where the work that is actually done by the spider is usually preformed. The `page` parameter contains the page contents.

```
public void processPage(HTTP page)
```

The `spiderComplete` method   Called when the spider has no work remaining.

```
public void spiderComplete()
```

Using the *Spider* Class

The Bot package's spider is implemented through the `Spider` class. Though this class is considered the actual spider, it is not the only class that makes up the spider. The other classes that make up the spider will be explored in Chapter 9, which explores how a high-volume spider can be constructed.

To use the `Spider` class in this chapter, you must first instantiate a `Spider` object. For this object to be instantiated, the constructor for the `Spider` class must be passed the initial URL, the spider manager, and the size of the thread pool. Once these are specified, the spider may begin processing.

The Bot package's spider is multithreaded, which makes it more efficient because it can look at more than one web page at once as a result (multithreading will be discussed in greater detail in Chapter 9). You do not need to be aware of how this spider internally processes the pages in order to use it. Instead, you just need to focus on what a spider is and what it does. The following is a list of methods supported by the `Spider` class; each of these methods is followed by a description and an example of how they might appear in code.

NOTE   Because of the complexity of the spider classes, Chapter 9 is dedicated to explaining how a high-volume spider actually works. Think of Chapter 9 as the "Under the Hood" section for this chapter.

The `Spider` constructor   This constructor prepares the spider so that it is ready to begin traversing a site. It also ensures that the basic information required to begin this journey is passed from the program using the spider. The constructor stores these values in the `Spider` class for later use.

In the code below, the parameters of this constructor function as noted. The `manager` parameter is the object to which this spider reports its findings. The `url` parameter is the URL at which the spider should begin. The `http` parameter is the HTTP handler used by this spider. The `poolsize` parameter specifies the size of the thread pool. The optional `w` parameter is a customized workload manager.

```
public Spider(ISpiderReportable manager,String url,HTTP http,int poolSize)
public Spider(ISpiderReportable manager,String url,HTTP http,int
    poolSize,IWorkloadStorable w)
```

The `addWorkload` method   Called to add a workload to the workload manager. This method will release a thread that was waiting for a workload, but it will do nothing if the spider has been halted. The `url` parameter is the URL to be added to the workload.

```
synchronized public void addWorkload(String url)
```

The `completePage` method   Called to request that a page be processed. This page was just downloaded by the spider. This method passes this call on to its manager. The `page` parameter of this method contains the page contents; the `error` parameter indicates if this page resulted in an error.

```
synchronized public void completePage(HTTP page,boolean error)
```

The `foundExternalLink` method   Called when the spider finds an external link. This method hands the link off to the manager and adds the URL to the workload if necessary. If this is a world spider, then external links are treated as internal links. The `url` parameter specifies the URL that was found by the spider. This method returns true if the spider should add this URL to the workload.

```
synchronized public boolean foundExternalLink(String url)
```

The `foundInternalLink` method   Called when the spider finds an internal link. This method hands the link off to the manager and adds the URL to the workload if necessary. The `url` parameter specifies the URL that was found by the spider. This method returns true if the spider should add this URL to the workload.

```
synchronized public boolean foundInternalLink(String url)
```

The `foundOtherLink` method   Called when the spider finds a type of link that does not point to another HTML page (for example a mailto link). This method hands the link off to the manager and adds the URL to the workload if necessary. The `url` parameter specifies the URL that was found by the spider. This method returns true if the spider should add this URL to the workload.

```
synchronized public boolean foundOtherLink(String url)
```

The `getMaxBody` method   Called to return the maximum body size that will be downloaded. This method returns the body size, or –1 for unlimited.

```
public int getMaxBody()
```

The getRemoveQuery method   Called by the spider to determine if query strings should be removed. By default, the spider always chooses to remove query strings, so true is returned. This method returns true if the query string should be removed.

```
synchronized public boolean getRemoveQuery()
```

The getSpiderDone method   Called to get the SpiderDone object used by this spider to monitor its progress. The SpiderDone object is used to determine when the spider's work is complete.

```
public SpiderDone getSpiderDone()
```

The getWorkload method   Called to get a workload from the workload manager. If no workload is available, this method will block until there is one. This method returns the next URL to be spidered.

```
synchronized public String getWorkload()
```

The getWorldSpider method   Called to return true if this is a world spider. A world spider does not restrict itself to a single site and will likely go on indefinitely.

```
public boolean getWorldSpider()
```

The halt method   Called to cause the spider to halt. This will not happen immediately, but once the spider is halted, the run method will return.

```
synchronized public void halt()
```

The processPage method   Called to process a page. This is where the work actually done by the spider is usually preformed. The page parameter contains the page contents.

```
synchronized public void processPage(HTTP page)
```

The run method   Called to request the spider to begin processing. This can be called directly, or the start method can be called to run as a background thread. This method will not return until there is no work remaining for the spider.

```
public void run()
```

The setMaxBody method   Called to set the maximum body size that will be downloaded. The i parameter specifies the maximum body size, or -1 for unlimited.

```
public void setMaxBody(int mx)
```

The setWorldSpider method   Called to specify this spider as either a world or a site spider. See getWorldSpider for more information about what a world spider is. The b parameter is true if this is a world spider.

```
public void setWorldSpider(boolean b)
```

The **spiderComplete method**   Called when the spider has no more work. This method just passes this event on to its manager.

```
synchronized public void spiderComplete()
```

GetSite Example

We will now examine an example spider, which will download all of the pages of the site that it is given. These files will be downloaded into a directory located on the local hard disk. Figure 8.4 shows this program running.

To begin this process, you should select a URL from which the spider will download. You should also select a path to which the web pages should be downloaded. Optionally, you may specify a path to write a log file to as well. Once you have entered this URL, you should click the Go button to begin the spider. Once the spider is running, you can cancel the process by clicking the Cancel button, which does not appear until the spider begins.

The source code for the GetSite example is shown in Listing 8.2. Once the Go button is clicked, the Go_actionPerformed method, which begins the spider threads, is called.

Listing 8.2   Downloading a Site (*GetSite.java*)

```java
import java.awt.*;
import java.util.*;
import javax.swing.*;
import java.io.*;
import com.heaton.bot.*;

/**
 * Example from Chapter 8
 *
 * This example program will download all of the HTML files
```

```
 * of a web site to a local drive. This shows how a spider can
 * be used to map/download a site.
 *
 * @author Jeff Heaton
 * @version 1.0
 */
public class GetSite extends javax.swing.JFrame implements ISpiderReportable
{

  /**
   * The underlying spider object.
   */
  Spider _spider = null;

  /**
   * The current page count.
   */
  int _pagesCount;

   /**
    * The constructor. Set up the visual Swing
    * components that make up the user interface
    * for this program.
    */
   public GetSite()
   {
      //{{INIT_CONTROLS
      setTitle("Download Site");
      getContentPane().setLayout(null);
      setSize(405,268);
      setVisible(false);
      D.setHorizontalTextPosition(
        javax.swing.SwingConstants.LEFT);
      D.setVerticalTextPosition(
        javax.swing.SwingConstants.TOP);
      D.setVerticalAlignment(
        javax.swing.SwingConstants.TOP);
      D.setText("Download pages of:");
      getContentPane().add(D);
      D.setBounds(12,12,384,24);
      JLabel2.setText("URL:");
      getContentPane().add(JLabel2);
      JLabel2.setBounds(12,36,36,24);
      getContentPane().add(_url);
      _url.setBounds(48,36,348,24);
      JLabel3.setText("Select local path to download files");
      getContentPane().add(JLabel3);
      JLabel3.setBounds(12,72,384,24);
      getContentPane().add(_save);
      _save.setBounds(12,96,384,24);
      _go.setText("GO!");
```

```
        getContentPane().add(_go);
        _go.setBounds(96,228,216,24);
        getContentPane().add(_current);
        _current.setBounds(12,204,384,12);
        JLabel4.setText("Number of pages:");
        getContentPane().add(JLabel4);
        JLabel4.setBounds(12,180,120,12);
        _pages.setText("0");
        getContentPane().add(_pages);
        _pages.setBounds(120,180,108,12);
        JLabel6.setText(
"Select local path(and filename) to write log to(optional):");
        getContentPane().add(JLabel6);
        JLabel6.setBounds(12,120,384,24);
        _logPath.setText("./spider.log");
        getContentPane().add(_logPath);
        _logPath.setBounds(12,144,384,24);
        _go.setActionCommand("jbutton");
        //}}

        //{{INIT_MENUS
        //}}

        //{{REGISTER_LISTENERS
        SymAction lSymAction = new SymAction();
        _go.addActionListener(lSymAction);
        SymWindow aSymWindow = new SymWindow();
        this.addWindowListener(aSymWindow);
        //}}
    }

    /**
     * Added by VisualCafe.
     *
     * @param b
     */
    public void setVisible(boolean b)
    {
        if (b)
            setLocation(50, 50);
        super.setVisible(b);
    }

    /**
     * Program entry point, causes the main
     * window to be displayed.
     *
     * @param args Command line arguments are not used.
     */
    static public void main(String args[])
    {
```

```
        (new GetSite()).setVisible(true);
}

/**
 * Added by VisualCafe.
 */
public void addNotify()
{
    // Record the size of the window prior
    // to calling parents addNotify.
    Dimension size = getSize();

    super.addNotify();

    if (frameSizeAdjusted)
        return;
    frameSizeAdjusted = true;

    // Adjust size of frame according to the insets and menu bar
    Insets insets = getInsets();
    javax.swing.JMenuBar menuBar =
getRootPane().getJMenuBar();
    int menuBarHeight = 0;
    if (menuBar != null)
    menuBarHeight = menuBar.getPreferredSize().height;
    setSize(insets.left +
      insets.right +
      size.width,
      insets.top +
      insets.bottom +
      size.height + menuBarHeight);
}

// Used by addNotify
boolean frameSizeAdjusted = false;

//{{DECLARE_CONTROLS
javax.swing.JLabel D = new javax.swing.JLabel();
javax.swing.JLabel JLabel2 = new javax.swing.JLabel();

/**
 * The URL to spider.
 */
javax.swing.JTextField _url = new javax.swing.JTextField();
javax.swing.JLabel JLabel3 = new javax.swing.JLabel();

/**
 * The directory to save the files to.
 */
javax.swing.JTextField _save = new javax.swing.JTextField();

/**
 * The Go button.
 */
```

```
    */
    javax.swing.JButton _go = new javax.swing.JButton();

    /**
     * Displays the current page.
     */
    javax.swing.JLabel _current = new javax.swing.JLabel();
    javax.swing.JLabel JLabel4 = new javax.swing.JLabel();

    /**
     * A count of how many pages have been
     * downloaded.
     */
    javax.swing.JLabel _pages = new javax.swing.JLabel();
    javax.swing.JLabel JLabel6 = new javax.swing.JLabel();

    /**
     * Used to specify the path to store the
     * log to.
     */
    javax.swing.JTextField _logPath = new javax.swing.JTextField();
    //}}

    //{{DECLARE_MENUS
    //}}


    /**
     * An event handler class, generated by VisualCafe.
     *
     * @author VisualCafe
     */
    class SymAction implements java.awt.event.ActionListener
    {
        public void actionPerformed(java.awt.event.ActionEvent event)
        {
            Object object = event.getSource();
            if (object == _go)
                Go_actionPerformed(event);
        }
    }


    /**
     * As the files of the web site are located,
     * this method is called to save them to disk.
     *
     * @param file The HTTP object corresponding to the page
     * just visited.
     */
    protected void processFile(HTTP file)
    {
```

```
    try
    {
      if(_save.getText().length()>0)
      {
        int i = file.getURL().lastIndexOf('/');

        if(i!=-1)
        {
          String filename = file.getURL().substring(i);
          if(filename.equals("/"))
            filename="root.html";
          FileOutputStream fso
            = new FileOutputStream(
            new File(_save.getText(),filename) );
          fso.write( file.getBody().getBytes("8859_1") );
          fso.close();
        }
      }
    }
    catch(Exception e)
    {
      Log.logException("Can't save output file: ",e);
    }
  }

  /**
   * This is where most of the action takes place. This
   * method is called when the Go button is pressed.
   *
   * @param event The event
   */
  void Go_actionPerformed(java.awt.event.ActionEvent event)
  {
    IWorkloadStorable wl = new SpiderInternalWorkload();
    if(_spider!=null)
    {

      Runnable doLater = new Runnable()
      {
        public void run()
        {
          _go.setText("Canceling...");
        }
      };
      SwingUtilities.invokeLater(doLater);

      _spider.halt();
      return;
    }

    try
    {
```

```
   if(_url.getText().length()>0)
    {
     HTTPSocket http = new HTTPSocket();
     http.send(_url.getText(),null);
    }
    else
    {
      _current.setText("<<distributed mode>>");
    }
  }
  catch(Exception e)
  {
   JOptionPane.showMessageDialog(this,
     e,
     "Error",
     JOptionPane.OK_CANCEL_OPTION,
     null );

     return;
  }

  Runnable doLater = new Runnable()
  {
    public void run()
    {
       _go.setText("Cancel");
       _current.setText("Loading....");
    }
  };
  SwingUtilities.invokeLater(doLater);

   // Prepare to start the spider
   _pagesCount = 0;
   if(_logPath.getText().length()>0)
   {
     File file = new File(_logPath.getText());
     file.delete();
     Log.setLevel(Log.LOG_LEVEL_NORMAL);
     Log.setFile(true);
     Log.setConsole(false);
     Log.setPath(_logPath.getText());
   }

// NOTE: To use SQL-based workload management,
// uncomment the following lines and include a
// valid data source.
/*
   try
   {
     wl = new SpiderSQLWorkload(
       "sun.jdbc.odbc.JdbcOdbcDriver",
```

```
              "jdbc:odbc:WORKLOAD");
          }
          catch(Exception e)
          {
           JOptionPane.showMessageDialog(this,
             e,
             "Error",
             JOptionPane.OK_CANCEL_OPTION,
             null );
          }
     */


     _spider
        = new Spider( this,
          _url.getText(),
          new HTTPSocket(),
          100,
          w1);
     _spider.setMaxBody(200);
     _spider.start();

   }

  /**
   * This method is called by the spider when an
   * internal link is found.
   *
   * @param url The URL of the link that was found. This
   * link is passed in fully resolved.
   * @return True if the spider should add this link to
   * its visitation list.
   */
  public boolean foundInternalLink(String url)
  {
     return true;
  }

  /**
   * This method is called by the spider when an
   * external link is found. An external link is
   * one that points to a different host.
   *
   * @param url The URL of the link that was found. This
   * link is passed in fully resolved.
   * @return True if the spider should add this link to
   * its visitation list.
   */
  public boolean foundExternalLink(String url)
  {
     return false;
```

```java
}

/**
 * This method is called by the spider when an
 * other type link is found. Links such as e-mail
 * addresses are sent to this method.
 *
 * @param url The URL of the link that was found. This
 * link is passed in fully resolved.
 * @return True if the spider should add this link to
 * its visitation list.
 */
public boolean foundOtherLink(String url)
{
  return false;
}

/**
 * A simple class used to update the current
 * URL target. This is necessary because Swing
 * only allows GUI components to be updated by the
 * main thread.
 *
 * @author Jeff Heaton
 * @version 1.0
 */

class UpdateTarget implements Runnable
{
  public String _t;
  public void run()
  {
    _current.setText(_t);
    _pages.setText( "" + _pagesCount );
  }
}

/**
 * Called by the spider when a page has been
 * loaded and should be processed. For
 * example, this method will save this file
 * to disk.
 *
 * @param page The HTTP object that corresponds to the
 * page just visited.
 */
public void processPage(HTTP page)
{
  _pagesCount++;
  UpdateTarget ut = new UpdateTarget();
```

```
      ut._t = page.getURL();
      SwingUtilities.invokeLater(ut);
      processFile(page);
    }


    /**
     * Not used. This must be implemented because
     * of the interface. Called when a page completes.
     *
     * @param page The page that just completed.
     * @param error True if the completion of this page
     * resulted in an error.
     */
    public void completePage(HTTP page,boolean error)
    {
    }


    /**
     * This method is called to determine if
     * query strings should be stripped.
     *
     * @return Returns true if query strings(the part of
     * the URL after the ?) should be stripped.
     */
    public boolean getRemoveQuery()
    {
      return true;
    }


    /**
     * This method is called once the spider
     * has no more work to do.
     */
    public void spiderComplete()
    {
      if(_spider.isHalted())
      {
      JOptionPane.showMessageDialog(this,
          "Download of site has been canceled. " +
          "Check log file for any errors.",
          "Done",
          JOptionPane.OK_CANCEL_OPTION,
          null );
      }
      else
      {
      JOptionPane.showMessageDialog(this,
          "Download of site is complete. " +
          "Check log file for any errors.",
          "Done",
          JOptionPane.OK_CANCEL_OPTION,
```

```
      null );
    }
    _spider=null;

    Runnable doLater = new Runnable()
    {
      public void run()
      {
        _go.setText("GO!!");
      }
    };
    SwingUtilities.invokeLater(doLater);
  }


  /**
   * An event handler class generated by VisualCafe.
   *
   * @author VisualCafe
   */
  class SymWindow extends java.awt.event.WindowAdapter
  {
      public void windowClosed(java.awt.event.WindowEvent event)
      {
        Object object = event.getSource();
        if (object == GetSite.this)
          GetSite_windowClosed(event);
      }
  }
  /**
   * Called to close the window.
   *
   * @param event The event.
   */

  void GetSite_windowClosed(java.awt.event.WindowEvent event)
  {
      System.exit(0);
  }


}
```

Examining the *GetSite* Example

The code just presented provides a simple spider that can be used to download every page from a site. You will now be shown how this example works. First several objects must be setup before the spider can begin.

Setting Up

In Listing 8.2 the `Go_actionPerformed` method begins by specifying that the spider will use an internal workload manager, which will use the computer's RAM to maintain the queues. (Refer to Chapter 9 to see how SQL database can be used to store these queues). The following code creates a memory resident workload storage system.

```
IWorkloadStorable wl = new SpiderInternalWorkload();
```

Canceling the Spider

There is only one push button on the spider's frame window. Its functionality alternates between starting and canceling the spider. Initially, it starts the spider, however, once the spider begins, the button becomes a cancel button.

When this button is pressed, the `Go_actionPerformed` method is called. This method handles both canceling and starting the spider. In order to determine if it should perform a cancel or start procedure, the method checks to see if the spider is already running. If there is no spider running, then the user is requesting that one should be started. If there is a spider running, then the user is likely trying to cancel it.

To make this determination, you should check the `_spider` variable to see if a spider already exists. If one does, the user has attempted to cancel the spider download. If this is the case, the Go button's text is changed to the text "Canceling..." using the `invokeLater` method of Swing. This method must be used whenever there is a chance that a thread, other than the main thread, will be updating a GUI component. The text is changed to "Canceling..." because it will likely take a few seconds for all of the spider's threads to exit properly. The spider's shut down process is then initiated by calling `_spider.halt()`, as shown here:

```
if(_spider!=null)
{

  Runnable doLater = new Runnable()
  {
    public void run()
    {
      _go.setText("Canceling...");
    }
  };
  SwingUtilities.invokeLater(doLater);

  _spider.halt();
  return;
}
```

Starting the Spider

The Go_actionPerformed method can also start the spider. If this method was not called, then you must find out why. To do this, first verify that a valid URL was entered. You can do this by opening an HTTPSocket connection to the specified URL. If the URL fails to load properly, or it is blank, an error message will be displayed, as is shown here:

```
try
{
  if(_url.getText().length()>0)
  {
    HTTPSocket http = new HTTPSocket();
    http.send(_url.getText(),null);
  }
  else
  {
    _current.setText("<<distributed mode>>");
  }
}
catch(Exception e)
{
  JOptionPane.showMessageDialog(this,
    e,
    "Error",
    JOptionPane.OK_CANCEL_OPTION,
    null );

  return;
}
```

If no exception was generated, we have now verified that a valid URL has been entered. The spider can now be started. Once the spider starts up the text, the Go button becomes a Cancel button. In code, you accomplish this change by using Java method invokeLater.

The following code is responsible for changing the current status indicator, which is a JText component, to "Loading....". This is done to signify that the spider is about to start up and will soon be reporting pages. The code also changes the Go button to a Cancel button. These calls to change the status and button text are wrapped in a class to be passed to invokeLater. This is necessary when Swing components, such as buttons, are changed from inside secondary threads.

NOTE   As the program stands, the invokeLater calls used in this method are not required, but they are put in as a precaution because they are required in nearly every other method of this example. This placement ensures commutability in case the go method was called from a background thread.

```
Runnable doLater = new Runnable()
{
  public void run()
  {
     _go.setText("Cancel");
     _current.setText("Loading....");
  }
};
SwingUtilities.invokeLater(doLater);
```

Once the button has been changed from Go to Cancel, logging is enabled if a log file path was specified. In this segment, normal level logging has been specified, with the output directed to a file.

```
// Prepare to start the spider
_pagesCount = 0;
if(_logPath.getText().length()>0)
{
  File file = new File(_logPath.getText());
  file.delete();
  Log.setLevel(Log.LOG_LEVEL_NORMAL);
  Log.setFile(true);
  Log.setConsole(false);
  Log.setPath(_logPath.getText());
}
```

Finally, the spider is constructed and started. In the code below, you will notice that the value 100 is used to specify that the thread pool will have 100 threads. A few lines later, the w1 parameter specifies what workload manager this spider will be using. Then the setMaxBody method specifies the largest page (in kilobytes) that can be downloaded. This prevents the spider from downloading huge multimedia files that it might encounter. Finally, the start method is called, which starts the spider up as a separate thread.

```
_spider
  = new Spider( this,
    _url.getText(),
    new HTTPSocket(),
    100,
    w1);
_spider.setMaxBody(200);
_spider.start();
```

Workload Management

As previously mentioned, the spider must track every URL that it encounters and the management of this URL list referred to as *workload management*. By default, the spider uses the computer's RAM to store the workload. If the site is very large, it may be preferable to store the workload elsewhere, perhaps in a SQL database. Notice that the following code is commented out. This code can be uncommented to enable the spider to store its queues in a SQL database. (This topic will be covered in Chapter 9.) This code is designed to use a DSN called WORK-LOAD under the ODBC driver.

```
// NOTE: To use SQL-based workload management,
// uncomment the following lines and include a
// valid data source.
/*
    try
    {
      wl = new SpiderSQLWorkload(
        "sun.jdbc.odbc.JdbcOdbcDriver",
        "jdbc:odbc:WORKLOAD");
    }
    catch(Exception e)
    {
     JOptionPane.showMessageDialog(this,
       e,
       "Error",
       JOptionPane.OK_CANCEL_OPTION,
       null );
    }
*/
```

Monitoring the Spider's Progress

As the spider processes the sites, it calls the events methods of the ISpiderReportable inter-face (discussed earlier), which is implemented by the GetSite object (shown in Listing 8.2). For example, the processPage method is called to save each page. Also, in order to update the GUI, the internal class UpdateTarget is used, and then it is invoked later. A small method named processFile is called to save the page to disk. Most of the work performed by a spider is done by the processFile method. This method is passed the page that was just downloaded. It simply saves the contents of the page to disk. The processFile method is shown in Listing 8.2.

NOTE   In past chapters, this section was used to describe the internal workings of the Bot package classes that were shown earlier in the chapter. This chapter is different, however. Due to the complexity of the spider classes, Chapter 9 has been devoted to explaining how they actually function, so in a sense, Chapter 9 functions as one huge "Under the Hood" section for this chapter. Chapter 9 also explains some advanced tasks you can perform using spiders, such as using an SQL database to store the queues.

Summary

A spider is a specialized bot that follows links as it searches for pages. In this chapter, we explored the concept of a spider, we built a spider that could download all of the HTML files for a website, and we learned of the most basic ways of using such a spider.

A spider is designed to take HTML output from a website and trace its links. By using this process, the spider soon finds other links. This is a recursive operation because a spider is endlessly following these links. The spider in this chapter has been built without recursion, however. Recursion would have stack requirements that are too great for a large site. The spider presented in this chapter maintains a list of links found. This list is then distributed amount several concurrent threads.

Another design consideration for spiders is making sure that they are doing something with the content they receive from sites. Simply looking at pages is not enough, most likely you will want to actually do something with the data encountered by the spider. The ISpiderReportable interface is a tool that can accomplish this by reporting back what the spider finds as it is navigating web pages. When you implement this interface you will receive events while the spider finds links, explores pages, and eventually finishes its search.

In the following chapter, we will look at what makes the spider that we created in this chapter processes data as fast is it does. In addition, we will review threads, thread synchronization, and how to use JDBC, and we will learn how to combine all of these features into a high-volume spider.

CHAPTER 9

Building a High-Volume Spider

- Using threads

- Accessing data with ODBC

- Scheduling threads

- Creating a high-volume spider

The job of a spider may seem never ending sometimes. As a spider visits pages, it locates other pages to visit, and when it visits those, still other sites pop up. As a result, the spider's workload begins to grow exponentially. Because of this, it is very important that the spider is built as efficiently as possible.

In the previous chapter, we saw how to use a couple of the Bot package classes to construct a spider. This chapter continues dealing with the construction of a spider, but it focuses more on why those classes were constructed the way that they were, and what performance considerations were taken during their development. It also spends a lot more time discussing how a spider can be programmed to be more efficient, which was not discussed in the previous chapter.

Multithreading, which is so important to the performance and efficiency of a spider, will be reviewed at the beginning of this chapter. Then thread synchronization, which shows how threads can work together to produce an aggregate result, will be discussed.

Workload management is also very important to a high-performance spider. This is because the spider must track thousands of web pages that it has visited. The spider described in the previous chapter stored its workloads in memory. This is effective for small sites, but it isn't very effective for very large sites. This chapter will show you another approach—how to use Java Database Connectivity (JDBC) to make a SQL database to store the workload.

Using the techniques just described, a highly efficient spider will be developed. This chapter will begin by discussing how to use multithreading.

What Is Multithreading?

Before we get into the details of how to use threads, we must examine what exactly threads are. Basically, a *thread* is a path of execution through a program. Most programs written today run as a single thread, and thus they have just one path of execution. This can cause problems when multiple events or actions need to occur at the same time, however. For example, a single threaded program is not capable of downloading data from the network while it is also responding to mouse or keyboard input from the user. Instead, such a program must give its full attention to either the keyboard input or the network download. The ideal solution to this problem is the seamless execution of two or more sections of a program at the same time. This is the problem that giving a program multiple threads was designed to solve.

Multithreading is a program's ability to run more than one task at a time. This should not be confused with the older technology, *multitasking*, which is a computer's ability to run more than one program at a time. To clarify, multithreading is internal to a program and multitasking is internal to a computer. Multithreading's ability to run more than one program task at a time is very important to the efficiency of the spider. Because multithreading is occurring internal to the program, threads can very easily share data because they both use the same memory space.

One of the most common ways to optimize a program is to identify and speed up *bottlenecks*. A bottleneck is the slowest portion of the program that sets the pace for everything else. It does not matter how much the rest of the program is optimized; if there is a bottleneck, the program will still have to wait on its slowest part.

To explain how multithreading might help with efficiency, consider the following example. A spider has to download ten pages. To do this, the spider must request and then receive those pages from a server. While the spider is awaiting a response, a bottleneck occurs. This happens because the spider has requested the page and now must wait for the request to travel through the Internet to the web server. It is in this type of situation that implementing multithreading can help. In this case, numerous threads would allow the wait times of these ten pages to be combined, rather than having them be executed one after another. It is inefficient for the spider to be just waiting on one single page. Multithreading allows the spider to wait on a large number of pages simultaneously. Next you will be shown how to use multithreading in a Java application.

Multithreading with Java

Threads are a feature supported by many different programming languages. Java has its own way of handling threads. Before you can create a spider that makes effective use of multithreading, you must first understand how to write a multithreaded program in Java. With a firm understanding of the fundamentals of Java thread programming, you will be able to create a spider that uses multithreading, but you must first learn how to create a thread in Java.

Creating Threads

A thread's job is to execute some part of the program in the background, while the rest of the program continues to run. When a thread is created in Java, that thread must be told exactly what code it should execute in the background. This code is isolated in one single method of the Java thread—the run method. Depending on where this run method is located within the code, Java handles multithreading in one of two ways.

The first way to handle multithreading is by subclassing the Thread object. The Thread object is the object that Java provides to encapsulate a thread. If you subclass the Thread class, then you must override the run method in this class to provide the code that should be executed by this particular thread. Another benefit of handling multithreading by subclassing is that Java, which does not support multiple inheritance, only allows a class to subclass one class. If your class needs to subclass another class, then you will not be able to subclass the Thread object.

The second way of handling multithreading is by implementing the Runnable interface that is provided by Java and then creating a run method in that class. A Java class can implement as many interfaces as needed, so this way does not have the limitations of the previous one. However, your run method is now no longer a descendant of the Thread class, and as a result, it does not have direct access to the Thread methods.

It is important to understand both ways of handling multithreading with Java. We will continue by discussing the first way, which involves extending the Thread class.

NOTE   The Thread class is defined in the java.lang package, so it does not need to be imported (java.lang is always automatically imported by Java).

Subclassing the *Thread* Class

You can create a thread by directly subclassing the Thread class. This is done using the extends keyword of Java, as shown in the code sample below. This allows you to create a self-contained thread object that contains both your run method and the methods you need to control the execution of your run method. The following Java program demonstrates how to create a thread by extending the Thread class.

```
public class ExtendThread extends Thread
{
  public void run()
  {
    for(int i=0;i<=1000;i++)
    {
      System.out.println("Counting..." + i );
    }
  }

  public static void main(String args[])
  {
    ExtendThread t = new ExtendThread();
    t.start();
  }
}
```

The above program creates a thread that counts from 0 to 1000. The loop that actually does this work is placed in the run method. To begin execution, the main method instantiates our class of ExecuteThread and calls the start method, which was inherited from the Thread class. As previously stated, extending the Thread class does not allow you to extend from any other class. To alleviate this problem, Java includes a second way of creating a thread.

Implementing the *Runnable* Interface

The second way that Java allows threads to be created is by implementing the Runnable interface. But before you can be shown how to do this, you will need to be more familiar with interfaces.

Java interfaces do no real work themselves, instead, they specify prototypes for methods that will ultimately do the work. Interface names generally end in the -able prefix and the rest of their name usually describes what they show you how to do. (For example, the Runnable interface specifies how to run a thread.) When you implement an interface, you must include the methods that the interface requires. For the Runnable interface, this means that you must include a run method. The following code shows the same example as the one in the previous section, but in this case, a Runnable interface is being used instead of a Thread class.

```
public class ImplementRunnable implements Runnable
{
  public void run()
  {
    for(int i=0;i<=1000;i++)
    {
      System.out.println("Counting..." + i );
    }
  }

  public static void main(String args[])
  {
    ImplementRunnable runnable = new ImplementRunnable();
    Thread t = new Thread(runnable);
    t.start();
  }
}
```

In the code above, you can see that a thread that is created by implementing the Runnable interface is started slightly differently than a thread that subclassed with the Thread object. For such a thread to be created, the class that implements the Runnable interface must first be instantiated. After that task is completed, a Thread object must be instantiated. The Thread object is then passed the runnable object as an argument to its constructor. Once the new Thread object has been instantiated, the thread can begin its work by calling the start method. It is important to note that the run method that is actually called is that of the class implementing the Runnable interface, not the run method of the Thread object.

Now that you know how to create a thread, you need to be shown how to control its execution; this includes knowing how to start, stop, and pause it.

Controlling the Thread's Execution

Now that we have examined the different ways to create an instance of a thread, we will discuss ways to begin and end its execution. We will also look at a short example program that uses several threads that remain synchronized.

In order for a thread to begin execution, the `start` method must be called.

```
Public static void main(String args[])
{
  MyRunnable run = new MyRunnable();
  Thread t = new Thread(run);
  t.start();
}
```

Suspending and Resuming Threads

There are several ways to stop a thread from executing, such as sleeping or suspending the thread. The preferred method is to cause the thread's `run` method to return. For example, the following `run` method would simply print out "hello" and then terminate by returning.

```
public void run()
{
  System.out.println("Hello");
}
```

Also, take a look at the code in the previous section. If this code is called, a new thread is created; this new thread will begin its job by executing the `run` method of the `ImplementRunnable` class. But once this method is running, you should call `sleep` or `yield` at some point so that the thread won't consume all the CPU time for the process, which may result in it not allowing any other threads to be executed.

A thread's execution can be paused by calling the `sleep` method of the `Thread` object. The `sleep` method will cause the thread to stop executing for a specified number of milliseconds. This method is declared as a static method and must be called as follows.

```
Thread.sleep(1500);
```

The above line would cause the currently executing thread to sleep for 1,500 milliseconds (1.5 seconds). You may not execute the `sleep` method on any but the currently executing thread. If you need to cause a thread other than the currently executing one to temporarily stop executing, the `suspend` and `resume` methods of the `Thread` class must be used.

To temporarily halt a thread's execution you should call that thread's `suspend` method. This will stop the thread from executing and taking up processor time. Once you wish the thread to resume, you should call the thread's `resume` method.

If you simply want to pause your thread to give other threads a chance to execute, you might want to consider using the `Thread.yield` method. This method does not wait a specific amount of time like `sleep` does, but instead it will yield to any threads that might have been waiting to execute. The `yield` method call is typically put inside of the `run` method that executes a lengthy task. The following `run` method illustrates this:

```
public void run()
{
```

```
for(int x=0;x<100000;x++)
{
  // perform some lengthy task
  Thread.yield(); // yield to any other threads so this // thread won't
monopolize the processor.
  }
}
```

WARNING It is not generally recommended to stop threads by calling the stop method. The stop method abruptly halts a thread. This could leave resources locked that the thread was using. It is better to let the thread stop itself by allowing the run method to return.

Synchronizing Threads

Up to this point, we have only talked about independent, asynchronous threads—those that are self contained and don't need any outside resources or methods to run. Instead, such threads may run at their own pace, and they don't need to be concerned with the state or activities of any other threads that may be running in the background.

However, this type of thread is the exception rather than the rule. Most threads must usually work with other related threads. When such threads work together, they must not only share data, but they must also be aware of the state and activities of other threads. The threads used to create a multithreaded spider share data this way. In order to make the spider run efficiently, the work of the spider (examining many web pages) is broken down into smaller subtasks, and these tasks are given to individual threads. These threads must communicate with each other to make sure that new work is obtained and no new work duplicates work already completed.

Object Locking

Java provides several mechanisms to facilitate this thread synchronization. Most Java synchronization centers around the mechanism of *object locking*. Every object in Java that descends from the object named Object has an *individual* lock. And because every object in Java must descend from Object, every object in Java has its own lock, which allows it to be coordinated among threads to be shared.

Another way Java facilitates thread synchronization is through the use of the synchronized keyword. Java uses the synchronized keyword to define sections of the program that require thread synchronization. The most basic operation performed by using the synchronized keyword is defining each section that needs such treatment as a *critical section*. In a critical section, only one thread can be executing at a time.

Most object orientated programs use get and set methods to get and set the values of properties. These methods are ideal candidates to use with the synchronized keyword. This is because the get method reads the internal state of any object and the set method changes the internal state of an object. You do not want the state changing right in the middle of a get operation. Likewise, you do not want the state to change while another thread is changing the state with the set operation. The following code shows just such an example.

```
public class MySynchronizedObject
{
  int myInt;

  public synchronized int getMyInt()
  {
    return myInt;
  }

  public synchronized void putMyInt(int value)
  {
    myInt = value;
  }
}
```

In this code, the method declarations for both putMyInt() and getMyInt() make use of the synchronized keyword. As a result, the system creates a unique lock with every instantiation of MySynchronizedObject. Whenever a thread enters a synchronized method, all other threads must wait to access that method. No two threads can be inside of a synchronized method at the same time.

Once a thread calls either putMyInt() or getMyInt(), that thread owns the lock of that instance of MySynchronizedObject, until the putMyInt() or getMyInt() method exits. Java automatically handles the acquisition and release of this lock.

NOTE   Each object only has one lock that is shared by all synchronized areas of that program. A common misconception is that each synchronized area contains its own lock.

Examining Thread Synchronization

You will now be shown an example of thread synchronization and object locking. In the next few sections, we will develop a simple object that uses object locking and synchronized sections to allow itself to be accessed by multiple threads. First, we will look at a conventional non-locking class to see why locking is needed.

A Non-Locking Example

The MySynchronizedObject stores its contents variable. A Boolean variable, named available, is also declared. This variable has a value of true when the value has just been put but has not yet been gotten, and it is false when the value has been gotten but not yet put. We will first consider a simple implementation of synchronized get and put methods.

```
public synchronized int getMyInt()
{
  if (available == true)
  {
    available = false;
    return myInt;
  }
}
public synchronized void putMyInt(int value)
{
  if (available == false)
  {
    available = true;
    myInt = value;
  }
}
```

In the code above, these two methods will not work. First consider the get method. What happens if nothing has yet been put in the MySynchronizedObject and available isn't true? In this case, get doesn't do anything. Likewise, if something is put into the object before the get method was called, the put method does nothing.

In this case, what is needed is for the caller of the get method to wait until there is something to read. Likewise, the caller of the put method should wait until there is no data and it is safe to store its value. To allow this to work, the two methods must coordinate their actions. You will now be shown how to do this.

A Locking Example

Consider this new implementation in which both get and put wait on their class's lock and notify each other of their activities:

```
public synchronized int getMyInt()
{
  while (available == false)
  {
    try
    {
      // wait for a different thread to put a value
      wait();
    }
    catch (InterruptedException e)
    {
    }
  }
  available = false;
  // notify all remaining threads seeking this object that value has been
retrieved
```

```
    notifyAll();
    return myInt;
  }

  public synchronized void putMyInt(int value)
  {
    while (available == true)
    {
      try
      {
        // wait for a different thread to get value
        wait();
      }
      catch (InterruptedException e)
      {
      }
    }
    myInt = value;
    available = true;
    // notify that value has been set
    notifyAll();
  }
```

Here, the get method loops until the put method has been called and there is data to read. The wait method is also called each time through this loop. When the wait method is called, the lock held on the MySynchronizedObject is relinquished (thereby allowing other threads to lock and update the MySynchronizedObject) as the thread waits for a notify method to be called. Once something is put in the MySynchronizedObject, it notifies any waiting threads by calling notifyAll(). These waiting threads will then come out of the wait state, and the available variable will be set to true, causing the loop to exit. All of this will cause the get method to return the value in the MySynchronizedObject.

NOTE   The put method works in a similar fashion, waiting for a thread to consume the current value before allowing the other threads to add more values.

Calling the notifyAll() method, as mentioned above, will wake any threads that are waiting on the MySynchronizedObject that called notifyAll(). The code just demonstrated uses notifyAll() in both the get and set methods to release any threads that might have been waiting for these methods to finish. In addition to the notifyAll() method there is a method named notify() that will select a single thread to release. You have no way to influence this selection, however. You may only release one seemingly random thread, or all the threads. As a result you cannot control exactly which thread will be released.

Using a Database

If a spider is to access large web sites, there must be an efficient way to store the queues of sites that drive the spider. These queues, which were discussed in the last chapter, manage the large lists of web pages that a spider must maintain. To manage such large lists requires the use of a *Database Management System (DBMS)*. A DBMS is a software application that manages data. Examples of DBMSs include Oracle, IBM DB2, and Microsoft SQL Server. Java provides a set of classes, known collectively as *Java Database Connectivity (JDBC)* to access a DBMS.

As you are shown how to access a database through Java, three different standards will be discussed. First is *Structured Query Language (SQL)*, which allows you to specify what data you would like returned from a database. Java Database Connectivity (JDBC) is what a Java program uses to submit SQL commands to a database. JDBC can also use an *Open Database Connectivity (ODBC)* driver to communicate with a database. ODBC is a very popular, widely used protocol developed by Microsoft.

The spider provided for this book supports the use of a SQL database to store the queues. As long as the database is compatible with JDBC and can be accessed using SQL, it will be supported. There are JDBC drivers available for most databases, and nearly every modern database supports SQL. The specific database that we will examine in this chapter is Microsoft Access, which is a very common, inexpensive database. The SQL code used by the spider is not tied to MS Access because it is written to be generic enough to be used by any SQL database.

The SQL Language

The purpose of JDBC is to allow SQL statements to be sent to a database. Before you learn how to use JDBC, however, you first need to be familiar with some of the basic SQL commands that will be used by the spider provided by the Bot package.

The *SELECT* Statement

The SELECT statement is one of the first statements that SQL programmers use. The basic syntax of the SQL SELECT statement is as follows:

```
SELECT [Field1],[Field2],[Fieldx] FROM [TABLE] WHERE [FieldX] = [Value]
```

Immediately following the SELECT statement are the fields that you would like returned. Don't use all of these fields because by doing so, you will slow the DBMS connection. Once the fields are specified, you must use the FROM clause to tell JDBC which table contains these fields. After you have specified the table, you can use the optional WHERE clause to filter the amount of data being retrieved and to perform comparisons on the fields. The following is an example SQL SELECT statement:

```
SELECT URL FROM tblWorkload WHERE Status = 'W';
```

This statement would return the URLs of all records in the `tblWorkload` table where the status was equal to `W`.

The *DELETE* Statement

The `DELETE` statement is used to remove rows from a table. This statement shares many syntactical similarities to the `SELECT` statement. The basic syntax of the SQL `DELETE` statement is as follows:

```
DELETE FROM [TABLE] WHERE [FieldX] = [Value]
```

In this case, a table must be specified from which to delete a row. A single `DELETE` statement cannot delete from more than one table. If the optional `WHERE` clause is not provided, the `DELETE` statement will delete all of the rows in that table. The following is an example of a `DELETE` statement that will delete every row from the `tblWorkload` table where the `Status` field is equal to `'W'`.

```
DELETE FROM tblWorkload WHERE Status = 'W';
```

The *INSERT* Statement

The `INSERT` statement is used to insert values into a table. This process should not be confused with the process of changing data that is already stored in the table. If you wish to modify data that is stored in the table, the `UPDATE` statement (discussed next) must be used. The `INSERT` statement is used only when new data needs to be inserted into the DBMS for the first time. The basic syntax of the SQL `INSERT` statement is as follows:

```
INSERT INTO [Table]([Field1],[Field2],[FieldX]) VALUES
([Value1],[Value2],[ValueX]);
```

In this code, the table must first be specified as should the fields that will be initially filled. The values, which are the actual data to be inserted into the table, will then be copied to the fields in the same order in which they were specified. The following `INSERT` statement will insert a URL with the status of W into the table:

```
INSERT INTO tblWorkload(URL,Status) VALUES ('http://www.heat-on.com','W');
```

The *UPDATE* Statement

The SQL `UPDATE` statement is used to change data that is already in the table. This statement can change any number of rows. The `UPDATE` uses a `WHERE` clause that is in the same format as the `SELECT` statement. The basic syntax of the SQL `UPDATE` statement is as follows:

```
UPDATE [table] SET [Field1] = [Value1], [Field2] = [Value2], [FieldX] = [ValueX]
WHERE [WhereField] = [WhereValue];
```

The `UPDATE` statement must specify the table to be updated. The `SET` clause allows a series of comma-separated name-value pairs that specify the values to be updated. Finally, the `WHERE` clause is used to specify which rows should be updated. If the `WHERE` clause is not used, every row in the table will be updated. The following is an example of an UPDATE statement that will set the status to C for every row in the database that has a URL of http://www.heat-on.com:

```
UPDATE tblWorkload SET Status = 'C' WHERE URL = 'http://www.heat-on.com/';
```

NOTE   It is important to note that if no records satisfy the where clause, then no rows will be updated.

Selecting and Configuring the Database

Before you can learn to create the Java code necessary to access a database, the database must be configured. First you will need to choose what DBMS you are going to be using, and what sort of driver. The spider provided by the Bot package supports either JDBC or Open Database Connectivity (ODBC) drivers, and the examples given in this chapter will use the Microsoft Access database. Before you can configure the database you must make sure it will support either JDBC or ODBC.

JDBC and ODBC

We must first discuss the difference between JDBC and ODBC. JDBC is a well-defined application program interface (API) for accessing databases using Java. To use a database with JDBC, you must have a JDBC driver. One problem with using JDBC is that it is a new standard and there are not always drivers to support your particular database.

This is where ODBC comes into play. ODBC is one of the most common database drivers, and there is an ODBC driver available for nearly every database. Though ODBC does work similarly to JDBC (it is an API for database access), it is quite different from JDBC in that it is only available on the Windows platform, and it cannot be directly called from a Java program.

NOTE   Microsoft and a consortium of other companies developed the ODBC standard, and there-fore, ODBC is very common on the Microsoft platforms.

Though ODBC is not directly compatible with Java, it can be used with Java through the use of a *bridge driver*. An ODBC bridge driver allows Java programs to get to ODBC data-bases by using a JDBC driver that works with any ODBC database. This driver is called the *JDBC to ODBC bridge*. By using this driver, you can take advantage of the many ODBC drivers in existence.

Though the Bot package will work with any JDBC driver without ODBC, for the purposes of this chapter, we will first discuss how to use the JDBC to ODBC bridge driver with Microsoft Access. We will then discuss how to use other databases. Of course, you will have to have either a JDBC or an ODBC driver for any database you wish to use.

> **TIP** It is not necessary to own a copy of Microsoft Access to use the example in this chapter. Instead, you will just need to install the Microsoft Data Access (MDAC) package in order for the example from this chapter to be able to run. This package can be downloaded from http://www.microsoft.com/data/.

Using Microsoft Access

In order to use a Microsoft Access database with the spider provided by the Bot package, you must specify a Data Source Name (DSN). Microsoft Windows uses this DSN to identify databases that will be used with ODBC. In order to use the SQL version of the spider provided by the Bot package, you will need to set up a DSN entry so that the Microsoft Access database can be located. The Microsoft Access database needed for this chapter (SpiderWorkload .mdb) can be found with the example code for this chapter on the companion CD.

> **WARNING** Do not try to use the SpiderWorkload.mdb database directly from the CD-ROM because it requires read/write access. Copy the database from the CD to your hard drive and use this copy.

ODBC DSNs are set up using the ODBC Data Source Administrator. To access this administrator, select the Control Panel from the Windows Start menu, and look for an icon named Data Sources (ODBC). If you don't see the ODBC icon here, look for the Administrative Tools icon. Some of the newer versions of Windows, such as Windows XP, store the ODBC icon here instead of in the main folder.

Once you start the ODBC Administrator, you will be presented with a screen similar to the one shown in Figure 9.1.

FIGURE 9.1:
ODBC Data Source
Administrator

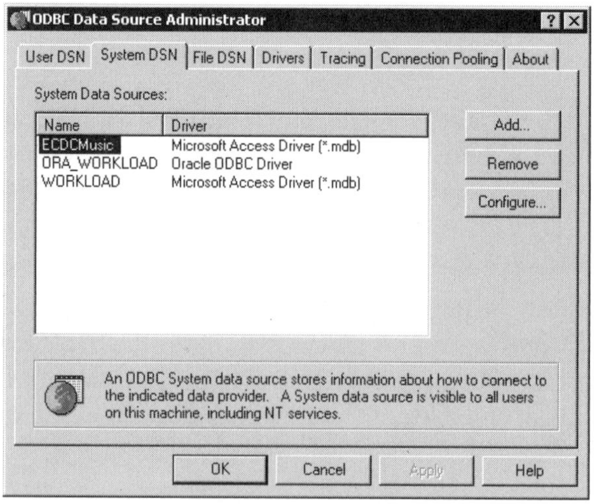

The first thing you should notice is that there are three distinct types of DSNs that can be configured. These three different DSN types are represented as tabs at the top of the dialog box in Figure 9.1.

User DSN   The user DSN will only give the current user access to your DSN.

System DSN   Every user who has access to this computer can use your DSN.

File DSN   Your DSN is available to all users, and it is stored in a file rather than in the Registry.

The type of DSN that we will be creating will be a system DSN. By choosing this type, you will be allowed to use this DSN regardless of what user is logged in. Also any *NT Service* running on the computer can use a system DSN. An NT Service is a program that runs in the background without the user noticing it. A common example of such a service is a web server. Figure 9.1 already has the System DSN tab selected. From here, in order to start the process of using a system DSN, you should click the Add button.

After you click the Add button, you will see a screen that looks like Figure 9.2; it is here that you configure the access to your DSN. First enter **WORKLOAD** (the name specified for use with the SpiderWorkload.mdb database and the one that the example program that appears later in this chapter expects) into the Data Source Name box. This name is what other programs will use to access the DSN you are setting up.

In addition to the name of the DSN, you must also specify the location of the database file. This should be done by clicking the Select button. This button will open a standard Windows file browser that allows you to choose the MDB file that will be associated with this DSN. Navigate to where you stored your SpiderWorkload.mdb file, and select it. Again, remember to choose the copy you saved to your hard drive rather than choosing the CD copy, which wouldn't work.

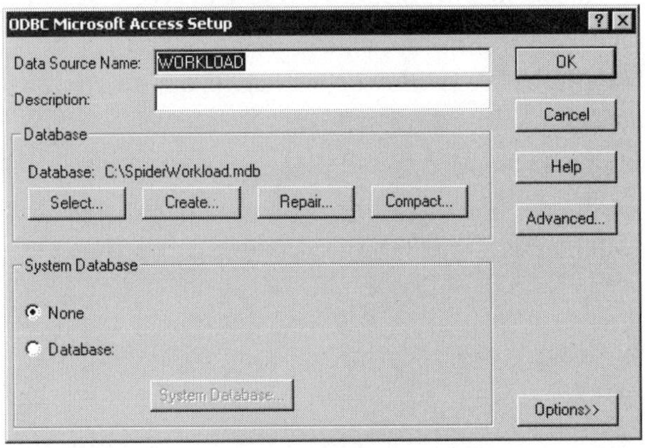

FIGURE 9.2:
ODBC Microsoft Access setup

Using Other Databases

Microsoft Access is not the only database supported by the spider provided by the Bot package. Furthermore, ODBC is not the only type of driver that the spider can use. In order to use other databases, you must perform whatever steps are required to set up a DSN for that database. The SQL code used by the spider is very generic and should work under any SQL DBMS.

Most databases will offer some sort of ODBC driver when they are running under Microsoft Windows. It may take a few extra setups to set them up, however. Though ODBC is the easiest way to use the high-performance spider under the Windows operating system, another method is to use a use a JDBC driver for the database of your choice. This is the only option that will be available if you are running the high-performance spider under a UNIX operating system. The instructions for installing JDBC drivers vary from vendor to vendor, so be sure to check with the vendor before proceeding with the installation.

If you do use another database, you will have to reconstruct the tblWorkload table that is used by the spider. The structure of the tblWorkload is very simple; it has two fields—URL and status. Here is a summary of the two fields, their types, and their lengths:

Field	Type	Length
URL	Varchar	255
Status	Varchar	1

Some databases will require you to issue a CREATE TABLE command in order to construct a suitable table. The following is a CREATE TABLE statement that will create a valid workload table.

```
CREATE TABLE Workload(
  URL VARCHAR(255),
  status char 1 );
```

Programming with JDBC

As previously stated, JDBC allows Java to access a DBMS. We will now examine the basics of how this works.

Basically, before JDBC can be used in your program, you must import it using the following command:

```
import java.sql.*;
```

This will make the objects that you need in order to use JDBC available to your program. We will now examine the objects that make up JDBC

The Connection Objects

Connection objects are the highest-level JDBC objects. A connection object represents the actual connection to the DBMS. The syntax for creating a connection is shown here.

```
Connection conn;
Class.forName("sun.jdbc.odbc.JdbcOdbcDriver");
conn = DriverManager.getConnection("jdbc:odbc:WORKLOAD");
```

The first line of this code creates a variable of the type `Connection`, which will be used later to obtain a statement object. The command in the following line, `Class.forName`, registers the JDBC driver that will be used. The string `sun.jdbc.odbc.JdbcOdbcDriver` identifies the driver that we are using. This is the JDBC to ODBC bridge driver that was mentioned earlier. When it is using this driver, a Java program can access any ODBC data source. If you were going to use a JDBC driver other than the ODBC bridge, its name would be inserted here. Refer to your DBMS documentation for the correct driver string.

Finally, in the last line of this code, the connection is opened. Where you see the string `WORKLOAD` is where the DSN name should be inserted. If you plug in any valid DSN string, this code will attempt to gain access to that DBMS. Now that we have a connection object we can obtain a statement object.

The Statement Object

Statement objects represent individual SQL statements, or commands, that will be executed against a connection object. For the spider in this chapter, we use a special type of statement called a *prepared statement*. A prepared statement stores its SQL in a compiled state so that it can be more quickly executed. This is particularly valuable if a SQL statement must be executed repeatedly. In this case, the SQL statement would have to be compiled each time it was executed. Using a prepared statement alleviates this overhead.

A prepared statement is stored in a `PreparedStatement` object. The following lines of code will create a prepared statement designed to execute the SQL command `SELECT * FROM tblWORKLOAD WHERE status = ?`.

```
PreparedStatement prep;
prep = conn.prepareStatement(
"SELECT * FROM tblWORKLOAD WHERE status = ?");
```

First, the `prep` variable is declared. Next, a prepared statement is generated using the connection object named `conn`. The prepared statement is now ready to be used and is stored in the `prep` variable.

A SQL statement such as the one above is used to retrieve rows from a database. This entire statement is valid SQL except for the question mark. This question mark is used to fill in a parameter. To use this parameter, the `setString()` call of the `PreparedStatement` object must be used. The `setString` method is used to work with string data. The `PreparedStatement` object also supports methods for other data types, such as `setAsciiStream()`, `setBigDecimal()`, `setBinaryStream()`, `setBoolean()`, `setByte()`, `setBytes()`, `setDate()`, `setDouble()`, `set-Float()`, `setInt()`, `setLong()`, `setNull()`, `setObject()`, `setShort()`, `setString()`, `setTime()`, `setTimestamp()`, and `setUnicodeStream()`. The following code would set the parameter to the character `W`.

```
prep.setString(1, "W");
```

The first parameter specifies the number of the parameter to set. If there had been multiple question marks in the SQL string, 1 would indicate the first, 2 the second, and so on. The second parameter (`W`) is the value that will be inserted for the first question mark in the SQL.

Now that we have seen how to create a prepared statement we will examine how to execute a SQL statement and retrieve a result set.

The *ResultSet* Object

Some SQL commands will return data, which is then held by *result sets*. The JDBC object `ResultSet` is one such result set. A `ResultSet` object is only used if you are expecting the SQL statement to return data. If the SQL statement is not going to return data the `executeUpdate` method of the prepared statement should be used, rather than the `executeQuery` statement shown here.

The SQL `SELECT` statement is the only SQL statement that will return data. The other SQL commands (`INSERT`, `DELETE`, and `UPDATE`) will not return data because they are not requesting data. The following code would be used when a `SELECT` statement is executed and you receive data back:

```
rs = prep.executeQuery();

while( rs.next() )
{
    System.out.println( rs.getString("URL"));
}
```

When you call the `executeQuery` method of the prepared statement, as shown here, a result set will be returned. In the following line, the `next` method must be called in order to retrieve the first row returned by the query. The `next` method will return false when another row could not be acquired. In the following line, the `getString` method is being used to retrieve the columns or fields of the requested table. The `URL` string in this line specifies the field name to be retrieved in this particular result set.

If no data is to be returned from the SQL statement, the process is somewhat different. In this case, the `executeUpdate()` method is used instead of an `executeQuery()` because there is no return value from this method. The SQL is simply executed. If an error happens, then an exception is thrown. The following shows how to execute a prepared statement that does not return a `ResultSet`.

```
prep.executeUpdate();
```

The High-Performance Spider

The example program for this chapter implements a spider that can use a SQL-based queue instead of a memory-based queue. This is the only difference between this example and the example program you saw in Chapter 8. Both the SQL-based queue discussed here and the memory-based queue are useful; which you use depends on what you need for a particular situation. The memory-based queue spider of Chapter 8 is useful when you are running a program that may not have direct access to a SQL database. On the other hand, if your spider is to access large amounts of pages or many sites, then a SQL-based spider is more effective.

TIP   From tests on my own computer I found that the memory-based spider becomes less effective on jobs that will cause the such a spider to visit 10,000 pages or more. Jobs that require more than 10,000 pages should be handled by the SQL-based spider.

As stated, the changes to this program from the way it appeared in Chapter 8 are minimal. This is because the source code that is necessary to use a SQL database for queue management was already contained in Chapter 8's example in the form of commented text. These lines of code just need to be uncommented to produce a spider that uses a SQL DBMS rather than a memory-based one.

Because the `GetSite.java` file is nearly the same as that of Chapter 8, it will not be reprinted here. Instead, you only need to take a look at the following lines of code, the ones that should be uncommented:

```
// NOTE: To use SQL based workload management,
// uncomment the following lines and include a
// valid data source.

    try
    {
      wl = new SpiderSQLWorkload(
        "sun.jdbc.odbc.JdbcOdbcDriver",
        "jdbc:odbc:WORKLOAD");
    }
    catch(Exception e)
```

```
{
  JOptionPane.showMessageDialog(this,
    e,
    "Error",
    JOptionPane.OK_CANCEL_OPTION,
    null );
}
```

By uncommenting this code, you are allowing this code to do several things. First, this code specifies that the `SpiderSQLWorkload` manager must use a SQL database to manage the queues. If a workload is not specified, the memory-based spider, implemented through the `SpiderInternalWorkload` class, will be used.

This code also asks that the constructor of `SpiderSQLWorkload` take two parameters. The first of these is the name of the JDBC driver. In this case, we are using the JDBC to ODBC bridge driver, which is denoted by the string `"sun.jdbc.odbc.JdbcOdbcDriver"`. The second parameter specifies the information to be used to open a connection; this is denoted by the string `"jdbc:odbc:WORKLOAD"`.

Once this new workload manager has been specified, the spider will attempt to use a SQL DBMS to manage the queues. Before you go any further, make sure that you have the database properly configured, as described earlier in this chapter. Now that you have seen the high-performance spider in action and know how to use it, you will be shown how it was constructed.

Under the Hood

The high-performance spider makes extensive use of threads and its SQL database. We will now examine each of the classes that make up this spider in detail. In addition to these classes, the spider is designed to communicate with external classes provided by the programmer. In this section, you will see how all of this works. First, you will be presented with an overview of how the various classes fit together. Next, this section will explain the finer points of each class. Figure 9.3 shows how all of the spider related classes fit together.

FIGURE 9.3:

The spider classes

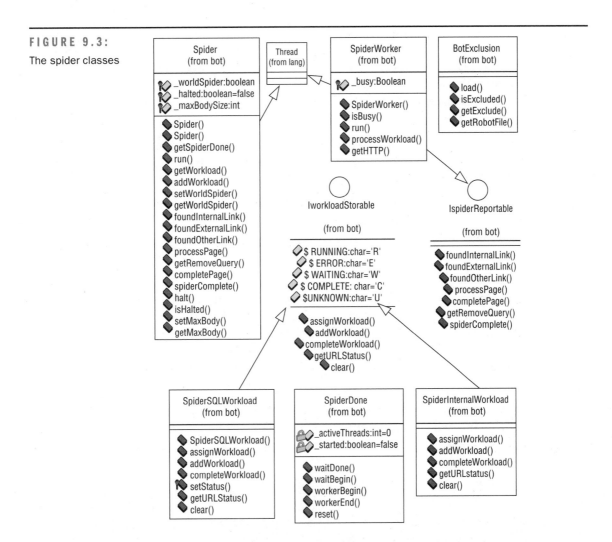

The Spider Class   The Spider class is the class that you will work with as you create a spider of your own. This class contains many methods that act as the interface, through which you command the spider. The spider class allows two additional classes, defined by the ISpiderReportable and IWorkloadStorable interfaces, to be used to customize the operation of the spider.

The ISpiderReportable Interface   This interface defines a consumer for web pages that the spider locates. A spider by itself simply traverses through web pages. This alone serves little purpose. The spider should actually do something with each page that it encounters. Any object that implements the ISpiderReportable interface can receive pages from the spider.

The `IWorkloadStorable` Interface   The `IWorkloadStorable` interface is the second interface that allows you to customize the behavior of the spider. One major task for the spider is to organize the lists of sites visited, and those it has yet to visit. These lists are called the *workload*. This interface defines an object that can store and retrieve pages in the workload. The Bot package includes the following two workload managers: `SpiderSQLWorkload` and `SpiderInternalWorkload`.

The `SpiderSQLWorkload` Class   The `SpiderSQLWorkload` class is one of the built-in workload managers. This workload manager can store the workload in a SQL database. Using a SQL database, this workload manager can handle very large sites.

The `SpiderInternalWorkload` Class   The `SpiderInternalWorkload` class is one of the built-in workload managers. This workload manager can store the workload in the computer's memory. Because it uses the computer's memory, this workload manager does not require a database to be set up. Though self contained, this approach may not work on extremely large sites.

The `SpiderWorker` Class   The spider makes extensive use of multithreading, and must break the task into many smaller tasks. The basic task of the spider is to download a web site and add any links that the page has to the workload. This `SpiderWorker` class implements this basic task. When the spider starts up, it creates a pool of `SpiderWorker` classes that will handle the pages found by the spider.

The `SpiderDone` Class   With many concurrent threads it is difficult to tell exactly when the spider is done. There needs to be an object that tracks exactly how many threads are still running, and one that provides an efficient way to wait for that count to reach zero. This is the purpose of the `SpiderDone` class.

The *Spider* Class

The `Spider` class is meant to serve three goals. First, it acts as the interface to the spider and provides methods for using the spider. In addition to this, this object manages the thread pool and it reports the findings of the spider back to the object that started the spider. (In this section, we will examine how the a `Spider` object communicates with the `SpiderWorker` objects.) Finally, it is the job of the `Spider` class to determine when the spider is done.

NOTE   This object's methods were documented in Chapter 8, as was the interface between this class and an application using the spider.

The primary task that the `Spider` class provides for the `SpiderWorker` objects is management of the workload. The workload is the list of all URLs that the spider has interacted with so far.

The purpose of the SpiderWorker objects is to process URLs that the spider must visit. When a SpiderWorker object first starts up, it requires a URL process. The SpiderWorker objects call the getWorkload() method of the Spider object. The getWorkload method will return a new URL that was waiting to be checked. If no URL is waiting, the getWorkload method will wait for work to become available.

In addition to managing the workload, the Spider class must also keep track of when the spider is done. This task is delegated to the SpiderDone class. A SpiderDone object is made available to each of the SpiderWorker objects. This SpiderDone object keeps track of the SpiderWorker objects and can determine when the spider is done.

When you call the Spider object from another class, you expect to get back pages that the spider has found. The last task accomplished by the Spider class is the return of these pages. When the Spider object was first constructed, a manager object to which the pages would be handed off to was specified. This manager object, which must implement the ISpider-Reportable interface, should be set up in your program to handle pages returned. The process for creating such a class was discussed in Chapter 8.

Listing 9.1 shows such a spider manager. This particular spider manager is used to download the contents of a site to files. For each page encountered by the spider, this manager will save that page to a file.

Listing 9.1   **The Spider Manager (*Spider.java*)**

```
/**
 * The Spider class is the main organizational class for
 * spidering. It delegates work to the SpiderWorker class.
 *
 * Copyright 2001 by Jeff Heaton
 *
 * @author Jeff Heaton
 * @version 1.0
 */
package com.heaton.bot;
import java.util.*;
import java.io.*;
import com.heaton.bot.*;

public class Spider extends Thread implements ISpiderReportable
{
    protected IWorkloadStorable _workload;
    protected SpiderWorker _pool[];
    protected boolean _worldSpider;
    protected ISpiderReportable _manager;
    protected boolean _halted = false;
    protected SpiderDone _done = new SpiderDone();
```

```
protected int _maxBodySize;


/**
 * This constructor prepares the spider to begin.
 * Basic information required to begin is passed.
 * This constructor uses the internal workload manager.
 *
 * @param manager The object to which this spider reports its findings.
 * @param url The URL at which the spider should begin.
 * @param http The HTTP handler used by this spider.
 * @param poolsize The size of the thread pool.
 */
public Spider(ISpiderReportable manager,String url,HTTP http,int poolSize)
{
  this(manager,url,http,poolSize,new SpiderInternalWorkload());
}

/**
 * This constructor prepares the spider to begin.
 * Basic information required to begin is passed.
 * This constructor allows the user to specify a
 * customized workload manager.
 *
 * @param manager The object to which this spider reports its findings.
 * @param url The URL at which the spider should begin.
 * @param http The HTTP handler used by this spider.
 * @param poolsize The size of the thread pool.
 * @param w A customized workload manager.
 */
public Spider(ISpiderReportable manager,String url,HTTP http,int
poolSize,IWorkloadStorable w)
{
  _manager = manager;
  _worldSpider = false;

  _pool = new SpiderWorker[poolSize];
  for(int i=0;i<_pool.length;i++)
  {
    HTTP hc = http.copy();
    _pool[i] = new SpiderWorker( this,hc );
  }
  _workload = w;
  if(url.length()>0)
  {
    _workload.clear();
    addWorkload(url);
  }
}

/**
```

```
 * Get the SpiderDone object used by this spider
 * to determine when it is done.
 *
 * @return Returns SpiderDone object.
 */
public SpiderDone getSpiderDone()
{
  return _done;
}

/**
 * The main loop of the spider. This can be called
 * directly, or the start method can be called to
 * run as a background thread. This method will not
 * return until there is no work remaining for the
 * spider.
 */
public void run()
{
  if(_halted)
    return;
  for(int i=0;i<_pool.length;i++)
    _pool[i].start();

    try
    {
      _done.waitBegin();
      _done.waitDone();
      Log.log(Log.LOG_LEVEL_NORMAL,"Spider has no work.");
      spiderComplete();

      for(int i=0;i<_pool.length;i++)
      {
          _pool[i].interrupt();
          _pool[i].join();
          _pool[i] = null;
      }

    }
    catch(Exception e)
    {
      Log.logException("Exception while starting spider", e);
    }

}


/**
 * This method is called to get a workload
 * from the workload manager. If no workload
 * is available, this method will block until
```

```
 * there is one.
 *
 * @return Returns the next URL to be spidered.
 */
synchronized public String getWorkload()
{
  try
  {
    for(;;)
    {
      if(_halted)
        return null;
      String w = _workload.assignWorkload();
      if(w!=null)
        return w;
      wait();
    }
  }
  catch( java.lang.InterruptedException e)
  {
  }
  return null;
}

/**
 * Called to add a workload to the workload manager.
 * This method will release a thread that was waiting
 * for a workload. This method will do nothing if the
 * spider has been halted.
 *
 * @param url The URL to be added to the workload.
 */
synchronized public void addWorkload(String url)
{
  if(_halted)
    return;
  _workload.addWorkload(url);
  notify();
}

/**
 * Called to specify this spider as either a world
 * or site spider. See getWorldSpider for more information
 * about what a world spider is.
 *
 * @param b True to be a world spider.
 */
public void setWorldSpider(boolean b)
{
  _worldSpider = b;
}
```

```
/**
 * Returns true if this is a world spider; a world
 * spider does not restrict itself to a single site
 * and will likely go on "forever."
 *
 * @return Returns true if the spider is done.
 */
public boolean getWorldSpider()
{
  return _worldSpider;
}


/**
 * Called when the spider finds an internal
 * link. An internal link shares the same
 * host address as the URL that started
 * the spider. This method hands the link off
 * to the manager and adds the URL to the workload
 * if necessary.
 *
 * @param url The URL that was found by the spider.
 * @return true - The spider should add this URL to the workload.
 * false - The spider should not add this URL to the workload.
 */
synchronized public boolean foundInternalLink(String url)
{
  if(_manager.foundInternalLink(url))
    addWorkload(url);
  return true;
}

/**
 * Called when the spider finds an external
 * link. An external link does not share the
 * same host address as the URL that started
 * the spider. This method hands the link off
 * to the manager and adds the URL to the workload
 * if necessary. If this is a world spider, then
 * external links are treated as internal links.
 *
 * @param url The URL that was found by the spider.
 * @return true - The spider should add this URL to the workload.
 * false - The spider should not add this URL to the workload.
 */
synchronized public boolean foundExternalLink(String url)
{
  if(_worldSpider)
  {
    foundInternalLink(url);
    return true;
```

```
    }
    if(_manager.foundExternalLink(url))
      addWorkload(url);
    return true;
  }

  /**
   * Called when the spider finds a type of
   * link that does not point to another HTML
   * page (for example a mailto link). This method
   * hands the link off to the manager and adds
   * the URL to the workload if necessary.
   *
   * @param url The URL that was found by the spider.
   * @return true - The spider should add this URL to the workload.
   * false - The spider should not add this URL to the workload.
   */
  synchronized public boolean foundOtherLink(String url)
  {
    if(_manager.foundOtherLink(url))
      addWorkload(url);
    return true;
  }

  /**
   * Called to process a downloaded page.
   *
   * @param page The page contents.
   *
   */

  synchronized public void processPage(HTTP page)
  {
    _manager.processPage(page);     }


  /**
   * This method is called by the spider to determine if
   * query strings should be removed. By default the spider
   * always chooses to remove query strings, so true is
   * returned.
   *
   * @return true - Query string should be removed.
   * false - Leave query strings as is.
   */
  synchronized public boolean getRemoveQuery()
  {
    return true;
  }
```

```
/**
 * Called to request that a page be processed.
 * This page was just downloaded by the spider.
 * This message passes this call on to its
 * manager.
 *
 * @param page The page contents.
 * @param error true - This page resulted in an HTTP error.
 * false - This page downloaded correctly.
 */
synchronized public void completePage(HTTP page,boolean error)
{
    _workload.completeWorkload(page.getURL(),error);
}


/**
 * Called when the spider has no more work. This method
 * just passes this event on to its manager.
 */
synchronized public void spiderComplete()
{
    _manager.spiderComplete();
}


/**
 * Called to cause the spider to halt. The spider will not halt
 * immediately. Once the spider is halted, the run method will
 * return.
 */
synchronized public void halt()
{
    _halted = true;
    _workload.clear();
    notifyAll();
}


/**
 * Determines if the spider has been halted.
 *
 * @return Returns true if the spider has been halted.
 */
public boolean isHalted()
{
    return _halted;
}

/**
 * This method will set the maximum body size
 * that will be downloaded.
 *
 * @param i The maximum body size, or -1 for unlimted.
```

```
  */
 public void setMaxBody(int mx)
 {
   _maxBodySize = mx;
   for(int i=0;i<_pool.length;i++)
     _pool[i].getHTTP().setMaxBody(mx);
 }

 /**
  * This method will return the maximum body size
  * that will be downloaded.
  *
  * @return The maximum body size, or -1 for unlimted.
  */
 public int getMaxBody()
 {
   return _maxBodySize;
 }

}
```

The *ISpiderReportable* Interface

The ISpiderReportable interface (discussed in detail in Chapter 8) is one of the two interfaces that you can use to customize the operation of the spider. This interface defines the
methods used by the spider to report its findings. Listing 9.2 shows the source code for the
IspiderReportable interface.

Listing 9.2   **Reporting progress (*ISpiderReportable.java*)**

```
package com.heaton.bot;

/**
 * This interface represents a class to which
 * the spider can report. As the spider
 * does its job, events from this interface
 * will be called.
 *
 * Copyright 2001 by Jeff Heaton
 *
 * @author Jeff Heaton
 * @version 1.0
 */
public interface ISpiderReportable {

  /**
   * Called when the spider finds an internal
   * link. An internal link shares the same
```

```
 * host address as the URL that started
 * the spider.
 *
 * @param url The URL that was found by the spider.
 * @return true - The spider should add this URL to the workload.
 * false - The spider should not add this URL to the workload.
 */
public boolean foundInternalLink(String url);

/**
 * Called when the spider finds an external
 * link. An external link does not share the
 * same host address as the URL that started
 * the spider.
 *
 * @param url The URL that was found by the spider.
 * @return true - The spider should add this URL to the workload.
 * false - The spider should not add this URL to the workload.
 */
public boolean foundExternalLink(String url);

/**
 * Called when the spider finds a type of
 * link that does not point to another HTML
 * page(for example a mailto link).
 *
 * @param url The URL that was found by the spider.
 * @return true - The spider should add this URL to the workload.
 * false - The spider should not add this URL to the workload.
 */
public boolean foundOtherLink(String url);

/**
 * Called to process a downloaded page.
 *
 * @param page The page contents.
 *
 */
public void processPage(HTTP page);

/**
 * Called to request that a page be processed.
 * This page was just downloaded by the spider.
 *
 * @param page The page contents.
 * @param error true - This page resulted in an HTTP error.
 * false - This page downloaded correctly.
 */
public void completePage(HTTP page,boolean error);

/**
```

```
    * This method is called by the spider to determine if
    * query strings should be removed. A query string
    * is the text that follows a ? on a URL. For example:
    *
    * http://www.heat-on.com/cgi-bin/login.jsp?id=a;pwd=b
    *
    * Everything to the right of, and including, the ? is
    * considered part of the query string.
    *
    * @return true - Query string should be removed.
    * false - Leave query strings as is.
    */
   public boolean getRemoveQuery();

   /**
    * Called when the spider has no more work.
    */
   public void spiderComplete();
 }
```

The *IWorkloadStorable* Interface

The IWorkloadStorable is the second interface that allows you to customize the operation of the spider. This interface implements the basic functionality required to store the four queues that manage the spider's workload. There are two implementations of the IWorkloadStorable interface provided by the Bot package.

SpiderInternalWorkload   Stores the contents of the workload in memory.

SpiderSQLWorkload   Stores the contents of the workload in a SQL database.

As the IWorkloadStorable interface stores and processes URLs, they are assigned status codes that specify which of the four queues a workload entity is currently in. These statuses are defined in Table 9.1.

TABLE 9.1: Spider Workload Statuses

Status Code	Description
RUNNING	A workload entry has a status of RUNNING if the spider worker is opening or downloading that page. This state usually goes to COMPLETE or ERROR.
ERROR	Processing this URL resulted in an error.
WAITING	This URL is waiting for a spider worker to take it on.
COMPLETE	This page is complete and should not be downloaded again.
UNKNOWN	The specified URL is not in any of the queues.

The following methods are defined by the IWorkloadStorable interface. Using these methods, URLs can be added and removed from the queues. After these methods are described, the listing for this interface will appear (see Listing 9.3).

The addWorkload method   Adds a new URL to the workload and assigns it a status of WAITING. The url parameter specifies a new URL to be added.

```
public void addWorkload(String url);
```

The assignWorkload method   Requests a URL to process. This method will return a WAITING URL and set that URL to a status of RUNNING.

```
public String assignWorkload();
```

The completeWorkload method   Marks this URL as either COMPLETE or ERROR. The url parameter specifies the URL to complete. If the error parameter is true, this workload is assigned a status of ERROR; if it is false, this workload is assigned a status of COMPLETE.

```
public void completeWorkload(String url,boolean error);
```

The clear method   Clears the contents of this workload store.

```
public void clear();
```

The getURLStatus method   Gets the status of a URL. The url parameter specifies the URL. Returns either RUNNING, ERROR, WAITING, or COMPLETE. If the URL does not exist in the database, the value of UNKNOWN is returned.

```
public char getURLStatus(String url);
```

Listing 9.3   **Storing the Workload *(IWorkloadStorable.java)***

```
package com.heaton.bot;

public interface IWorkloadStorable
{
  public static final char RUNNING = 'R';
  public static final char ERROR = 'E';
  public static final char WAITING = 'W';
  public static final char COMPLETE = 'C';
  public static final char UNKNOWN = 'U';

  public String assignWorkload();
  public void addWorkload(String url);
  public void completeWorkload(String url,boolean error);
  public char getURLStatus (String url);
  public void clear();
}
```

The *SpiderSQLWorkload* Class

The SpiderSQLWorkload class is an implementation of the IspiderWorkloadStorable inter-face that stores the workload in a SQL database. When using this approach, the spider can use a SQL DBMS to maintain its store of queues. The SpiderSQLWorkload object, shown in Listing 9.4, does this. This object implements the IWorkloadStorable interface and provides all of the methods required by that interface.

The SpiderSQLWorkload object works by preparing several SQL statements that can be used to create, add, update, and delete workload entries. One internal method, setURLStatus(), is declared. This method will first check to see if any status exists for the specified URL. If no status exists, one will be created. If a status does exist, it will be updated. The following listing shows how a SQL based workload is managed.

Listing 9.4   **Managing a SQL-Based Workload (*SpiderSQLWorkload.java*)**

```java
package com.heaton.bot;
import java.util.*;
import java.sql.*;


/**
 * This class uses a JDBC database
 * to store a spider workload.
 *
 * @author Jeff Heaton
 * @version 1.0
 */
public class SpiderSQLWorkload implements IWorkloadStorable
{

  /**
   * The JDBC connection.
   */
  Connection _connection;

  /**
   * A prepared SQL statement to clear the workload.
   */
  PreparedStatement _prepClear;

  /**
   * A prepared SQL statement to assign a workload.
   */
  PreparedStatement _prepAssign;

  /**
   * A prepared SQL statement to get the status of
```

```
 * a URL.
 */
PreparedStatement _prepGetStatus;

/**
 * A prepared SQL statement to set the status.
 */
PreparedStatement _prepSetStatus1;

/**
 * A prepared SQL statement to set the status.
 */
PreparedStatement _prepSetStatus2;

/**
 * A prepared SQL statement to set the status.
 */
PreparedStatement _prepSetStatus3;

/**
 * Create a new SQL workload store and
 * connect to a database.
 *
 * @param driver The JDBC driver to use.
 * @param source The driver source name.
 * @exception java.sql.SQLException
 * @exception java.lang.ClassNotFoundException
 */
public SpiderSQLWorkload(String driver, String source)
  throws SQLException, ClassNotFoundException
{
  Class.forName(driver);
  _connection = DriverManager.getConnection(source);
  _prepClear = _connection.prepareStatement("DELETE FROM tblWorkload;");
  _prepAssign = _connection.prepareStatement("SELECT URL FROM tblWorkload
WHERE Status = 'W';");
  _prepGetStatus = _connection.prepareStatement("SELECT Status FROM
tblWorkload WHERE URL = ?;");
  _prepSetStatus1 = _connection.prepareStatement("SELECT count(*) as qty FROM
tblWorkload WHERE URL = ?;");
  _prepSetStatus2 = _connection.prepareStatement("INSERT INTO
tblWorkload(URL,Status) VALUES (?,?);");
  _prepSetStatus3 = _connection.prepareStatement("UPDATE tblWorkload SET
Status = ? WHERE URL = ?;");
}

/**
 * Call this method to request a URL
 * to process. This method will return
 * a WAITING URL and mark it as RUNNING.
 *
```

```
 * @return The URL that was assigned.
 */
synchronized public String assignWorkload()
{
  ResultSet rs = null;

  try
  {
    rs = _prepAssign.executeQuery();

    if( !rs.next() )
      return null;
    String url = rs.getString("URL");
    setStatus(url,RUNNING);
    return url;
  }
  catch(SQLException e)
  {
    Log.logException("SQL Error: ",e );
  }
  finally
  {
    try
    {
      if(rs!=null)
        rs.close();
    }
    catch(Exception e){}
  }
  return null;
}

/**
 * Add a new URL to the workload, and
 * assign it a status of WAITING.
 *
 * @param url The URL to be added.
 */
synchronized public void addWorkload(String url)
{
  if(getURLStatus(url)!=UNKNOWN)
    return;
  setStatus(url,WAITING);

}

/**
 * Called to mark this URL as either
 * COMPLETE or ERROR.
 *
 * @param url The URL to complete.
```

```
 * @param error true - assign this workload a status of ERROR.
 * false - assign this workload a status of COMPLETE.
 */
synchronized public void completeWorkload(String url,boolean error)
{
  if(error)
    setStatus(url,ERROR);
  else
    setStatus(url,COMPLETE);

}


/**
 * This is an internal method used to set the status
 * of a given URL. This method will create a record
 * for the URL if one does not currently exist.
 *
 * @param url The URL for which to set the status.
 * @param status What status to set.
 */
protected void setStatus(String url,char status)
{
  ResultSet rs = null;

  try
  {
// first see if one exists
    _prepSetStatus1.setString(1,url);
    rs = _prepSetStatus1.executeQuery();
    rs.next();
    int count = rs.getInt("qty");

    if( count<1)
    {// Create one
      _prepSetStatus2.setString(1,url);
      _prepSetStatus2.setString(2,(new Character(status)).toString());
      _prepSetStatus2.executeUpdate();
    }
    else
    {// Update it
      _prepSetStatus3.setString(1,(new Character(status)).toString());
      _prepSetStatus3.setString(2,url);
      _prepSetStatus3.executeUpdate();
    }
  }
  catch(SQLException e)
  {
    Log.logException("SQL Error: ",e );
  }
  finally
```

```
      {
        try
        {
          if(rs!=null)
            rs.close();
        }
        catch(Exception e){}
      }
    }


    /**
     * Get the status of a URL.
     *
     * @param url Returns either RUNNING, ERROR
     * WAITING, or COMPLETE. If the URL
     * does not exist in the database,
     * the value of UNKNOWN is returned.
     * @return Returns either RUNNING, ERROR,
     * WAITING, COMPLETE, or UNKNOWN.
     */
    synchronized public char getURLStatus(String url)
    {
      ResultSet rs = null;

      try
      {
      // first see if one exists
        _prepGetStatus.setString(1,url);
        rs = _prepGetStatus.executeQuery();

        if( !rs.next() )
          return UNKNOWN;

        return rs.getString("Status").charAt(0);
      }
      catch(SQLException e)
      {
        Log.logException("SQL Error: ",e );
      }
      finally
      {
        try
        {
          if(rs!=null)
            rs.close();
        }
        catch(Exception e){}
      }
      return UNKNOWN;
    }
```

```
/**
 * Clear the contents of the workload store.
 */
synchronized public void clear()
{
  try
  {
    _prepClear.executeUpdate();
  }
  catch(SQLException e)
  {
    Log.logException("SQL Error: ",e );
  }
}
}
```

The *SpiderInternalWorkload* Class

The SpiderInternalWorkload class is an implementation of the IspiderWorkloadStorable interface that stores the workload in memory. When using this approach, the spider does not require a SQL DBMS to maintain its store of queues. This allows the spider to operate as a completely self-contained unit. The SpiderSInternalWorkload object, shown in Listing 9.5, does this. This object implements the IWorkloadStorable interface and provides all of the methods required by that interface.

The SpiderInternalWorkload object works by preparing several Vectors that will contain each of the workload queues. As the methods defined by the ISpiderWorkloadStorable interface are called, the URLs are moved between the Vectors that represent the queues.

Listing 9.5　　　**Handling the Internal Workload (*SpiderInternalWorkload.java*)**

```
package com.heaton.bot;
import java.util.*;

/**
 * This class is used to maintain an internal,
 * memory-based workload store for a spider. This
 * workload store will be used by default if no
 * other is specified.
 *
 * Copyright 2001 by Jeff Heaton
 *
 * @author Jeff Heaton
 * @version 1.0
 */
public class SpiderInternalWorkload implements IWorkloadStorable {
```

```
/**
 * A list of complete workload items.
 */
Hashtable _complete = new Hashtable();

/**
 * A list of waiting workload items.
 */
Vector _waiting = new Vector();

/**
 * A list of running workload items.
 */
Vector _running = new Vector();

/**
 * Call this method to request a URL
 * to process. This method will return
 * a WAITING URL and mark it as RUNNING.
 *
 * @return The URL that was assigned.
 */
synchronized public String assignWorkload()
{
  if ( _waiting.size()<1 )
    return null;

  String w=(String)_waiting.firstElement();
  if ( w!=null ) {
    _waiting.remove(w);
    _running.addElement(w);
  }
  Log.log(Log.LOG_LEVEL_TRACE,"Spider workload assigned:" + w);
  return w;
}

/**
 * Add a new URL to the workload and
 * assign it a status of WAITING.
 *
 * @param url The URL to be added.
 */
synchronized public void addWorkload(String url)
{
  if ( getURLStatus(url) != IWorkloadStorable.UNKNOWN )
    return;
  _waiting.addElement(url);
  Log.log(Log.LOG_LEVEL_TRACE,"Spider workload added:" + url);
}

/**
```

```
   * Called to mark this URL as either
   * COMPLETE or ERROR.
   *
   * @param url The URL to complete.
   * @param error true - assign this workload a status of ERROR.
   * false - assign this workload a status of COMPLETE.
   */
  synchronized public void completeWorkload(String url,boolean error)
  {
    if ( _running.size()>0 ) {
      for ( Enumeration e = _running.elements() ; e.hasMoreElements() ; ) {
        String w = (String)e.nextElement();
        if ( w.equals(url) ) {
          _running.remove(w);
          if ( error ) {
            Log.log(Log.LOG_LEVEL_TRACE,"Spider workload ended in error:" +
url);
            _complete.put(w,"e");
          } else {
            Log.log(Log.LOG_LEVEL_TRACE,"Spider workload complete:" + url);
            _complete.put(w,"c");
          }
          return;
        }
      }
    }
    Log.log(Log.LOG_LEVEL_ERROR,"Spider workload LOST:" + url);

  }

  /**
   * Get the status of a URL.
   *
   * @param url Returns either RUNNING, ERROR,
   * WAITING, or COMPLETE. If the URL
   * does not exist in the database,
   * the value of UNKNOWN is returned.
   * @return Returns either RUNNING, ERROR,
   * WAITING, COMPLETE or UNKNOWN.
   */
  synchronized public char getURLStatus(String url)
  {
    if ( _complete.get(url)!=null )
      return COMPLETE;

    if ( _waiting.size()>0 ) {
      for ( Enumeration e = _waiting.elements() ; e.hasMoreElements() ; ) {
        String w = (String)e.nextElement();
        if ( w.equals(url) )
          return WAITING;
      }
```

```
      }

    if ( _running.size()>0 ) {
      for ( Enumeration e = _running.elements() ; e.hasMoreElements() ; ) {
        String w = (String)e.nextElement();
        if ( w.equals(url) )
          return RUNNING;
      }
    }

    return UNKNOWN;
  }

  /**
   * Clear the contents of the workload store.
   */
  synchronized public void clear()
  {
    _waiting.clear();
    _complete.clear();
    _running.clear();
  }
}
```

The *SpiderWorker* Class

Because the spider is multithreaded, it must have a way of dividing tasks up among different threads. The basic unit of work is the SpiderWorker object, as seen in Listing 9.6. After the listing, the code will be discussed.

Listing 9.6   **The Worker Threads (*SpiderWorker.java*)**

```
package com.heaton.bot;
import com.heaton.bot.*;
import java.net.*;

/**
 * The SpiderWorker class performs the actual work of
 * spidering pages. It is implemented as a thread
 * that is created by the spider class.
 *
 * Copyright 2001 by Jeff Heaton
 *
 * @author Jeff Heaton
 * @version 1.0
 */
public class SpiderWorker extends Thread
{
```

```java
/**
 * The URL that this spider worker
 * should be downloading.
 */
protected String _target;

/**
 * The owner of this spider worker class
 * should always be a Spider object.
 * This is the class to which this spider
 * worker will send its data.
 */
protected Spider _owner;

/**
 * Indicates if the SpiderWorker is busy or not.
 * true = busy
 * false = idle
 */
protected boolean _busy;

/**
 * A descendant of the HTTP object that
 * this class should be using for HTTP
 * communication. This is usually the
 * HTTPSocket class.
 */
protected HTTP _http;

/**
 * Constructs a spider worker object.
 *
 * @param owner The owner of this object, usually
 * a Spider object.
 * @param http
 */
public SpiderWorker(Spider owner,HTTP http)
{
  _http = http;
  _owner = owner;
}

/**
 * Returns true or false to indicate if
 * the SpiderWorker is busy or idle.
 *
 * @return true = busy
 * flase = idle
 */
public boolean isBusy()
{
```

```
            return _busy;
    }

    /**
     * The run method causes this thread to go idle
     * and wait for a workload. Once a workload is
     * received, the processWorkload method is called
     * to handle the workload.
     */
    public void run()
    {
        for(;;)
        {
          _target = _owner.getWorkload();
          if(_target==null)
            return;
          _owner.getSpiderDone().workerBegin();
          processWorkload();
          _owner.getSpiderDone().workerEnd();
        }
    }

  protected void processWorkload()
  {
    try
    {
      _busy = true;
      Log.log(Log   /**
     * The run method actually performs the
     * the workload assigned to this object.
     */
.LOG_LEVEL_NORMAL,"Spidering " + _target );
        _http.send(_target,null);

        HTMLParser parse = new HTMLParser();
        parse._source = new StringBuffer(_http.getBody());
        _owner.processPage(_http);

        // find all the links
        while( !parse.eof() )
        {
          char ch = parse.get();
          if(ch==0)
          {
            HTMLTag tag = parse.getTag();
            Attribute href = tag.get("HREF");
            if(href==null)
              continue;

            URL target=null;
            try
```

```
          {
            target = new URL(new URL(_target),href.getValue());
          }
          catch(MalformedURLException e)
          {
            Log.log(Log.LOG_LEVEL_TRACE,
              "Spider found other link: " + href );
            _owner.foundOtherLink(href.getValue());
            continue;
          }

          if(_owner.getRemoveQuery())
            target = URLUtility.stripQuery(target);
          target = URLUtility.stripAnchor(target);


          if(target.getHost().equalsIgnoreCase(
            new URL(_target).getHost()))
          {
            Log.log(Log.LOG_LEVEL_NORMAL,
              "Spider found internal link: " + target.toString() );
            _owner.foundInternalLink(target.toString());
          }
          else
          {
            Log.log(Log.LOG_LEVEL_NORMAL,
              "Spider found external link: " + target.toString() );
            _owner.foundExternalLink(target.toString());
          }

          _owner.completePage(_http,false);
        }
      }
    }
    catch(java.io.IOException e)
    {
      Log.log(Log.LOG_LEVEL_ERROR,
        "Error loading file("+ _target +"): " + e );
    }
    catch(Exception e)
    {
      Log.logException(
        "Exception while processing file("+ _target +"): ", e );
    }
    finally
    {
      _owner.completePage(_http,true);
      _busy = false;

    }
  }
```

```
/**
 * Returns the HTTP descendant that this
 * object should use for all HTTP communication.
 *
 * @return An HTTP descendant object.
 */
public HTTP getHTTP()
{
  return _http;
}
}
```

Through this object, the spider maintains a *thread pool*, which alleviates the spider of the task of creating and destroying thread objects. In this code, you saw that each SpiderWorker object began in the run method of the Spider object as its start() method was called.

The run method then began a wait until there was a workload for it. Once a workload had been acquired from the spider manager, the SpiderDone class was notified that the thread was no longer idle. At that point, the workload was passed off to the processWorkload() method to be handled.

In this code, the processWorkload() method did much of the work you would normally associate with a spider. The processWorkload() method began by downloading the specified page. If the download completed without error, the method would then parse the HTML and add every link to the waiting queue. Finally, the page was passed on to the manager object for this spider.

The *SpiderDone* Class

Usually it's pretty easy for an application to tell when it is done. In the case of a multithreaded spider, however, this is not the case. There are two main criteria that must be met before the spider can consider itself done.

No Active Worker Threads   There shouldn't be any threads that are currently downloading. If they are, they may very well add URLs to the waiting queue, which would cause the spider to continue searching.

No Waiting Queue   There shouldn't be any data in the waiting queue. If there is, then the worker threads will soon be processing it, in which case the spider cannot be considered finished.

The SpiderDone class is shown in Listing 9.7. After the code listing you will be shown how this class works.

Listing 9.7   **Are We Done Yet? (*SpiderDone.java*)**

```java
package com.heaton.bot;

/**
 * This is a very simple object that
 * allows the spider to determine when
 * it is done. This object implements
 * a simple lock that the spider class
 * can wait on to determine completion.
 * Done is defined as the spider having
 * no more work to complete.
 *
 * Copyright 2001 by Jeff Heaton
 *
 * @author Jeff Heaton
 * @version 1.0
 */
class SpiderDone
{

  /**
   * The number of SpiderWorker object
   * threads that are currently working
   * on something.
   */
  private int _activeThreads = 0;

  /**
   * This Boolean keeps track of whether
   * the very first thread has started
   * or not. This prevents this object
   * from falsely reporting that the spider
   * is done, just because the first thread
   * has not yet started.
   */
  private boolean _started = false;
  /**
   * This method can be called to block
   * the current thread until the spider
   * is done.
   */

  synchronized public void waitDone()
  {
    try
    {
      while(_activeThreads>0)
      {
        wait();
```

```
      }
    }
    catch(InterruptedException e)
    {
    }
}
/**
 * Called to wait for the first thread to
 * start. Once this method returns, the
 * spidering process has begun.
 */

synchronized public void waitBegin()
{
  try
  {
    while(!_started)
    {
      wait();
    }
  }
  catch(InterruptedException e)
  {
  }
}


/**
 * Called by a SpiderWorker object
 * to indicate that it has begun
 * working on a workload.
 */
synchronized public void workerBegin()
{
  _activeThreads++;
  _started = true;
  notify();
}

/**
 * Called by a SpiderWorker object to
 * indicate that it has completed a
 * workload.
 */
synchronized public void workerEnd()
{
  _activeThreads-;
  notify();
}

/**
```

```
   * Called to reset this object to
   * its initial state.
   */
  synchronized public void reset()
  {
    _activeThreads = 0;
  }

}
```

The SpiderDone object is used to determine when there are no active threads and nothing is waiting to be processed. Often an object will want to wait for these two events to occur. By being in a separate object, the SpiderDone object will have its own lock, and thus objects can wait on the SpiderDone class. Because the SpiderDone object has its own lock, other objects are allowed to wait; this results in minimal CPU time being consumed, until the spider is done.

The following methods make up the SpiderDone class.

The reset method   The reset method will reset the SpiderDone object to its initial state—when no threads are running.

```
    synchronized public void reset()
```

The waitBegin method   The waitBegin method will wait for the spider to begin processing.

```
    synchronized public void waitBegin()
```

The waitDone method   The waitDone method will wait until the spider has no workload. Make sure you call the waitBegin method first so that you don't get a false Done reading because the spider has not been started yet.

```
    synchronized public void waitDone()
```

The workerBegin method   When a thread worker begins, it should call this method. Calling this method allows the SpiderDone object to keep an accurate count of how many threads are active.

```
    synchronized public void workerBegin()
```

The workerEnd method   When a thread worker ends, it should call this method. Calling this method allows the SpiderDone object to keep an accurate count of how many threads are active.

```
    synchronized public void workerEnd()
```

Summary

Threads allow a program to process more than one task at once. This is particularly useful for a spider because it may need to download multiple pages simultaneously. When the spider uses threads, a spider can execute more easily in the background and it does not need to consume unnecessary CPU cycles.

When you use threads, they must be synchronized. Synchronization can be achieved by using several built-in features of Java. Java provides support for object locking and critical sections. By making use of these tools, the programmer can cause portions of the spider to wait on others without having to enter idle loops, so the spider does not consume unnecessary CPU cycles.

In addition to threads, a SQL database must also be used to create a more successful high-volume spider. JDBC allows Java to access such a database. Java also provides a JDBC to ODBC bridge that allows Java programs to access an ODBC data source as though it were a JDBC driver. This in turn allows JDBC to access SQL databases that only provide an ODBC driver.

By bringing together the technologies of threads, thread synchronization, and JDBC, you are able to create a high-performance spider. It may not be appropriate to use all of the high-performance features all of the time, however. For example, you may wish to create a small spider that will not have access to a SQL database. The Bot package allows you to optionally use either a memory- or SQL-based queue store.

Now that we have seen how to create a spider, we will continue to build on this knowledge by creating more bots in the following chapter. Some of the more advanced bots introduced in the next chapter will use a spider-like process to seek out the specific information needed.

CHAPTER 10

Building a Bot

- Using a traditional bot

- Weaknesses inherent in bots

- Recognizing common pages

- Creating an adaptive bot

A *bot* is an Internet-aware program that can retrieve information for the user in an autonomous way. Though bots have been used already in several of the preceding chapters, after summarizing the bot techniques already presented, this chapter goes one step further, by showing how bots are designed to retrieve data from more than just one individual site.

To understand how many bots function, you should know that most bots are designed specifically to retrieve information from one specific website. Basically, these bots are tied to the particular user-interface nuances that are built into this site. This chapter introduces a new type of bot, called a CatBot, which is designed to operate across an entire category of sites.

A normal bot is programmed with very intricate and specific information about a particular site; a *CatBot*, on the other hand, is programmed with broad general information about the type of site it will be examining. The Internet is filled with many such site categories. Such categories could include those sites that handle shipping packages, e-mail accounts, online banking information, or even weather information. A CatBot is designed to retrieve data, from many sources, that is based on the broad-ranging characteristics that all the sites in a particular category might share.

A CatBot also overcomes many of the limitations that are inherent in bots that are designed to work closely with the user interface of just one site. A common problem that such bots face is the volatility of the sites from which they are designed to retrieve information. (By volatility, I mean the constant state of flux most websites seem to be in.) Because most bots look for specific features, or landmarks, as they travel through their intended site, if you remove one or more of these landmarks, the bot will likely get lost.

In this chapter, we will examine some of the characteristics of both regular bots and CatBots. First, we will begin by looking at how to construct a regular bot. We will then explore the limitations of this process, and then we will extend this normal bot into a CatBot. By doing so, we will develop a bot that works with a much larger set of websites and is more responsive to changes in the underlying site.

Constructing a Typical Bot

Before we create an automated CatBot, we must first examine how to create a regular bot. Before we begin, remember that a regular bot is constructed specifically to access one type of site, and therefore, any changes to that underlying site will likely result in changes to the bot program.

Introducing the WatchBBS Bot

Many websites operate bulletin boards to which users can post messages. These bulletin boards allow for ongoing discussions among the website's visitors. My own website has one such discussion area. To examine it, visit the URL http://heat-on.com/cgi-bin/ubb/ultimatebb.cgi, or take a look at Figure 10.1.

FIGURE 10.1:

Discussion area at
JeffHeaton.com

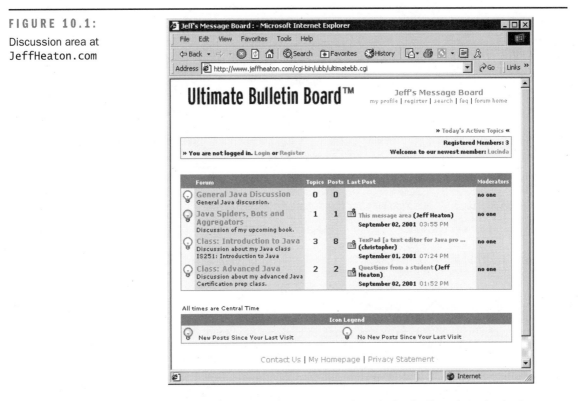

The first bot that we create will be designed to work with this bulletin board, which uses the Ultimate Bulletin Board system that was developed by the company InfoPop (http:// www.infopop.com). Because this system is a common BBS package that is used by many websites, it is the example bot that will be created here. In addition to working with my site, it should work with any site that uses the Ultimate Bulletin Board system.

This bot program has been designed to run in the background and monitor the bulletin board for a user to post a new message to the board. Once the bot notices that a new message has been posted by one of the users, a pop-up window will alert the user that is running the bot. This program can be seen running in Figure 10.2, and its source code can be seen in Listing 10.1.

NOTE   This program does not use any new features of the Bot package; it simply uses the HTTP and HTML parsing classes, discussed in previous chapters, to look for new messages posted to the discussion board.

FIGURE 10.2:

The WatchBBS
application

Listing 10.1   **Watching for Messages (*WatchBBS.java*)**

```
import java.awt.*;
import java.util.*;
import javax.swing.*;
import com.heaton.bot.*;

/**
 * Example from Chapter 10
 *
 * This is a simple bot program that is designed
 * to work with one specific site. Later we will
 * see CatBots, which are designed to function across
 * an entire category of sites.
 *
 * This Bot is designed to scan the bulletin board hosted
 * at my site, http://www.jeffheaton.com, and look for new
 * messages. When a new message is located, the user is
 * informed that there are new messages waiting.
 *
 * @author Jeff Heaton
 * @version 1.0
 */
public class WatchBBS extends javax.swing.JFrame implements Runnable {

  /**
   * The time of the latest message posted.
   */
  Date _latest = null;

  /**
   * The time of the next poll.
   */
  Date _nextPoll;

  /**
   * The background thread.
```

```
 */
Thread _thread;

/**
 * The constructor. Used to setup all of the Swing
 * controls.
 */
public WatchBBS()
{
  //{{INIT_CONTROLS
  setTitle("Watch BBS");
  getContentPane().setLayout(null);
  setSize(398,210);
  setVisible(false);
  JLabel1.setText("Message board URL to watch:");
  getContentPane().add(JLabel1);
  JLabel1.setBounds(12,12,384,12);
  _url.setText(
  "http://www.jeffheaton.com/cgi-bin/ubb/ultimatebb.cgi");
  getContentPane().add(_url);
  _url.setBounds(12,36,372,24);
  JLabel2.setText("Polling Frequency(how often should we check):");
  getContentPane().add(JLabel2);
  JLabel2.setBounds(12,72,384,12);
  _minutes.setText("5");
  getContentPane().add(_minutes);
  _minutes.setBounds(12,96,96,24);
  JLabel3.setText("minutes");
  getContentPane().add(JLabel3);
  JLabel3.setBounds(120,108,240,12);
  _start.setText("Start");
  _start.setActionCommand("Start");
  getContentPane().add(_start);
  _start.setBounds(60,168,84,24);
  _stop.setText("Stop");
  _stop.setActionCommand("Stop");
  _stop.setEnabled(false);
  getContentPane().add(_stop);
  _stop.setBounds(156,168,84,24);
  _go.setText("Poll Now");
  _go.setActionCommand("Poll Now");
  _go.setEnabled(false);
  getContentPane().add(_go);
  _go.setBounds(252,168,84,24);
  _status.setText("Not started");
  getContentPane().add(_status);
  _status.setBounds(12,132,384,12);
  //}}

  //{{INIT_MENUS
  //}}
```

```
//{{REGISTER_LISTENERS
SymAction lSymAction = new SymAction();
_start.addActionListener(lSymAction);
_stop.addActionListener(lSymAction);
_go.addActionListener(lSymAction);
SymWindow aSymWindow = new SymWindow();
this.addWindowListener(aSymWindow);
//}}
}

/**
 * Added by VisualCafe.
 *
 * @param b True if the window is visible.
 */
public void setVisible(boolean b)
{
  if ( b )
    setLocation(50, 50);
  super.setVisible(b);
}

/**
 * The program entry point.
 *
 * @param args Command line arguments are not used.
 */
static public void main(String args[])
{
  (new WatchBBS()).setVisible(true);
}

/**
 * Added by VisualCafe.
 */
public void addNotify()
{
  // Record the size of the window prior to calling parents addNotify.
  Dimension size = getSize();

  super.addNotify();

  if ( frameSizeAdjusted )
    return;
  frameSizeAdjusted = true;

  // Adjust size of frame according to the insets and menu bar
  Insets insets = getInsets();
  javax.swing.JMenuBar menuBar = getRootPane().getJMenuBar();
  int menuBarHeight = 0;
  if ( menuBar != null )
    menuBarHeight = menuBar.getPreferredSize().height;
```

```
        setSize(insets.left
                + insets.right
                + size.width,
                insets.top + insets.bottom
                + size.height + menuBarHeight);
    }

    // Used by addNotify
    boolean frameSizeAdjusted = false;

    //{{DECLARE_CONTROLS
    javax.swing.JLabel JLabel1 =
      new javax.swing.JLabel();

    /**
     * The URL of the BBS to scan.
     */
    javax.swing.JTextField _url =
      new javax.swing.JTextField();
    javax.swing.JLabel JLabel2 =
      new javax.swing.JLabel();

    /**
     * The polling frequency.
     */
    javax.swing.JTextField _minutes =
      new javax.swing.JTextField();
    javax.swing.JLabel JLabel3 =
      new javax.swing.JLabel();

    /**
     * The Start button.
     */
    javax.swing.JButton _start =
      new javax.swing.JButton();

    /**
     * The Stop button.
     */
    javax.swing.JButton _stop =
      new javax.swing.JButton();

    /**
     * The "Poll Now" button.
     */
    javax.swing.JButton _go =
      new javax.swing.JButton();

    /**
     * The displayed status.
     */
    javax.swing.JLabel _status =
      .
```

```
  new javax.swing.JLabel();
//}}

//{{DECLARE_MENUS
//}}


/**
 * Added by VisualCafe.
 *
 * @author VisualCafe
 */
class SymAction implements java.awt.event.ActionListener {
  public void actionPerformed(java.awt.event.ActionEvent event)
  {
    Object object = event.getSource();
    if ( object == _start )
      Start_actionPerformed(event);
    else if ( object == _stop )
      Stop_actionPerformed(event);
    else if ( object == _go )
      Go_actionPerformed(event);
  }
}

/**
 * Called when the start button is clicked.
 * This method starts up the background thread
 * and determines the date of the latest post,
 * at this time. This time will later be used
 * as a reference to determine if there are any
 * new messages.
 *
 * @param event The event.
 */
void Start_actionPerformed(java.awt.event.ActionEvent event)
{
  if ( _latest==null ) {
    _latest = getLatestDate();
    if ( _latest==null )
      return;
  }
  if ( !setNextPoll() )
    return;
  _thread = new Thread(this);
  _thread.start();
  _start.setEnabled(false);
  _stop.setEnabled(true);
  _go.setEnabled(true);
}

/**
```

```
 * Called when the stop button is clicked.
 * This method stops the background thread.
 *
 * @param event
 */
void Stop_actionPerformed(java.awt.event.ActionEvent event)
{
  _thread.stop();
  _start.setEnabled(true);
  _stop.setEnabled(false);
  _go.setEnabled(false);
}

/**
 * Called when the Poll Now button is cliked. Also
 * called when the background thread determines that
 * it is time to poll again.
 *
 * @param event The event.
 */
void Go_actionPerformed(java.awt.event.ActionEvent event)
{
  setNextPoll();
  Date update = getLatestDate();
  if ( !update.toString().equalsIgnoreCase(_latest.toString()) ) {
    _latest = update;
    Runnable doit = new Runnable()
    {
      public void run()
      {
        JOptionPane.showMessageDialog(null,
          "There are new messages at:" + _url.getText(),
          "New Messages",
          JOptionPane.OK_CANCEL_OPTION,
          null );
      }
    };

    SwingUtilities.invokeLater(doit);

  }
}

/**
 * Added by VisualCafe
 *
 * @author VisualCafe
 */
class SymWindow extends java.awt.event.WindowAdapter {
  public void windowClosed(java.awt.event.WindowEvent event)
  {
    Object object = event.getSource();
```

```java
      if ( object == WatchBBS.this )
        WatchBBS_windowClosed(event);
    }
  }

  /**
   * Called when the window is closed.
   *
   * @param event The event.
   */
  void WatchBBS_windowClosed(java.awt.event.WindowEvent event)
  {
    System.exit(0);

  }

  /**
   * Called to get the latest date that
   * a message was posted at the specified
   * BBS.
   *
   * @return A Data class of the last message date.
   */
  protected Date getLatestDate()
  {
    HTTPSocket http;
    Date latest = new Date(0,0,0);
    try {
      http = new HTTPSocket();
      http.send(_url.getText(),null);
    } catch ( Exception e ) {
      JOptionPane.showMessageDialog(this,
        e,
        "Error",
        JOptionPane.OK_CANCEL_OPTION,
        null );
      return null;
    }
    HTMLParser parse = new HTMLParser();
    parse._source = new StringBuffer(http.getBody());

    int foundTag = 0;
    String date = "";


    // find all the links
    while ( !parse.eof() ) {
      char ch = parse.get();
      if ( ch==0 ) {
        HTMLTag tag = parse.getTag();
        if ( tag.getName().equalsIgnoreCase("B") ) {
          foundTag = 2;
```

```
          date="";
        } else if ( tag.getName().equalsIgnoreCase("/FONT") ) {
          foundTag--;
          if ( foundTag==0 ) {
            Date d = parseDate(date);
            if ( d!=null ) {
              if ( d.after(latest) )
                latest = d;
            }
          }
        }
      } else {
        if ( (ch=='\r') || (ch=='\n') )
          ch=' ';
        date+=ch;
      }
    }
    return latest;
}

/**
 * Parse a date of the form:
 *
 * September 2, 2001 5:30 PM
 *
 * @param str The string form of the date.
 * @return A Date object that was parsed.
 */
Date parseDate(String str)
{
  String months[] = {"jan","feb","mar","apr","may",
    "jun","jul","aug","sep","oct","nov","dec"};
  Date rtn;
  try {
    rtn = new Date();
    // month
    String mth = str.substring(0,str.indexOf(' '));
    for ( int i=0;i<months.length;i++ ) {
      if ( mth.toLowerCase().startsWith(months[i]) ) {
        rtn.setMonth(i);
        break;
      }
    }

    // day

    str = str.substring(str.indexOf(' ')+1);
    String day = str.substring(0,str.indexOf(','));
    rtn.setDate(Integer.parseInt(day));

    // Year
```

```
        str = str.substring(str.indexOf(',')+1).trim();
        String year = str.substring(0,str.indexOf(' '));
        rtn.setYear(Integer.parseInt(year)-1900);

        // Hour

        str = str.substring(str.indexOf(' ')+1).trim();
        String hour = str.substring(0,str.indexOf(':'));
        rtn.setHours(Integer.parseInt(hour));

        // Minute

        str = str.substring(str.indexOf(':')+1).trim();
        String minutes = str.substring(0,str.indexOf(' '));
        rtn.setMinutes(Integer.parseInt(minutes));
        rtn.setSeconds(0);

        // AM or PM
        str = str.substring(str.indexOf(' ')+1).trim();
        if ( str.toUpperCase().charAt(0)=='P' )
          rtn.setHours(rtn.getHours()+12);

        return rtn;
      } catch ( Exception e ) {
        return null;
      }
    }

  /**
   * This run method is called to execute
   * the background thread.
   */
  public void run()
  {
    while ( true ) {
      Runnable doit = new Runnable()
      {
        public void run()
        {
          Date d = new Date();
          long milli = (_nextPoll.getTime()-d.getTime())/1000;
          _status.setText("Will poll in " + milli + " seconds.");
        }
      };

      if ( _nextPoll.before(new Date()) ) {
        Go_actionPerformed(null);
      }

      SwingUtilities.invokeLater(doit);
      try {
        Thread.sleep(1000);
```

```
      } catch ( InterruptedException e ) {
      }
    }
  }

  /**
   * Called to determine the next time
   * that a poll will take place.
   *
   * @return True on success, false on failure.
   */
  public boolean setNextPoll()
  {
    try {
      int minutes = Integer.parseInt(_minutes.getText());
      Date d = new Date();
      d.setMinutes(d.getMinutes()+minutes);
      _nextPoll = d;
      return true;
    } catch ( Exception e ) {
      JOptionPane.showMessageDialog(this,
        e,
        "Invalid Polling Time",
        JOptionPane.OK_CANCEL_OPTION,
        null );
      return false;
    }
  }
}
```

We will now examine how this program works and what limitations it has.

How the WatchBBS Bot Works

The WatchBBS example must sit in the background and scan the targeted BBS. To accomplish this, the program uses threads. As soon as the Start button is clicked, a background thread is started, and it begins scanning the BBS system. This thread continues until the Stop button is clicked, but the scanning is not continuous. A polling frequency is specified by the user to determine how often the bot should run.

The actual bot portion of this program can be found in the section of code that uses the getLatestDate() method. This method is called to determine the date on which the latest message was posted. By comparing this value taken at different times, the program can determine if any new messages have been posted since its last visit. As shown below, this program begins by setting an internal variable, named latest, to a zero date, and then it opens a connection to the URL that is specified by the edit field. If any error occurs while this initial connection to the site is being made, the error will be displayed in a window.

```
HTTPSocket http;
Date latest = new Date(0,0,0);
try
{
 http = new HTTPSocket();
 http.send(_url.getText(),null);
}
catch(Exception e)
{
 JOptionPane.showMessageDialog(this,
   e,
   "Error",
   JOptionPane.OK_CANCEL_OPTION,
   null );
 return null;
}
```

Next, the data that was downloaded from the site must be parsed. To do this, an HTMLParser object is allocated. This will allow us to loop through all of the tags.

```
HTMLParser parse = new HTMLParser();
parse._source = new StringBuffer(http.getBody());

int foundTag = 0;
String date = "";
```

Now the code must loop through all of the tags, as is shown in the code segment below. If you refer back to Figure 10.1, you will notice that several dates are displayed. Each of the message areas maintains a separate time for the last posted message.

```
// find all the tags
while( !parse.eof() )
{
  char ch = parse.get();
  if(ch==0)
  {
    HTMLTag tag = parse.getTag();
```

One by one, the tags are read through until the date is reached.

If you look at the HTML for a date, you will see that it is of the following form:

```
<FONT size="1" face="Verdana, Helvetica, sans-serif"><B>September 03,
2001</B></FONT>
```

Items of text that match this pattern are located. As each is found, they are run through the `parseDate` method to determine if they are in a date format that is valid for the bulletin board.

```
if(tag.getName().equalsIgnoreCase("B"))
{
  foundTag = 2;
  date="";
}
else if(tag.getName().equalsIgnoreCase("/FONT"))
{
  foundTag--;
  if(foundTag==0)
  {
    Date d = parseDate(date);
    if(d!=null)
    {
      if(d.after(latest))
        latest = d;
    }
  }
}
```

This process results in a date displayed by the BBS that is in a form that cannot be parsed by `DateFormat`—Java's own date parsing class. (The BBS expresses dates in the form "September 2, 2001 5:30 PM.") Because of this, we must parse this date internally in the program. In this case, the code was set up so that the `parseDate()` method accepts a string containing a date formatted the way the BBS expresses it, and it then changes it into the format that the Java `Date` class uses.

As date after date is located, they are compared with previous dates, and from each of the message areas, the last date is located. Changes in these values will indicate that a user has posted a message. Whenever the date of the last posted message changes, it indicates that a new message has been posted to the discussion board.

Bot Weaknesses

The above bot may seem pretty effective, but there are several issues that it and other bots will face in their lifetimes that make them less than ideal. First is the reliability of the underlying sites that typical bots will be exploring. A bot must rely on a site to provide data in a reliable and consistent manner. If the site is down, the bot cannot retrieve its information. The bot must make adaptations so it doesn't crash when it experiences such events. If the bot is running unattended, it is unacceptable for it to crash if the target site fails to respond.

Another issue involves the volatility of site content. An event that can devastate a bot is a change, or redesign, of the underlying site. A bot, such as the `WatchBBS` bot that we just examined, is programmed to look for certain landmark features of the HTML code for a particular site. If these features are removed, or changed to the point where they are no longer recognizable, it is unlikely that the bot will succeed in finding its data. Because of this, it is important to build as much adaptability into the bot as possible. In the next section, we will examine a new type of bot, one that actually contains no data specific to the underlying site; this allows it to avoid the pitfalls mentioned here.

Using the CatBot

The Bot package on the companion CD contains a special kind of bot called a CatBot. A CatBot, or category bot, is designed to be able to operate on an entire category of websites. By using the CatBot classes, you can create CatBots for a wide variety of sites. The example that we will examine in this chapter is a shipping bot that retrieves status information about a package that has been shipped.

CatBot Recognizers

CatBots navigate a website by using a series of classes called *recognizers*. A recognizer is a class specifically designed to recognize, and then interact with, a specific type of web page. If at least one recognizer is present for each type of page that the CatBot will encounter, then the CatBot will be successful.

We will work with several kinds of recognizers to create the second example program for this chapter. First, let's consider the type of site that might benefit from such a CatBot.

There are many companies available that can ship packages. When you ship a package with one of these carriers, you are provided with a tracking number. By entering this tracking number into the carrier's website, you can get the exact status of your package.

Though a bot that could obtain the status of a tracking number could be very useful, several design challenges may need to be considered. One potential challenge is that there are many different carriers available. Each of these carriers has their own websites. Each of these websites is likely laid out differently. This is a problem because a bot is normally only designed to handle one individual site. Also, many companies use a combination of the available carriers. It would be convenient to use one single bot for all carriers. It would be useful, therefore, to create a CatBot that can handle any carrier that is likely to be encountered.

You may have to visit several different pages of a carrier's website before you are actually allowed to enter the tracking number. Some carriers may even want to know what country you are accessing their site from first. But some carriers have a box in which to enter your tracking number right on their home page. To be successful in navigating all of these possibilities, a shipping CatBot must contain a recognizer for each of these situations. First, let's examine the types of pages for which you are apt to need recognizers.

Pick your country (`RecognizeCountry`)   The `RecognizeCountry` recognizer can recognize a page that typically displays a list of countries and asks you to identify yours. Some carriers use such a page on their site, but it is not necessarily just tied to shipping. Any page where you are presented with a list of countries and are made to choose one could be a candidate for this recognizer.

Find a link (`RecognizeLink`)   The `RecognizeLink` recognizer can recognize a page that has a certain type of link on it. This link is of the type that leads you to the next page that you might be interested in. This is a very general recognizer that can be used any time you must seek out a text link that may take you to a new page. For instance, when you are tracking shipments, you might be seeking a link that contains the text "Click here to track shipment," or something similar.

Enter tracking number (`RecognizePackagePage`)   The `RecognizePackagePage` recognizer can recognize a page in which you need to enter a tracking number. This page would only exist on a shipping site, and thus this recognizer is not very general. The shipping bot example that is examined later in this chapter, under the section "An Example CatBot" shows how this comes in to play.

Starting the CatBot

When the CatBot is first started, it is given three things. First, the CatBot is given a URL from which to begin its search. Second, the CatBot is given a series of recognizers with which to work. Finally, one of the recognizers is identified as the prime recognizer. The *prime recognizer* can recognize the type of data that is the ultimate goal of the CatBot. If the prime recognizer is satisfied, the CatBot considers its job done, regardless of whether the other recognizers were satisfied.

The CatBot begins at its starting URL. First, the prime recognizer is applied to the URL. If the data needed happens to be on the first page, then it is gathered, and the job is done. If it isn't, all remaining recognizers are applied to the page. If none of them recognize it, then the CatBot gives up and stops. If one recognizer does recognize the page, then that recognizer is allowed to interact with that page. This recognizer knows how to move on to a new page, where the recognition process will start over again. The process will continue until the CatBot finds what it's looking for, or a page is reached that no recognizers recognize. This process is summarized in Figure 10.3.

FIGURE 10.3:

The recognition process flowchart

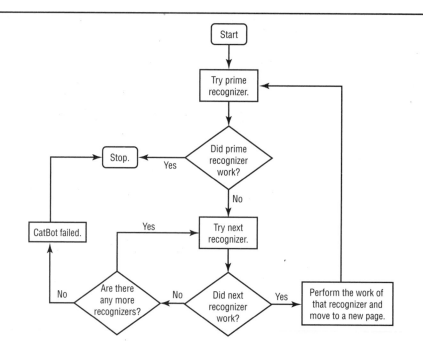

The *CatBot* Class

The CatBot class forms the foundation of any CatBot. This class contains several abstract methods and is therefore an abstract class. Because of this, you never work with an instance of the CatBot class; you use classes that are descendants of the CatBot class instead. The CatBot class only exists to provide a base class for other CatBots, such as the ShipBot that we will soon be examining.

CatBot Properties

The CatBot class contains several important properties, and any CatBot that you create will likely require you to use these. The class level properties of the CatBot class are summarized in Table 10.1.

TABLE 10.1: CatBot Properties

Property	Meaning
_country	This property is used to store the country from which the CatBot is operating. Usually some value such as "UK" or "USA". May not be used by some implementations of the CatBot.

Continued on next page

TABLE 10.1 CONTINUED: CatBot Properties

Property	Meaning
_http	The HTTP object that this CatBot will be using for web communication.
_uid	If the site that the CatBot is accessing requires a user ID to be entered, it is stored here. May not be used by some implementations of the CatBot.
_pwd	A password for the CatBot to use. May not be used by some implementations of the CatBot.
_primeRecognizer	The prime recognizer that will recognize the ultimate information that the CatBot is seeking. Once the prime recognizer recognizes a page, the work of the CatBot is done.
_recognizers	This property represents a list of recognizers. See the Recognize class for more information on what a recognizer is.
_url	The URL at which the CatBot starts.

CatBot Class Methods

The CatBot class also contains several methods. Some of these methods are marked as abstract and must be defined by child classes of this object. A complete list of the CatBot methods and the constructor for this class are summarized here.

The CatBot constructor   Sets up the CatBot. The http parameter specifies an HTTP object that should be used for communication.

```
public CatBot(HTTP http)
```

The getCountry method   Gets a country that the CatBot may have been using. This method returns the user ID that the CatBot was using.

```
public String getCountry()
```

The getHTTP method   Returns the HTTP object being used by this CatBot.

```
public HTTP getHTTP()
```

The getPWD method   Gets a password that the CatBot may have been using.

```
public String getPWD()
```

The getRecognizers method   Gets the list of recognizers that should be used by this CatBot. This method will return the list of recognizers used by this CatBot.

```
public Vector getRecognizers()
```

The getUID method   Gets a user ID that the CatBot may have been using.

```
public String getUID()
```

The `setCountry` method   Sets a country for the CatBot to use. This parameter may or may not be used, depending on the type of CatBot. The `uid` parameter specifies a user ID for the CatBot to use.

```
public void setCountry(String country)
```

The `setPWD` method   Sets a password for the CatBot to use. This parameter may or may not be used, depending on the type of CatBot. The `pwd` parameter specifies a password for the CatBot to use.

```
public void setPWD(String pwd)
```

The `setUID` method   Sets a user ID for the CatBot to use. This parameter may or may not be used, depending on the type of CatBot. The `uid` parameter specifies a user ID for the CatBot to use.

```
public void setUID(String uid)
```

The `setURL` method   Sets the URL that this CatBot should start on. The `url` parameter specifies this URL.

```
public void setURL(String url)
```

The `standardRecognition` method   Causes the CatBot to begin moving through the site with a set of recognizers. The CatBot will continue until the prime recognizer recognizes something, or all recognizers have been exhausted. This method returns true if the recognition was successful.

```
protected HTMLPage standardRecognition
    throws java.io.IOException,
    javax.swing.text.BadLocationException
```

The *Recognize* Class

The `Recognize` class is the class from which all recognizers descend. As mentioned earlier, the use of recognizers is an important concept for the CatBot. These classes can recognize and extract data from certain types of page, and then they can provide these pages with the needed information so that the CatBot can continue. The following methods are provided by the `Recognize` class.

The `Recognize` constructor   Stores the CatBot controller for this recognizer. The parameter `controller` specifies the CatBot controller for this object.

```
public Recognize(CatBot controller)
```

The `findOption` method   Finds the specified option in an HTML "select list." The `list` parameter specifies the component list to search. The `search` parameter specifies the search string. Only a partial match is needed.

```
public String findOption(AttributeList list,String search)
```

The findPrompt method   Finds a form prompt based on a partial search string. The form parameter specifies the form to search. The search parameter specifies the form text that is being searched for.

```
public String findPrompt(HTMLForm form,String search)
```

The has method   Returns true if the specified form has a component that matches the name passed to this method. The form parameter specifies the form object that is to be searched for. The hasWhat parameter specifies the search string. This method returns the component found.

```
public HTMLForm.FormElement has(HTMLForm form,String hasWhat)
```

The internalPerform method   Performs the process of interacting with this page when called internally. This is an abstract method that must be implemented by child classes. The parameter page specifies the page to perform against. This method returns true if successful.

```
abstract protected boolean internalPerform(HTMLPage page)
   throws java.io.IOException,
   javax.swing.text.BadLocationException;
```

The isRecognizable method   Returns true if this page is recognized. The parameter page specifies the page to look at. This method returns true if this page is recognized.

```
abstract public boolean isRecognizable(HTMLPage page);
```

The isRecognized method   Returns true if this page has already been recognized.

```
abstract public boolean isRecognized();
```

The perform method   Performs whatever task is done by this Recognize object.

```
public boolean perform(HTMLPage page)
```

An Example CatBot

Package delivery is an important business service. In the last few years, delivery companies have enabled their websites to track the status of these packages. By logging on to your shipping company's website and entering your tracking number, you can see the exact status of your package. The example program we will examine here (called ShipBot) is designed to be given a package tracking number and return the status of that package.

This example program is implemented as a JSP page, which allows the user to enter a tracking number and the carrier's website and then see the package status. Before you see ShipBot in action, you will first be shown how the JSP is structured.

WARNING   As always, you should verify that running a program such as this does not violate the *current* rules, regulations, and terms of service of the target company.

Running a JSP Page

The program that we will examine here is implemented as a JSP page. To run JSP pages, you will need a web server, such as Tomcat, running. (For information about installing Tomcat, refer to Appendix D, "Installing Tomcat.") The example program can be seen running in Figure 10.4, and the code for the main JSP page can be seen in Listing 10.2.

FIGURE 10.4:

The package tracker running

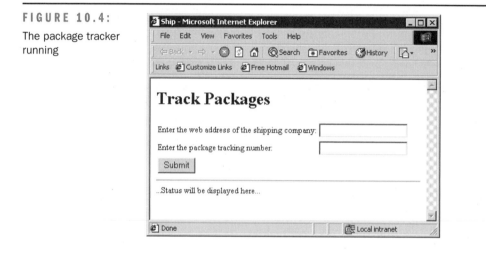

Listing 10.2   **Checking the Status of a Shipment (*ship.jsp*)**

```
<%@page import="com.heaton.bot.ship.*" %>
<h1>Track Packages</h1>
<table border=0>
<form method=post>
<tr><td>Enter the web address of the shipping company:</td>
<td><input name="url" value="<%=request.getParameter("url")%>"></td></tr>
<tr><td>Enter the package tracking number:</td>
<td><input name="track" value="<%=request.getParameter("track")%>"></td></tr>
<tr><td colspan="2">
<input type="submit" value="Submit"></td></tr>
</form>
</table>
<hr>
<%
if(request.getParameter("url")==null)
{%>
...Status will be displayed here...
<%
}
else
{
    String str
```

```
      = FindPackage.findPackage(
        request.getParameter("url"),
        request.getParameter("track"),
        "U.S.A.");
    out.println(str);
  }%>
```

This `ship.jsp` page will be displayed two times. The first time that the `ship.jsp` is called, it displays a form that allows a user to enter the tracking number, shipping carrier web address, and the country the package was sent from. This is accomplished by the HTML seen at the top of Listing 10.2. The JSP seen near the bottom will not activate until the second time this JSP page is called, when the user completes the form and clicks Submit. As a result of this action, the contents of the form are posted right back to `ship.jsp`. When these contents are posted, the form is redisplayed, and the JSP code near the bottom begins to execute. First the JSP code checks to see if it should execute.

```
<%
if(request.getParameter("url")==null)
{%>
...Status will be displayed here...
<%
}
else
{
```

The above code checks to see if there is a value in the `url` parameter. If there is no value, then the form has not yet been posted, and this is the first time the `ship.jsp` page has been displayed. This is because the parameters do not get filled until the form is posted. If there are no parameters, and this is the first time, then `ship.jsp` simply reports "… status will be displayed here…."

If there is a value contained in the `url` parameter, then the posted contents of the form will be evaluated. This is done with the following lines of code:

```
    String str
      = FindPackage.findPackage(
        request.getParameter("url"),
        request.getParameter("track"),
        "U.S.A.");
    out.println(str);
```

Here, the `findPackage` method of the `FindPackage` class is called, and the URL, tracking number, and country of origin are all passed. This program defaults to "U.S.A." for simplicity, but any nation could be entered here. The `findPackage` method will return a string that contains the status of that package, which is displayed below the form. Now that you have seen how the JSP works, you will now be shown how the `FindPackage` class works.

Connecting JSP to the Bot Package

As previously stated, the FindPackage class allows the JSP to communicate with the Bot package. You will now be shown how the FindPackage class was constructed. (The FindPackage class can be seen in Listing 10.3.) This class contains a single static method called findPackage(); this method is called to start the ShipBot program. The findPackage method accepts three parameters—the URL of the shipping carrier, the tracking number, and the country the package was shipped from. These are the same three parameters with which the JSP page passed with the findPackage method was called. The findPackage method does no more than instantiate a ShipBot object and called the lookup method from ShipBot. How ShipBot was constructed will be covered in the next section.

Listing 10.3   **Finding the Status of a Tracking Number (*FindPackage.java*)**

```
package com.heaton.bot.ship;
import com.heaton.bot.*;
import com.heaton.bot.catbot.*;

public class FindPackage
{
  public static String findPackage(String url,String code,String country)
  {
    try
    {
      ShipBot ship = new ShipBot(new HTTPSocket());
      ship.setURL(url);
      ship.setCountry(country);
      return ship.lookup(code);
    }
    catch(Exception e)
    {
      return e.toString();
    }
  }
}
```

Recognizing HTML

The RecognizePackagePage recognizer class accomplishes a great deal of the ShipBot's work. This recognizer class (shown in Listing 10.4) is used to recognize an HTML page that is laid out to allow the entry of tracking numbers.

The two methods that are most active in this class are the isRecognizable() method and the interalPerform method. The isRecognizable() method that is called in the code determines if this page is actually a tracking entry page. It does this by looping through all forms and components on the page. Once one is located that contains either the text number or track, that page is assumed to be a tracking number entry page. The `internalPerform()` method is called to interact with the page once it has been identified. This method will fill in the tracking number and submit the form. The resulting page is returned.

Listing 10.4   **Identifying a Shipping Page (*RecognizePackagePage.java*)**

```java
package com.heaton.bot.ship;
import com.heaton.bot.*;
import com.heaton.bot.catbot.*;
import java.util.*;

public class RecognizePackagePage extends Recognize
{
  HTMLForm _targetForm = null;
  String _targetControl;

  public RecognizePackagePage(CatBot controller)
  {
    super(controller);
  }

  public boolean isRecognized()
  {
    return(_targetForm!=null);
  }


  public boolean isRecognizable(HTMLPage page)
  {
    if(page.getForms()==null)
      return false;

    Vector forms = page.getForms();
    for (Enumeration e = forms.elements() ; e.hasMoreElements() ;)
    {
      HTMLForm form = (HTMLForm)e.nextElement();
      String target = findPrompt(form,"track");
      if(target!=null)
      {
        _targetForm = form;
        _targetControl = target;
        Log.log(Log.LOG_LEVEL_NORMAL,"Recognized a package page");
        return true;
      }
      target = findPrompt(form,"number");
      if(target!=null)
      {
        _targetForm = form;
        _targetControl = target;
        Log.log(Log.LOG_LEVEL_NORMAL,"Recognized a package page");
```

```
      return true;
    }
  }
  return false;
}

protected boolean internalPerform(HTMLPage page)
  throws java.io.IOException
{
  if(_targetForm==null)
    return false;
  _targetForm.set(_targetControl,
    ((ShipBot)_controller).getPackageID() );
  page.post(_targetForm);

  return true;
}

}
```

The *ShipBot* Class

The ShipBot class (shown in Listing 10.5) provides the framework for the shipping bot, but there is little real work performed in this class.

The main method that is active in this class, the lookup() method, should be called to perform the actual lookup of shipping information. This method is then passed a tracking number, and with this information, it returns the status screen as HTML data. The status screen is the page that the shipping company provides in response to the given tracking number.

The lookup() method assembles the link, country, and shipping recognizers. The shipping recognizer is designated as the prime recognizer. Then the standardRecognition() method is called to begin the process of searching for the shipping page.

Listing 10.5   ShipBot Framework (*ShipBot.java*)

```
package com.heaton.bot.ship;
import com.heaton.bot.*;
import com.heaton.bot.catbot.*;
import java.net.*;
import java.io.*;
import javax.swing.text.*;

import com.heaton.bot.*;

public class ShipBot extends CatBot
{
  protected String _packageID;
```

```
public ShipBot(HTTP http)
{
  super(http);
}

String getPackageID()
{
  return _packageID;
}

public String lookup(String packageID)
  throws IOException, BadLocationException
{
  _packageID = packageID;

  RecognizeCountry rcountry = new RecognizeCountry(this);
  RecognizeLink rlink = new RecognizeLink(this);
  rlink.setSearch("track");
  RecognizePackagePage rship = new RecognizePackagePage(this);
  _recognizers.addElement(_primeRecognizer=rship);
  _recognizers.addElement(rlink);
  _recognizers.addElement(rcountry);
  HTMLPage page = standardRecognition();
  if(page==null)
    return "Failed to understand site: " + _url;
  return page.getHTTP().getBody();

}
}
```

Under the Hood

We will now examine how the more low-level classes of the CatBot function. The first one we shall examine is the CatBot class itself. This class provides the framework for other CatBots. We will begin by examining the CatBot class. This class forms the framework for a CatBot and is the primary class that you will use in your own programs that will use a CatBot.

The *CatBot* Class

The CatBot class serves two primary purposes. First, it serves as a holder for many of the common properties that all CatBots will have. It holds such variables as the user ID, password, country, and starting URL.

The second main use for the CatBot class is to hold the standardRecognition method. This method is used to loop through the website and recognizers until the desired data is found. A prime recognizer (notated by the _primeRecognizer variable) must be designated. This prime recognizer can recognize the final page that the bot is looking for. Once the primary recognizer's search is satisfied, the CatBot's run is complete. Figure 10.3, shown earlier in this chapter, is a flowchart of this process. Listing 10.6 shows the CatBot class.

Listing 10.6   **The CatBot (*CatBot.java*)**

```java
package com.heaton.bot.catbot;
import java.util.*;
import com.heaton.bot.*;

/**
 * A CatBot is a bot that is designed to be able
 * to get information from a variety of sites in
 * the same category. This class lays the framework
 * for CatBots.
 *
 * @author Jeff Heaton
 * @version 1.0
 */
public class CatBot
{

  /**
   * A user ID for the CatBot to use.
   * May not be used by some implementations
   * of the CatBot.
   */
  protected String _uid = "";

  /**
   * A password for the CatBot to use.
   * May not be used by some implementations
   * of the CatBot.
   */
  protected String _pwd = "";

  /**
   * A country for the CatBot to use.
   * May not be used by some implementations
   * of the CatBot.
   */
  protected String _country = "";

          protected String _state = "";


  /**
   * The URL at which the CatBot starts.
   */
  protected String _url = "";
```

```
/**
 * The HTTP object to be used by this
 * CatBot.
 */
protected HTTP _http;

/**
 * A list of recognizers. See the Recognize class
 * for more info on what a Recognizer is.
 */
protected Vector _recognizers = new Vector();

/**
 * The prime recognizer that will recognize the
 * ultimate information that the CatBot is
 * seeking.
 */
protected Recognize _primeRecognizer;

/**
 * The constructor. Sets up the CatBot.
 *
 * @param http An HTTP object that should be used for
 * communication.
 */
public CatBot(HTTP http)
{
  _http = http;
}

/**
 * Sets a user ID for the CatBot to use. This
 * parameter may or may not be used, depending
 * on the type of CatBot.
 *
 * @param uid A user ID for the CatBot to use.
 */
public void setUID(String uid)
{
  _uid = uid;
}

/**
 * Gets a user ID that the CatBot may have been
 * using.
 *
 * @return A user ID that the CatBot was using.
 */
public String getUID()
{
  return _uid;
```

```
}


/**
 * Sets a country for the CatBot to use. This
 * parameter may or may not be used, depending
 * on the type of CatBot.
 *
 * @param uid A user ID for the CatBot to use.
 */
public void setCountry(String country)
{
  _country = country;
}

/**
 * Gets a country that the CatBot may have been
 * using.
 *
 * @return A country that the CatBot was using.
 */
public String getCountry()
{
  return _country;
}


/**
 * Sets a password for the CatBot to use. This
 * parameter may or may not be used, depending
 * on the type of CatBot.
 *
 * @param pwd A password for the CatBot to use.
 */
public void setPWD(String pwd)
{
  _pwd = pwd;
}

/**
 * Gets a password that the CatBot may have been
 * using.
 *
 * @return A user ID that the CatBot was using.
 */
public String getPWD()
{
  return _pwd;
}

/**
 * Set the URL that this CatBot should start on.
```

```
 *
 * @param url The URL that this CatBot should start on.
 */
public void setURL(String url)
{
  _url = url;
}

/**
 * Get the HTTP object to use.
 *
 * @return The HTTP object being used by the
 * CatBot.
 */
public HTTP getHTTP()
{
  return _http;
}

/**
 * Get the list of recognizers that should
 * be used by this CatBot.
 *
 * @return The list of recoginzers used by this
 * CatBot.
 */
public Vector getRecognizers()
{
  return _recognizers;
}
/**
 * This method can be called to cause the CatBot
 * to begin moving through the site with a set of
 * recognizers. The CatBot will continue until the
 * prime recognizer recognizes something, or all
 * recognizers have been exhausted.
 *
 * @return HTMLPage reference if the recognition was successful, null if
unsuccessful.
 * @exception java.io.IOException
 * @exception javax.swing.text.BadLocationException
 */

protected HTMLPage standardRecognition()
  throws java.io.IOException,
  javax.swing.text.BadLocationException
{
  boolean recognizedOne;

  HTMLPage page = new HTMLPage(_http);
  page.open(_url,null);
```

```
      // loop so long as the prime recognizer is not
      // satisfied and all other recognizers have
      // not been exhausted.
      do
      {
        recognizedOne = false;
        // first try the prime recognizer
        if(_primeRecognizer.perform(page))
          return page;
        for (Enumeration e = _recognizers.elements() ;
          e.hasMoreElements() ;)
        {
          Recognize rec = (Recognize)e.nextElement();
          if(!rec.isRecognized() && rec.perform(page))
          {
            // one was found, thats enough
            // the one that was just found moved
            // us to a new page so we must break
            // to restart the process.
            recognizedOne = true;
            break;
          }
        }
      } while( recognizedOne && !_primeRecognizer.isRecognized() );

      // if successful return the page
      if( _primeRecognizer.isRecognized() )
        return page;
      else
        return null;
  }

}
```

Inside the *Recognize* Class

The Recognize class is the parent of all recognizer classes. This class contains many methods that you can use to recognize pages. This class also defines a common interface so that the recognition process, explained in the previous section "The CatBot Class," can execute new recognizers.

This class contains two important abstract methods that must be implemented. These two methods were discussed earlier under the section "The Recognize Class." The first is the isRecognizable() method, which will return true if the specified page is recognizable. The second is the internalPerform() method, which must be implemented by a subclass of the Recognize class. The internalPeform method implemented in the subclass actually processes the current page.

In addition to these two abstract methods, the `Recognize` class also contains several useful utility methods. Many of these methods perform specialized searches for items such as option lists or user prompts. These methods are part of the public interface, and were documented earlier in this chapter under "The `Recognize` Class." The base recognizer class is shown in Listing 10.7.

Listing 10.7   **Recognizing a Page (*Recognize.java*)**

```java
package com.heaton.bot.catbot;

import com.heaton.bot.*;

/**
 * This class forms the base class for all
 * recognizers. Recognizers are an important
 * concept for the CatBot.
 * A recognizer is a class that can recognize
 * and extract data from certain types of page.
 * The recognizer will provide the page with the
 * needed information so that the CatBot can
 * continue.
 *
 * @author Jeff Heaton
 * @version 1.0
 */
abstract public class Recognize
{

  /**
   * The CatBot object that controls this object.
   */
  protected CatBot _controller;

  /**
   * Returns true if this page is recognized.
   *
   * @param page The page to look at.
   * @return Returns true if this page is recognized.
   */
  abstract public boolean isRecognizable(HTMLPage page);

  /**
   * This method is called internally to perform
   * the process of interacting with this page.
   * This is an abstract class that must be implemented
   * by child classes.
   *
   * @param page The page to perform against.
   * @return True if successful.
   * @exception java.io.IOException
   * @exception javax.swing.text.BadLocationException
   */
```

```java
abstract protected boolean internalPerform(HTMLPage page)
  throws java.io.IOException,
  javax.swing.text.BadLocationException;

/**
 * Returns true if this page has already been
 * recognized.
 *
 * @return True if this page has already been recognized.
 */
abstract public boolean isRecognized();

/**
 * The constructor. This method stores the CatBot
 * controller for this recognizer.
 *
 * @param controller The CatBot controller for this object.
 */
public Recognize(CatBot controller)
{
  _controller = controller;
}

/**
 * Perform whatever task is done by this Recognize
 * object.
 *
 * @param page
 */
public boolean perform(HTMLPage page)
{
  try
  {
  if(!isRecognizable(page))
    return false;
  return internalPerform(page);
  }
  catch(java.io.IOException e)
  {
    Log.logException("CatBot IO exception during perform:",e);
    return false;
  }
  catch(javax.swing.text.BadLocationException e)
  {
    Log.logException("CatBot HTML Parse exception during perform:",e);
    return false;
  }
}

/**
 * Returns true if the specified form has
 * the specified type of component.
 *
```

```
 * @param form The form object that is to be searched.
 * @param hasWhat The search string
 * @return The component found.
 */
public HTMLForm.FormElement has(HTMLForm form,String hasWhat)
{
  if(form==null)
    return null;
  for(int i=0;i<form.length();i++)
  {
    HTMLForm.FormElement element = (HTMLForm.FormElement)form.get(i);
    if(element.getType().equalsIgnoreCase(hasWhat) )
      return element;
  }
  return null;
}

/**
 * Find the specified option in a select list.
 *
 * @param list The component list to search.
 * @param search The search string. Only a partial match is needed.
 */
public String findOption(AttributeList list,String search)
{
  if(list==null)
    return null;
  search = search.toUpperCase();
  for(int i=0;i<list.length();i++)
  {
    Attribute element = list.get(i);
    if( element.getName().toUpperCase().indexOf(search)!=-1 )
      return element.getValue();
  }
  return null;
}

/**
 * Find a form prompt based on a partial
 * search string.
 *
 * @param form The form to search.
 * @param search The form text we are searching for.
 */
public String findPrompt(HTMLForm form,String search)
{
  search = search.toUpperCase();
  for(int i=0;i<form.length();i++)
  {
    HTMLForm.FormElement element =
      (HTMLForm.FormElement)form.get(i);
    String name = element.getName();
    if(name==null)
```

```
      continue;
    if( name.toUpperCase().indexOf(search)!=-1 )
    {
      return element.getName();
    }
  }
  return null;
  }
}
```

Built-In Recognizers

There are a couple of built-in recognizers supported by the CatBot. These are the `Recognize-Country` and `RecognizeLink` classes. This section will describe how these two classes were constructed.

The *RecognizeCountry* Recognizer

The `RecognizeCountry` class (shown in Listing 10.8) is used to recognize a page that contains a list of countries. From this list, the user must select their country. In addition to recognizing such a page, `RecognizeCountry` can complete it. You will now see how it works. Like any recognizer class, the `RecognizeCountry` class must implement two very important methods: the `isRecognizeable` method must be implemented to determine if the current page is actually a country selection page, and the `internalPerform` method must also be implemented to actually request the correct country. It is the use of these two methods that makes this class a recognizer.

The `isRecognizable()` method does most of the work; it scans the forms on the page and looks for one that appears to be a list of countries. Several known countries' non-compound names are then chosen. (A *compound name* is a country such as the United States. It can be referred to as "US," "USA," "United States," "United States of America," or just "America.") Once such a list is found, it is remembered so that the `internalPerform` method can execute it.

The `internalPerform()` method is used to actually submit the country choice to the website. The country choice is chosen by attempting to match the country that was selected earlier using the `CatBot.setCountry()` method.

Listing 10.8   **Recognizing a Country Selection Page (*RecognizeCountry.java*)**

```
package com.heaton.bot.catbot;

import java.io.*;
import java.util.*;
import com.heaton.bot.*;

/**
 * This recognizer is called to handle a page that
```

```
 * contains a large list of countries. The country
 * that was specified in the CatBot class will be
 * located and used.
 *
 * @author Jeff Heaton
 */
public class RecognizeCountry extends Recognize
{

  /**
   * The targeted form, if recognized.
   */
  protected HTMLForm _targetForm = null;

  /**
   * The target form component, if recognized.
   */
  protected HTMLForm.FormElement _targetElement = null;

  /**
   * The constructor. Passes the controller to the
   * parent constructor.
   *
   * @param controller The CatBot controller object.
   */
  public RecognizeCountry(CatBot controller)
  {
    super(controller);
  }

  /**
   * Used to indicate if this recognizer has
   * already recognized the country specified.
   *
   * @return Returns true if the country has been recognized.
   */
  public boolean isRecognized()
  {
    return(_targetForm!=null);
  }

  /**
   * Returns true if the specified page can
   * be recognized to be a country page.
   *
   * @param page The page to look at.
   * @return Returns true if the page is recognized.
   */
  public boolean isRecognizable(HTMLPage page)
  {
    if(page.getForms()==null)
      return false;
```

```java
      Vector forms = page.getForms();
      for (Enumeration e = forms.elements() ; e.hasMoreElements() ;)
      {
        HTMLForm form = (HTMLForm)e.nextElement();
        HTMLForm.FormElement element = has(form,"select");
        if(element!=null)
        {
          // look for a few known countries. USA is a bad example
          // is it USA? United States? America?
          // United States of America? We will use a few common ones
          // that do not have many name combinations:
          // Canada, France, Japan, Egypt.
          if( (findOption(element.getOptions(),"france")!=null ) ||
           (findOption(element.getOptions(),"canada")!=null ) ||
           (findOption(element.getOptions(),"japan")!=null ) ||
           (findOption(element.getOptions(),"egypt")!=null ) )
          {
            _targetForm = form;
            _targetElement = element;
            Log.log(Log.LOG_LEVEL_NORMAL,"Recognized a country page");
            return true;
          }
        }
      }
    return false;
  }

  /**
   * The internalPerform method will transmit
   * our country choice back to the web server.
   *
   * @param page The page to look at.
   * @return True if successful.
   * @exception java.io.IOException
   */
  protected boolean internalPerform(HTMLPage page)
    throws java.io.IOException
  {
    if(_targetForm==null)
      return false;
    String code = findOption(
      _targetElement.getOptions(),
      _controller.getCountry());
    _targetForm.set(_targetElement.getName(),code);
    page.post(_targetForm);
    return true;
  }

}
```

The *RecognizeLink* Recognizer

The last provided recognizer is the `RecognizeLink` class (see Listing 10.9. This class attempts to find a link contained on the current page. This recognizer works on text links such as "Click here to read your e-mail" or "Click here to view your tracking numbers."

The link recognizer should be given a partial name to use to search links. Using the provided partial name, the `RecognizeLink` class will scan through all links on the current page looking for a partial or complete match. This is done with the following lines of code. Here, the program loops through every link contained on the current page. The ALT, HREF, and prompt text are all obtained for comparison. (The *prompt* text is the text that you must click to activate the link.)

```
for(Enumeration e = page.getLinks().elements() ; e.hasMoreElements() ;)
{
  Link link = (Link)e.nextElement();
  String alt = link.getALT();
  String href = link.getHREF();
  String prompt = link.getPrompt();

  if(prompt==null)
    prompt="";
  if(alt==null)
    alt="";
  if(href==null)
    continue;
```

Once the ALT, HREF, and prompt text are all obtained for the current link, these values are compared against the value you are searching for. This value is part of the prompt, for example the word "tracking."

```
if( ( alt.toUpperCase().indexOf(_search)!=-1) ||
    ( prompt.toUpperCase().indexOf(_search)!=-1) ||
    ( href.toUpperCase().indexOf(_search)!=-1) )
{
  _targetHREF = link.getHREF();
  Log.log(Log.LOG_LEVEL_NORMAL,"Recognized a link:" + _search);
  return true;
}
```

The above code checks to see if the value being searched for (_search) is contained in any of the prompts. This is done with the `indexOf` calls contained in the `if` statement. Once the link is located, the `_targetHREF` variable is set to contain the target of the link.

Listing 10.9   **Finding a Link (*RecognizeLink.java*)**

```
package com.heaton.bot.catbot;

import java.util.*;
```

```java
import com.heaton.bot.*;

/**
 * The link recognizer is used to search for a specific
 * text or graphic link on the page. To locate this link
 * the recognizer uses alt tags, the text linked, and
 * even the HREF itself to establish the identity of
 * the link.
 *
 * @author Jeff Heaton
 * @version 1.0
 */
public class RecognizeLink extends Recognize
{

  /**
   * The string that is being searched for.
   */
  String _search;

  /**
   * The HREF found in the target link.
   */
  String _targetHREF;

  /**
   * The constructor. Pass the controller on
   * to the parent.
   *
   * @param controller
   */
  public RecognizeLink(CatBot controller)
  {
    super(controller);
  }

  /**
   * Returns true if the link has already been
   * recognized.
   *
   * @return True if the link has already been recognized.
   */
  public boolean isRecognized()
  {
    return(_targetHREF!=null);
  }


  /**
   * Returns the search string being used to find
   * the link.
   *
```

```
 * @return The search string being used to find the
 * link.
 */
public String getSearch()
{
  return _search;
}

/**
 * Sets the search string being used to find the link.
 *
 * @param s The search string being used to find the link.
 */
public void setSearch(String s)
{
  _search = s.toUpperCase();
}


/**
 * Returns true if this page can be recognized.
 *
 * @param page The page to look at.
 * @return True if this page can be recognized.
 */
public boolean isRecognizable(HTMLPage page)
{
  for(Enumeration e = page.getLinks().elements() ; e.hasMoreElements() ;)
  {
    Link link = (Link)e.nextElement();
    String alt = link.getALT();
    String href = link.getHREF();
    String prompt = link.getPrompt();
    if(prompt==null)
      prompt="";
    if(alt==null)
      alt="";
    if(href==null)
      continue;

    if( ( alt.toUpperCase().indexOf(_search)!=-1) ||
        ( prompt.toUpperCase().indexOf(_search)!=-1) ||
        ( href.toUpperCase().indexOf(_search)!=-1) )
    {
      _targetHREF = link.getHREF();
      Log.log(Log.LOG_LEVEL_NORMAL,"Recognized a link:" + _search);
      return true;
    }
  }
  return false;
}
```

```
/**
 * The internal perform of this class will scan
 * all forms of links on the page searching for
 * the text specified by the setSearch method. This
 * is the method that actually performs the data
 * collection; because it is a protected method it is only
 * called internally.
 *
 * @param page The page to look at.
 * @return True if successful.
 * @exception java.io.IOException
 * @exception javax.swing.text.BadLocationException
 */
protected boolean internalPerform(HTMLPage page)
  throws java.io.IOException,
    javax.swing.text.BadLocationException
{
  if(_targetHREF!=null)
  {
    page.open(_targetHREF,null);
    return true;
  }
  else return false;
}

}
```

Summary

Standard bots are designed to retrieve data from specific web pages. By scanning the web page for HTML codes near the desired data, the bot can locate the data that it needs.

But there are several weaknesses that hinder most bots. Bots are particularly prone to problems arising from changes made to the underlying site. This is because a bot is typically programmed to look for landmarks from the underlying site. If these landmarks are changed or altered, this could cause the bot to not be able to handle the new site.

A CatBot (category bot) is a bot that can extract information from every site that is in the same category. It can look at a category of bots rather than one specific bot because no specific information about the underlying sites is programmed into the CatBot. CatBots are usually very accepting in their responses to changes that are made in the underlying sites.

Now that we can build bots, we will take this one step further in the following chapter. In this chapter, you will be introduced to an aggregator, which is a program that takes the data collected from several sites and combines them into one report. The next chapter will show you how to do this by building an aggregator that consolidates a city's temperature guide.

CHAPTER 11

Building an Aggregator

- Accessing online aggregation

- Running offline aggregation

- Creating an aggregator

There are numerous sites on the Web that fulfill similar functions, and the data that appears on such sites may be quite comparable. Such data may be obtained from sites such as those that deal with the status of a package being shipped, online e-mail, bank account information, or weather reports. Users who need to access this type of information probably have several web sources for such information; they may maintain several online e-mail accounts, ship using several vendors, and do business with many different financial accounts. To keep track of such information, they may use an *aggregator*.

An aggregator is a bot or a collection of bots that is/are designed to collect data from several similar websites and present that data in a consolidated format. If the user has accounts across an entire category of sites, the aggregator bot will visit each of them and present the user with an aggregated view of the data it retrieved from the sites.

An aggregator may be made up of a collection of regular bots or one CatBot (discussed in the previous chapter) that is sent to many sites. The reason a collection is required when you are using normal bots is that one regular bot will be required for each website that could potentially be added to the list of aggregated sites. On the other hand, a CatBot can very easily be converted into an aggregator. The CatBot is simply run against several sites, and when it has gathered all the data, new programming is introduced to combine the results into the aggregated view.

The aggregator presented in this chapter will aggregate data that is contained on several web pages. This example program will retrieve weather data for several cities and present one consolidated listing.

Online versus Offline Aggregation

Currently, there are two common ways to facilitate the aggregation process—online and offline. Here, we will explore both, as well as the important distinctions between them.

Online Aggregation

Online aggregation doesn't require any special software for the user's machine. The user simply logs in to the aggregator site. Once they are in the aggregator site, the user gives the aggregator all of the IDs, PINs, and passwords necessary to access their accounts. This information is stored on a central computer, and then later on, the aggregation program will go out and download from all of the sites specified by the user.

Online aggregation presents several advantages. First, an online aggregator can be implemented as a *thin client application*, meaning that no special software is installed on the user's PC. Secondly, an online aggregator can be accessed from anywhere or from any number of computers.

The main disadvantage to this approach is that user IDs, PINs, and passwords must be disclosed to the aggregation company that controls the site, which could pose a security risk.

Another disadvantage is that if the online aggregation company that you were using went out of business, you would no longer have access to their aggregator because it is run completely from their web server.

An example of online aggregation is Yodlee (http://www.yodlee.com). Many companies contract with Yodlee to provide online aggregation. Yodlee's current clients include Yahoo, Charles Schwab, Bank of America, and others. Yodlee stores your account access information for a variety of financial service companies, and presents you with an aggregated view of your balances.

Offline Aggregation

Offline aggregation works by providing the user with an aggregation program that they must install on their local computer system. This program works like a conventional client-server program in that it downloads all of its information from the web server. In offline aggregation, all of the bot's work is concentrated in the user's own PC. A program like this, which must be installed onto a user's PC, is often called a thick, or fat, client, because much of the software must be loaded onto the client machine.

The main advantage to this approach is that the user IDs, PINs, and passwords remain in the sole custody of the user. An additional benefit of this approach is that this aggregator does not depend on another company to function like an online aggregator does.

The main disadvantage to offline aggregation is that the user has to install software onto their machine rather than simply accessing it on a web page.

Intuit's Quicken financial package (http://www.quicken.com) is an example of offline aggregation. Quicken is installed onto your PC and it goes out and retrieves all of your accounts. The information gathered by Quicken is then stored on your PC.

NOTE The industry trend seems to lean toward the using thin-client web-enabled applications. Even though it is unlikely that every type of application will need to be run as an Internet application, most aggregation applications seem to be of the online variety. Because of this trend, this chapter will deal primarily with online aggregation.

Building the Underlying Bot

Remember that an aggregator is nothing more than a collection of bots that are designed to present data in the same way. Take, for example, an aggregator designed to display an aggregated view of checking accounts from three popular banks. To do this you would first create three bots, each designed to access a different bank. These bots would then present the financial transactions to the aggregator, which would then produce a consolidated report.

Before we build the aggregator for this chapter, we will build a regular bot that can read weather information. This bot will be implemented using the Bot package and a JSP page. This JSP page can be incorporated into any website that supports JSP in order to provide local weather information.

Using Data from the National Weather Service

The bot shown in this chapter uses the United States National Weather Service (NWS) website (`http://www.nws.noaa.gov/`). As a result, it will only report weather conditions for areas inside the United States. If you want to later modify this so that it will report weather conditions in other countries, you should be able to do this with little difficulty.

The mission statement of the National Weather Service is quoted here:

The National Weather Service™ (NWS) provides weather, hydrologic, and climate forecasts and warnings for the United States, its territories, adjacent waters and ocean areas, for the protection of life and property and the enhancement of the national economy. NWS data and products form a national information database and infrastructure that can be used by other governmental agencies, the private sector, the public, and the global community.

This mission statement contains two very important pieces of information. First, it describes the scope of information that can be obtained from the NWS. This means that, as of this printing, this site allows its data to be used by bots. Second, it states that this data can be reused. It is very important that you do not create bots that use copyrighted information illegally.

Planning the Weather Bot

The first step in creating a bot is to define exactly what data you would like the bot to retrieve. In the case of the NWS, you could get current weather reports for many locations throughout the United States. As an example of the type of information you can receive, take a look at the report for St. Louis, Missouri, which can be seen in Figure 11.1. In the example bot we are working on, this is this page that contains the information that we would like to acquire.

Once you have found the data that you would like to retrieve, the next step is to use a browser and trace the path to that information. At each step, note the URL at the top of the page. Table 11.1 shows how to get to the page in Figure 11.1 from the NWS home page.

TABLE 11.1: Getting St. Louis Weather from the NWS

Page	URL	Purpose
Home Page	`http://www.nws.noaa.gov/`	This is the home page for the site. From here click the Weather Data link.
Weather Data	`http://www.nws.noaa.gov/data.html`	This is the page for weather data. From here click the Current Conditions link.
Current Conditions	`http://weather.noaa.gov/weather/curcond.html`	This is the page for current weather conditions. From here click the Current Weather Conditions in the United States link. This link is near the top of the screen.
United States Weather	`http://weather.noaa.gov/weather/ccus.html`	This page displays a drop-down list that allows you to enter a US state. Select Missouri.
Missouri Weather	`http://weather.noaa.gov/weather/MO_cc_us.html`	This page displays a drop-down list that allows you to chose any of several weather stations that are located in Missouri. From the drop-down list under current weather conditions, choose St. Louis, Lambert-St. Louis International Airport.
Current Weather Conditions...	`http://weather.noaa.gov/weather/current/KSTL.html`	You made it. This page lists the current weather conditions for St. Louis (see Figure 11.1). Now you must parse the data on this page.

FIGURE 11.1:

NWS weather data

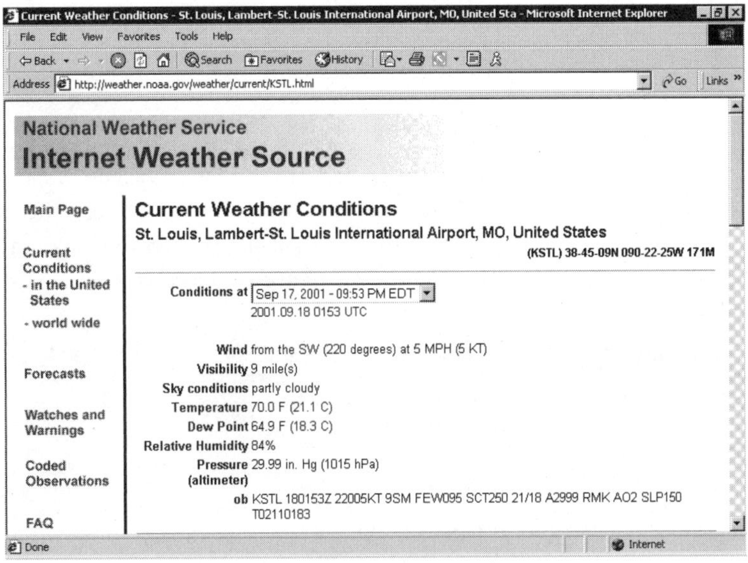

As you can see, there were five intermediary pages that had to be crossed before the target page was reached. You now must determine if it is necessary for the bot to actually cross all of those pages. Often, the bot does not need to take the exact path as a user. A little experimentation is the only way to find out.

Extracting Data for the Weather Bot

If you examine the final URL in Table 11.1, you can see that there is some identifying information. The last few letters are KSTL.html. This code is likely some meteorological code for the St. Louis Lambert Airport. To determine if that URL can be directly accessed, you should close the browser you were using to reach that site. Now open a new browser and enter that URL, http://weather.noaa.gov/weather/current/KSTL.html. Does the browser go right to the St. Louis weather page, or does it return an error? If an error is returned, it is most likely caused by cookies. Many sites store cookies as you progress through the internal pages on the site. If the site uses cookies, it is unlikely that an attempt at direct access like this will work; however, in the case of the NWS, a direct link works. In this case, the bot will be able to directly access this page, which will save time when the bot executes.

The page that you just examined contains all of the information you would need to determine the current temperature at the selected city (refer back to Figure 11.1). By parsing through the HTML, the current temperature can be determined.

NOTE   HTML parsing, which was discussed in Chapter 4, "HTML Parsing," is the process by which a bot makes sense of the data contained on an HTML document.

Building the Weather Bot

Now we must actually build a weather bot that can access the current temperature for a city. To do this, we must create a getTemp method that can read the current temperature for any city. This method is part of the Weather class, which is shown in Listing 11.1. Following this listing, you will be shown how the getTemp method works.

Listing 11.1   **The Weather Aggregation Class (*Weather.java*)**

```
package com.heaton.bot.weather;
import com.heaton.bot.*;
import java.io.*;

/**
 * Example from Chapter 11
 *
 * A simple weather aggregator. This bot will download the
 * current temperatures from several different US cities. This
```

```
 * aggregator can either return the list or write HTML
 * to a file.
 */
public class Weather
{

  /**
   * The city name
   */
  public String city;

  /**
   * The temperature in degrees Fahrenheit.
   */
  public double deg;

  /**
   * Called to get the current temperature.
   *
   * @param code A weather code for the city.
   * @return The temperature in degrees Fahrenheit.
   */
  public static double getTemp(String code)
  {
    try
    {
      String url;
      url = "http://weather.noaa.gov/weather/current/";
      url += code.toUpperCase();
      url += ".html";
      HTTPSocket http = new HTTPSocket();
      http.send(url,null);
      int i = http.getBody().indexOf("Temperature")+11;
      while( !Character.isDigit(http.getBody().charAt(i)) )
        i++;
      String str = http.getBody().substring(i,
        http.getBody().indexOf(' ',i) );
      return Double.parseDouble(str);
    }
    catch(Exception e)
    {
    }
    return 0;
  }

  /**
   * A list of cities to aggregate.
   */
  static String _city[] = {
    "Anchorage, AK|PANC",
    "Atlanta, GA|KATL",
```

```
      "Chicago, IL|KCGX",
      "Denver, CO|KDEN",
      "Honolulu, HI|PHNL",
      "Los Angeles, CA|KLAX",
      "New Orleans, LA|KMSY",
      "New York, NY|KNYC",
      "Orlando, FL|KSFB",
      "Phoenix, AZ|KPHX",
      "St. Louis, MO|KSTL",
      "Washington, DC|KDCA" };


  public static Weather[] getList()
  {
    Weather array[] = new Weather[_city.length];
    for(int i=0;i<_city.length;i++)
    {
      array[i] = new Weather();
      array[i].city = _city[i].substring(0,
        _city[i].indexOf("|") );
      array[i].deg = getTemp(
        _city[i].substring( _city[i].indexOf("|") + 1));
    }
    return array;
  }


  /**
   * Aggregate this list of cities to a file.
   *
   * @param path Where to write the HTML file.
   */
  public static void fileAggregate(String path)
  {
    try
    {
      FileOutputStream fw = new FileOutputStream(path,true);
      PrintStream ps = new PrintStream(fw);
      ps.println("<html><head><title>Current Weather</title></head>");
      ps.println("<body>");
      ps.println("<h1>Current Weather</h1><table border=0>");
      Weather wx[] = getList();
      for(int i=0;i<wx.length;i++)
      {
        ps.println("<tr><td>" + wx[i].city + "</td><td>"
          + wx[i].deg + "</td></tr>");
      }
      ps.println("</table></body></html>");
      ps.close();
      fw.close();
    }
    catch(Exception e)
```

```
      {
      }

    }
  }
```

The `getTemp` method is designed so that it can be passed a city code and in response it will return the temperature. The method begins as follows:

```
public static double getTemp(String code)
{
  try
  {
```

As you can see in the code above, the method is designed to accept `String code`, which is a city code, and returns a `double`, which is the current temperature. The city code is used to determine the URL. This is because the NWS stores weather information in a URL consistent with the city code. For example, St. Louis, which is KSTL, is stored at the URL `http://weather`
`.noaa.gov/weather/current/KSTL.html`.

```
String url;
url = "http://weather.noaa.gov/weather/current/";
url += code.toUpperCase();
url += ".html";
```

Once the URL is determined, an `HTTPSocket` class is instantiated and instructed to retrieve the URL.

```
HTTPSocket http = new HTTPSocket();
http.send(url,null);
```

After the HTML is downloaded, it must be parsed. Somewhere in the body of this `HTTP-Socket` class is the correct temperature. The process for determining the temperature is relatively straightforward. First, a scan is done looking for the word Temperature. Once it is located, the program advances until a digit is found. Once a digit is found, the string is truncated up to the next space. The result is the string value of the temperature.

```
int i = http.getBody().indexOf("Temperature")+11;
while( !Character.isDigit(http.getBody().charAt(i)) )
  i++;
String str = http.getBody().substring(i,
  http.getBody().indexOf(' ',i) );
```

Finally, all that remains is converting the string to the Java primitive type of `double`. A `double` was chosen because it can hold decimal places. This double value is then returned to the calling method.

```
return Double.parseDouble(str);
```

The `getTemp` method shown in Listing 11.1 is a complete bot. A program could easily use it independent of the aggregator. For example, the following code would display the current temperature in St. Louis.

```
System.out.println("Temperature in St Louis is: " + Weather.getTemp("KSTL"));
```

Building the Weather Aggregator

The previous section showed you how to create a bot that can get a city's current temperature. Now you will be shown how to aggregate many city temperatures into one report. The example program produced in this section (see Listing 11.2) will display the current temperature for several US cities. To display data for these cities, you must find their weather code. You can do this by manually exploring the site so that you can find this code for each city. For example, when you request the weather data for New York, NY, you are given the URL of http:// weather.noaa.gov/weather/current/KNYC.html. This implies that New York's weather code is KNYC. Table 11.2 shows the listing of city codes for several other cities.

TABLE 11.2: City Weather Codes

City	Code
Anchorage, AK	PANC
Atlanta, GA	KATL
Chicago, IL	KCGX
Denver, CO	KDEN
Honolulu, HI	PHNL
Los Angeles, CA	KLAX
New Orleans, LA	KMSY
New York, NY	KNYC
Orlando, FL	KSFB
Phoenix, AZ	KPHX
St. Louis, MO	KSTL
Washington, DC	KDCA

The aggregator that we will produce will aggregate the current temperature from these cities into an aggregate report, which can be seen in Figure 11.2.

FIGURE 11.2:
The city Weather aggregator

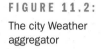

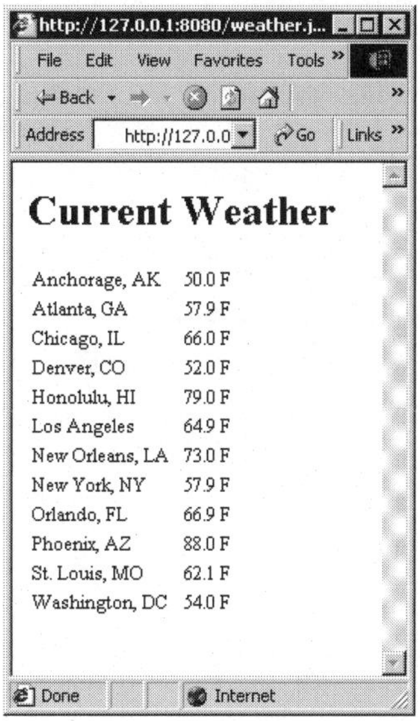
http://127.0.0.1:8080/weather.j...
File Edit View Favorites Tools
Back
Address http://127.0.0 Go Links
Current Weather
Anchorage, AK 50.0 F
Atlanta, GA 57.9 F
Chicago, IL 66.0 F
Denver, CO 52.0 F
Honolulu, HI 79.0 F
Los Angeles 64.9 F
New Orleans, LA 73.0 F
New York, NY 57.9 F
Orlando, FL 66.9 F
Phoenix, AZ 88.0 F
St. Louis, MO 62.1 F
Washington, DC 54.0 F
Done
Internet

The Weather aggregator consists of two parts. The first is the JSP page that will display the aggregate report of cities to the user. The second is the `Weather` class that is used to actually perform this aggregation. You will now be shown how these two parts were constructed, starting with the JSP page.

The Weather JSP Page

The Weather aggregator must display a list of cities and temperatures to the web users. This is accomplished by using a JSP page. The JSP page allows the data, produced by the aggregator, to be formatted in a way that fits in with the rest of the website. The JSP used in this example, shown in Listing 11.2, shows how to present this list. After the listing, you will be shown how the JSP page was constructed.

Listing 11.2 Displaying Aggregate Weather Data (*weather.jsp*)

```
<%@page import="com.heaton.bot.weather.*" %>

<html><head><title>Current Weather</title></head>
<body>
<h1>Current Weather</h1>
<table border=0>
<%
    Weather a[] = Weather.getList();
    for(int i=0;i<a.length;i++)
    {%>
```

```
<tr><td><%=a[i].city%>  </td><td><%=a[i].deg%> F</td></tr>
<%  }

    Weather.fileAggregate("wxtest.html");
%>
</table>
</body>
</html>
```

All of the methods that the Weather aggregator must use are contained in the Weather class, which will be discussed in the next section. All of the Weather class methods are static and should be called directly from the class (i.e., Weather.getList()). The JSP page must also know what cities to display. The Weather object also doubles as a data container and holds the list of cities that the aggregator will display.

The JSP page begins by importing the com.heaton.bot.weather package. This package, which will be explained in the section "The Weather Class," is used to retrieve a list of cities and their temperatures. Next, the JSP page gets a list of all of the cities and their temperatures. Calling the getList() method executes the aggregation process and connects to the NWS.

```
Weather a[] = Weather.getList();
for(int i=0;i<a.length;i++)
   {%>
<tr><td><%=a[i].city%>  </td><td><%=a[i].deg%> F</td></tr>
```

Now that you have seen how to create the JSP page needed by the Weather aggregator using the Weather class (which did most of the work), you will now see how this class was constructed.

The *Weather* Class

The Weather class is a simple aggregator that is designed to operate in two modes. First it can be called from a JSP page to provide a real-time capture of the temperatures for the selected cities. This is the mode that will now be examined. The next section shows how the Weather class can also be used in an offline mode to write the weather data to a file for later viewing.

The *Weather* Class and Online Aggregation

Earlier in the chapter, we developed a bot that could get the current temperature for cities. Now that this bot has been developed to download an individual temperature, it must be used to create an aggregator.

To do this, the getList() method is called to retrieve a list of values. The implementation of this method is relatively straightforward. The method simply enters a loop and calls getTemp() for each of the cities.

First, an array is allocated to hold the list of cities that will be built. An internal array, named _city, is kept to hold a list of the cities to display.

```
Weather array[] = new Weather[_city.length];
```

Next, calling the getTemp method will fill in the array elements. Each element of the _city array contains a city name and weather code. The city code is separated from the city name by a pipe (|) delimiter. Using this notation, the city of St. Louis, MO, with the weather code of KSTL, would be stored as "St. Louis, MO|KSTL".

```
for(int i=0;i<_city.length;i++)
{
  array[i] = new Weather();
  array[i].city = _city[i].substring(0,
    _city[i].indexOf("|") );
  array[i].deg = getTemp(
    _city[i].substring( _city[i].indexOf("|") + 1));
}
return array;
```

Once the array is complete it is returned to the calling page.

The *Weather* Class and Batch Online Aggregation

You were just shown how the Weather class could be used for an online aggregator. This class was also designed to be used as an offline aggregator because it is inefficient to retrieve the same information from the NWS for every user. This section will discuss how to use the Weather class in a more efficient batch system.

The way in which weather data was collected in the previous section causes the web server to poll the NWS every time a user hits the JSP page. If your site gets a large amount of volume, this can be very taxing on system resources. At this point, you will have to determine whether having the second-to-second real-time weather data provided by the last example is necessary.

Most likely, your site can suffice with weather data that is updated at a certain polling frequency, for example, every 15 minutes. Now the weather data would be stored in a regular HTML file that will be displayed by the web server. However, this regular HTML file would be updated periodically with new temperature information. This file will look similar to the following:

```
<html><head><title>Current Weather</title></head>
<body>
<h1>Current Weather</h1><table border=0>
<tr><td>Atlanta, GA</td><td>57.9</td></tr>
<tr><td>Anchorage, AK</td><td>50.0</td></tr>
<tr><td>Honolulu, HI</td><td>80.1</td></tr>
<tr><td>Chicago, IL</td><td>66.0</td></tr>
```

```
<tr><td>New Orleans, LA</td><td>73.0</td></tr>
<tr><td>New York, NY</td><td>57.0</td></tr>
<tr><td>Denver, CO</td><td>55.9</td></tr>
<tr><td>Washington, DC</td><td>55.9</td></tr>
<tr><td>Los Angeles</td><td>64.0</td></tr>
<tr><td>Orlando, FL</td><td>66.0</td></tr>
<tr><td>Phoenix, AZ</td><td>88.0</td></tr>
<tr><td>St. Louis, MO</td><td>62.1</td></tr>
</table></body></html>
```

The fileAggregate() method is called to create this file. This method is passed a name that specifies where to create this file. The fileAggregate() method begins by opening the correct streams and filters.

```
FileOutputStream fw = new FileOutputStream(path,true);
PrintStream ps = new PrintStream(fw);
```

Once the file is open, the HTML header information is written out. The data written here could be replaced by HTML that seamlessly integrates with the website that is displaying this information.

```
ps.println("<html><head><title>Current Weather</title></head>");
ps.println("<body>");
ps.println("<h1>Current Weather</h1><table border=0>");
```

Now the weather data is actually retrieved and displayed. First, the getList() method is called to retrieve a list of cities and temperature values. Then the array is displayed as an HTML table.

```
Weather wx[] = getList();
for(int i=0;i<wx.length;i++)
{
  ps.println("<tr><td>" + wx[i].city + "</td><td>"
    + wx[i].deg + "</td></tr>");
}
```

After the data is displayed, the final HTML data is displayed. Just like the header, this information can be customized to provide seamless integration with the main website.

```
ps.println("</table></body></html>");
```

Finally the files are closed.

```
ps.close();
fw.close();
```

NOTE   Most chapters of the book use this section to describe the internal workings of the Bot package classes that were introduced in the chapter. This chapter focuses more on an application of the Bot packages (the aggregator) rather than the classes themselves. As a result, no new Bot classes are introduced, so this chapter does not contain an "Under the Hood" section.

Summary

Data you may need to digest may be spread across many web pages. An aggregator takes this disjointed data and combines it so that it can be presented as one cohesive report. Aggregation can be done in two ways—online and offline.

Online aggregation occurs when a web page does not require the user to install aggregation software on their computer. This type of aggregation is advantageous because the aggregation website can be accessed from anywhere and no software installation is required on the user's PC. The main disadvantage of this type or aggregation is the loss of control the user experiences—they must give up their login information, and they cannot run the aggregator independently of the aggregation website.

Offline aggregation occurs when the user installs an aggregator onto their PC. The main advantage to offline aggregation is that the user maintains control of the process. Using this type of aggregation, the user does not have to disclose login information to a third party. The main disadvantage is that the data is only accessible from the user's PC and the user must install the aggregator onto their PC.

In the example that was created in this chapter using the United States National Weather Service (NWS), both of these processes were highlighted. You were shown how to download weather while a user was connected to the website, and you were also shown how to download weather data just once for all users.

You have learned to create advanced spiders, bots, and aggregators. We will now discuss the ethical use of such programs, and we will see how we can examine bots, and how to refrain from using them against sites that electronically request that they not be accessed by a bot.

CHAPTER 12

Using Bots Conscientiously

- Dealing with websites

- Understanding webmaster actions

- Interpreting the robots.txt file

- Spidering conscientiously

It is easy to think of a website as an inanimate collection of information to be harvested by a bot, spider, or aggregator. However, you need to keep in mind that there is a human webmaster or company behind every website, and websites are designed to provide information to human visitors. Because of this, you need to proceed very carefully so that you design a bot that respects everyone's wishes. If your bot interferes with the mission of the website it is exploring, then it will likely be unwelcome by the webmaster, which almost guarantees that it will get you into trouble.

Even if your bot does not interfere with the normal operation of the site, it is not necessarily in the clear. This is because there are various laws that govern the use and access of websites. For instance, there are copyright laws that protect the content of the site, and there is contract law, which governs the use and access of the website. Contract law is enforced by the website's *terms of use*. The terms of use make up a contract that most websites have that specifies the terms under which you may use the site. Most of the time, you agree to the terms of use simply by your continued use of the site.

As a bot creator, it is your responsibility to ensure that your bot is compliant with these laws and does not adversely affect the operation of websites. This chapter explores what issues you should be aware of as both a bot programmer, and as a webmaster. While this chapter does give some general information about website contracts, the intention is not to convey legal advice. Always consult an attorney when you are not sure about the legality of using a program in a given situation.

We will begin by looking at how a spider, bot, or aggregator could adversely affect a website. Next, we will see how to read the bot exclusion header. This header acts as a no trespassing sign that can be posted for the benefit of visiting spiders and bots. Finally, we will look at things from the webmaster's point-of-view and see how spiders, bots, and aggregators can be blocked. We will not explore counter measures to these blocks because a bot programmer should never try to side-step security put in place to keep bots out. This underscores the main point of this chapter—when you are creating spiders, bots, and aggregators, *always* respect the wishes of the webmaster.

Dealing with Websites

As a bot writer, you must be a courteous visitor to the websites from which information is gathered. We will now explore some of the common problems that bots can inadvertently create for websites. We will then examine how bots can be designed to avoid these bad habits. Finally, this section will examine physical warnings that sites can post that restrict the use of bot programs.

Hammering

Hammering is a form of denial-of-service attack. A *denial-of-service attack* seeks to bring down a website by using up all available resources. When a bot program is involved in hammering, it issues vast numbers of requests to the target site; this dramatically increases the load that is placed upon the web server. Soon, the web server is so busy filling the requests from the attacking bot that it has no processor time remaining to fulfill legitimate requests coming from the site's human users. Hammering has much the same effect as a maliciously planned denial-of-service attack, but it is unintentional. Both prevent the site from servicing user requests by overwhelming the site with non-user requests.

Surprisingly, bots that have been designed specifically to waste websites' resources do have a place outside the arsenal of a website hacker. Such a denial-of-service attack bot can be very useful when you are trying to determine the capacity of your own website. By using such a bot, you can ratchet up the concurrent requests until your server reaches its breaking point. It is much better to see the breaking point of your web server under this controlled environment than during your company's busy season. One such bot is Mindcraft's WebStone, which can be found at `http://www.mindcraft.com/webstone/`.

With the exception of the Mindcraft example mentioned here, none of the example programs presented in this book are specifically designed to hammer a website. However, the programs that appear in the Bot package could be quite easily altered to do so. This is not to say that all bot programs serve dishonest purposes. Like many things, it all depends on who is using them. In the hands of a farmer, fertilizer can be used to produce healthier crops that will feed larger numbers of people. In the wrong hands, though, fertilizer can be used to construct a bomb.

It is easy to just think that you have no intention of using bots maliciously, and therefore, you don't need to give the matter any further thought. In fact, this chapter assumes that you do intend to use your bots with probity. But this chapter's goal is to make you aware of how easily a bot can inadvertently become a denial-of-service attack even if you didn't design it with that intention.

Types of Hammering

The two types of hammering that we will explore in this chapter are isolated and distributed hammering. We will first examine each of these hammering techniques and then we will examine ways in which a bot can keep from committing each type.

Isolated Hammering

Isolated hammering occurs when a bot repeatedly requests information from the same site. Of course these requests could just as easily come from browsers, but few webmasters complain about legitimate user traffic. These requests occur from the same computer that hosts the bot, and they can be traced to a single IP address. This can occur if there is a large amount of data to download, or if the polling frequency is set too small. The *polling frequency* is the amount of time a bot waits before it sends its next request to the server.

Isolated hammering can become particularly bad when the bot is used more and it becomes multithreaded. Consider a website that uses a bot to find the lowest price between several online vendors. When a user requests a price listing on a certain item, the website's bot will visit each catalog and locate the lowest price. If this site becomes very popular and many users are asking for the lowest price on a product concurrently, the amount of traffic delegated to the online catalog grows as a result. Now the price searching site has thousands of users performing searches on a broad range of products. The spider employed by this price search site will now be consuming more and more traffic from the underlying sites that contain the actual prices. The bot will now show up very clearly on the catalog site's log files and may not be a welcome presence.

Distributed Hammering

Distributed hammering must be considered if the bot is to be embedded into a program that will be distributed to other users. Distributed hammering is when many bots, as opposed to just one, consume a great deal of bandwidth from a site. Many bots can consume far more bandwidth than just one; as a result, distributed hammering is almost always more damaging than isolated hammering. Consider the WatchBBS example program from Chapter 9, "Building a High-Volume Spider." This program was designed to poll a web-hosted discussion board every so many minutes. Consider a large discussion board with 50,000 users. If 25 percent of them are using this program, and they all poll once a minute, there will be 12,500 requests every minute. If the page being requested is approximately 4KB in length, this will mean that the web host must transfer 49MB of data every minute, or nearly 3GB/hr. And this is in addition to the normal traffic that the site must handle. This is a huge amount of additional traffic, and it will likely prove detrimental to the site. Yet it is unlikely that the bot programmer ever thought that the bot would be damaging.

How to Avoid Hammering

As a bot designer, you must strive to reduce the effects of hammering in the bots you produce. As you might have guessed by now, the consequences of hammering can be severe and can get you in a lot of trouble. At the very least, webmasters can take a number of precautions to block your bot from accessing their websites. In order to prevent this from happening, you should design your bots in such a way so that they do not give a webmaster a reason to block them.

Setting the Polling Frequency

The most obvious way to reduce hammering is by intelligently setting the polling frequency of the bot program. Does a bot really need to access a website every minute? Perhaps every hour, or just a few times a day is sufficient. Of course, this all depends on the use of the bot.

Consider a program that is designed to read news stories from several sources, for example. Does this program need to access these sites with great frequency? If the user is likely to just review the collection of news stories on a daily basis, then accessing the site a few times a day may be sufficient. But consider a program that must make use of stock quotes throughout the day. Stock quotes change continually all day long. A long polling frequency may not be acceptable for such a program. Other options should be considered, such as contracting with a quote service company to provide quote data at a price.

Cooperation with Websites

Another thing you should consider when you are designing your bot is how you can make it cooperate with the site it is exploring. For instance, if you are releasing a program that will be used by the general Internet community, a webmaster may be willing to make accommodations for your bot program if you are willing to help make their site more visible. Your bot could help bring additional visitors by providing a link back to the site in the bot itself. Such cases must be evaluated on a case-by-case basis.

If a webmaster is willing cooperate with you over the use of your bot, there are several options that can be pursued. For instance, a smaller specialized web page can be produced on your targeted site. This page would give your bot all of the information it needs to determine if any new information must be downloaded. When the bot only accesses this page, the load on the entire site is reduced considerably. By using this smaller specialized page, the bot can avoid wading through other pages on the underlying site in order to find the page that actually contains the desired data. If the webmaster provides such a page, your bot can directly access this page without consuming much bandwidth getting there.

There are other ways that a bot programmer can cooperate with a webmaster. These can include limiting bot access to just certain sections of the site. Others might include programming to bots to only access the site at certain times of the day. This is really just an agreement between the bot programmer and webmaster that is mutually beneficial to both.

Terms of Service

If you do not reach a specialized agreement with the webmaster, as discussed in the previous section, then you are bound by the website's terms of service. Websites often publish contractual *terms of service* that specify the means by which they can be legally accessed. As a bot programmer, you must be aware of these terms of service. If a site specifies that bots may not be used with this site, then that's the end of the story. You should not access such a site with a bot. This section shows you some of the language commonly used by terms of service contracts.

WARNING   It is beyond the scope of this book to explain the intricacies of Contract or Internet law. Whenever in doubt, consult an attorney.

Some terms-of-service contracts go out of their way to express open use of their site; bots can freely access such sites. Government sites in particular are often of this type. Many government agencies make certain information available for free public use.

The following example is an excerpt from such a contract on the National Weather Service's website (http://www.nws.noaa.gov/). This contract specifies that the information contained on this site can be used for nearly any means.

> *Data and products form a national information database and infrastructure which can be used by other governmental agencies, the private sector, the public, and the global community.*

Some sites are much more restrictive. Some are very specific about what bot access they permit, if any. If a site specifically says that bots should not be used, then this site should not be used. The following is an example expert from such a contract; this is a generic representation from no particular site.

> *User will not access any software or data provided via indirect means or any method not intended or agreed upon by this site. Robot programs (automated query systems) are strictly prohibited and any use of such systems will result in immediate termination of access.*

TIP   It is very important to verify that it is legal to access the site that you are designing your bot to access. Nothing is worse than designing a complete spider, only to find out that the owners of that site will not allow your bot to access the site. This is the kind of information that should be determined before you spend the time developing your bot.

Bot Identification

All browsers have a way to reveal their identity to the web server that they are accessing. Because a bot emulates a browser, it can identify itself by the same means. There are several different ways that a bot or spider can identify itself: a bot may identify itself anonymously, it may imitate a popular browser, or it may identify itself as a bot. You will now be shown the means by which a bot identifies itself.

Using HTTP Headers

Part of the HTTP headers that are sent with every request identify the type and version of software that initiated the request. The User-Agent HTTP header field identifies the client software in use. A typical block of HTTP headers can be seen here.

```
GET /response.asp?MT=www.gsu1.com&srch=5&prov=&utf8 HTTP/1.1
Accept: application/vnd.ms-powerpoint, application/vnd.ms-excel,
application/msword, image/gif, image/x-xbitmap, image/jpeg, image/pjpeg, */*
```

```
Accept-Language: en-us
Accept-Encoding: gzip, deflate
User-Agent: Mozilla/4.0 (compatible; MSIE 5.5; Windows NT 4.0)
Host: auto.search.msn.com
Connection: Keep-Alive
Cookie: MC1=V=2
```

As you can see, the code above sets the user agent field to `Mozilla/4.0 (compatible;` `MSIE 5.5; Windows NT 4.0)`. This is the identifier for Microsoft Internet Explorer 5.5. You can easily instruct the Bot package to use any text you would like for the user agent. Calling the `setAgent` method contained in the `HTTP` class does this. (The `HTTP` class was described in Chapter 2, "Examining the Hypertext Transfer Protocol.") To change the user agent to `MySpider` you would use the following command:

```
HTTP http = new HTTPSocket();
http.setAgent("MySpider");
```

In addition to using the headers, there are several other things to consider when you are choosing what type of name your bot will use. The first option we will explore is having your bot remain anonymous.

Anonymous Identification

To make your bot virtually indistinguishable from normal user traffic, *anonymous identification* can be used. To use anonymous identification, your bot will need to report a User-Agent field that matches a popular browser, such as Microsoft Internet Explorer or Netscape Navigator.

There are no rules or policies that govern what web client software must report for the User-Agent field. As you can see from the above examples, both Internet Explorer and Netscape identify themselves as Mozilla. *Mozilla* is a code word for early versions of Netscape, and Microsoft Internet Explorer uses this to state its compatibility with the original HTML protocols.

One of the primary reasons for using anonymous identification is for compatibility with websites. Many websites have been programmed to customize themselves based on your User-Agent field. In fact, some of these websites will display a page requesting that you update your browser if an unrecognized User-Agent response is generated. This "please update your browser" screen would be a dead end to the spider and prevent it from accessing the needed data.

But how do Microsoft Internet Explorer and Netscape Navigator identify themselves? Microsoft Internet Explorer reports its username in the following line:

```
User-Agent: Mozilla/4.0 (compatible; MSIE 5.5; Windows NT 4.0)
```

Netscape Navigator, on the other hand, would use a line like the following:

```
User-Agent: Mozilla/5.0 (Windows; U; WinNT4.0; en-US; rv:0.9.2) Gecko/20010726
Netscape6/6.1
```

By default, the bot provided in the Bot package uses anonymous identification, and it simply reports itself as "Mozilla/4.0." You can use the `setAgent` method of the `HTTP` class to easily configure this.

Unique Identification

You may choose to identify your bot or spider by a unique name. This could be the name of your company or a product that uses your spider or bot. If you chose to do this, you would be in good company because many of the popular Internet search engines give unique names to their spiders. Table 12.1 shows a listing of the spider names used by these sites.

But this method of identification has some drawbacks. For instance, some firewall software will restrict outbound requests to those that specify a recognized user agent. This prevents users from running unauthorized browsers. If you attempt to run a bot that has a unique identification from such a network, all of your requests will be blocked. If you must run your bot or spider in such an environment, you may not be able to use unique identification.

As you can see, unique identification has its own set of benefits and pitfalls. In your relationship with webmasters, you may find that if your bot is considered to be beneficial to many users, if it is a search engine, for instance, it will often be welcomed. If your bot gains a poor reputation as a resource hog, however, a unique name may be detrimental.

TABLE 12.1: Popular Spider Names

Popular Site	Bot Name (Reported by User-Agent)
AltaVista	Scooter
HotBot	Slurp
Excite	AlphaCONNECT
Infoseek	Infoseek Sidewinder
Google	Googlebot

Combined Identification

It is possible to combine elements from unique and anonymous identification. For example, the following user agent header may be used:

```
Mozilla/4.0(compatible; MyBot 1.0; WinNT 4.0)
```

The above User-Agent specifies that the bot is compatible with Mozilla 4.0. The bot's name is MyBot, and the operating system is Windows NT v4.0. The advantage of this approach is that you still state compatibility with a certain browser, yet you also identify your bot. This should also prevent websites from thinking that your bot is not compatible.

Webmaster Actions

There are many steps that webmasters can take to thwart bot activity. As a bot programmer, you need to be aware of these actions, and you should never try to circumvent any of them. The webmasters are the ultimate authorities on how their sites may be accessed. If the webmaster is using one of these techniques to stop your bot, you should respect this. Alternatively, you may wish to contact the webmaster to see if you can work out some access agreement. This section will show you some of the methods that are used to restrict bot usage.

The Bot Exclusion File

The *bot exclusion file* allows webmasters to provide standardized access policies to visiting bots and spiders. This file acts as a No Trespassing sign for certain areas of the website. The Bot package provides a class, called BotExclusion that can read and understand this file. When they use this class, spiders built from the Bot package automatically comply with the bot exclusion file. First we will look at the format for this file.

The bot exclusion file is named robots.txt. This file must be stored at the root level of the website because this is where all bots are designed to look for it. Even if you frequently access the website from a sub directory, the robots.txt file must be in the root. For example, the URLs http://www.jeffheaton.com/java/ and http://www.jeffheaton.com/ would both rely on a robots.txt file stored at http://www.jeffheaton.com/robots.txt. The following listing shows an example robots.txt file.

```
# robots, scram

User-agent: *
Disallow:   /cgi-bin
Disallow:   /development
Disallow:   /keepOut

User-agent:   Slurp
Disallow:   /cgi-bin
Disallow:   /development
Disallow:   /keepSlurpOut

User-agent:   Scooter
Disallow:   /cgi-bin
Disallow:   /development

User-agent: Ultraseek
Disallow:   /cgi-bin
Disallow:   /development
Disallow:   /keepUltraseekOut
```

```
User-agent: GoogleBot
Disallow:   /cgi-bin
Disallow:   /development
Disallow:   /keepGoogleOut
```

There are only three kinds of lines in a `robots.txt` file. The first type is a comment line. Comment lines begin with the pound sign (#) and have no direct effect on the file. Comments sometimes contain messages to bot programmers.

The other two types of lines always end in a colon. These lines are contained in sections that specify the instructions for each sort of bot. The first type is a `User-agent` command line; each instructional section begins with one of these. This command tells to which bot the following disallow exclusion lines (the final line type) apply. This bot name, listed after the `User-agent` command, is the same one that is specified using the `setAgent` method of the `HTTP` class (discussed earlier in this chapter under "Bot Identification"). If the bot name is given as an asterisk (*), then all bots must heed the disallow statements that follow.

After the `User-agent` line, one or more disallow commands will follow. These commands specify portions of the website's hierarchy that should not be accessed using a spider. When a directory name is specified, the entire directory is excluded.

TIP   To see the robot exclusion file for any site, just use a browser and enter the URL followed by `robots.txt`. For example, the URL `http://abcnews.go.com/robots.txt` can be used to view the `robots.txt` file for the ABC News site.

Thwarting Bot Access

Webmasters can also take steps to curtail the use of spiders on their sites. Some of these actions are general and therefore they affect all spiders and bots. However, if you come to the attention of the webmaster in a bad way, some of these methods can be applied directly to a single spider—yours!

Bot Detection

If webmasters are going to do anything to thwart the access of a bot, first they must detect it. There are several ways to do this; here are three of them:

User agent name   If a large number of accesses are seen from a particular user agent name, the webmaster can see that this is a specific bot. If a bot is using anonymous access, this method of bot detection will not work, however.

Frequency of access   A bot will typically access just a few pages, but those pages that the bot does access will be accessed in great volume. Also, a bot will likely always come from the same IP address. A very large volume of accesses from the same IP address is usually a telltale sign of a bot or spider.

Access method   How is the bot accessing the site? Is it only pulling text files and not downloading any images? Web browsers being used by human users will almost always download all of the images too. A bot typically only goes after the text.

Website Hostility

Webmasters do not need to sit idly by and see their sites accessed in ways that they do not approve of. There are several ways that a webmaster can thwart your spider or bot.

Usenet postings   The webmaster can make Usenet postings to defame your bot and website. If your bot is an annoyance, most webmasters will want to warn other webmasters.

Legal measures   If you are violating their terms of service, they may bring legal action against you.

Bot exclusion file   We've already examined the `robots.txt` file. By using this file, the webmaster can request your spider to leave the site alone. This is the least subtle means of thwarting a spider or bot. If this method fails, a more severe alternative will likely be pursued.

Filter based on IP   If a large volume of traffic is coming from a single IP address, that IP address could be denied access.

Filter based on agent name   If a large volume of traffic is coming from a single agent name, that agent name can be denied access.

A Conscientious Spider

We will now see how a conscientious spider can be created. This spider will examine the `robots.txt` file to ensure that only allowed portions of the site are being accessed. A class, named `BotExclusion`, is provided by the Bot package to assist you in compliance with the `robots.txt` file. You will now be shown how to use the `BotExclusion` class.

The *BotExclusion* Class

The `BotExclusion` class, which was introduced earlier, contains several methods that can be used to load and then interpret a `robots.txt` file. Once the file is loaded, new URLs can be queried to see if they should be excluded. These methods are listed below with brief descriptions and examples of how they might appear in code.

The `getExclude` method   Returns a list of URLs to be excluded. This method returns a vector of URLs to be excluded.

```
public Vector getExclude()
```

The `getRobotFile` method   This method returns the full URL of the `robots.txt` file.

```
public String getRobotFile()
```

The isExcluded method   This is the main worker method for this class. This method can be called to determine if the specified URL should be excluded. The url parameter specifies the URL to be checked. This method returns true if the specified URL is to be excluded, otherwise it returns false.

```
public boolean isExcluded(String url)
```

The load method   The load method will load a robots.txt file from the given URL. The http parameter specifies an HTTP object to use. The url parameter specifies the web-site from which to load the robots.txt file.

```
public void load(HTTP http,String url)
    throws MalformedURLException,
        UnknownHostException,
        java.io.IOException
```

A Spider Example

We will now look at an example of a conscientious spider. This spider is built upon the same spider example that was shown in Chapter 8, "Building a Spider." Unlike that spider, this spider will first read the robot.txt file and then exclude those lines that are specified. This program can be seen in Figure 12.1. The program's listing can be found in Listing 12.1.

FIGURE 12.1:

The conscientious
spider

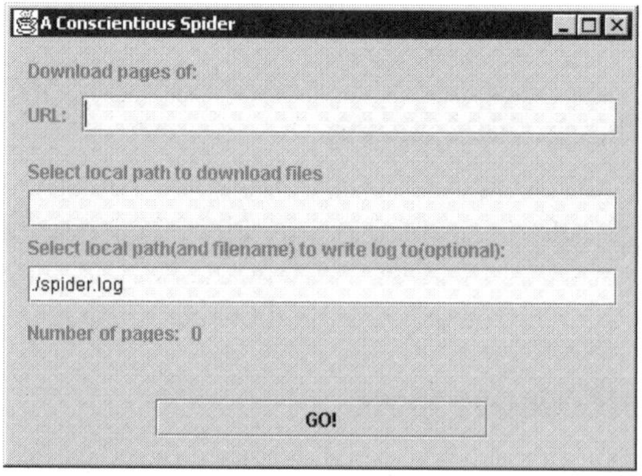

The main code differences between this spider and the one you saw in Chapter 8 will be highlighted before you see this full listing.

First, a new bot exclusion class is allocated and instructed to load from the URL that was given.

```
http.send(_url.getText(),null);
_exclude = new BotExclusion();
_exclude.load(new HTTPSocket(),_url.getText());
```

Now that the `robots.txt` file has been loaded, the `isExcluded` method can be called to query whether a given URL should be excluded. This is accomplished by causing the `foundInternal-Link` method to return false when an excluded URL is found. When `foundInternalLink` returns false, that URL is not added to the workload of sites to be spidered.

```java
public boolean foundInternalLink(String url)
{
  return(!_exclude.isExcluded(url));
}
```

Other than these changes, the example from this chapter is the same as the spider presented in Chapter 8. The code listing for the conscientious spider appears below.

Listing 12.1   **The Conscientious Spider (*GetSite.java*)**

```java
import java.awt.*;
import java.util.*;
import javax.swing.*;
import java.io.*;
import com.heaton.bot.*;

/**
 * Example program from Chapter 12
 * Programming Spiders, Bots, and Aggregators in Java
 * Copyright 2001 by Jeff Heaton
 *
 *
 * This example program will download all of the HTML files
 * of a web site to a local drive. This shows how a spider can
 * be used to map/download a site. This example is very similar
 * to the example from chapter 8. This program processes the
 * bot exclusion header and does not "spider" the areas that
 * are disallowed.
 *
 * @author Jeff Heaton
 * @version 1.0
 */
public class GetSite extends javax.swing.JFrame implements ISpiderReportable
{
  /**
   * The bot exclusion object.
   */
  BotExclusion _exclude = null;

  /**
   * The underlying spider object.
   */
  Spider _spider = null;

  /**
```

```
   * The current page count.
   */
  int _pagesCount;

  /**
   * The constructor. Set up the visual Swing
   * components that make up the user interface
   * for this program.
   */
  public GetSite()
  {
    //{{INIT_CONTROLS
    setTitle("A Conscientious Spider");
    getContentPane().setLayout(null);
    setSize(405,268);
    setVisible(false);
    D.setHorizontalTextPosition(
      javax.swing.SwingConstants.LEFT);
    D.setVerticalTextPosition(
      javax.swing.SwingConstants.TOP);
    D.setVerticalAlignment(
      javax.swing.SwingConstants.TOP);
    D.setText("Download pages of:");
    getContentPane().add(D);
    D.setBounds(12,12,384,24);
    JLabel2.setText("URL:");
    getContentPane().add(JLabel2);
    JLabel2.setBounds(12,36,36,24);
    getContentPane().add(_url);
    _url.setBounds(48,36,348,24);
    JLabel3.setText("Select local path to download files");
    getContentPane().add(JLabel3);
    JLabel3.setBounds(12,72,384,24);
    getContentPane().add(_save);
    _save.setBounds(12,96,384,24);
    _go.setText("GO!");
    getContentPane().add(_go);
    _go.setBounds(96,228,216,24);
    getContentPane().add(_current);
    _current.setBounds(12,204,384,12);
    JLabel4.setText("Number of pages:");
    getContentPane().add(JLabel4);
    JLabel4.setBounds(12,180,120,12);
    _pages.setText("0");
    getContentPane().add(_pages);
    _pages.setBounds(120,180,108,12);
    JLabel6.setText(
"Select local path(and filename) to write log to(optional):");
    getContentPane().add(JLabel6);
    JLabel6.setBounds(12,120,384,24);
    _logPath.setText("./spider.log");
```

```
        getContentPane().add(_logPath);
        _logPath.setBounds(12,144,384,24);
        _go.setActionCommand("jbutton");
        //}}

        //{{INIT_MENUS
        //}}

        //{{REGISTER_LISTENERS
        SymAction lSymAction = new SymAction();
        _go.addActionListener(lSymAction);
        SymWindow aSymWindow = new SymWindow();
        this.addWindowListener(aSymWindow);
        //}}
    }

/**
 * Added by VisualCafe.
 *
 * @param b
 */
public void setVisible(boolean b)
{
    if (b)
        setLocation(50, 50);
    super.setVisible(b);
}

/**
 * Program entry point, causes the main
 * window to be displayed.
 *
 * @param args Command line arguments are not used.
 */
static public void main(String args[])
{
    (new GetSite()).setVisible(true);
}

/**
 * Added by VisualCafe.
 */
public void addNotify()
{
    // Record the size of the window prior
    // to calling parents addNotify.
    Dimension size = getSize();

    super.addNotify();

    if (frameSizeAdjusted)
```

```
      return;
    frameSizeAdjusted = true;

    // Adjust size of frame according to the insets and menu bar
    Insets insets = getInsets();
    javax.swing.JMenuBar menuBar = getRootPane().getJMenuBar();
    int menuBarHeight = 0;
    if (menuBar != null)
    menuBarHeight = menuBar.getPreferredSize().height;
    setSize(insets.left +
      insets.right +
      size.width,
      insets.top +
      insets.bottom +
      size.height + menuBarHeight);
}

// Used by addNotify
boolean frameSizeAdjusted = false;

//{{DECLARE_CONTROLS
javax.swing.JLabel D = new javax.swing.JLabel();
javax.swing.JLabel JLabel2 = new javax.swing.JLabel();

/**
 * The URL to spider.
 */
javax.swing.JTextField _url = new javax.swing.JTextField();
javax.swing.JLabel JLabel3 = new javax.swing.JLabel();

/**
 * The directory to save the files to.
 */
javax.swing.JTextField _save = new javax.swing.JTextField();

/**
 * The Go button.
 */
javax.swing.JButton _go = new javax.swing.JButton();

/**
 * Displays the current page.
 */
javax.swing.JLabel _current = new javax.swing.JLabel();
javax.swing.JLabel JLabel4 = new javax.swing.JLabel();

/**
 * A count of how many pages have been
 * downloaded.
 */
javax.swing.JLabel _pages = new javax.swing.JLabel();
```

```java
javax.swing.JLabel JLabel6 = new javax.swing.JLabel();

/**
 * Used to specify the path to store the
 * log to.
 */
javax.swing.JTextField _logPath = new javax.swing.JTextField();
//}}

//{{DECLARE_MENUS
//}}


/**
 * An event handler class, generated by VisualCafe.
 *
 * @author VisualCafe
 */
class SymAction implements java.awt.event.ActionListener
{
    public void actionPerformed(java.awt.event.ActionEvent event)
    {
        Object object = event.getSource();
        if (object == _go)
            Go_actionPerformed(event);
    }
}


/**
 * As the files of the web site are located,
 * this method is called to save them to disk.
 *
 * @param file The HTTP object corresponding to the page
 * just visited.
 */
protected void processFile(HTTP file)
{
  try
  {
    if(_save.getText().length()>0)
    {
      int i = file.getURL().lastIndexOf('/');

      if(i!=-1)
      {
        String filename = file.getURL().substring(i);
        if(filename.equals("/"))
          filename="root.html";
        FileOutputStream fso
          = new FileOutputStream(
```

```
          new File(_save.getText(),filename) );
        fso.write( file.getBody().getBytes("8859_1") );
        fso.close();
      }
    }
  }
  catch(Exception e)
  {
    Log.logException("Can't save output file: ",e);
  }
}

/**
 * This is where most of the action takes place. This
 * method is called when the Go button is pressed.
 *
 * @param event The event
 */
void Go_actionPerformed(java.awt.event.ActionEvent event)
{
  IWorkloadStorable wl = new SpiderInternalWorkload();
  if(_spider!=null)
  {

    Runnable doLater = new Runnable()
    {
      public void run()
      {
        _go.setText("Canceling...");
      }
    };
    SwingUtilities.invokeLater(doLater);

    _spider.halt();
    return;
  }

  try
  {
    if(_url.getText().length()>0)
    {
     HTTPSocket http = new HTTPSocket();
     http.send(_url.getText(),null);
     _exclude = new BotExclusion();
     _exclude.load(new HTTPSocket(),_url.getText());

    }
    else
    {
      _current.setText("<<distributed mode>>");
    }
```

```
        }
      catch(Exception e)
      {
       JOptionPane.showMessageDialog(this,
         e,
         "Error",
         JOptionPane.OK_CANCEL_OPTION,
         null );

         return;
      }

     Runnable doLater = new Runnable()
     {
        public void run()
        {
          _go.setText("Cancel");
          _current.setText("Loading....");
        }
     };
     SwingUtilities.invokeLater(doLater);

      // Prepare to start the spider
      _pagesCount = 0;
      if(_logPath.getText().length()>0)
      {
        File file = new File(_logPath.getText());
        file.delete();
        Log.setLevel(Log.LOG_LEVEL_NORMAL);
        Log.setFile(true);
        Log.setConsole(false);
        Log.setPath(_logPath.getText());
      }

// NOTE: To use SQL-based workload management,
// uncomment the following lines and include a
// valid data source.
/*
     try
     {
        wl = new SpiderSQLWorkload(
         "sun.jdbc.odbc.JdbcOdbcDriver",
         "jdbc:odbc:WORKLOAD");
     }
     catch(Exception e)
     {
       JOptionPane.showMessageDialog(this,
         e,
         "Error",
         JOptionPane.OK_CANCEL_OPTION,
         null );
```

```
        }
    */

    _spider
      = new Spider( this,
        _url.getText(),
        new HTTPSocket(),
        100,
        wl);
    _spider.setMaxBody(200);
    _spider.start();

  }

  /**
   * This method is called by the spider when an
   * internal link is found.
   *
   * @param url The URL of the link that was found. This
   * link is passed in fully resolved.
   * @return True if the spider should add this link to
   * its visitation list.
   */
  public boolean foundInternalLink(String url)
  {
    return(!_exclude.isExcluded(url));
  }

  /**
   * This method is called by the spider when an
   * external link is found. An external link is
   * one that points to a different host.
   *
   * @param url The URL of the link that was found. This
   * link is passed in fully resolved.
   * @return True if the spider should add this link to
   * its visitation list.
   */
  public boolean foundExternalLink(String url)
  {
    return false;
  }

  /**
   * This method is called by the spider when another
   * type link is found. Links, such as e-mail
   * addresses, are sent to this method.
   *
   * @param url The URL of the link that was found. This
   * link is passed in fully resolved.
   * @return True if the spider should add this link to
```

```
 * its visitation list.
 */
public boolean foundOtherLink(String url)
{
  return false;
}

/**
 * A simple class used to update the current
 * URL target. This is necessary, because Swing
 * only allows GUI components to be updated by the
 * main thread.
 *
 * @author Jeff Heaton
 * @version 1.0
 */

class UpdateTarget implements Runnable
{
  public String _t;
  public void run()
  {
    _current.setText(_t);
    _pages.setText( "" + _pagesCount );
  }
}

/**
 * Called by the spider when a page has been
 * loaded and should be processed. For
 * example, this method will save this file
 * to disk.
 *
 * @param page The HTTP object that corresponds to the
 * page just visited.
 */
public void processPage(HTTP page)
{
  _pagesCount++;
  UpdateTarget ut = new UpdateTarget();

  ut._t = page.getURL();
  SwingUtilities.invokeLater(ut);
  processFile(page);
}

/**
 * Not used. This must be implemented because
 * of the interface. Called when a page completes.
 *
 * @param page The page that just completed.
```

```
 * @param error True if the completion of this page
 * resulted in an error.
 */
public void completePage(HTTP page,boolean error)
{
}

/**
 * This method is called to determine if
 * query strings should be stripped.
 *
 * @return Returns true if query strings (the part of
 * the URL after the ?) should be stripped.
 */
public boolean getRemoveQuery()
{
  return true;
}

/**
 * This method is called once the spider
 * has no more work to do.
 */
public void spiderComplete()
{
  if(_spider.isHalted())
  {
  JOptionPane.showMessageDialog(this,
      "Download of site has been canceled. " +
      "Check log file for any errors.",
      "Done",
      JOptionPane.OK_CANCEL_OPTION,
      null );
  }
  else
  {
  JOptionPane.showMessageDialog(this,
      "Download of site is complete. " +
      "Check log file for any errors.",
      "Done",
      JOptionPane.OK_CANCEL_OPTION,
      null );
  }
  _spider=null;

  Runnable doLater = new Runnable()
  {
    public void run()
    {
      _go.setText("GO!!");
    }
```

```
        };
        SwingUtilities.invokeLater(doLater);
    }


    /**
     * An event handler class, generated by VisualCafe.
     *
     * @author VisualCafe
     */
    class SymWindow extends java.awt.event.WindowAdapter
    {
        public void windowClosed(java.awt.event.WindowEvent event)
        {
            Object object = event.getSource();
            if (object == GetSite.this)
                GetSite_windowClosed(event);
        }
    }
    /**
     * Called to close the window.
     *
     * @param event The event.
     */

    void GetSite_windowClosed(java.awt.event.WindowEvent event)
    {
        System.exit(0);
    }
}
```

Under the Hood

Reading the robots.txt file is the first and most important step to using the BotExclusion class. This is because the BotExclusion class, discussed earlier, provides all of the support for the robots.txt file through several method calls. This source file used to read the robots.txt file is shown in Listing 12.2. Once this relatively simple class is provided with a URL, it loads the robots.txt file from the root of that URL. The robots.txt file tells the spider which URLs the webmaster wishes to be excluded from the spider's scan. This list of URLs, which is read from robots.txt, is stored in the _robotFile property.

Listing 12.2   **Reading the *robots.txt* File (*BotExclusion.java*)**

```
package com.heaton.bot;
import java.util.*;
import java.net.*;
```

```
import java.io.*;

/**
 * The bot exclusion class is used to read and
 * process a robots.txt file from a web site.
 * Using this file, a bot can make sure it is
 * obeying this public policy file.
 *
 * @author Jeff Heaton
 * @version 1.0
 */
public class BotExclusion
{

    /**
     * The full URL of the robots.txt file.
     */
    protected String _robotFile;

    /**
     * A list of full URLs to exclude.
     */
    protected Vector _exclude = new Vector();

    /**
     * @param http An HTTP object to use.
     * @param url A URL from the web site to load the robots.txt file from.
     */

    public void load(HTTP http,String url)
      throws MalformedURLException,
        UnknownHostException,
        java.io.IOException
    {
      String str;
      boolean active = false;

      URL u = new URL(url);
      URL u2 = new URL(
        u.getProtocol(),
        u.getHost(),
        u.getPort(),
        "/robots.txt");
      _robotFile = u2.toString();
      http.send(_robotFile,null);

      StringReader sr = new StringReader(http.getBody());
      BufferedReader r = new BufferedReader(sr);
      while( (str=r.readLine()) != null )
      {
        str = str.trim();
```

```
        if(str.length()<1)
          continue;
        if(str.charAt(0)=='#')
          continue;
        int i = str.indexOf(':');
        if(i==-1)
          continue;
        String command = str.substring(0,i);
        String rest = str.substring(i+1).trim();
        if(command.equalsIgnoreCase("User-agent"))
        {
          active = false;
          if(  rest.equals("*") )
            active = true;
          else
          {
            if(rest.equalsIgnoreCase(http.getAgent()))
              active = true;
          }
        }
        if(active)
        {
          if(command.equalsIgnoreCase("disallow"))
          {
            URL u3 = new URL(new URL(_robotFile),rest);
            if(!isExcluded(u3.toString()))
              _exclude.addElement(u3.toString());
          }
        }
      }
    }
}

/**
 * This is the main worker method for this class.
 * This method can be called to determine if the
 * specified URL should be excluded.
 *
 * @param url The URL to be checked.
 * @return Returns true if the specified URL is to be excluded.
 * Returns false if not.
 */
public boolean isExcluded(String url)
{
  for(Enumeration e = _exclude.elements();
    e.hasMoreElements() ;)
  {
    String str = (String)e.nextElement();
    if(str.startsWith(url))
      return true;
  }
  return false;
```

```
    }


    /**
     * Returns a list of URLs to be excluded.
     *
     * @return A vector of URLs to be excluded.
     */
    public Vector getExclude()
    {
      return _exclude;
    }
    /**
     * Returns the full URL of the robots.txt file.
     *
     * @return The full URL of the robots.txt file.
     */

    public String getRobotFile()
    {
      return _robotFile;
    }
  }
```

Once the robot.txt file is loaded, the isLoaded method can be called to determine if the URL is covered by one of the URLs that was specified in the bot exclusion file. This is done using the load method, which must be passed the URL that corresponds to the site that the spider is about to visit. As previously stated, a robots.txt file is always stored in the root of the web host. The load method starts off by transforming the URL back down to just the root, and appending the filename robots.txt. Then a connection is opened to that file using the send method.

```
URL u = new URL(url);
URL u2 = new URL(
    u.getProtocol(),
    u.getHost(),
    u.getPort(),
    "/robots.txt");
robotFile = u2.toString();
http.send(_robotFile,null);
```

Next, the load method prepares to parse the file. Wrapping the file's contents (which are retrieved by the getBody method) in a Java BufferedReader object does this. A while loop is then used to loop through the file and retrieve all of the lines contained in the robots.txt file.

```
StringReader sr = new StringReader(http.getBody());
BufferedReader r = new BufferedReader(sr);
while( (str=r.readLine()) != null )
{
```

Each line of the robots.txt file is processed individually. First the line is trimmed of any leading or trailing spaces. Then, if the line is blank (length less than 1), no further processing is done on the line. Likewise, if the line starts with a pound sign (#) the line is skipped—such lines are comments. What we are really looking for is the agent header lines that end in a colon. If the line does not contain a colon, then it is skipped. For more information on the colon lines, refer to the section entitled "The Bot Exclusion File."

```
str = str.trim();
if(str.length()<1)
  continue;
if(str.charAt(0)=='#')
  continue;
int i = str.indexOf(':');
if(i==-1)
  continue;
```

The code continues on because it has now found a block of exclusions for an agent. First, any text found to the left of the colon is assumed to be the command and is stored in a variable named command. The rest of the line, after the command, is stored in a variable named rest. Take for example the following line, found in a robots.txt file.

```
Disallow:    /keepOut
```

In this example, the variable command would be set to Disallow and the variable rest would be set to /keepOut. If the command is User-agent, then we have found a new block of paths that the spider should avoid. We must now compare to see if this block is talking about our bot. First we check to see if the bot specified by the User-agent command is the asterisk (*). If it is, then this block applies to every spider and we must parse it. If not, we compare it to the agent string we are using (obtained by calling http.getAgent()). If either of the two if statements apply, the active variable is set to true. Setting this variable to true will cause this method to begin adding the methods to the list of paths to exclude.

```
String command = str.substring(0,i);
String rest = str.substring(i+1).trim();
if(command.equalsIgnoreCase("User-agent"))
{
  active = false;
  if( rest.equals("*") )
    active = true;
  else
  {
    if(rest.equalsIgnoreCase(http.getAgent()))
      active = true;
  }
```

The following lines of code are regulated by the variable named `active`. Once the code shown immediately above sets `active` to true, any lines that begin with `disallow` will now be added to the list of excluded URLs.

```
if(active)
{
  if(command.equalsIgnoreCase("disallow"))
  {
    URL u3 = new URL(new URL(_robotFile),rest);
    if(!isExcluded(u3.toString()))
      exclude.addElement(u3.toString());
  }
}
```

The `load` method then continues reading through the file until the end is reached. The URLs collected by the `load` method will be stored to direct the spider.

Summary

Whether on purpose or not, a bot programmer might eventually find that their bot has gotten them into trouble. One of the most common causes of this is when a spider accidentally hammers a website—it requests data in such a large volume that it degrades that website's performance. Because it is so easy to get into trouble, the bot programmer must strive to create bots and spiders that use their powers conscientiously.

A bot programmer must also decide how to identify their bot to the websites. Like all web access clients, bots identify themselves using the HTTP header called User-Agent. Bots may also emulate the User-Agent of popular browsers and thereby run anonymously.

The User-Agent header is not the only way that bots can come to the attention of webmasters, however. In fact, webmasters can detect bots relatively easily. Certain things, such as IP addresses, access patterns, and User-Agent names can allow webmasters to detect the presence of a bot.

There are several ways that a webmaster can prevent a bot from accessing their website; these include adding the bot to the bot exclusion file, taking legal action, and performing IP address blocking.

A bot exclusion file named `robots.txt` specifies which parts of the site, if any, bots may access. This file should be read by a spider to determine which parts of the site should be avoided.

The next chapter of this book, which is also the last chapter, will discuss the future directions that bots might take. A new technology called Simple Object Access Protocol (SOAP) may make the life of a bot much easier by providing standardized access to underlying sites.

CHAPTER 13

The Future of Bots

- XML files

- XML in motion: SOAP

- Describing SOAP services with WSDL

- What SOAP means to bots

The last chapter of this book will focus on the future role of spiders, bots, and aggregators, and how current and emerging technologies will affect their functions. The main technology that will be highlighted in this chapter is the Simple Object Access Protocol (SOAP), which is based on the Extensible Markup Language (XML). The primary function of SOAP is to enable computers on the Internet to share information in a standardized way. This is done using a well-defined XML protocol.

The primary function of a SOAP application is very similar to that of the bots that we examined in this book. A bot attempts to retrieve information from a site that contains the desired information. SOAP makes certain aspects of this data retrieval easier. As you have seen in this book, this retrieval process is not always an easy task. The procedures that may be necessary to access such information and the format that such information may take can vary greatly from site to site. SOAP addresses this by providing a standard XML protocol that is used to request data from websites.

This chapter will begin by describing the evolution of the Internet and how this lead to development of SOAP. We will then examine the origins of SOAP and XML. The exact structure of SOAP and how it uses HTTP will also be discussed. Finally, this chapter will conclude with a discussion of how, one day, much of what we now rely on bots for might be replaced by SOAP.

Internet Information Transfer

If we examine the evolution of networked computers—from computers that were barely connected to today's Internet, which is a vast network of computers from around the world—an interesting trend can be observed. When the earliest personal computers began to appear in the late 1970s there were many disjointed computer systems. Each individual computer system had different sorts of data but did not share it. When this was the case, the only way to transfer data between systems was using sneakernet—copying data on to a disk, and manually transferring it to the other system. Because data between systems needed to be shared, the search for a better way to transfer data began. In the process, local area networks (LANs), which allow the computers of a single company to share information, were developed. Ultimately, after this, the goal became to create the Internet, which emerged as a way to connect all of these LANs into one global network.

Basically, this evolution transformed the user's ability to access a wealth of data, but it didn't solve all problems. Though the user who once only had access to a small amount of data can now access a virtual universe of data, this data is still in very different forms, and there is no uniform way to access it. There are two ways to solve this basic problem. One is to write an aggregator to make all data appear to conform to a single standard. The second way is to actually make all data conform to a single standard.

By attempting to bring some commonality to the vast quantities of information available through the Internet, technologies such as SOAP and XML try to create such a standard. This standard allows webmasters to control the access of SOAP programs to their data, which creates a much more corporative environment than that of bots.

In order to clarify how these technologies work together to support the standard that bots need to access universal data, this chapter will first look at what XML is and how it is being applied to SOAP. This chapter will then conclude with a discussion of the role of bots when they are used in conjunction with these new technologies.

Understanding XML

SOAP is based on XML. Because of this, a review of XML is necessary. First, we will take a look at what an XML file actually looks like.

Viewing a Typical XML File

Listing 13.1, which contains a student list, is a short example of an XML file. An XML file can always be identified by examining the first line of the file, which indicates to which version of XML this file adheres. Currently, version 1.0 is the only version in use.

NOTE   The exact structure of an XML file was discussed in Chapter 6, "Interpreting Data."

Listing 13.1   **A Simple XML File (*test.xml*)**

```
<?xml version="1.0" ?>
<studentList>
  <student>
    <first>John</first>
    <last>Smith</last>
    <phone>314-555-1212</phone>
    <id>1</id>
  </student>
  <student>
    <first>Jane</first>
    <last>Smith</last>
    <phone>636-555-1200</phone>
    <id>1</id>
  </student>
</studentList>
```

If such an XML file is stored on a Microsoft platform, it can be viewed using Internet Explorer. If you choose to view such a file using Internet Explorer, you will see a display similar to the one in Figure 13.1.

FIGURE 13.1:

Viewing an XML file

FIGURE 13.1:

Viewing an XML file

What Is XML?

Now that you have been reminded of what an XML file looks like and how it may be viewed, you can refresh your memory on exactly what XML is, and what it is not. You can begin examining the key points of XML by exploring the text file into which XML data is placed.

XML Stores Data Hierarchically

A text file is normally considered *flat*; this means that there is no implied hierarchy to the information displayed or conveyed in such a file. Instead, data is simply stored in a line-by-line format. XML was developed to allow data to be stored hierarchically in a file.

Before we get into the details of XML, we must first examine what exactly is meant by the term *hierarchical*. Hierarchical data forms a hierarchy—that is, there can be many levels. The basic unit of an XML file is the *node*. A node has a name, a value, and zero or more child nodes. The node's name is simply used to retrieve that node. The node's value is the data associated with that node. As mentioned, the node can also have zero or more child nodes, which continue the hierarchy. This is illustrated by the following:

```
<XMLNodeName>The value</XMLNodeName>
<XMLParentNode>
  <XMLChildNode>Value 1</XMLChildNode>
  <XMLChildNode>Value 2</XMLChildNode>
</XMLParentNode>
```

Hierarchical files are nothing new. Programs that need to store such data often store it to disk in binary, non-human readable format. (A *format* is nothing more than a set of rules that specifies how to read and write from a file.) Because of this, when this method is used, such data can only be accessed by another program that understands the format in which this data was stored. Usually, the only such program is the one that the user used to create the file.

The programmers who developed XML attempted to solve this problem by making XML embody a universal set of formatting rules for such files. XML files are always text files—always human readable. This is because an XML file is composed only of printable ASCII codes. For example, the value 1000 would be stored textually as the four characters "1000" and not as some binary representation of the number.

Also, because XML files are text files, programmers can more easily debug applications that use them, and they can use a simple text editor to fix broken XML files. This is because a text file can easily be opened in an editor such as Notepad, whereas a binary file cannot. However, the rules for XML files are much more strict than those for HTML. For instance, a forgotten tag or an attribute without quotes can make the file unusable, whereas such practice is often acceptable in HTML. As the official XML specification (from `http://www.w3c.org`) states, "applications are not allowed to try to second-guess the creator of a broken XML file; if the file is broken, an application has to stop right there and issue an error."

XML Appears Similar to HTML

At first glance, an XML file looks very similar to an HTML file because both make use of tags and attributes, as was discussed in Chapter 6. But this is as far as the similarity goes. Though HTML goes to the trouble of specifying what each tag and attribute means, XML contains no predefined tag names; it is up to the programmer to define meaningful tag names. The actual interpretation of these tags is left completely to the application that reads it. For example, if you see a <i> tag inside an XML file, do not assume that it is a tag for italics, as it is in HTML. This tag could be assigned any purpose.

XML is Easily Human Readable

XML is a text format. Because of this, it uses tags to delimit the data. Because it takes several bytes to store each one of these XML tags, XML files are nearly always larger than comparable binary formats. XML developers made this design decision intentionally because the advantages of a text format, described earlier, outweigh the disadvantages for this larger file size.

In addition to the benefits of text format, there are others. For instance, because of constant technological improvements, disk space isn't as expensive as it used to be, and programs like zip can compress files very efficiently. Not only are such programs available for nearly all platforms, but they are usually free. Additionally, communication protocols are now built into modem hardware and HTTP/1.1, and these protocols can compress data behind the scenes, without the web programmer being concerned with it. This saves bandwidth as effectively as a binary format would.

XHTML 1: A Stricter HTML

XHTML 1 is the latest version of the HTML. This new version of HTML attempts to make HTML documents a subset of XML, which has several important features that are described in a moment. Basically, this system works by using a standard XML parser to parse HTML documents, rather than requiring that HTML and XML parsers be separate programs. As a result of this development, tools that previously only worked with XML can be used with XHTML documents as well. Here are several of the other features:

Tag names are now consistent in case.   In HTML 3.2, tag names could be of any case, but under XHTML, case is significant. For example, the tags <img>, <Img>, and <IMG> would all be considered to be logically the same tag name in HTML 3.2. Under XHTML, these would all be different tag names.

Attributes must delineate their values.   In HTML 3.2, attributes did not need to be delineated by quotes, but such delineation is required in XHTML. For example, in HTML 3.2, the tag <img src=image.gif> would be acceptable. Under XHTML, this same tag must be expressed as <img src="image.gif">.

XML-like hierarchy must be enforced.   HTML 3.2 did not enforce strict hierarchies. For example, the tag sequence <p><b>hello</p></b> would be legal. Under XHTML, this sequence would be illegal because the p and b tags overlap. Under XHTML, this should be written as <p><b>hello</b></p>.

Most of the features added in XHTML are extra constraints that may seem limiting to an HTML programmer. The main motivation behind XHTML was to make HTML compatible with XML, not to simplify HTML development.

XML Is Based on SGML

The development that was needed to produce XML began in 1996, but it wasn't until 1998 that the World Wide Web Consortium(W3C) made it a standard. Because this all took place fairly recently, you may think that XML is a bit immature as far as technologies go. But in fact, the technology behind XML is not very new at all. That is because XML is based on Standard Generalized Markup Language (SGML), which was developed in the early 1980s. In fact, SGML became an ISO standard in 1986, more than a decade before XML became one, and it is widely used for large documentation projects.

NOTE   As you may have guessed, HTML is also rooted in SGML. Its development began in 1990, several years before XML.

XML is much simpler to use than SGML. As XML was created, the designers took many of the best features from SGML to create XML. This, combined with what was learned through years of HTML usage, allowed them to create XML. Basically, the current differences between the uses of SGML and XML are that SGML is mostly used for technical documentation and it is used much less for other kinds of data, and XML is the exact opposite. XML is designed to be able to handle all forms of data.

XML Is a Free Open Standard

XML is an open standard that is not controlled by just one company. XML was produced by a consortium of companies represented by the W3C. XML is an idea, a way of representing data; it is not a software package. Because of this, you can obtain XML solutions from any number of vendors.

XML and Bots

XML is a very relevant technology to the bot programmer. One of the hardest tasks facing any bot programmer is gleaning the desired data from all of the other HTML contained on a site. XML brings some standard to web data and makes it easier for the bot to find what it is looking for.

Bot programmers must usually create elaborate parsing programs that scan through many HTML documents. If this data is XML, then a standard DOM parser, like the one discussed in Chapter 6, can be used to parse the XML data.

Of course, to take advantages of these features, the target site must support XML. Currently, most of the sites support HTML only, and it is unlikely that a vast majority of the sites will support XML any time soon. For many information sites that do not seek to directly appeal to bots, there is no compelling reason to make their data available as XML.

XML is only a means of encoding data; it specifies nothing about how the data is transferred. An XML message needs some other technology to move it from its source to its destination. You could think of XML as a message that you give to the postal service for delivery. For XML documents, the postal service is SOAP. In the next section, you will see how SOAP can be used to move XML messages from one site to the next.

Transferring XML Data

XML provides a standard way to store data, and it is this storage of data that is the only thing that XML is directly concerned with. For data to be of any use, however, it must be able to be both transmitted and received. This function can be accomplished using SOAP. As the previous section stated, SOAP is much like a post office for XML messages. While there are other ways to deliver XML messages, SOAP is the predominant message delivery system.

What Is SOAP?

SOAP is an XML-based, lightweight protocol that is used for information exchange. This protocol is designed to work in environments that are both decentralized and distributed. SOAP is decentralized in that the provider of a SOAP service and the consumer program can be running on two different computers. SOAP is distributed in that many different computers can provide the same SOAP service, which allows these computers to balance the load of requests to achieve maximum performance.

SOAP consists of three main parts: an envelope that describes what is in a message and how to process it, a set of encoding rules for expressing the applications data types, and a convention for exposing the methods of the remote application. These parts are summarized here.

SOAP envelope   The SOAP envelope portion of the message contains addressing information, much like a real envelope. A SOAP envelope contains a target address that specifies the server that the SOAP message is targeted for. It also includes a return address that specifies where the server should send its response. The encoding rules are specified by the XML attribute `SOAP-ENV:Envelope`.

Encoding rules   Every SOAP message contains the encoding rules used to encode it. These rules specify what version of SOAP was used and how different components of the SOAP message are represented. The encoding rules are specified by the XML attribute `SOAP-ENV:encodingStyle`.

Method call   To cause a Java program to execute, that Java program's methods are executed. The same principle applies to a SOAP message. When a SOAP message is sent, pat of the message specifies what methods the server should execute. The method being invoked is specified inside of the `SOAP-ENV:Body` XML tag.

SOAP can potentially be used with a variety of protocols, though in reality, SOAP is almost always used in conjunction with only HTTP. It is this pairing that we will examine in this chapter.

How SOAP Transfers Data

In essence, SOAP messages are one-way transmissions from a sender to a receiver. First, a SOAP request is sent from the client to the server. At some point, the sever may respond with a response back to the client. This response is asynchronous, in that considerable time may elapse before the response is sent. This pattern of request followed by response is how SOAP communication is carried out.

Though SOAP is not tied to any specific network protocol, SOAP messages are almost always delivered using HTTP, as mentioned previously. As a result, SOAP implementations can be optimized to exploit the unique characteristics of particular network systems, such as

HTTP. For example, the HTTP-based SOAP implementations can be created so that SOAP response messages are delivered as HTTP responses, using the same connection as the inbound request. This two-way connection is not always available.

SOAP messages can also be transferred using Simple Mail Transfer Protocol (SMTP). Under this scheme, SOAP messages are actually e-mailed to the server that is to fulfill the request. Any response that the server gives is then e-mailed back to the calling program. A considerable amount of time may elapse between the message being requested and its eventual receipt.

SOAP specifies the structure that XML messages will have, but it does not do anything to actually communicate the structure of this exchange. SOAP allows you to call methods, just like you call a method on a regular Java object. But how do you know these method names? For example, would a method used to retrieve the current temperature be called `GetCurrent-Temperature` and perhaps just `GetTemperature`? The name of this method could follow any number of naming conventions. In order for the correct name to be determined, there needs to be a file that defines what services are offered by a web service such as this. Web Service Definition Language (WSDL) fills this need. Every SOAP service should have a WSDL file that defines the protocol template for communicating with it.

The Structure of SOAP

We will first examine a simple example of SOAP being used with HTTP. This example transmits a `GetCurrentTemperature` SOAP request to a `CurrentTemperature` service (see Listing 13.2). The request takes a string parameter, `city code`, which represents the city for which you wish to retrieve the temperature. The SOAP server that receives this request will return a floating point number that corresponds to the current temperature in the requested city.

Now we will examine the request and response in greater detail. As you can see from Listing 13.2, the SOAP Envelope element, `SOAP-ENV:Envelope` is the top element of the XML document representing the SOAP message. XML *namespaces*, short names that prefix tag names, are used to ensure that SOAP identifiers are not confused with application specific identifiers. For example, the tag `<SOAP-ENV:Envelope>` is using a namespace of `SOAP-ENV`.

Listing 13.2   **SOAP Message Embedded in HTTP Request (*SOAPRequest.txt*)**

```
POST /GetTemperature HTTP/1.1
Host: www.temperatureserver.com
Content-Type: text/xml; charset="utf-8"
Content-Length: nnnn
SOAPAction: "Some-URI"

<SOAP-ENV:Envelope
  xmlns:SOAP-ENV="http://schemas.xmlsoap.org/soap/envelope/"
  SOAP-ENV:encodingStyle="http://schemas.xmlsoap.org/soap/encoding/">
```

```
<SOAP-ENV:Body>
    <m:GetCurrentTemperature xmlns:m="Some-URI">
        <symbol>KSTL</symbol>
    </m: GetCurrentTemperature >
</SOAP-ENV:Body>
</SOAP-ENV:Envelope>
```

The `SOAP-ENV:Body` section is what contains the actual method call. Here a method named `GetCurrentTemperature` is being called. A return address should be provided where you see the text `"Some-URI"`. This specifies the return address to which the SOAP server will send the response message. This URI parameter is actually a URL when HTTP is used as the transport mechanism. If SMTP were used, the URI would specify a return e-mail address. After the method name, the parameters that are used to call this method appear. Here a single parameter, named `symbol`, is sent to indicate the desired city.

Once this message is sent to the temperature server, the temperature server will respond with the temperature. It is important to note that this is a completely asynchronous response; it occurs with a second `POST` and is not a part of the initial `POST` shown in Listing 13.2. Listing 13.3 shows this response.

Listing 13.3   SOAP Message Embedded in HTTP Response (*SOAPResponse.txt*)

```
HTTP/1.1 200 OK
Content-Type: text/xml; charset="utf-8"
Content-Length: ###

<SOAP-ENV:Envelope
  xmlns:SOAP-ENV="http://schemas.xmlsoap.org/soap/envelope/"
  SOAP-ENV:encodingStyle="http://schemas.xmlsoap.org/soap/encoding/"/>
  <SOAP-ENV:Body>
      <m: GetCurrentTemperature xmlns:m="Some-URI">
          <Temperature>34.5</GetCurrentTemperature>
      </m: GetCurrentTemperature>
  </SOAP-ENV:Body>
</SOAP-ENV:Envelope>
```

The response to a SOAP message looks very similar to the request. Inside of the `SOAP-ENV: Body` tag are the results of any method calls. The method, in this case `GetCurrentTemperature`, is presented just as it was in the request. The data returned by the method, in this case a `Temperature` tag, follows the method.

As you can see, there is certain information that you must have in order to properly send a SOAP message and process the response. The address of the SOAP server must be known so that you know where to send the message. The name of the method you are calling, and its parameters, must be known. Finally, you must know what kind of data is to be returned from the SOAP server. SOAP provides for a standardized way of representing this information. The standardized representation, called WSDL, will be covered in the next section.

A Template for SOAP: WSDL

WSDL is an XML format that is used to describe network services. The operations of the underlying web service are described abstractly, and then they are bound to a concrete network protocol and message format so that an actual physical service provider, called an endpoint, can be defined. WSDL is designed so that you do not need to be aware of what server is handling your request. The WSDL file is programmed with what servers can handle the request and does not require the programmer to specify the exact server that will be used.

NOTE   This section provides only a general overview of WSDL. For a complete discussion of WSDL refer to its actual specification, which can be found at `http://www.w3.org/TR/wsdl`.

Communications protocols and message formats are becoming standardized in the web community. As a result, it is now possible to describe the communications in some structured way. WSDL addresses the need for structured communications by defining an XML grammar that is used to describe network services as collections of communication endpoints that are capable of sharing information by exchanging messages. A WSDL document not only provides information for distributed systems, but it also serves as a recipe for automating the details involved in applications communication.

Using SOAP in Java

The SOAP messages we have examined in this chapter could easily apply to any computer language that supports SOAP. Each computer language has their own way of providing an interface into SOAP. The Microsoft programs use .NET (pronounced dot NET) to provide this interface. This section will show you how a Java program interfaces to SOAP.

There are several class libraries available to Java programs so that they can implement SOAP. For instance, Sun makes one available called the *Java API for XML Messaging (JAXM)*. JAXM is a class library that can be downloaded from the Java section of the Sun website.

Basically, the JAXM package enables applications so that they can send and receive document oriented XML messages using a pure Java API. In fact, JAXM implements SOAP 1.1, which allows developers to build applications rather than requiring them to learn the low-level intricate details of XML messaging that were only briefly touched on in the previous section.

TIP   For more complete information about JAXM and other Sun XML products visit this website at `http://java.sun.com/xml/`.

Bots and SOAP

Bots and SOAP applications are very closely related because they both are designed to retrieve information using HTTP. The primary difference between a bot and a SOAP application is that a SOAP application gets its data in a nice, well defined form and the bot must instead deal with data in a wide variety of formats. If every site on the Internet supported SOAP, we would not need the bots that were presented in this book. In essence, bots would be replaced by SOAP applications that connect to well-defined providers for the data that the bots sought. This would make the creation of information exchange applications much easier. The problem is that this will only work if the website supports SOAP.

You may be wondering why this hasn't already happened. In fact, it is doubtful that we will see this idealistic world anytime soon. This is because there is already a tremendous amount of traditional HTML data available on the Internet, and as a result, it is likely that much of this data will likely stay in this format for the foreseeable future. For many existing sites, the cost that would be incurred in order to switch to SOAP for messages does not justify the gains.

To completely switch a website from a traditional HTML design to SOAP would require a complete restructuring of the entire site. Further, it may be beyond the means of the webmaster. Putting up an HTML website only involves creating HTML pages and posting them to a web host. Creating a SOAP-enabled website requires the webmaster to be a competent programmer.

This means that for the foreseeable future, web-enabled applications will likely be using a mixture of SOAP and bot technology. If a website does not support SOAP, then it will still be necessary to bots and HTML parsers to gather the needed information.

Summary

Bots are not the only way to retrieve information from web servers. New technologies such as SOAP and XML allow data to be retrieved from a website in a much more standardized way than bots do. This chapter explored XML and SOAP and their ability to retrieve information from the Internet.

Extensible Markup Language (XML) is a standard language that can be used to represent hierarchical data in a text file. XML is designed according to strict rules that ensure that the XML data will be interpretable by any application that supports XML.

Simple Object Access Protocol (SOAP) is a protocol that traffics XML messages between web service providers and clients. Just as XML provides a consistent interface for reading files, SOAP provides a consistent means for accessing data from sites.

Web Service Definition Language (WSDL) is a language used to describe web services that use SOAP. WSDL documents the method signatures of the web service. This allows someone implementing a SOAP application to know what data should be sent, and what data should be returned.

But what does the future hold for bots and XML? If every website supported SOAP, there would be no need for the kinds of bots described in this book. This is an unlikely scenario anytime in the near future. For some time, we will likely see a mix of websites and SOAP compliant web services.

The remainder of the book is comprised of the appendices and glossary. Here you will find a listing of all of the bot classes and methods, several charts that show the various responses and requests that web servers expect, and some basic installation information for the Tomcat web server.

Appendix A

The Bot Package

One of the main features of this book is the Bot package, which is part of the companion CD. This package contains many reusable classes that can be used to create your own spiders, bots, and aggregators. This appendix provides a quick overview of these classes. For more in-depth information on any of these classes, please refer to the appropriate chapter of the book.

This appendix also contains figures that show the inheritance structure of the bot classes. These figures are in the Uniform Modeling Language (UML) format. Due to the complexity of the diagrams, only the generalizations (inheritance) are shown.

Utility Classes

The utility classes are those classes that do not fall easily into any category. The Bot package uses several utility classes to assist the other classes, and these classes are shown in Figure A.1. The classes that fall into this category include `Base64OutputStream`, `Link`, `Log`, and `URLUtility`.

NOTE   UML diagrams often reference built-in Java classes, such as `FilterOuputStream` in Figure A.1. A UML diagram always identifies the source of an object. You can easily identify the source because it will have the words (from x), just below the class title, where x is the place that the class resides. Classes provided by the Bot package will always have the words (from bot) below their class names.

The *Base64OutputStream* Class

This filter is used to 64-bit encode the specified string. This class allows a string to be displayed with only ASCII characters, and it is also used to provide HTTP authorization. The methods for this class are shown in Table A.1, along with the method signature, which lists the method name and parameters used to call the method.

TABLE A.1: Base64OutputStream Methods

Method Name	Method Signature
Base64OutputStream	Public Base64OutputStream(OutputStream out)
flush	public void flush()
write	public void write(int c) throws IOException

FIGURE A.1:

The utility classes

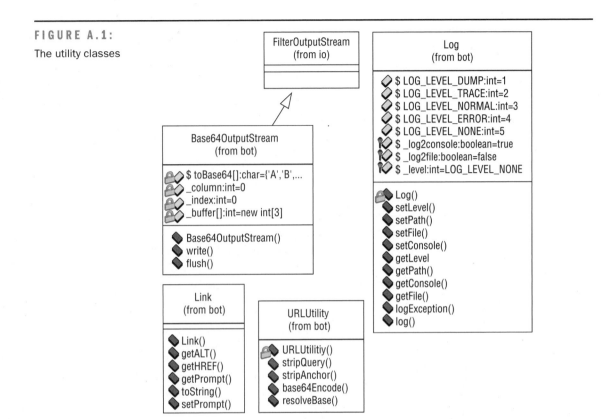

The *Link* Class

This is a very simple data class that holds HTML links. This class holds both the actual link URL, as well as the ALT tag. The methods for this class are shown in Table A.2.

TABLE A.2: Link Methods

Method Name	Method Signature
getALT	public String getALT()
getHREF	public String getHREF()
getPrompt	public String getPrompt()
Link	public Link(String alt,String href,String prompt)
setPrompt	public void setPrompt(String prompt)
toString	public String toString()

The *Log* Class

The Log class is used to write out log information. The methods for this class are shown in Table A.3.

TABLE A.3: Log Methods

Method Name	Method Signature
getConsole	static public boolean getConsole()
getFile	static public boolean getFile()
getLevel	static public int getLevel()
getPath	static public String getPath()
Log	private Log()
log	synchronized static public void log(int level,String event)
logException	static public void logException(String event,Exception e)
setConsole	static public void setConsole(Boolean b)
setFile	static public void setFile(boolean b)
setLevel	static public void setLevel(int l)
setPath	static public void setPath(String s)

The *URLUtility* Class

This simple static class contains several methods that are used to manipulate URLs. The methods for this class are shown in Table A.4.

TABLE A.4: URLUtility Methods

Method Name	Method Signature
base64Encode	static public String base64Encode(String s)
resolveBase	static public String resolveBase(String base,String rel)
stripAnchor	static public URL stripAnhcor(URL url)
stripQuery	static public URL stripQuery(URL url)
URLUtility	private URLUtility()

HTTP Classes

The HTTP classes (shown in Figure A.2) are used to send HTTP requests to the web server. These classes provide all of the communication needed by the Bot package. The classes that fall into this category are HTTP and HTTPSocket.

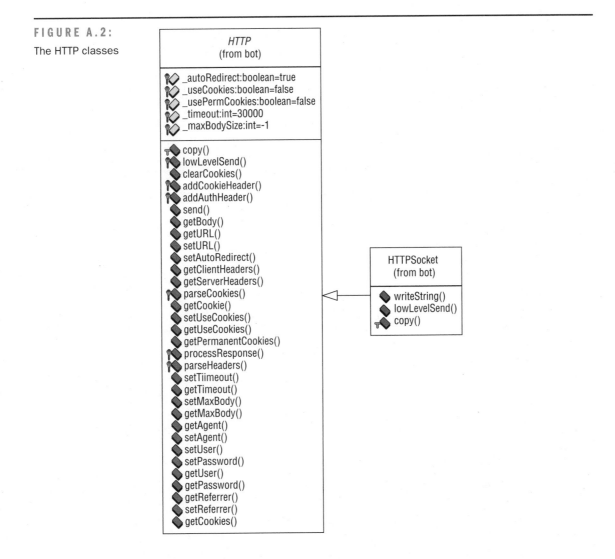

The HTTP classes

The *HTTP* Class

This class implements an HTTP handler. This class handles these specific issues:

- Cookies

- The referrer tag

- HTTP user authentication

- Automatic redirection

- Parsing headers

The low-level details of how the data is actually transmitted are left to a derived class. Most likely, you will be using the HTTPSocket class, which derives from the HTTP class, more often. This is because the HTTPSocket class is designed to actually communicate using sockets, which is the primary way of using HTTP. The methods for the HTTP class are shown in Table A.5.

TABLE A.5: HTTP Methods

Method Name	Method Signature
addAuthHeader	protected void addAuthHeader()
addCookieHeader	protected void addCookieHeader()
clearCookies	public void clearCookies()
copy	Abstract HTTP copy();
getAgent	public String getAgent()
getBody	public String getBody()
getClientHeaders	public AttributeList getClientHeaders()
getCookie	public CookieParse getCookie(String name)
getCookies	public AttributeList getCookies()
getMaxBody	public int getMaxBody()
getPassword	public String getPassword()
getPerminantCookies	public boolean getPerminantCookies()
getReferrer	public String getReferrer()
getServerHeaders	public AttributeList getServerHeaders()
getTimeout	public int getTimeout()
getURL	public String getURL()
getUseCookies	public boolean getUseCookies()
getUser	public String getUser()
lowLevelSend	abstract protected void lowLevelSend(String url,String post)
parseCookies	protected void parseCookies()
parseHeaders	protected void parseHeaders()
processResponse	protected void processResponse(String name)
send	public void send(String url,String post)
setAgent	public void setAgent(String a)
SetAutoRedirect	public void SetAutoRedirect(boolean b)
setMaxBody	public void setMaxBody(int i)

Continued on next page

TABLE A.5 CONTINUED: HTTP Methods

Method Name	Method Signature
setPassword	`public void setPassword(String p)`
setReferrer	`public void setReferrer(String p)`
setTimeout	`public void setTimeout(int i)`
setUrl	`public void setURL(String u)`
setUseCookies	`public void setUseCookies(boolean session,boolean perm)`
setUser	`public void setUser(String u)`

The *HTTPSocket* Class

The HTTPSocket class provides the socket-based implementation of HTTP. This is the main class used for HTTP communication in the Bot package. The methods for this class are shown in Table A.6.

TABLE A.6: HTTPSocket Methods

Method Name	Method Signature
copy	`HTTP copy()`
lowLevelSend	`synchronized public void lowLevelSend(String url,String post)`
writeString	`Public void writeString (OutputStream out, String str)`

The Parsing Classes

The parsing classes are used to parse a variety of data. There are specialized classes provided to parse cookies and HTML. The parsing classes that are included in the Bot package are shown in Figure A.3. The classes that fall into this category are Attribute, AttributeList, CookieParse, HTMLForm, HTMLForm.FormElement, HTMLPage, HTMLParse, HTMLParser, HTMLTag, and Parse.

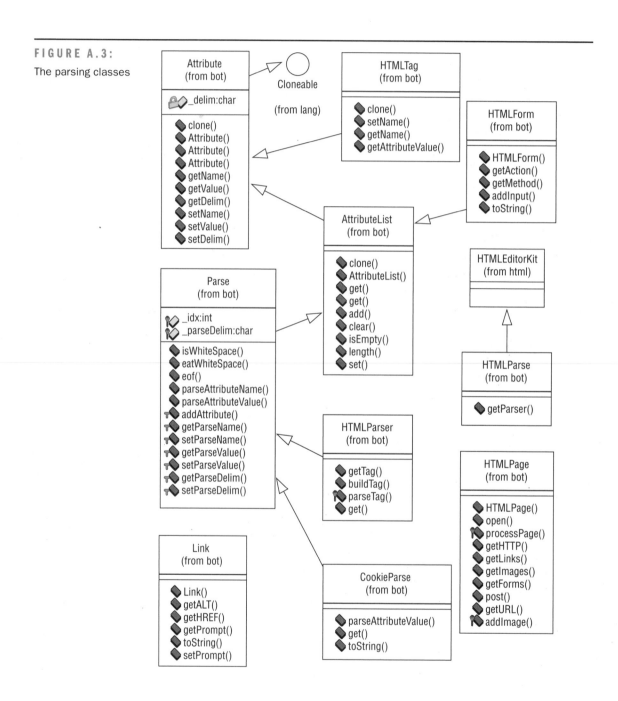

The *Attribute* Class

The Attribute class stores a list of named-value pairs. Optionally, the value can have delimiters such as ' or ". The methods for this class are shown in Table A.7.

TABLE A.7: Attribute Methods

Method Name	Method Signature
Attribute	public Attribute()
Attribute	public Attribute(String name,String value)
Attribute	public Attribute(String name,String value,char delim)
clone	public Object clone()
getDelim	public char getDelim()
getName	public String getName()
getValue	public String getValue()
setDelim	public void setDelim(char ch)
setName	public void setName(String name)
setValue	public void setValue(String value)

The *AttributeList* Class

The AttributeList class is used to store lists of Attribute classes. The methods for this class are shown in Table A.8.

TABLE A.8: AttributeList Methods

Method Name	Method Signature
add	synchronized public void add(Attribute a)
AttributeList	public AttributeList()
clear	synchronized public void clear()
clone	public Object clone()
get	synchronized public Attribute get(int id)
get	synchronized public Attribute get(String id)
isEmpty	synchronized public Boolean isEmpty()
length	synchronized public int length()
set	synchronized public void set(String name,String value)

The *CookieParse* Class

This class is used to parse cookies that are transmitted with the HTTP headers. The methods for this class are shown in Table A.9.

TABLE A.9: CookieParse Methods

Method Name	Method Signature
get	public boolean get()
parseAttributeValue	public void parseAttributeValue()
toString	public String toString()

The *HTMLForm* Class

The HTMLForm class is used to create a response to an HTML form and then transmit it to a web server. The methods for this class are shown in Table A.10.

TABLE A.10: HTMLForm Methods

Method Name	Method Signature
addInput	public void addInput(String name,String value,String type,String prompt,AttributeList options
getAction	public String getAction()
getMethod	public String getMethod()
HTMLForm	public HTMLForm(String method,String action)
toString	public String toString()

The *HTMLForm.FormElement* Class

This class holds a single form element, and it was created as the inner class of the HTMLForm class. *Inner classes* are a Java programming technique in which a class is created inside of another class. In this case, the FormElement class was created inside of the HTMLForm class. The methods for this class are shown in Table A.11.

TABLE A.11: FormElement Methods

Method Name	Method Signature
getOptions	public AttributeList getOptions()
getPrompt	public String getPrompt()
getType	public String getType()

Continued on next page

TABLE A.11 CONTINUED: FormElement Methods

Method Name	Method Signature
setOptions	`public void setOptions(AttributeList options)`
setPrompt	`public void setPrompt(String str)`
setType	`public void setType(String t)`

The *HTMLPage* Class

The HTMLPage class is used to parse an HTML page and store that page, in a parsed form. The methods for this class are shown in Table A.12.

TABLE A.12: HTMLPage Methods

Method Name	Method Signature
addImage	`protected void addImage(String img)`
getForms	`public Vector getForms()`
getHTTP	`public HTTP getHTTP()`
getImages	`public Vector getImages()`
getLinks	`public Vector getLinks()`
getURL	`public String getURL()`
HTMLPage	`public HTMLPage(HTTP http)`
open	`public void open(String url,HTMLEditorKit.ParserCallback callback)`
post	`public void post(HTMLForm form)`
processPage	`protected void processPage(HTMLEditorKit.ParserCallback callback)`

The *HTMLParse* Class

This is a very simple class. The only purpose of the HTMLParse class is to be a descendant of the HTMLEditorKit class. This allows the HTMLParse class to make the getParser method public. This is because Java allows descendant classes to make methods contained in the parent class have a more public access attribute. This is necessary so that we can call the getParser method. The method for this class is shown in Table A.13.

TABLE A.13: The HTMLParse Method

Method Name	Method Signature
GgetParser	`Public HTMLEditorKit.Parser getParser()`

The *HTMLParser* Class

The HTMLParse class is used to parse an HTML page. This is a very simple class that does not store any values, and it is used to provide some basic utility methods to the other HTML parsing methods described in this section. The methods for this class are shown in Table A.14.

TABLE A.14: HTMLParser Methods

Method Name	Method Signature
buildTag	Public String buildTag()
get	Public char get()
parseTag	protected void parseTag()
getTag	Public HTMLTag getTag()

The *HTMLTag* Class

The HTMLTag class is used to store an HTML tag, including its name and any attributes. The methods for this class are shown in Table A.15.

TABLE A.15: HTMLTag Methods

Method Name	Method Signature
clone	public Object clone()
getAttributeValue	public String getAttributeValue(String name)
getName	public String getName()
setName	public void setName(String s)

The *Parse* Class

The Parse class is the low-level text parsing class that all other parsing classes are based on. The methods for this class are shown in Table A.16.

TABLE A.16: Parse Methods

Method Name	Method Signature
addAttribute	void addAttribute()
eatWhiteSpace	public void eatWhiteSpace()
eof	public boolean eof()
getParseDelim	char getParseDelim()

Continued on next page

TABLE A.16 CONTINUED: Parse Methods

Method Name	Method Signature
getParseName	String getParseName()
getParseValue	String getParseValue()
isWhiteSpace	public static boolean isWhiteSpace(char ch)
parseAttributeName	public void parseAttributeName()
parseAttributeValue	public void parseAttributeValue()
setParseDelim	void setParseDelim(char s)
setParseName	void setParseName(String s)
setParseValue	void setParseValue(String s)

Spider Classes

The spider classes (see Figure A.4) are used to create a bot that can crawl from one page to the next. The classes and interfaces that fall into this category include BotExclusion, ISpider-Reportable, IWorkloadStorable, Spider, SpiderDone, SpiderInternalWorkload, SpiderSQL-Workload, and SpiderWorker.

The *BotExclusion* Class

The BotExclusion class is used to read and process a robots.txt file from a website. When a bot uses this class, it can make sure it is obeying this public policy file. This policy, which sites store in a file named robots.txt, allows the webmaster to govern which directories a bot may access. The methods for this class are shown in Table A.17.

TABLE A.17: BotExclusion Methods

Method Name	Method Signature
getExclude	Public Vector getExclude()
getRobotFile	public String getRobotFile()
isExcluded	public boolean isExcluded(String url)
load	public void load(HTTP http,String url)

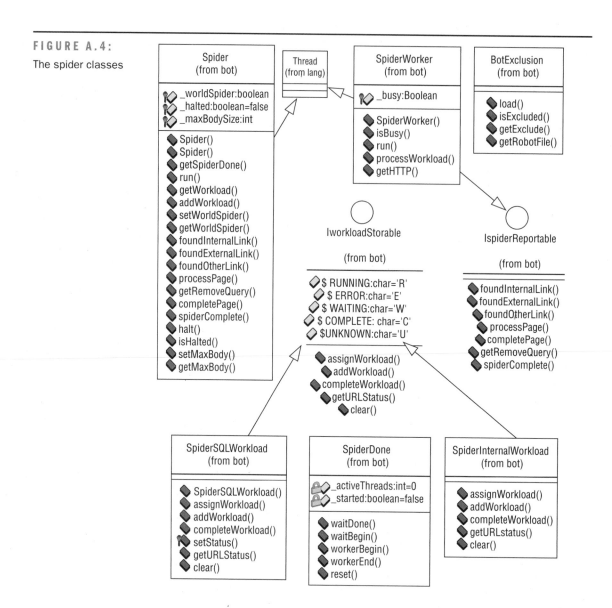

The *ISpiderReportable* Interface

This interface represents an interface to which the spider can report. As the spider does its job, events from this interface will be called. The methods for this interface are shown in Table A.18.

TABLE A.18: ISpiderReportable Methods

Method Name	Method Signature
foundInternalLink	public boolean foundInternalLink(String url);
foundExternalLink	public boolean foundExternalLink(String url);
foundOtherLink	public boolean foundOtherLink(String url);
processPage	public void processPage(HTTP page);
completePage	public void completePage(HTTP page,boolean error);
getRemoveQuery	public boolean getRemoveQuery();
spiderComplete	public void spiderComplete();

The *IWorkloadStorable* Interface

This interface defines a class that can be used to store a spider's workload. The Bot package currently supports two different workload stores:

SpiderInternalWorkload   Stores the contents of the workload in memory.

SpiderSQLWorkload   Stores the contents of the workload in a SQL database.

The methods for this class are shown in Table A.19.

TABLE A.19: IWorkloadStorable Methods

Method Name	Method Signature
assignWorkload	public String assignWorkload();
addWorkload	public void addWorkload(String url);
completeWorkload	public void completeWorkload(String url,Boolean error);
getURLStatus	public char getURLStatus(String url);
cear	public void clear();

The *Spider* Class

The Spider class is the main organizational class for spidering. It delegates work to the SpiderWorker class. The methods for this class are shown in Table A.20.

TABLE A.20: Spider Methods

Method Name	Method Signature
addWorkload	synchronized public void addWorkload(String url)
completePage	synchronized public void completePage(HTTP page,boolean error)
foundExternalLink	synchronized public Boolean foundExternalLink(String url)
foundInternalLink	synchronized public Boolean foundInternalLink(String url)
foundOtherLink	synchronized public boolean foundOtherLink(String url)
getMaxBody	public int getMaxBody()
getRemoveQuery	synchronized public boolean getRemoveQuery()
getSpiderDone	public SpiderDone getSpiderDone()
getWorkload	synchronized public String getWorkload()
getWorldSpider	public boolean getWorldSpider()
halt	synchronized public void halt()
isHalted	public boolean isHalted()
processPage	synchronized public void processPage(HTTP page)
run	public void run()
setMaxBody	public void setMaxBody(int mx)
setWorldSpider	public void setWorldSpider(boolean b)
Spider	public Spider(ISpiderReportable manager,String url,HTTP http,int poolSize)
Spider	public Spider(ISpiderReportable manager,String url,HTTP http,int poolSize,IWorkloadStorable w)
spiderComplete	synchronized public void spiderComplete()

The *SpiderDone* Class

This is a very simple class that allows the spider to determine when it is done. This class implements a simple lock that the spider class can wait on to determine completion. Done is defined as the spider having no more work to complete. The methods for this class are shown in Table A.21.

TABLE A.21: SpiderDone Methods

Method Name	Method Signature
reset	synchronized public void reset()
waitBegin	synchronized public void waitBegin()
waitDone	synchronized public void waitDone()
workerBegin	synchronized public void workerBegin()
workerEnd	synchronized public void workerEnd()

The *SpiderInternalWorkload* Class

This class is used to maintain an internal, memory-based workload store for a spider. This workload store will be used by default if no other store is specified. The methods for this class are shown in Table A.22.

TABLE A.22: SpiderInternalWorkload Methods

Method Name	Method Signature
assignWorkload	synchronized public String assignWorkload()
addWorkload	synchronized public void addWorkload(String url)
clear	synchronized public void clear()
completeWorkload	synchronized public void completeWorkload(String url,boolean error)
getURLStatus	synchronized public char getURLStatus(String url)

The *SpiderSQLWorkload* Class

This class uses a JDBC database to store a spider workload. The methods for this class are shown in Table A.23.

TABLE A.23: *SpiderSQLWorkload* Methods

Method Name	Method Signature
addWorkload	synchronized public void addWorkload(String url)
assignWorkload	synchronized public String assignWorkload()
clear	synchronized public void clear()
competeWorkload	synchronized public void completeWorkload(String url,boolean error)
getURLStatus	synchronized public char getURLStatus(String url)
setStatus	protected void setStatus(String url,char status)
SpiderSQLWorkload	public SpiderSQLWorkload(String driver, String source)

The *SpiderWorker* Class

The SpiderWorker class performs the actual work of spidering pages. It is implemented as a thread that is created by the Spider class. The methods for this class are shown in Table A.24.

TABLE A.24: SpiderWorker Methods

Method Name	Method Signature
getHTTP	public HTTP getHTTP()
isBusy	public Boolean isBusy()
processWorkload	protected void processWorkload()
run	public void run()
SpiderWorker	public SpiderWorker(Spider owner,HTTP http)

APPENDIX B

Various HTTP Related Charts

HTTP consists of headers, status codes, and the actual data of the message. The charts contained in this appendix can provide a quick lookup for codes that you might encounter while you are using HTTP. For more information about HTTP, see Chapter 2, "Examining the Hypertext Transfer Protocol."

The ASCII Chart

ASCII, which is pronounced "ask-key," is a code that represents letters and symbols with numbers. Most web pages store their HTML information as ASCII characters. ASCII is an acronym for the American Standard Code for Information Interchange. ASCII is the standard seven-bit code that was accepted as an international standard in 1963 by the American National Standards Institute (ANSI). Other standards that document ASCII are ISO-14962-1997 and ANSI-X3.4-1986 (sR1997).

ASCII codes range from 0-127. There are also many special control codes, which have special meaning to the older computer terminals. However, these special meanings have no real meaning to web applications. Table B.1 lists each ASCII code and the corresponding letter or special meaning.

TABLE B.1: ASCII Codes and Their Meanings

Decimal	Hexadecimal	Character	Special Meaning
0	00	NUL	Null
1	01	SOH	Start of heading
2	02	STX	Start of text
3	03	ETX	End of text
4	04	EOT	End of transmission
5	05	ENQ	Enquiry
6	06	ACK	Acknowledge
7	07	BEL	Play a tone
8	08	BS	Back space
9	09	HT	Horizontal tab
10	0a	LF	Line feed
11	0b	VT	Vertical tab
12	0c	FF	Form feed
13	0d	CR	Carriage return
14	0e	SO	Shift out
15	0f	SI	Shift in

Continued on next page

TABLE B.1 CONTINUED: ASCII Codes and Their Meanings

Decimal	Hexadecimal	Character	Special Meaning
16	10	DLE	Data link escape
17	11	DC1	Device control 1
18	12	DC2	Device control 2
19	13	DC3	Device control 3
20	14	DC4	Device control 4
21	15	NAK	Negative acknowledge
22	16	SYN	Synchronous idle
23	17	ETB	End of transmission block
24	18	CAN	Cancel
25	19	EM	End of medium
26	1a	SUB	Substitute
27	1b	ESC	Escape
28	1c	FS	File separator
29	1d	GS	Group separator
30	1e	RS	Record separator
31	1f	US	Unit separator
32	20	(space)	
33	21	!	
34	22	" " " "	
35	23	#	
36	24	$	
37	25	%	
38	26	&	
39	27	'	
40	28	(	
41	29	)	
42	2a	*	
43	2b	+	
44	2c	" , "	
45	2d	-	
46	2e	.	
47	2f	/	
48	30	0	
49	31	1	
50	32	2	

Continued on next page

TABLE B.1 CONTINUED: ASCII Codes and Their Meanings

Decimal	Hexadecimal	Character	Special Meaning
51	33	3	
52	34	4	
53	35	5	
54	36	6	
55	37	7	
56	38	8	
57	39	9	
58	3a	:	
59	3b	;	
60	3c	<	
61	3d	=	
62	3e	>	
63	3f	?	
64	40	@	
65	41	A	
66	42	B	
67	43	C	
68	44	D	
69	45	E	
70	46	F	
71	47	G	
72	48	H	
73	49	I	
74	4a	J	
75	4b	K	
76	4c	L	
77	4d	M	
78	4e	N	
79	4f	O	
80	50	P	
81	51	Q	
82	52	R	
83	53	S	
84	54	T	
85	55	U	

Continued on next page

TABLE B.1 CONTINUED: ASCII Codes and Their Meanings

Decimal	Hexadecimal	Character	Special Meaning
86	56	V	
87	57	W	
88	58	X	
89	59	Y	
90	5a	Z	
91	5b	[	
92	5c	\	
93	5d	]	
94	5e	^	
95	5f	_	
96	60	`	
97	61	a	
98	62	b	
99	63	c	
100	64	d	
101	65	e	
102	66	f	
103	67	g	
104	68	h	
105	69	i	
106	6a	j	
107	6b	k	
108	6c	l	
109	6d	m	
110	6e	n	
111	6f	o	
112	70	p	
113	71	q	
114	72	r	
115	73	s	
116	74	t	
117	75	u	
118	76	v	
119	77	w	
120	78	x	

Continued on next page

TABLE B.1 CONTINUED: ASCII Codes and Their Meanings

Decimal	Hexadecimal	Character	Special Meaning
121	79	y	
122	7a	z	
123	7b	{	
124	7c	|	
125	7d	}	
126	7e	~	
127	7f	DEL	

ASCII data is used in every part of the HTTP message. The actual body of the HTTP message that the user sees is ASCII. ASCII is also used to store components of the HTTP message that the user does not see. For instance, HTTP headers are stored in ASCII, yet they are not normally visible to the user. The next section describes HTTP headers.

HTTP Headers

HTTP headers are portions of an HTTP message that are rarely seen by a user. These headers take the form of a series of name-value pairs. The following code shows the HTTP headers sent by a web client (a browser) when it requests a page. The name of the header is on the left side of the colon, and the value is to the right.

```
GET /response.asp HTTP/1.0
@CodeSnippet:Accept: application/vnd.ms-powerpoint, application/vnd.ms-excel,
application/msword, image/gif, image/x-xbitmap, image/jpeg, image/pjpeg, */*
Accept-Language: en-us
Accept-Encoding: gzip, deflate
User-Agent: Mozilla/4.0 (compatible; MSIE 5.5; Windows NT 4.0)
Host: auto.search.msn.com
Connection: Keep-Alive
Cookie: MC1=V=2
```

The server will then respond with the appropriate HTML file and some headers of its own. Table B.2 lists common headers; shows whether these headers are sent from the client, the server, or both; and lists the meanings of each.

NOTE   The following table was based on RFC2616. You may refer to RFC2616 for additional information. RFC2616 may be viewed at this URL ftp://ftp.isi.edu/in-notes/rfc2616.txt.

TABLE B.2: Selected HTTP Headers

Header Field	Client or Server	Description
Accept	Client	Specifies the preferred media types by the browser.
Accept-Charset	Client	Specifies the preferred character set by the browser.
Accept-Encoding	Client	Specifies the preferred encoding method by the client.
Accept-Language	Client	Specifies the human language preferred by the client.
Allow	Server	Identifies the preferred methods for the requested resource.
Authorization	Client	Used to specify the user ID and password for user authentication.
Content-Encoding	Both	Specifies encoding and other additional formatting that applies to the response, in addition to what Content-Type indicates.
Content-Length	Server	Indicates the length, in bytes, of the body of the response being sent by the server.
Content-Type	Server	Specifies the mime-type of the response being sent by the server.
Date	Server	Specifies the time and date that the sever generated this response.
Expires	Server	Specifies a time and date after which the content is no longer considered valid. This value is used with browser caching.
From	Client	Specifies the e-mail address of the user of the browser. Not generally used.
Etag	Client	Used to specify the ID of this entity. (Stands for the entity tag.) Used in conjunction with the If-Match and If-None-Match.
Host	Client	Specifies the host that the browser is requesting. This header is used when multiple host names point to the same IP address.
If-Match	Client	Used to specify a conditional request. Server responds only if the correct Etag is specified.
If-Modified-Since	Client	Used to specify a conditional request. Server responds only if the site has been modified since the specified date.
If-None-Match	Client	Used to specify a conditional request. Server responds only if the specified Etag does not match.
If-Unmodified-Since	Client	Used to specify a conditional request. Server responds only if the page has not been modified since the specified date.
Last-Modified	Server	Specifies the date that the requested resource was last modified.
Location	Server	Used to perform a server-side redirection. This header will cause the browser to request a new page.
Max-Forwards	Client	Specifies the maximum number of gateways this request is allowed to pass through.
MIME-Version	Server	Specifies the mime version of the server.
Public	Server	Lists non-standard other than GET, POST, HEAD) supported by this resource. These could be any sort of request a programmer decided to implement. This is a rarely used feature.

Continued on next page

TABLE B.2 CONTINUED: Selected HTTP Headers

Decimal	Hexadecimal	Character	Special Meaning
Pragma	Client	Specifies server directives.	
Proxy-Authenticate	Server	Describes a proxy authentication.	
Referrer	Client	Specifies the page that the browser was currently on before linking or being posted here.	
Retry-After	Server	Used to specify when a server that is down will be available.	
Server	Server	Specifies the version of server software in use.	
User-Agent	Client	Specifies the version of the browser or bot.	
Vary	Server	Specifies the names of fields to be used to determine page caching for future requests and responses.	
Warning	Server	Allows additional warning information to be returned from the server.	
WWW-Authenticate	Server	Challenges the requestor to resubmit the request with authentication information.	

HTTP headers are sent at the top of an HTTP message. In addition to HTTP headers, a status code is always transmitted at the very top of the HTTP response. These status codes are discussed in the next section.

HTTP Status Codes

Every response from a web server will contain a status, or response, code. The *response code* is a numeric identifier that allows you to determine the status of the request. There are several groups into which status codes fall. Some status codes indicate success, others indicate various types of failure, and some are purely informational. You can determine the group that a status code falls into by the digit that occupies the hundreds position.

The tabular entries in this section are also based on RFC2616, as was the table in the previous section. You may refer to RFC2616 for additional information. RFC2616 may be viewed at this URL `ftp://ftp.isi.edu/in-notes/rfc2616.txt`. The following is the complete copyright statement from RFC2616.

Copyright (C) The Internet Society (1999). All Rights Reserved.

Informational—1*xx*

Status codes that contain a 1 in the hundreds digit are informational. They indicate that the request is continuing and are simply an in-progress status. Here are a couple of examples of this type of code:

Code	Meaning
100	Continue
101	Switching protocols

Successful—2*xx*

Status codes that contain a 2 in the hundreds digit indicate a successful conclusion to the transaction. The most common is code 200, which is what is usually transmitted upon successful download.

Code	Meaning
200	OK
201	Created
202	Accepted
203	Non-authoritative information
204	No content
205	Reset content
206	Partial content

Redirection–3*xx*

Status codes that contain a 3 in the hundreds digit indicate a redirection. Redirections ask the web client (browser) to request an alternate page.

Code	Meaning
300	Multiple choices
301	Moved permanently
302	Moved temporarily
303	See other
304	Not modified
305	Use proxy
306	Unused
307	Temporary redirect

Client Error–4*xx*

Status codes that contain a 4 in the hundreds digit indicate an error that was the fault of the web client (browser).

Code	Meaning
400	Bad request
401	Unauthorized
402	Payment required
403	Forbidden
404	Not Found
405	Method not allowed
406	Not acceptable
407	Proxy authentication required
408	Request timeout
409	Conflict
410	Gone
411	Length required
412	Precondition failed

Continued on next page

Code	Meaning
413	Request entity too Large
414	Request-URI too long
415	Unsupported media type
416	Requested range not satisfiable
417	Expectation failed

Server Error—5xx

Status codes that contain a 5 in the hundreds digit indicate an error that was the fault of the web server.

Code	Meaning
500	Internal server error
501	Not implemented
502	Bad gateway
503	Service unavailable
504	Gateway timeout
505	HTTP version not supported

Status codes and headers are stored at the top of the HTTP message and are not visible to the web browser's user. Not all codes are invisible to the user, however. For instance, HTML provides for character constants to encode special characters. These codes are mixed with the HTML that is displayed to the user. The next section explains how to use HTML character constants.

HTML Character Constants

HTML allows certain special characters to be embedded using HTML character constants. HTML character constants begin with an ampersand (&) and end with a semicolon (;). For example, to display the text <html> you would encode "<html>".

Table B.3 is a list of some of the most useful, and most commonly used, character constants and what they represent.

TABLE B.3: Selected HTML Character Constants

HTML Code	Character	Note
&quot;	"	Quotation mark
&amp;	&	Ampersand
&lt;	<	Less-than sign
&gt;	>	Greater-than sign
		Non-breaking space
&iexcl;	¡	Inverted explanation mark
&cent;	¢	Cent sign
&pound;	£	Pound sterling sign
&current;	¤	General currency sign
&yen;	¥	Yen sign
&brvbar;	¦	Broken vertical bar
&sect;	§	Section sign
&uml;	¨	Umlaut
&copy;	©	Copyright symbol
&ordf;	ª	Feminine ordinal
&laquo;	«	Left angle quote
&not;	¬	Not sign
&shy;	-	Soft hyphen
&reg;	®	Registered trademark symbol
&macr;	¯	Macron accent
&deg;	°	Degree symbol
&plusmn;	±	Plus or minus
&sup2;	?	Superscript two
&sup3;	?	Superscript three
&acute;	´	Acute accent
&micro;	µ	Micro sign
&para;	¶	Paragraph sign
&middot;	·	Middle dot

    This appendix contains many of the status codes, headers, and other information you might need when you are programming spiders, bots, and aggregators, so keep it in mind when you are looking for a quick way to lookup a particular value or code.

APPENDIX C

Troubleshooting

U nfortunately, there are numerous things that can go wrong while you are trying to run the example programs from the chapters. To avoid such difficulties, first take a look at this book's introduction, which describes how your environment should be set up to properly execute examples from this book. If, after following the instructions in the introduction, you are still having problems running the examples, this appendix may help you to resolve the issue.

WIN32 Errors

The following is an error that might commonly occur when you are using the Windows platform. Problems listed here can also occur under UNIX, but the error messages and/or solutions are different. This section focuses exclusively on the WIN32 platform.

Java not Part of the Path

The Java compiler must be in the system path if you are to execute Java programs. If it is not, you will encounter the following error.

Problem: `'javac' is not recognized as an internal or external command.` You may encounter the following condition when you try to build one of the examples. The following command line session shows an attempt to build an example from Chapter 1, "Java Socket Programming," without the JDK as part of the system path.

```
C:\book\examples\ch1\Lookup>build

C:\book\examples\ch1\Lookup>javac Lookup.java
'javac' is not recognized as an internal or external command,
operable program or batch file.
```

Solution: Make Java part of the system path. This error comes up because the Java compiler (javac) can't be found. This means that you do not have the BIN directory of Java as part of your system path. To correct this, you will first need to make sure that you have JDK installed. If you do not, there is a copy on the companion CD that came with this book. JDK can also be downloaded from `http://java.sun.com`. The examples in this book will work with all JDK versions 1.2 and higher. The book's introduction contains more information about making JDK part of your system path.

UNIX Errors

The following are errors that might commonly occur when using the UNIX platform. Problems listed here can also occur under WIN32, but the error messages and/or solutions are different. This section focuses exclusively on the UNIX platform.

The Bot package and examples from the book are fully UNIX compatible, and were tested using the Red Hat V7.0 distribution of Linux. Figure C.1 shows an example from Chapter 2, "Examining the Hypertext Transfer Protocol," running under Linux.

FIGURE C.1:

An example program running under Linux

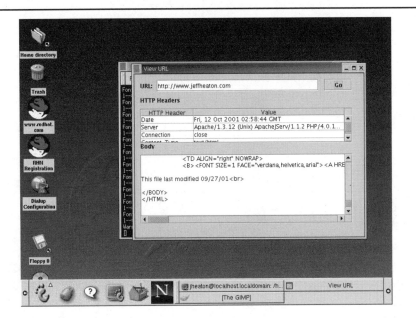

Java not Part of the Path

The Java compiler must be in the path environmental variable if you are to execute Java programs. If it is not, you will encounter the following error.

Problem: /build.sh: javacc: command not found.   You may encounter the following condition when you try to build one of the examples. The following command line session shows an attempt to build:

```
> ./build.sh
./build.sh: javac: command not found
```

Solution: Make Java part of the system path.   This problem develops because the Java compiler (javac) can't be found. This means that you do not have the BIN directory of Java as part of your system path. On a UNIX system, the JDK is usually installed under the /usr/ directory. The full path on my system is /usr/java/j2sdk1.4.0/. You must add this to your profile.

What your profile is and how to edit it depends on what shell you're using. By default, Linux uses the bash shell. If you are using the bash shell, your profile is stored in your home directory in a file named .bash_profile. The .bash_profile file contains the path statement that defines your system path. You should add Java binary directory (usually /usr/java/j2sdk1.4.0/bin/ or similar) to the path statement contained in .bash_profile.

Figure C.2 shows the .bash_profile file being edited, with a correct change.

FIGURE C.2:

Adding Java to the
bash shell

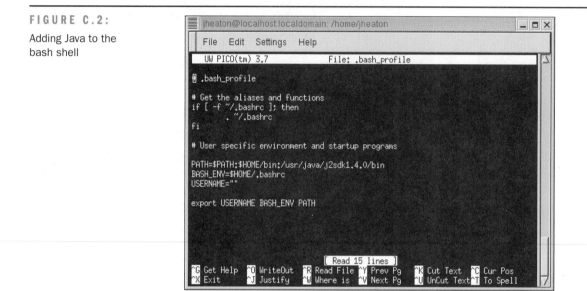

X-Windows Not Loaded

The examples contained in the chapters are Windows-based and thus require X-Windows in order to run. If you are trying to run the examples outside of X-Windows you will get the following error.

Problem: `Can't connect to X11 window server`. You may encounter the following condition if you try to run an example program from a telnet shell or from the console without X-Windows loaded.

```
> ./run.sh
Exception in thread "main" java.lang.InternalError: Can't connect to X11 window
server using ':0.0' as the value of the DISPLAY variable.
    at sun.awt.X11GraphicsEnvironment.initDisplay(Native Method)
    at sun.awt.X11GraphicsEnvironment.<clinit>(X11GraphicsEnvironment.java:70)
    at java.lang.Class.forName0(Native Method)
    at java.lang.Class.forName(Class.java:135)
    at java.awt.GraphicsEnvironment.getLocalGraphicsEnvironment
➥(GraphicsEnvironment.java:65)
```

```
    at java.awt.Window.init(Window.java:211)
    at java.awt.Window.<init>(Window.java:255)
    at java.awt.Frame.<init>(Frame.java:401)
    at java.awt.Frame.<init>(Frame.java:366)
    at javax.swing.JFrame.<init>(JFrame.java:153)
    at ViewURL.<init>(ViewURL.java:34)
    at ViewURL.main(ViewURL.java:96)
```

Solution: Load X-Windows.   The example programs require the use of X-Windows for all versions of UNIX. To start X-Windows under Linux, you should use the `startx` command. To configure X-Windows, you should use the Xconfigurator program included with Linux.

Many Warnings

Warnings can occur when compiling or running an application. Certain warnings, like those about `font.properties`, can be safely ignored.

Problem: `Font specified in font.properties not found`.   When you attempt to run the examples from this book, you may see several warnings like those shown here.

```
Font specified in font.properties not found [--standard symbols
➥1-medium-r-normal--*-%d-*-*-p-*-urw-fontspecific]
Font specified in font.properties not found [--standard symbols
➥1-medium-r-normal--*-%d-*-*-p-*-urw-fontspecific]
Font specified in font.properties not found [--standard symbols
➥1-medium-r-normal--*-%d-*-*-p-*-urw-fontspecific]
Font specified in font.properties not found [--standard symbols
➥1-medium-r-normal--*-%d-*-*-p-*-urw-fontspecific]
```

Solution: Ignore the warning.   Warnings about fonts not being found can occur when running GUI Java applications under Linux, these warnings can be ignored.

Cross-Platform Errors

The following are errors that might occur on either the WIN32 or UNIX platforms. The error messages tend to be the same between the two platforms.

Can't Find the Bot Package

The Bot package is contained in a file named `bot.jar`. Java must be able to locate `bot.jar` if any of the examples are to compile or run.

Problem: `package com.heaton.bot does not exist`.   If you try to build an example program and you see an error about `com.heaton.bot` not existing, or you see `class not found` errors on classes such as HTTP, then it is unlikely that the example program is finding the Bot package. If this is the case, you will likely see output similar to the following:

```
C:\book\examples\ch2\ViewURL>build

C:\book\examples\ch2\ViewURL>javac ViewURL.java
ViewURL.java:4: package com.heaton.bot does not exist
import com.heaton.bot.*;
^
ViewURL.java:25: cannot resolve symbol
symbol  : class HTTP
location: class ViewURL
  HTTP _http;
      ^
ViewURL.java:35: cannot resolve symbol
symbol  : class HTTPSocket
location: class ViewURL
    _http = new HTTPSocket();
                ^
3 errors
```

Solution: Set up CLASSPATH or use `buildNOJAR.bat` (or `buildNOJAR.sh` for UNIX).
The book's introduction contains information about how to set up your CLASSPATH so that the Bot package can be located. It is important that you set bot.jar to be part of the CLASSPATH as specified in the introduction.

If you can't seem to get the CLASSPATH set up correctly, you do have one remaining option. In addition to the build and run script files contained in every example directory, there are also buildNOJAR and runNOJAR scripts. The NOJAR scripts make use of a copy of bot.jar that is already placed in the example directory.

Can't Resolve Symbol

If the bot.jar file cannot be located, you may encounter symbol errors. These errors likely specify that Bot package classes, such as HTTP or HTTPSocket, can't be resolved.

Problem: `Cannot resolve symbol`.   If you get this error on symbols that are part of the Bot package, then it is likely that the Bot package can't be found.

```
C:\book\examples\ch2\ViewURL>build

C:\book\examples\ch2\ViewURL>javac ViewURL.java
ViewURL.java:25: cannot resolve symbol
symbol  : class HTTP
location: class ViewURL
  HTTP _http;
      ^
```

```
ViewURL.java:35: cannot resolve symbol
symbol  : class HTTPSocket
location: class ViewURL
    _http = new HTTPSocket();
                 ^
```

2 errors

Solution: Set up CLASSPATH or use buildNOJAR.bat (or buildNOJAR.sh for UNIX)
See previous section "Can't Find the Bot Package" for solutions to this problem.

JDK Less Than 1.2

The examples contained in this book will not compile and execute on versions of JDK prior to 1.2. It is recommended that you use only JDK 1.3 or higher.

Problem: Unable to initialize threads: cannot find class java/lang/Thread.
You may encounter this condition when you try to build one of the examples. The following command line session shows an attempt to build that results in this error. In general, you will get errors related to Java classes (particularly Swing classes).

```
> ./run.sh
./run.sh: javac: command not found
Unable to initialize threads: cannot find class java/lang/Thread
```

Solution: Get the latest version of JDK. The classes contained in this book will work on JDK 1.2, but they would fail on anything lower. To resolve this issue, get the latest version of JDK from http://java.sun.com/.

How to Use the *NOBOT* Scripts

In addition to the normal build and run scripts discussed in the book's introduction, there are also two additional scripts. These scripts, named buildNOBOT and runNOBOT, are designed not to require that the CLASSPATH be set up properly. If you are having trouble with build and run, you might consider the NOBOT variants.

APPENDIX D

Installing Tomcat

M any of the examples in this book use Java Server Pages (JSP). In order to execute an example program that uses JSP, you must use a web server that supports JSP. There are many that do. This appendix presents a brief tutorial concerning the installation of one such web server.

Tomcat, which is a part of the Apache project, is a free web server that can process JSP pages. Tomcat is usually configured with another web server and used only to process JSP pages and servlets (which are used to make Java classes directly respond to web requests). But for the purposes of this book, we will only examine the use of Tomcat as a stand-alone web server.

NOTE   There are many settings and options that can be configured on a Tomcat system. There are entire books written just about Tomcat. To cover all of these topics is beyond the scope of a book about programming spiders, bots, and aggregators. For additional information, you should refer to the documentation included with Tomcat. One book that I found particularly helpful for Tomcat is *Apache Jakarta-Tomcat*, by James Goodwill (Apress, 2001).

Tomcat is an open source product that requires no licensing fees. A copy of Tomcat v4.0 is included on the companion CD for this book; it can also be downloaded from the Apache project at the URL `http://jakarta.apache.org/tomcat/`. If you choose to download this product from the Web, select one of the "binary releases." The Apache project separates builds into four categories: release builds, milestone builds, nightly builds, and demo builds. It is strongly suggested that you download a release build because these are the most stable.

Installing and Starting Tomcat

The Tomcat file that you download will likely be contained in a ZIP file. If you are using Windows, you should refer to `http://www.winzip.com` if you are unfamiliar with how to unzip files. UNIX users should download one of the gzip archives. For more information about uncompressing files using UNIX, refer to the gzip man pages, using the command `man gzip`.

Starting With Windows

When Tomcat is extracted, it will copy itself to a directory named `Jakarta-tomcat` followed by a version number. For example, if you downloaded Tomcat v4.0, it will extract to the directory `jakarta-tomcat-4.0`.

Tomcat requires that the environmental variable JAVA_HOME be set to point to your JDK directory (likely `c:\jdk1.4\` or something similar). If this is not done, JDK will fail to execute. The following two Appendices describe how to set environmental variables on several platforms.

When Tomcat 4.0 installs, a new item, called "Apache Tomcat 4.0," is added under your Start menu. In this folder, you will find the commands to start and stop Apache Tomcat.

Click the Start Apache item to start Apache. If Tomcat starts properly, you will see a console window with the following output.

```
Starting service Tomcat-Standalone
Apache Tomcat/4.0.1
Starting service Tomcat-Apache
Apache Tomcat/4.0.1
```

WARNING When Tomcat is running, a console (DOS) window will be visible on your computer. If you close this window, Tomcat will no longer be running.

Starting Using UNIX

If you are using UNIX, then Tomcat is started using a startup script located in the `bin` (/jakarta-tomcat-4.0/bin/) directory. This startup script is called `startup.sh`.

If you attempt to start Tomcat without the JAVA_HOME environmental variable set, you will get the following output:

```
% startup
You must set JAVA_HOME to point at your Java Development Kit installation
```

If Tomcat is properly started, you will see the following output:

```
% ./startup.sh
Using CATALINA_BASE: ..
Using CATALINA_HOME: ..
Using CLASSPATH:      ..\bin\bootstrap.jar;c:\jdk1.4\lib\tools.jar
Using JAVA_HOME:      c:\jdk1.4
```

Testing Your Installation

To test to see if Tomcat has loaded successfully, you should point a browser to the address `http://localhost:8080/`. This instructs the browser to access the web server running on the current machine using port 8080. By default, this is the port that Tomcat uses. Tomcat can be configured to use any port, however. To learn how to do this, refer to the Tomcat instructions that come with the product. If your installation and startup of the Tomcat server was successful, your browser should look similar to Figure D.1.

FIGURE D.1:

Browsing your Tomcat
installation

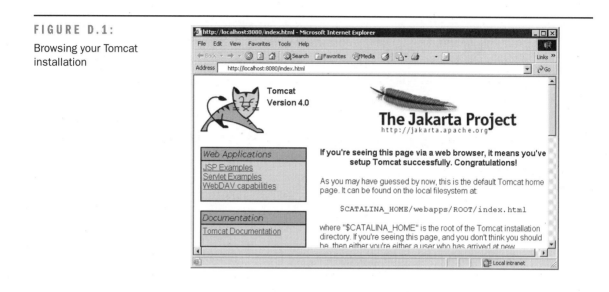

A JSP Example

Chapter 4, "HTML Parsing," contains an example JSP application that can translate any
website into Pig Latin. We will now examine how to properly install this translation example.
The Chapter 4 example directory, contained on the companion CD, contains all of the files
you will need.

WARNING The installation instructions presented here apply to the release version of Tomcat 4.0.
Earlier versions have different directions. Tomcat does have a way of changing the layout
of the Tomcat script files and directories from version to version. It is very important that
you check with the documentation for the version of Tomcat that you are using.

The first thing that you must do to use examples with Tomcat is to create a directory that
will contain the classes and packages needed. A complete version of this directory (named
TomCatClasses) is contained on the companion CD under this chapter. For simplicity, I will
assume that you have copied this directory to C:\TomCatClasses\. In reality, however, this
directory can be placed almost anywhere. If you do place this directory in a location other
than C:\TomCat\ you will have to use this new directory in the instructions below.

Now that you have a TomCatClasses directory created, you must request Tomcat to use it.
Unfortunately, the newest version of Tomcat completely ignores the CLASSPATH. This
means that the script file that starts Tomcat will have to be modified to accept our packages.
The file that you must modify is named catalina.bat. It is usually stored in the C:\Program
Files\Apache Tomcat 4.0\bin directory. Open it with any normal text editor, such as Notepad.

You will need to scroll down to where the CLASSPATH is being defined. You should see a section that looks similar to the following.

```
rem --- Set Up The Runtime Classpath ----------------------------------------

set CP=%CATALINA_HOME%\bin\bootstrap.jar;%JAVA_HOME%\lib
\tools.jar
if "%JSSE_HOME%" == "" goto noJsse
set CP=%CP%;%JSSE_HOME%\lib\jcert.jar;%JSSE_HOME%\lib\
➥jnet.jar;%JSSE_HOME%\lib\jsse.jar
:noJsse
set CLASSPATH=%CP%
echo Using CATALINA_BASE: %CATALINA_BASE%
echo Using CATALINA_HOME: %CATALINA_HOME%
echo Using CLASSPATH:     %CLASSPATH%
echo Using JAVA_HOME:     %JAVA_HOME%
```

You must modify the first line that begins with `set CP=%CATALINE…`. The text `;c:\TomCatClasses\;c:\TomCatClasses\bot.jar` should be appended to the end of the command, resulting in the following:

```
set CP=%CATALINA_HOME%\bin\bootstrap.jar;%JAVA_HOME%\lib
➥\tools.jar;c:\TomCatClasses\;C:\TomCatClasses\bot.jar
```

WARNING The `set` command is shown as two lines here. This is not actually the case. In your `catalina.bat` file, the `set` command must be one long line and not break as shown above.

This takes care of installing the packages needed to run the Translate example. You must also copy `translate.jsp`, which is also provided on the companion CD. The file `translate.jsp` must be copied to the Tomcat root directory; this is usually `C:\Program Files\Apache Tomcat 4.0\webapps\ROOT`.

If the `translate.jsp` file and the `TomCatClasses` directory from the examples are copied as instructed, you should now be able to execute this example. Point your browser to `http://localhost:8080/translate.jsp` to see this example in action.

NOTE This appendix presents only a brief overview of Tomcat. For more complete troubleshooting information, refer to the Tomcat installation.

How to Compile Examples Under Windows

ll of the Java code provided by this book will compile and execute correctly under the Windows platforms. This appendix shows you how to do this.

There are two primary ways that you can compile Java programs found in this book under Windows. The first is by using the JDK provided by Sun Microsystems. The second is by using any of several integrated development environments (IDEs) that are available. This appendix will discuss one in particular, WebGain's VisualCafé.

This appendix begins by showing you how to compile examples under the JDK. If you are interested in using VisualCafé, there is information on this later in this Appendix to help you do so.

Using the JDK

The JDK is an environment provided by Sun that allows you to compile and execute Java programs. The JDK can be downloaded, free of charge, from the Sun website at `http://java.sun.com`. A copy of the JDK can also be found on the companion CD. If you are using the JDK, there are several steps that you must take before the Java code from this book will work properly.

The steps that must be taken to correctly install and use JDK are as follows:

1. Install JDK 1.3 or higher on your system.
2. Make sure that the JDK bin directory (usually `C:\jdk1.3_01\bin\`) is part of the system path.
3. Copy the `bot.jar` file to the ext directory (usually `C:\jdk1.3\jre\lib\ext\`).
4. Add the path to the `bot.jar` (usually `C:\jdk1.3\jre\lib\ext\bot.jar`) to the CLASS-PATH. The process to do this will be covered in the later section entitled "Adding to the CLASSPATH and System Path."

The following sections will explain some of these steps in greater detail.

Locating the *bot.jar* File

The companion CD for this book contains a file called `bot.jar`. This file contains the compiled version of the Bot package provided by this book, which all the examples in this book require in order to run. The complete source code to this package is also provided on the companion CD.

As you progressed through the chapters of this book, you saw exactly how this package was created. For the purposes of this discussion, however, just use the compiled version. Now you will be shown how to use this file.

If this file is to be used, it *must* be accessible from the CLASSPATH. The CLASSPATH specifies to Java the locations of JAR files that Java should search in order to locate classes used by Java programs that are being executed. You should copy the `bot.jar` file to the extensions directory of your JDK folder using the path `c:\jdk1.3\jre\lib\ext\`. (If you do not have an ext directory, create one.) Once this directory is present, the `bot.jar` file should be copied into it. You must now add that file to the CLASSPATH.

Finding JDK's *bin* Directory

The `bin` directory of the JDK folder must be in the system path; you can easily find out whether it is or isn't. To do so, open a DOS or command prompt (depending on your version of Windows). From the command prompt window, type the command **javac**. If JDK is in the system path, you will see more than a page of instructions scrolling past. If you are given a "bad command or filename" message (or a similar error message), then JDK is *not* in the system path of your computer. If this is the case, you must first determine where the `bin` directory is located under the JDK folder.

JDK itself is usually stored in the `c:\jdk1.3\` folder. If this folder is not in the C drive, do a search to find this folder's location elsewhere on your computer. After the drive name, this folder will always be named so that it starts with JDK and is followed by a version number; in this case, the version number is 1.3. If you still can't find it, do a Windows file search for `javac.exe`. The `javac.exe` file is located in the `bin` directory of the JDK—most likely, you will find this in the `c:\jdk1.3\bin\` directory, which you must make part of the system path.

Adding to the CLASSPATH and System Path

The process for adding directories to both the CLASSPATH and system path is different depending on what version of Windows you are running. Specific examples are given for each version.

System Path and CLASSPATH under Windows 95/98/Me

To modify the system path and CLASSPATH under these versions of Windows, the `autoexec.bat` file must be modified. Your `autoexec.bat` files may look like the one shown in Figure E.1, but they may not. It all depends on which system you use. However, no matter what your `autoexec.bat` looks like, you should be able to follow these steps to execute it regardless of which system you use.

1. Locate the `autoexec.bat` file in the root of your C drive. Open the file with Notepad. You may want to save a copy of your current `autoexec.bat` file to a backup, such as `autoexec.bak`.

2. Locate the `set classpath` command. If you cannot find this command, type it in (as it is shown in Figure E.1). Add the `bot.jar` to the CLASSPATH by appending the `bot.jar` path (usually `c:\jdk1.3\jre\lib\ext\bot.jar`) to the end of the `set classpath` command (make sure you use a semicolon [;] to separate individual paths as shown in the figure).

3. Locate the path statement and add the location of your `bin` directory. Figure E.1 shows a properly modified `autoexec.bat` file.

FIGURE E.1:

A properly configured `autoexec.bat` file

```
@echo off
SET SOUND=C:\PROGRA~1\CREATIVE\CTSND
SET BLASTER=A220 I5 D1 H5 P330 E620 T6
Prompt $p$g
path=c:\dos;c:\windows\;c:\jdk1.3\bin\
set Temp=C:\TEMP
set classpath = .;c:\jdk1.3\ext\bot.jar
```

WARNING   Your autoexec.bat file will look slightly different than this example. This example is shown primarily to give you an idea of how it should look. Always make sure that the current directory—represented by a dot (.)—is part of the CLASSPATH. Without the current directory as part of the CLASSPATH, no Java program will correctly execute.

The information provided here is meant to give you a general idea of how Java should be set up. To completely describe how to configure the Java environment would be beyond the scope of this book. For more information on CLASSPATHs and installing JDK, please refer to the JDK installation instructions or a book about the Java programming language, such as *Java 2 Complete*, (Sybex, 1999).

System Path and CLASSPATH Under Windows NT/2000/XP

To modify the system and CLASSPATH under these versions of Windows, you must use the System Properties panel. There are several ways to bring up the System Properties panel. One way is by right-clicking the My Computer icon and selecting Properties. Next, you would click the Advanced tab of this panel. After you have done this, your screen should resemble Figure E.2.

FIGURE E.2:

The System Properties panel

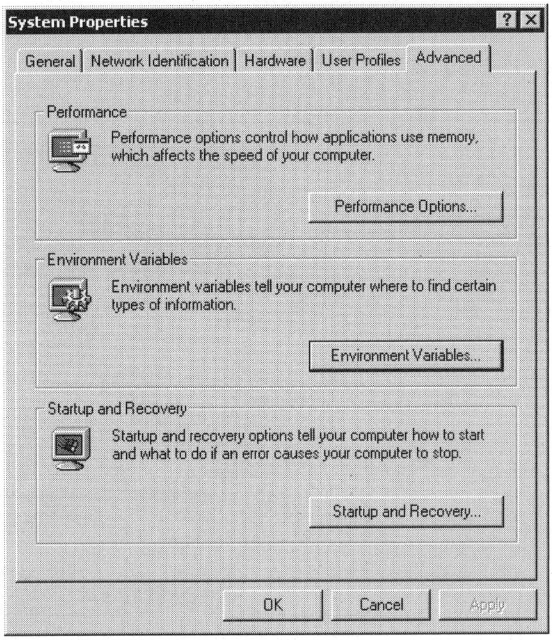

NOTE   The NT version of this screen will be slightly different because it has fewer tabs.

Now click the Environment Variables button in the Environment Variable section of this screen. When you do, you will see that there are two sets of environmental variables (shown in Figure E.3). The top set is for the current user. The bottom set is for the entire system. I suggest modifying them for the current user because this seems to be where most systems modify the CLASSPATH setting. To do so, follow these steps:

1. Find the path setting. If your JDK installation was not in the system path, you would have to add its `bin` directory to the system path. Add the location of the `bin` directory (usually `C:\jdk1.3\bin\`) to the PATH environmental variable. This is done by appending your `bin` directory to whatever currently exists in the PATH, as shown in Figure E.3.

2. Either create or append to the CLASSPATH setting the complete location of the `bot.jar` file (usually something like `C:\jdk1.3\jre\lib\ext\bot.jar`). Note that each path setting is delimited by a semicolon (;). If a CLASSPATH already exists, simply append the `bot.jar` path to the end; if there is no CLASSPATH, you must click New to create a CLASSPATH.

3. Click OK to accept your changes. This completes the process.

> **WARNING**   Make sure you include the dot (.) portion of your CLASSPATH. If you do not include the dot (.), which represents the current directory, no Java program will execute properly.

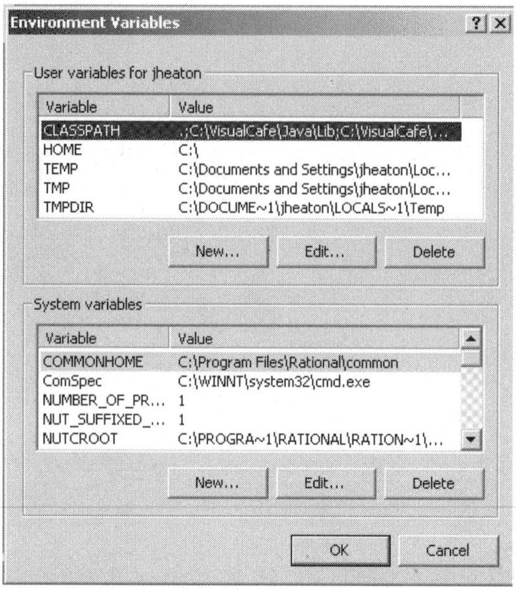

FIGURE E.3:

Changing the PATH and CLASSPATH with Windows 2000/NT/XP

Windows Installation Summary

To summarize, you must complete the following steps to be able to correctly use examples from this book:

1. Install JDK 1.3 or higher on your system.

2. Make sure that the JDK bin directory (C:\jdk1.3\bin\) is part of the system path.

3. Copy the bot.jar file to the ext directory (C:\jdk1.3\jre\lib\ext\) of the JDK home directory.

4. Add the bot.jar path to the CLASSPATH (C:\jdk1.3\jre\lib\ext\bot.jar).

> **WARNING**   The steps described here must be followed or the source code examples in this book will not work correctly.

Using VisualCafé

Every example program as well as the Bot package includes VisualCafé project files. These files are stored with the Java files located on the companion CD. Though complete information on the use of VisualCafé is beyond the scope of this book, I will highlight a few of the common pitfalls that you might encounter if you choose to run the examples from this book with VisualCafé. This section only shows you what you must do to use VisualCafé with the Bot package. For more information about VisualCafé, refer to VisualCafé's online help files.

First of all, if you want to use VisualCafé, do not try to execute the programs directly from the companion CD (remember, a CD-ROM is a read-only device) because this causes problems for VisualCafé. Instead, the entire book folder should be copied from the companion CD to your hard drive. When you are making this move, don't forget to mark the files as writeable. Generally, when files are copied from CD-ROM to a hard drive, these files have their read-only attribute set, which will also cause problems for VisualCafé.

Once you have moved these files, you will be able to open one of the examples. You should use VisualCafé to open the project file, which is the file that ends in the `.vpj` extension. With the project file open, you now must make sure that VisualCafé knows the location of the `bot.jar` file. You can access this dialog by selecting the Directories tab of the Project Options dialog box. Figure E.4 (next page) shows this tab. The complete path to your `bot.jar` file must be reflected here. For more information on where the `bot.jar` file should be located, refer to the earlier section entitled "Locating the `bot.jar` File."

FIGURE E.4:

Defining the location
of the `bot.jar` file for
VisualCafé

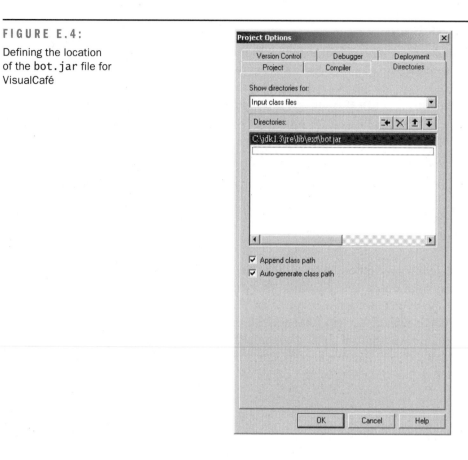

APPENDIX F

How to Compile Examples Under UNIX

The Bot package on the companion CD should be compatible with any version of UNIX. The package has been specifically tested by the author under Linux and BSD, and some limited testing was also conducted under Solaris. Though the Bot package runs correctly under the current version of Linux, it will not work with the current version of BSD. This is because there is only a 1.1 version of the JDK available for BSD. Once a 1.2 or higher version of JDK is made available for BSD, the examples in this book will likely work.

Just remember, to use the examples in this book, you need to use at least JDK 1.2, and JDK 1.3 is required for some of the example programs. Due to the number of shells and different configurations on UNIX, only general information will be presented here. Please consult the instructions that came with the JDK for your particular "flavor" of UNIX for more precise information.

To compile the Java code in this book under UNIX, you must obtain the JDK for your particular flavor of UNIX. Because there are several, they are not included on the companion CD. The JDK can be downloaded form the `http://java.sun.com` site.

Using the JDK

The JDK is an environment provided by Sun that allows you to compile and execute Java programs. The JDK can be downloaded, free of charge, from the Sun website at `http://java.sun.com`. If you are using the JDK, there are several steps that you must take before the Java code from this book will work properly.

The steps that must be taken to correctly install and use JDK are as follows:

1. Install JDK 1.3 or higher on your system. (Root access will be required to install for the entire system.)

2. Make sure that the JDK `bin` directory (`/usr/local/jdk1.3/`) is part of the system path.

3. Copy the `bot.jar` file to the `ext` directory (`/usr/local/jdk1.3/jre/lib/ext/`) of the JDK home directory.

4. Add the `bot.jar` path to the CLASSPATH (`/usr/local/jdk1.3/jre/lib/ext/bot.jar`).

The following sections will explain some of these steps in greater detail.

Locating the *bot.jar* File

The companion CD for this book contains a file called `bot.jar`. This file contains the compiled version of the Bot package provided by this book, which all the examples in this book require in order to run. The complete source code to this package is also provided on the companion CD.

NOTE   The bot.jar file that is used for Windows is also used for UNIX; this file is cross-platform compatible.

As you progressed through the chapters of this book, you saw exactly how this package was created. For the purposes of this discussion, however, just use the compiled version. Now you will be shown how to use this file.

If this file is to be used, it *must* be accessible from the CLASSPATH. The CLASSPATH specifies to Java the locations of JAR files that Java should search in order to locate classes used by Java programs that are being executed. You should copy the bot.jar file to the extensions directory of your JDK folder, using the path /usr/local/jdk1.3/jre/lib/ext/. (If you do not have an ext directory, create one.) Once this directory is present, the bot.jar file should be copied into it. You must now add that file to the CLASSPATH.

Finding JDK's *bin* Directory

The bin directory of the JDK folder must be in the system path; you can easily find out whether it is or isn't. To do so, open an XTERM or command prompt (depending on your UNIX system). From the command prompt window, type the command **javac**. If JDK is in the system path, you will see more than a page of instructions scrolling past. If you are given a "command not found" message (or a similar error message), then JDK is *not* in the system path of your computer. If this is the case, you must first determine where the bin directory is located under the JDK folder.

JDK itself is usually stored in the /usr/local/jdk1.3/ folder. If you cannot find this folder, do a search to find this folder's location elsewhere on your computer. After the drive name, this folder will always be named so that it starts with JDK and is followed by a version number; in this case, the version number is 1.3. If you still can't find it, execute the command "**find / |grep javac**" to locate it. The javac file is located in the bin directory of the JDK— most likely, you will find this in the /usr/local/jdk1.3/bin/ directory, which you must make part of the system path.

Adding Directories to the CLASSPATH and System Path

To modify the system path and CLASSPATH under UNIX, you must modify your profile file. The name of this file varies depending on what shell you are running. If you are using Linux, the name of this file is .bash_profile. A properly edited version of this profile file will look something like this.

```
# .bash_profile

# Get the aliases and functions
```

```
if [ -f ~/.bashrc ]; then
        . ~/.bashrc
fi

# User specific environment and startup programs

PATH=$PATH:$HOME/bin:/usr/local/jdk1.3/bin
CLASSPATH=./:/usr/local/jdk1.3/jre/lib/ext/bot.jar
BASH_ENV=$HOME/.bashrc
USERNAME=" "

export USERNAME BASH_ENV PATH CLASSPATH
```

In the above script, you can see that the bin directory for Java was added to the PATH statement. The following steps outline how to modify this file:

1. Locate the .bash_profile file in the root of your user directory. Open the file with a text editor. You may want to save a copy of your current .bash_profile file to a backup.

2. Locate the classpath command. If you cannot find this command, type it in (as it is shown in the listing above). Add the bot.jar to the CLASSPATH by appending bot.jar path (usually /usr/local/jdk1.3/jre/lib/ext/bot.jar) to the end of the set classpath command (make sure you use a colon [:] to separate individual paths as shown in the above listing).

3. Locate the path statement, and add the location of your bin directory.

WARNING   Your .bash_profile file will look slightly different than this example. This example is shown primarily to give you an idea of how it should look. Always make sure that the current directory—represented by a dot (.)—is part of the CLASSPATH. Without the current directory as part of the CLASSPATH, no Java program will correctly execute.

Recompiling the Bot Package

It is unlikely that you will need to recompile the Bot package at first. The bot.jar file included on the companion CD should work under any Java platform, and it should not need to be recompiled. You will only need to do this if you do want to make changes to or extend the bot framework.

Included on the companion CD is a directory called src. Located in that directory is a file called build.bat. This script file should be run to rebuild the Bot package. This file requires that the Java compiler be in the system path. (Refer to the "System Path and CLASSPATH under Windows 95/98/Me" section in Appendix E, "How to Compile Examples Under Windows," to see how to include the Java compiler in the system path.) Running this build script will recompile the entire Bot package.

WARNING   Remember that this type of activity should never be run directly from the companion CD. As with other similar activities, you should copy the build directory to a writeable drive before attempting to recompile it.

If there are any errors that occur during the recompilation, they will be shown as output. If you just double-click the build script icon, you will not be able to see this information. Instead, you will need to run the build command from a command window to see the output. If the build is successful, you should see output similar to that seen here.

```
D:\src>build
added manifest
adding: com/heaton/bot/Attribute.class(in = 1059) (out= 519)(deflated 50%)
adding: com/heaton/bot/AttributeList.class(in = 1539) (out= 866)(deflated 43%)
adding: com/heaton/bot/Base64OutputStream.class(in = 1423) (out= 852)(deflated 40%)
adding: com/heaton/bot/BotExclusion.class(in = 2313) (out= 1315)(deflated 43%)
adding: com/heaton/bot/CookieParse.class(in = 1553) (out= 838)(deflated 46%)
adding: com/heaton/bot/HTMLForm$FormElement.class(in = 1006) (out= 480)(deflated 52%)
adding: com/heaton/bot/HTMLForm.class(in = 1698) (out= 869)(deflated 48%)
adding: com/heaton/bot/HTMLPage$Parser.class(in = 4251) (out= 2165)(deflated 49%)
adding: com/heaton/bot/HTMLPage.class(in = 2803) (out= 1330)(deflated 52%)
adding: com/heaton/bot/HTMLParse.class(in = 428) (out= 266)(deflated 37%)
adding: com/heaton/bot/HTMLParser.class(in = 2723) (out= 1393)(deflated 48%)
adding: com/heaton/bot/HTMLTag.class(in = 1025) (out= 566)(deflated 44%)
adding: com/heaton/bot/HTTP.class(in = 6184) (out= 3102)(deflated 49%)
adding: com/heaton/bot/HTTPSocket.class(in = 4004) (out= 2282)(deflated 43%)
adding: com/heaton/bot/ISpiderReportable.class(in = 397) (out= 258)(deflated 35%)
adding: com/heaton/bot/IWorkloadStorable.class(in = 519) (out= 312)(deflated 39%)
adding: com/heaton/bot/Link.class(in = 709) (out= 375)(deflated 47%)
adding: com/heaton/bot/Log.class(in = 2732) (out= 1438)(deflated 47%)
adding: com/heaton/bot/Parse.class(in = 2394) (out= 1093)(deflated 54%)
adding: com/heaton/bot/Spider.class(in = 3647) (out= 1794)(deflated 50%)
adding: com/heaton/bot/SpiderDone.class(in = 773) (out= 477)(deflated 38%)
```

```
adding: com/heaton/bot/SpiderInternalWorkload.class(in = 2297) (out= 1185)(deflated 48%)
adding: com/heaton/bot/SpiderSQLWorkload.class(in = 3191) (out= 1684)(deflated 47%)
adding: com/heaton/bot/SpiderWorker.class(in = 3181) (out= 1631)(deflated 48%)
adding: com/heaton/bot/SSL.class(in = 1046) (out= 610)(deflated 41%)
adding: com/heaton/bot/URLUtility.class(in = 1833) (out= 988)(deflated 46%)
adding: com/heaton/bot/catbot/CatBot.class(in = 2142) (out= 1052)(deflated 50%)
adding: com/heaton/bot/catbot/Recognize.class(in = 1975) (out= 1032)(deflated 47%)
adding: com/heaton/bot/catbot/RecognizeCountry.class(in = 2048) (out= 1028)(deflated 49%)
adding: com/heaton/bot/catbot/RecognizeLink.class(in = 1967) (out= 1053)(deflated 46%)
```

If you get any errors, you must evaluate the cause. There are two types of errors you might encounter. First, there can be system configuration errors. As a result, I would suggest that you try to compile the package *before* you make any changes. By doing this, you will be able to isolate any configuration errors you might have before you recompile. Such errors are generally caused by not having Java in the correct path or having a missing setting. Information presented either in Appendix E or Appendix F can help you diagnose such errors. Second, you might encounter Java syntax errors that you have introduced by making your changes. You must debug these issues as you would any Java program that you created.

If the build script executes correctly, a new package will be generated, and it will be stored in a file called bot.jar. This file will be placed in the \book\lib directory. You must also copy this file to your CLASSPATH as specified either in Appendix E or Appendix F.

TIP   Try compiling the Bot package once before you make any changes. This will allow you to isolate any configuration/installation problems before you begin making changes of your own.

Glossary

NUMBER

8859_1   A character encoding that results in no transformations occurring in the text stream.

A

absolute URL   A URL that is fully qualified and not relative. An absolute URL would be of the form `http://www.jeffheaton.com/images/logo.gif`. Relative forms of that same URL would include `/images/logo.gif` and `logo.gif`.

agent   Often used as a generic term for an Internet client program. A web browser, bot, spider, aggregator, or intelligent agent could all be considered agents.

aggregate hammering   A form of hammering that occurs when several threads or processes are started that all access the same site. Accessing a site in this manner can request so many resources that the performance of the web server degrades.

aggregator   A collection of bots that gathers the same type of information from several sources. This disjointed information is then presented in one aggregated list. An example of an aggregator would be a program that displays account balances from several checking and savings accounts.

API   *See* application programming interface (API).

application programming interface (API)   A set of methods that is used to access functionality provided by a package.

artificial intelligence   Artificial intelligence (AI) is a group of computer programs that attempt to mimic the human mind. Though AI programs can solve problems that would be difficult for traditional programs, they do not provide human reasoning and logic.

authentication   The process by which the identity of an agent is determined.

B

base64   A simple form of encoding that prevents text from being human readable. Base64 encoding is trivial to decode and provides no real security. Nevertheless, it is the basis for HTTP authentication.

base URL   A base URL is an absolute URL that is used to resolve a relative URL. The base URL is generally the directory that holds the HTML file being displayed. This can be overridden by using the `<base>` HTML tag.

blocking   A thread blocks when it is waiting on a resource. This thread will continue to wait until it either times out, or gains access to the resource.

bot   An agent that does not require direct user interaction to execute. Generally, bots run unsupervised and retrieve information from websites. Bots are usually preprogrammed to only receive a certain type of information.

bot exclusion file   A simple text file that states the bot policies of a site. This file, named `robots.txt`, must be stored at the root level of a website. For example, the `robots.txt` file associated with

`www.jeffheaton.com` must be stored at `www`
`.jeffheaton.com/robots.txt`. Compliance with
this file is the honorary responsibility of the bot
or spider accessing the site.

Bot package   A collection of classes useful for creating bots that is presented by this book so that the
reader can begin bot programming. This package
may be freely used in other programs. The Bot
package is named `com.heaton.bot`.

bottleneck   If there are several portions of a network connection, the bottleneck is the slowest
one. This slowest segment then slows all of the
other segments down to its speed. When you are
seeking to speed up programs, you must first
locate the bottlenecks.

bridge driver   A driver that presents a known API
to a Java program and translates the database
commands to ones known by the underlying
database. A bridge driver can also be a JDBC
driver that allows JDBC to connect to another
type of driver. For example, the JDBC to ODBC
bridge driver allows any ODBC driver to be
used as a JDBC driver.

broadband   Connection speeds faster than the
traditional telephone system–based modem.
Broadband is usually provided by DSL, cable
modem, T1, or similar technologies.

buffering   Occurs when an intermediate buffer is
used to transmit or receive data in larger blocks.
This allows the data to be requested in whatever
size block is convenient for the program and
transmitted at an optimal block size.

C

cacerts   Security files used to implement a
specific security protocol.

CGI-BIN   One of the first ways to implement
interactive web pages. When a CGI-BIN
resource is accessed from a web browser, that
resource is executed rather than just transmitted.
The output from the CGI-BIN program is what
is actually sent to the web browser.

CLASSPATH   An environmental variable that is
set to contain a list of JAR and class files that the
Java virtual machine should use to locate classes.

client   The program in an Internet connection
that requests data. *See also* agent.

client headers   The HTTP headers that are
sent by the client (usually the web browser).

client socket   *See* socket.

clipping   The process by which certain kinds of
data are retrieved from a website. An example
would be a news story–clipping program.

connection   A connection is a communications
conduit between two sockets. A connection can
be between sockets on two different machines,
or between two sockets on the same machine. A
connection is bidirectional between the two sockets, and it is initiated by the client and accepted
by the server. *See* socket.

cookie   A small parcel of text data stored in an
agent, usually a web browser, by a web server.
The agent, or browser, stores this locally.

critical section   The section of a program that can only be accessed by one thread at a time. If a thread attempts to enter a critical section that is currently being occupied by another thread, the entering thread must block until the occupying thread leaves the critical section. Critical sections in Java are denoted by the `synchronized` keyword.

cross-platform   A program that can be executed on many computer systems. Java is considered cross-platform because a Java program can generally run on Windows, Macintosh, and UNIX.

D

daemon thread   A thread that continues to run even though the main thread of the process has terminated.

Database Management System (DBMS)   A term used to describe the software used to implement databases. Examples of DBMS systems would be Oracle and DB2.

DBMS   *See* Database Management System (DBMS).

denial of service (DOS) attack   A denial of service attack, sometimes referred to by the acronym DOS, is a malicious attempt to disrupt a website by bombarding it with requests. *See also* hammering.

DHCP   *See* Dynamic Host Configuration Protocol (DHCP).

distributed hammering   A form of hammering that occurs when many instances of a bot are run from many different computers. Though

one individual bot may not degrade a web server's performance, many thousands of such bots may.

DNS   *See* domain name service (DNS).

domain name service (DNS)   A server that will transform a hostname, such as `www.jeffheaton.com`, into an IP address, such as 192.1.1.10.

DOS   *See* denial of service (DOS) attack.

Dynamic Host Configuration Protocol (DHCP)   An Internet protocol for automating the configuration of computers that use TCP/IP.

E

emulation   Occurs when one system accepts the same input, and produces the same output, as another. Often a bot emulates a browser so that a web server cannot distinguish between it and a browser.

endpoint   The process that actually provides the information requested by a SOAP request.

Extensible Markup Language (XML)   Provides a hierarchical way to store data in a text file. XML is becoming the format of choice for many web-based documents.

external link   A link that points to a completely different web server. For example, the link `http://www.yahoo.com` would be considered an external link if it occurred on the page `http://www.jeffheaton.com/index.shtml`. *See also* internal link.

F

filter   A Java stream that acts on the data being sent through it.

firewall   Prevents external access to certain protected computers.

G

GET request   The most common of the HTTP requests. A GET request doesn't transmit any posted data to the web server; it just requests that a page be displayed.

H

hammering   Occurs when a bot unintentionally floods a web sever with requests that impair the normal operation of the web server. Intentional hammering is called a denial of service attack. *See also* denial of service (DOS) attack.

hard-code   Refers to inserting a literal number into several locations of a program rather than using a constant. This practice is discouraged because any change to that number will have to be reflected across the program.

hex   *See* hexadecimal.

hexadecimal   Hexadecimal numbers are represented as base16 numbers. Hexadecimal numbers in Java are usually prefixed with 0x. For example, 0xff is equal to 255.

hostname   An easy-to-remember alias for an IP address. Hostnames are resolved to IP addresses by DNS servers.

HREF   *See* hypertext reference (HREF).

HTML   *See* Hypertext Markup Language (HTML).

HTTP   *See* Hypertext Transfer Protocol (HTTP).

HTTP headers   Data items transferred before an HTTP request or response is sent.

HTTPS   A secured form of HTTP. HTTPS uses previously patented technology, and as a result, it is an add-on to Java. To use HTTPS in a Java program, JSSE must be used.

Hypertext Markup Language (HTML)   The language used to define most web pages.

hypertext reference (HREF)   A relative or absolute URL that specifies a page to link to. Because a spider travels from page to page, HREFs are of particular interest to the spider.

Hypertext Transfer Protocol (HTTP)   A means of requesting web-based resources.

I

Infoseek Sidewinder   The spider used by Infoseek.

intelligent agents   Bots that uses artificial intelligence to determine what pieces of information their user might be interested in. Intelligent agents also can interact with other intelligent agents.

interface   A Java programming construct that defines a set of method signatures and, optionally, constants, that a class may choose to implement. Classes that implement interfaces provide the method bodies. These methods can be called from another object that knows either the implementing object's object reference or the interface reference.

internal link   A hypertext reference that points to a page that shares the same web server as the page that contains the link.

Internet Protocol (IP)   A very low-level protocol used by TCP/IP.

IP   *See* Internet Protocol (IP).

isolated hammering   A form of hammering that occurs from one single source. *See also* hammering.

J

Java   A cross platform programming language introduced by Sun Microsystems. Java programs are compiled to byte code, which can then be run in a virtual machine (JVM) installed on the user's computer. The virtual machine is just a computer program that enables computer platforms to run Java. It is the JVM that is specific to each platform.

Java Database Connectivity (JDBC)   A series of classes and drivers that allows Java to access DBMS systems.

Javadoc   A utility that will take standardized comments from Java programs and create an HTML-based reference for those classes.

Java Messaging API (JAXM)   A package released by Sun that allows Java to communicate using SOAP.

JavaScript   A simplified version of Java that is executed by web clients. JavaScript should not be confused with JSP or Java; it is a related, but very different language. *See also* Java, Java server pages (JSP).

Java Secure Sockets Extensions (JSSE)   An add-on from Sun that allows Java to process HTTPS pages.

Java server pages (JSP)   Pages that are displayed like normal HTML files. JSP files contain embedded Java code that will be executed when these pages are displayed. The output from the embedded Java code contributes to what the page displays. JSP should not be confused with JavaScript. *See also* JavaScript.

JAXM   *See* Java Messaging API (JAXM).

JSP   *See* Java server pages (JSP).

JSSE   *See* Java Secure Sockets Extensions (JSSE).

L

link   A reference to a destination HTML page that is placed on a source HTML page.

listening   A socket is said to be listening when it is waiting for inbound connections.

M

Mozilla   Code name for early versions of the NCSA browser. Mozilla is still used as part of the browser version to specify Netscape compatibility.

multitasking   The ability of an operating system to run several programs at once.

multithreading   The ability for an operating system to allow a single program to have multiple points of execution.

N

name-value pair   A name-value pair implements a dictionary of sorts. A name is used to lookup a certain value.

National Center for Supercomputing Applications (NCSA)   A group that greatly contributed to the early versions of the NCSA Mosaic browser that would late form the foundation of Netscape. This group is located at the University of Illinois.

NCSA   *See* National Center for Supercomputing Applications (NCSA).

NT Service   *See* Windows NT Service.

O

object lock   Every object in Java contains a lock. This lock is set when the current thread enters a critical section. The lock is released when either a `wait` method is called or the critical section is left.

Open Database Connectivity (ODBC)   An API for accessing databases. Java generally accesses ODBC through a bridge driver.

Optical Character Recognition   A programming technique that allows computer programs to understand text that is stored as an image.

other link   A link of type other is neither internal nor external. An other type link connects to something such as an e-mail address.

P

package   A Java construct that is a collection of many related classes. Packages are usually designed to be reusable across many applications.

packet   A block of related data that is transmitted over a socket together.

parser   A computer program that examines textual data and makes sense of it.

patent   The ownership of intellectual property, granted by a government.

pattern recognition   An artificial intelligence technique used to recognize patterns in data. This allows the computer to tell the type of data, even if its format is altered somewhat.

peer-to-peer network   A network constructed so that there is little distinction between a client and a server. Any computer can function as a client, a server, or both a client and a server.

persistent   An object is said to be persistent if its contents can be stored to a medium more permanent than RAM.

persistent cookie   A cookie that is stored to disk by a browser. This cookie will remain even if the browser is restarted.

polling frequency   The frequency at which a bot scans its target site.

port   Every socket server must listen on a specific port. These port numbers define what service the listening server will perform. For example, HTTP is assigned to port 80.

POST request   An HTTP request that is usually sent in response to an HTML form being submitted. The HTTP POST request contains data, usually the form contents, that is sent to the web server.

prepared statement   A prepared SQL statement is one that is already compiled and can be executed rapidly. SQL statements that are going to be executed many times should be prepared.

process   A program that is executing on the computer. More than one process can execute at once if the operating system supports multitasking.

processor time   The measure of CPU time. The CPU has only a finite amount of processor time. Once this time has been exceeded, threads will have to wait for the CPU to become available again.

protocol   An agreed-upon set of rules by which a server and client communicate.

proxy   A system that connects to the Internet on behalf of a computer behind a firewall. Some companies use proxies to control access to the Internet. A proxy can cause problems for a Java application if Java is unaware that the proxy exists.

Q

query string   The portion of a URL that follows a question mark just behind the path. For example, `http://www.jeffheaton.com/cgi-bin/test.cgi?<query string>`

queue   A list of items waiting to be executed. Items added to a queue are usually retrieved in a first in, first out (FIFO) order. Therefore the older requests will be executed before the newer ones.

R

reader   A Java filter used to process a file in a certain way.

redirect command   Occurs when the web server uses the location header to specify an alternate page. The command causes the browser to redirect to an alternate page.

referrer   A page that contains a link to a new page. When the new page is loaded, the referrer header specifies the page that contained the link.

relative URL   A partial URL that must be combined with a base URL in order to be resolved to an absolute URL. For example, the relative URL `/images/logo.gif` is a relative URL because it does not specify the web host. This ambiguous relative URL can only be resolved by combining it with a base URL, such as `http://www.jeffheaton.com/`. If the relative URL `/images/logo.gif` were combined with the aforementioned base URL, the resulting absolute URL would be `http://www.jeffheaton.com/images/logo.gif`.

Request for Comments (RFC)   A document that formally specifies a protocol.

resource   Any item that can be accessed with a single URL. Usually a resource is a file, but a resource can also be the output of a script, such as a JSP page.

result set   A result set contains the rows returned from the SQL statement.

reverse DNS lookup   If you have only an IP address, a reverse DNS lookup can tell you what hostname is associated with that IP address.

RFC   *See* Request for Comments (RFC).

robots.txt   *See* bot exclusion file.

root document   The document that is retrieved when the path / is specified. For example, `http://www.jeffheaton.com/` would select the root document of `jeffheaton.com`.

S

scheme   The very first portion of the URL up to the first colon. The scheme specifies the protocol that should be used to download the specified resource. For example, `http://www.jeffheaton.com/` specifies the HTTP scheme.

Scooter   The spider used by AltaVista.

search engines   Search engines keep a list of websites, usually gathered from a spider, and allow the user to perform keyword searches.

Secure Socket Layer (SSL)   A special layer on top of a socket that encrypts its data. The HTTPS protocol is based on SSL.

server   A program that listens for incoming socket connections.

server headers   HTTP headers that are sent by a web server. These headers identify such information as what version of server software the web server is running.

servlet   A servlet is a Java class file that is executed from a URL and programmatically provides the requested resource.

session   A session begins when a user accesses a site. This allows the web server to associate all future requests with that user.

session cookie   A cookie that only remains active while the user is logged on.

SGML   *See* Structured General Markup Language (SGML).

Simple Mail Transfer Protocol (SMTP)   The Internet protocol that specifies how to send e-mail.

Simple Object Access Protocol (SOAP)   An XML-based protocol that allows objects to be accessed across the Internet.

Slurp   The spider used by Google.

SMTP   *See* Simple Mail Transfer Protocol (SMTP).

SOAP   *See* Simple Object Access Protocol (SOAP).

socket   The basic network connection upon which Internet protocols are built. A socket may both send and receive data.

spider   A bot that moves from site to site and finds new site pages for links. Those pages are also scanned for links, and the process continues.

SQL   *See* Structured Query Language (SQL).

SSL   *See* Secure Socket Layer (SSL).

state   State is something that a program remembers from one request to another. This allows a web server, for example, to remember which user is logged in.

stateless   Something is said to be stateless if nothing is remembered from one request to the next.

stream   A source or destination of bytes. Usually a stream originates from a socket or file.

Structured General Markup Language (SGML)   A broad document encoding method from which HTML (see HTML) and XML (see XML) both derive.

Structured Query Language (SQL)   A language used to access relational databases.

syntax   Rules by which you construct requests and responses to a protocol.

system path   Used by both UNIX and Windows to specify alternate directories that should be searched for an executable. For example, the introduction of this book recommends adding the bin directory of Java to the system path. If this is done, then the Java compiler (javac) can be executed from any directory. Both UNIX and Windows store the system path in the PATH environmental variable.

T

TCP/IP   *See* Transmission Control Protocol/Internet Protocol (TCP/IP).

terms of service (TOS)   The terms of service for a site specifies the way in which that site is to be used. Normally, you agree to the terms of service by clicking an I Agree button when you sign up for service.

terms of use   *See* terms of service (TOS).

thread   A point of execution within a program. A program can create many such points of execution and execute several portions of itself in parallel. Such a program is said to be multithreaded.

threading   A program is said to use threading if it uses threads.

thread pool   A thread pool is a collection of threads that will be reassigned to new tasks as they are created. This reassigning causes a program to maintain a consistent number of threads and not to have to endure the overhead of thread creation and destruction.

thread synchronization   The means by which threads coordinate their use of system resources.

TOS   *See* terms of service (TOS).

Transmission Control Protocol/Internet Protocol (TCP/IP)   TCP/IP is the combination of the TCP and IP protocols. TCP/IP is the protocol that sockets are generally used with.

U

Uniform Resource Identifier (URI)   A high-level address specification that includes the URL. A URI specifies only a scheme followed by a colon followed by protocol specific information. A URL is a special type of URI used for HTTP or HTTPS schemes.

Uniform Resource Locator (URL)   The address of a resource on the web.

URI   *See* Uniform Resource Identifier (URI).

URL   *See* Uniform Resource Locator (URL).

URL encoding   URL encoding consists of transforming certain characters into their ASCII equivalents. For example, the text "Hello World" would become "Hello%20World" when it was URL encoded. This is because the space would be URL encoded to its ASCII value, which is 32. This number is then converted to hex and prefixed with a percent (%).

W

W3C   *See* World Wide Web Consortium (W3C).

web application   An application designed to run completely from the Web.

webfarm   A webfarm is a collection of web servers that appear as one to an outside user. A webfarm is used to accept a very large volume of requests.

webmaster   The person, or people, responsible for the maintenance of a website.

Web Service Definition Language (WDSL)   Specifies the structure of a SOAP-accessible resource.

Windows NT Service   A program that runs in the background of Windows NT even when no user is logged in. Most web servers that are run on NT are run as services.

World Wide Web Consortium (W3C)   The body that defines many of the Internet document standard. The website for the W3C is `http://www.w3c.org`.

writer   A Java filter used to write data in some specific way.

WSDL   *See* Web Service Definition Language (WDSL).

XML   *See* Extensible Markup Language (XML).

Index

Note to the Reader: Throughout this index **boldfaced** page numbers indicate primary discussions of a topic. *Italicized* page numbers indicate illustrations.

A

a tags, 251
absolute URLs
    defined, 488
    for hyperlinks, **123–124**
Accept header, 451
Accept-Charset header, 451
Accept-Encoding header, 451
Accept-Language header, 451
accept method, 41
Access, **290–291**, *290–291*
access methods in bot detection, 395
action attribute, 194
actionPerformed method
    in GetImage, 142
    in GetSite, 265, 401
    in SecureGET, 104
    in SecurePrompt, 101
    in SendMail, 31
    in SiteSubmit, 187
    in ViewURL, 73
    in ViewURLCookie, 234
    in WatchBBS, 334
add method, 67, 435
addAttribute method, 238, 242, 438
addAuthHeader method, 113–114, 431
addCookieHeader method, 431
addImage method, 162, 437
addInput method, 178, 193–194, 436
addNotify method
    in GetImage, 141
    in GetSite, 264, 399–400
    in SecureGET, 103–104
    in SecurePrompt, 100
    in SendMail, 28–29
    in SiteSubmit, 184–185
    in ViewURL, 71–72
    in ViewURLCookie, 233
    in WatchBBS, 332

addresses
    in HTTP, **46–47**
    IP. *See* IP addresses
    in QIF files, 205
    of SMTP servers, 33
addWorkload method
    in IWorkloadStorable, 309, 441
    in Spider, 259, 302
    in SpiderDone, 442
    in SpiderInternalWorkload, 316, 443
    in SpiderSQLWorkload, 312, 443
Advanced tab, 474–475, *475*
agent headers, 63
agents, 488
aggregate hammering, 488
aggregation, **370**
    inline, **370–371**
    offline, **371**
aggregators
    defined, 488
    Weather aggregator, **378–379**, *379*
        Weather class for, **380–382**
        weather.jsp page for, **379–380**
    Weather bot for, **371–372**
        building, **374–378**
        extracting data from, **374**
        planning, **372–374**, *373*
AI (artificial intelligence), 488
Allow header, 451
AlphaCONNECT bot name, 392
alt attribute, 123, 132
AltaVista search engine, 179, 392
ampersands (&)
    for attributes, 195
    for forms, 177
    in URLs, 195
anchors
    for links, 251
    in URLs, 49
anonymous bot identification, **391–392**
Apache project, 466–467

S

T

TELL US WHAT YOU THINK!

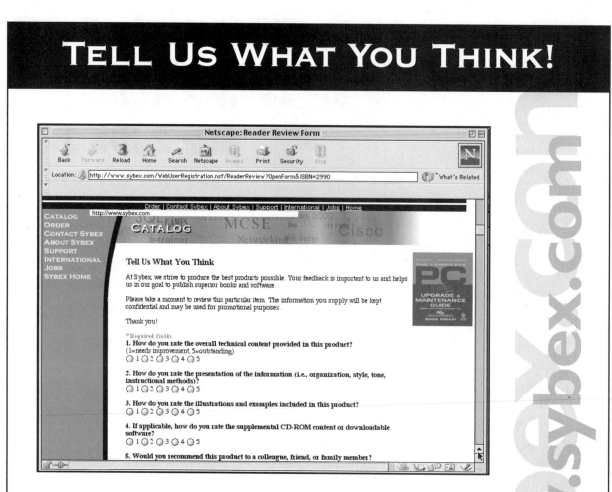

Your feedback is critical to our efforts to provide you with the best books and software on the market. Tell us what you think about the products you've purchased. It's simple:

1. Visit the Sybex website
2. Go to the product page
3. Click on **Submit a Review**
4. Fill out the questionnaire and comments
5. Click **Submit**

With your feedback, we can continue to publish the highest quality computer books and software products that today's busy IT professionals deserve.

www.sybex.com

SYBEX Inc. • 1151 Marina Village Parkway, Alameda, CA 94501 • 510-523-8233

The quotation on the bottom of the front cover is taken from the seventy-first chapter of Lao Tzu's Tao Te Ching, *the classic work of Taoist philosophy. This particular verse is from the translation by D. C. Lau (copyright 1963) and is part of a larger exploration of the qualities of the sage, who "meets with no difficulty...because he is alive to it."*

It is traditionally held that Lao Tzu lived in the fifth century B.C. in China, during the Chou dynasty, but it is unclear whether he was actually a historical figure. It is said that he was a teacher of Confucius. The concepts embodied in the Tao Te Ching *influenced religious thinking in the Far East, including Zen Buddhism in Japan. Many in the West, however, have wrongly understood the* Tao Te Ching *to be primarily a mystical work; in fact, much of the advice in the book is grounded in a practical moral philosophy governing personal conduct.*